A REFERENCE GUIDE
TO
EDMUND SPENSER

A REFERENCE GUIDE

TO

EDMUND SPENSER

By

FREDERIC IVES CARPENTER, PH.D.
Former Professor of English in the
University of Chicago

NEW YORK
PETER SMITH
1950

CONTENTS

I
INTRODUCTION

I.   INTRODUCTION

Many years ago I compiled and caused to be printed a brief Outline Guide to Spenser.   It has long been out of print.   Various requests for its reprinting together with a desire to make a more extended contribution to the study of a great English poet who has long been a delight to me have led me to undertake this book.

The apparatus for the study of the greater English poets has been accumulating for many years, but the present generation especially has seen it rapidly expanded, rounded out, and reduced to order.   Handbooks, concordances, bibliographies, annotations, and the whole *apparatus criticus*, are now reasonably complete for Chaucer, Shakespeare, Milton, and many of the later and even of the minor poets.   Spenser has had his share of attention. There are various handbooks, there is now an excellent concordance, he has been especially fortunate in the body of appreciative criticism which the lovers of his genius have written, and the body of annotations of his learned Muse is copious although defective in parts.   But there is lacking a comprehensive reference-list or bibliographical guide to his writings and the writings about him.   This lack I am here endeavoring to supply.

The compilation of references here presented does not pretend to be complete.[1]   My aim is attained if I have secured all the significant and important references.   There is a considerable mass of other stuff which I have not judged worth inclusion. I have briefly annotated the more important items.   Others of short scope and often sufficiently explained by their titles or of less importance I have entered without comment.   Some references of importance I have doubtless missed.   The field is

[1] Errors and omissions there will inevitably be.   I have striven to be accurate. May the Gentle Reader deal gently with all "faults escaped."   The abbreviations employed are thought to be self-explanatory.   Titles which I have not been able to verify are marked by an asterisk (*).

3

so large that a first attempt can scarcely hope to be quite comprehensive.

For the practical purpose of author and title finding I have supplied an index. For the study of special topics the classification of references in the body of the book, it is hoped, will be helpful. I have not attempted to compile a Spenser manual. The book is mainly a collection of references. In places I have added commentary which I trust will be found helpful. Each reference has been entered under the heading where it seems chiefly to belong. Under the headings I do not attempt to enter or index all pertinent passages from titles possibly appearing elsewhere. Cross references here have been interspersed, but it must be remembered that many passages bearing upon a given topic are likely to occur in entries under many headings, many of which cannot be indicated by a cross reference. The index here should help.

The captions under which references are classified might be largely extended. Thus there might be sections on "Spenser and Leicester," "Spenser and Burghley," "Rosalind," and many others. But the more classes the more complication and the more repetition.

I take pleasure in acknowledging the assistance and counsel which I have received from many persons. Mr. Henry R. Plomer has verified many references for me in England, and has searched out and supplied digests or transcripts of various documents. Messrs. J. B. Fletcher, C. G. Osgood, C. S. Northup, F. F. Covington, Jr., J. W. Draper, A. H. Tolman, J. M. Manly, J. D. Bruce, H. S. V. Jones, and Edwin Greenlaw have kindly checked over my lists and have supplied various additional entries. Suggestions and assistance of various sorts have been given by J. M. Manly, C. R. Baskervill, J. L. Lowes, F. F. Covington, Jr., E. Greenlaw, A. H. Tolman, Edith Rickert, J. M. Berdan, C. G. Osgood, Lane Cooper, C. S. Northup, James Westfall Thompson, Eleanor P. Hammond, and T. Peete Cross. And I am grateful for the courtesy and help rendered by the authorities of the Newberry Library, the Harvard Library, the

Boston Public Library, the Huntington Library, and the Yale Library. A few titles I have consulted at the British Museum; others there have been checked for me by Mr. Plomer.

Until the compilation of an allusion-book for Spenser such as we have for Chaucer and for Shakespeare, the materials for a History of Spenser's Literary Reputation lie scattered and many of them practically inaccessible.[1] The broad outlines of this history, however, are sufficiently known.

In his lifetime, at least in his last decade, Spenser was accepted as the great English poet of the age. His reputation was probably greater than that of Shakespeare.

In the seventeenth century his position in literary history became fixed. He began to be the poets' poet and to make a school. Cowley, Milton, and Dryden warmly praised him and received inspiration from his genius in their several ways. Almost all of his contemporaries who lived on after him acknowledged him. Many became his avowed disciples. Even those who went into reaction against the earlier Elizabethan poetic tradition, like Jonson and Donne, did not seriously contest his titles. A certain piety and tenderness of appreciation which attended him living persisted after his death. Scholars like Camden, Ware, and Johnston were concerned about his memorials and wrote brief, all too brief, sketches of his life. Hartlib and Worthington interested themselves in his vestigia and searched for his manuscript remains. A crop of Anecdota sprang up (Aubrey and others) to satisfy the general curiosity about him. It is true that there were only four editions of his poems in the century, but these were widely read. His works were among those to be found in a gentleman's library. And every scholar was supposed to know him.

In the eighteenth century there was no great change. Eight or nine editions indicate that he was generally read. And he is adopted into the collected editions of the English poets, although not into Dr. Johnson's. This is the period of the

[1] See Section IV ("Criticism, Influence, Allusions") infra. The collection of references thereunder is at best representative and does not aim at completeness.

Spenserian imitations, whether a sign, as Professor Beers and Professor Phelps think, of nascent romanticism or, as Dr. Cory holds, a sign that Spenser had now become adopted as a classic. At any rate like Milton he is regarded as one to be imitated, however far the imitations are from the true Spenserian manner.

Spenser has never been a popular poet, although always read by youth[1] and by poets, and pretty generally read also during most periods by all who aspire to culture. He has always interested the literati, and the middle and latter parts of the eighteenth century witnessed the growth of a body of annotations and commentary, occasionally rising into critical appreciation of permanent value. Hurd tried to fix his position as the great exemplar of romanticism. Thomas Warton, Upton, Birch, and various others made him the subject of voluminous commentary.

In the early part of the nineteenth century, however, Spenser comes most fully into his own. Todd's variorum edition attempts to codify the Spenser-lore of his day and marks his position as an English classic. And it is then that there begins the succession of illuminating and appreciative critiques, in which Spenser has been peculiarly fortunate, from the brilliant flashes of Coleridge, the gusto and insight of Hazlitt, the light touches of Leigh Hunt, the loyal devotion of Southey, and the sympathetic elaboration of John Wilson ("Christopher North"), through the company of commentators, antiquarians, and critics of the middle period of the century, J. P. Collier, Keightley, the various editors of his works, and G. L. Craik, most helpful, appreciative, and soundest of the Spenser critics of his day, down to our own times and the various and variously enlightening contributions of Taine, Ruskin, R. W. Church, Dowden, Aubrey DeVere, J. W. Hales, Grosart, Saintsbury, most fervent and forthright of Spenserians, J. W. Mackail, E. de Sélincourt, Lilian Winstanley, and even Courthope, neo-classicist and in turn perplexed *advocatus* and *advocatus diaboli*. America has

---

[1] For a very recent and striking example, see J. St. Loe Strachey, The Adventure of Living. N.Y. and Lond., 1922, pp. 77-78.

contributed its quota, from the essays in the early reviews, to the admirable appreciations of Lowell, Woodberry, and G. H. Palmer. In recent years especially American scholarship has developed a considerable school of Spenser interpretation and commentary and the various studies and contributions of Greenlaw, J. B. Fletcher, Dodge, Osgood, Long, Cory, Buck, Draper, Padelford, Baskervill, Jones, Higginson, Carrie A. Harper, and many others, have materially helped to elucidate the numerous puzzles and problems of Spenser's career and writings.[1]

I have aimed in this Reference Guide in some measure to indicate, record, classify, and codify most of the important topics and problems of Spenser criticism, solved and unsolved, the materials of which have been accumulating for some three centuries. These problems are many and various. Probably no modern poet offers a greater and more perplexing variety of them. Some of them, especially in the Shepherds' Calendar and the Faerie Queene, are deliberately posed and injected by the poet and by his friends, in part as a sort of camouflage and self-protective coloration, in part as a device of publicity, and as literary artifice. The list of them is too long to recite in full. Many of the titles referred to in this book deal with them. But something of their general nature may be suggested by the following examples, most of them still open questions:

The date of birth; parentage and family connections; other Spensers of the time, especially the other Edmund Spensers; the messenger from the English ambassador in France in 1569; the Turbervile allusions; Spenser's sojourn in "the north parts," and the Lancashire question; Spenser's relations to Sidney; to Leicester; to Burleigh; to Essex; relation to other contemporaries, and of his circle and associates; Spenser and Bryskett, and of the evidence from Bryskett's Discourse; the personages, allusions, and contemporary allegory of the Faerie Queene; of the Shepherds' Calendar; of Colin Clout's Come Home Again; interpretation of Muiopotmos, of the Amoretti, and of other works; Spenser and the Theatre of Worldlings;

[1] For an interesting summary of the recent discussion of many of these problems see J. W. Draper's Spenserian Biography: a Note on the Vagaries of Scholarship. Ingenious iconoclasm has become the mode. Perhaps it has been pushed too far. Most of the problems are very difficult, but the natural interpretation of the evidence is sometimes the right interpretation.

the Rosalind question; who was "E.K."?; the Areopagus question; the general interpretation and explanation of the entries under "Spenser" in the several Calendars of State Papers, etc.; explanation of the Spenser-Harvey letters; the early anecdotes and gossip (Aubrey, Ben Jonson, etc.); Spenser and Puritanism; the lost works; the lost continuation of the Faerie Queene; the Spenser Apocrypha; Spenser and the laureateship; the portraits; Spenser's autograph; Spenser and Shakespeare; Spenser's knowledge of Dante; Spenser's learning, reading, and use of his "sources"; Spenser and the law; Spenser as officeholder and man of affairs.

The list is almost without end. The following pages attempt to suggest the material at hand and the starting point for study and investigation of Spenser's career, writings, and literary history.

II
THE LIFE

II. THE LIFE

CHRONOLOGICAL OUTLINE OF THE LIFE

References, unless otherwise stated, are to those given under "Life, General References." The dates, except in quotations, are reduced to New Style. An attempt has been made to indicate by the use of larger type (eleven point) things documented and certain, by middle-sized type (nine point) things probable, and by smaller type (seven point) things possible.

PRINCIPAL PERIODS IN SPENSER'S LIFE

I. Birth, Family, and Boyhood.
II. University Life and Earliest Writings, 1569–76.
III. After graduation, in England, 1576–80.
IV. Life in Ireland, 1580–99.
    A. Chiefly in or near Dublin, 1580–86?
    B. Chiefly at Kilcolman, 1586?–98.
    C. Visits to England, 1589–90, 1595–97, 1598–99.

Few things are more difficult than to settle, at all satisfactorily, matters relating to chronology in Spenser's life and writings.—J. P. Collier.

The biography of Spenser is to a great extent a series of assumptions, or of assertions, repeated by one writer after another, but resting originally upon little or no evidence.—G. L. Craik.

THE GOVERNORS OF IRELAND, 1580–1600

(From Reports of the Deputy Keeper of Public Records in Ireland)

Aug. 1580— Sept. 1582: Lord Grey, Lord Deputy.
Sept. 1582— June 1584: Sir H. Wallop, Lord Justice.
21 June 1584—30 June 1588: Sir J. Perrot, Lord Deputy.
30 June 1588—11 Aug. 1594: Sir W. Fytzwylliam, Lord Deputy.
11 Aug. 1594—22 May 1597: Sir W. Russell, Lord Deputy.
22 May 1597—14 Oct. 1597: Thomas Lord Burgh, Lord Deputy.
Oct. 1597—27 Nov. 1597; Sir Thos. Norreys, Lord Justice.
Nov. 1597— Apr. 1599: Sir R. Gardener, Lord Justice.
15 Apr. 1599— Sept. 1599: Robert Earl of Essex, Lord Lieutenant.

1550–68. London as the place of Sp's birth is fixed by a passage in the Prothal. (ll. 127–29). Sp claimed affinity with the noble family of the Spencers (Prothal., ll. 130–31; cf. Ded. to MHT, to Muiop., and to T of M; cf. CCCHA, ll. 537–38).

That Sp's mother was named Elizabeth is stated in sonnet 74 of the Amoretti, ll. 5–6, 13.

Sp attended Merchant Taylors School, London (cf. Nowell), from which he proceeded to Cambridge in 1569 (Hist. MSS Comm. Reports).

1550–53. Nothing is definitely known about the year of Sp's birth. Some of the older biographers place it in 1553. Most of the recent writers assign it to 1552. Assuming that sixteen was the average age of college entrance in the period, Sp's matriculation at Cambridge in 1569 would approximately fit either date. The date 1552 is based on sonnet 60 of the Amoretti, the composition of which is conjecturally placed in 1593. Subtracting the "one year spent" (line 6) and "al those fourty which my life out-went," gives us 1552. Sp, however, is probably using round numbers ("al those fourty"), and P. W. Long and others suggest reasons for believing that the birth year may have been approximately 1550.

The original monument to Sp, erected c. 1620, by an obvious error gave Sp's dates as 1510–96.

The location of the birthplace in East Smithfield (London), near the Tower, is based on the authority of a MS note by Oldys, and one by Vertue. (On the date of birth cf. Grosart, I, 1–4.)

1550 ff. As to conjectures as to Sp's parents and descent see references under "Parents and Family"; also "Chief Lives of Spenser."

J. P. Collier conjectures that Sp's boyhood was spent partly in Warwickshire.

When he entered Merchant Taylor's School (Mulcaster master, Grindal "visitor" —founded 1561) is a matter of conjecture. Possibly in 1561. Wise and others suggest 1564.

Some connection of his parents and possibly of part of his boyhood, with North-ampton (the county in which is located Althorp, the seat of the noble family of the Spencers) has been suggested. See also below under 1576 as to the "North partes." See also the discussion of the Lancashire question and of Sp's possible connection with that locality.

1569

On Sp's life at Cambridge see the Spenser-Harvey Letters and the various biographies of Sp, esp. Grosart.

Publication of Van der Noodt's Theatre of Voluptuous Worldlings, with "Epigrams" and "Sonets," adopted as Sp's, with some altera-tions, in the Complaints volume of 1591. Sp's earliest published verse.

Verses addressed to "Spencer" by Turbervile in his Epitaphes and Sonnets, 1569, have been applied to Sp by Wood, Collier, and others.

Apr. 28. To Cambridge (cf. Nowell); receipt of ten shillings from Nowell. Easter Term. Sp matriculated as a sizar at Pembroke Hall, Cambridge (cf. Venn).

May 20. Matriculation (cf. DNB). John Young, whose secretary Sp became in 1578, master of Pembroke during Sp's college years.

July 7. Gifts from Nowell to "Edmunde Spenser" at Burnley in Lancashire (cf. Cartwright).

Oct. 18. Payment, on a "bill" signed on that date, to "Edmonde Spencer" as a bearer of letters from Sir Henry Norris, English ambassador to France, at Tours, to the queen (cf. Cunningham). The objections to this "Edmonde Spencer" being Spenser the poet are (1) that Sp at this time was a student at Cambridge (Cunningham suggests that the trip may have been taken during a college vacation), and (2) that Sp was only seventeen at the time. If Sp were born in 1550 he was nineteen; in any event the objection on the score of age would probably have seemed of less weight to men of the sixteenth century than now. Sp later was frequently a bearer of dispatches. Note Sp's knowledge of French in 1569 (translations in the Theatre of Worldlings) and his contact later with others of the Norris family.

1570–76

Allowances to Sp for illness ("aegrotanti") at Cambridge on five occasions—two and one-half weeks, four weeks, etc. (cf. Grosart, I, 36; DNB, XVIII, 794).

A.B. degree, 1572–73 (Venn). Sp eleventh in *ordo seniori-tatis* (Cooper).

A.M. degree, 1576 (Venn). Leaves Cambridge.

1576. Visit to "The North countrye," whence "for his more preferment" he returned to the south, perhaps in 1577 (Sh Cal, Gloss to June).

The North: conjecturally identified with (1) Lancashire, (2) Northamptonshire (Ralph Church), (3) Warwickshire (Drayton, Aubrey, J. B. Fletcher), (4) Cambridge (Higginson).

Harvey was in York in Aug. 1576 (Marginalia, 16, 84), and possibly accompanied Sp on his journey to the North.

1572–76. Composition of Virgil's Gnat (Fleay, etc.).

1574–75. Sp in trouble with the Cambridge authorities—Dr. Perne (Marginalia, 30).

1576–80

Period of poetic experimentation. Composition of the Sh Cal and of most of the Lost Works.

The Rosalind episode, followed by that of the "altera Rosalindula" (Harvey Letters; Sp's Works, passim; see refs. under "Life, Gen'l," "Sh Cal," etc.).

1576–77. Composition of first two of the Four Hymns—"in the greener times of my youth" (Grosart, Fleay, etc.). Harvey's connection with Leicester and Sidney, leading to Sp's reception by them (Marginalia, 18).

1577. Sp in Ireland in 1576–77, possibly as secretary to Sir Henry Sidney, or visiting Bryskett (V of I, Globe ed. of Sp, 636a)? Witnessed the execution of Murrogh O'Brein at Limerick, an event which took place in July, 1577 (cf. Calendar of 1575–88, p. 104). But cf. Ware's statement: "In Hiberniam *primùm* venit cum Arthuro Domino Grey." DNB suggests probably there as bearer of despatches from Leicester to Sir Henry Sidney, and that E. K.'s phrase "for long time farr estranged" [i.e., in strange parts] may refer to this absence (cf. Grosart, I, 65–66; Cal. of Carew MSS 1575–88, p. 104; Sélincourt, one-vol. ed. of Sp, p. xii).

Mr. Henry R. Plomer has made a search of the records in England likely to yield results, but has found no mention of Sp, or of Sir Philip Sidney, in Ireland in 1577. Sp is not mentioned in any of the extant correspondence of Lord Grey, or in the letters of Bryskett, although Mr. Plomer conjectures that Sp may have come to Ireland in 1577 on a visit to Bryskett.

1577–79. Writing of Sh Cal (Fleay).

1578. Secretary to John Young, Bishop of Rochester (Gollancz; Marginalia, 22 ff., 84).

Gift of copy of Turler's The Trauailer to Harvey by Sp Dec. 20. In London, gives copy of Howleglas to Harvey (now in Bodleian). (Macray; Marginalia, 23; see under "Sources, General").

1578–79. Attendance at Court (Letter to Harvey of 5 Oct. 1579)

1579. In London. In Leicester's service? (Marginalia, 27). Association with Sidney and Dyer.

FQ begun before 1580.

Apr. 10. E.K.'s Letter to Harvey, prefixed to Sh Cal.

Oct. 5. At Leicester House (body of letter states written in part Oct. 15–16 at Westminster). Letter of Sp to Harvey. Harvey writes to Sp from "Trinitie Hall, stil in my Gallerie, 23 Octob. 1579."

Dec. 5. Entry of Sh Cal in Stationer's Register (Arber). Published "1579" (=N.S. 1580?) anonymously, the authorship not generally known till some years later, although possibly hinted at in Harvey's letters 1580, and elsewhere.

Sp sacrificed by Leicester in a political exigency (Greenlaw).

Sp in 1579 expected to journey abroad; probably did not go at this time, as the known dates leave little time for the trip (Letters; cf. Marginalia, 29).

Composition of first version of MHT possibly in 1578–79 (Greenlaw; Keightley; Brit. Quart. Rev. suggests 1583–84, and Fleay 1576–77. "In the raw conceipt of my youth"). The MHT is one of the chief documents bearing on Sp's relations to Burghley.

1579–80. The "altera Rosalindula" episode (Letters; Grosart, I, 125–29; Collier, I, pp. lxvii f.: possibly Sp's first wife).

1580

Publication of Sh Cal. Dated 1579 (Old Style ?).

Appointed one of the secretaries to Lord Grey, Lord Deputy of Ireland (Calendars: several references to Sp as holding this office; treated as secretary to the Lord Deputy and the Council).

April 2. Sp writes to Harvey from Westminster (possibly = Leicester House). Harvey writes to Sp Apr. 7, and "From my place," Apr. 23.

June 30. Entry of Spenser-Harvey Letters in Stationers' Register (Arber). Published, 1580, by Bynneman.

August 1. A poem by Harvey dedicated to Edward Dyer by Benevolo = Sp (Marginalia, 26).

August. Lord Grey to Ireland, Sp doubtless accompanying. (Ware; Grosart, I, 133).

Sp's sister Sarah probably accompanied him to Ireland and later resided with him at Kilcolman. She married John Travers, receiving as dower from Sp part of the Kilcolman lands (on authority of a descendant of the Travers family, in G. L. Craik, III, 250).

1580–82. Sp probably accompanies Lord Grey in his journeys about Ireland. Note the Irish place-names in Sp's writings. Sp present at the massacre at Fort-del-Ore, Smerwick, in November (V of I).

Sept. 5. Complaint of Justice Pelham to Lord Grey that a letter by the latter's secretary (=Spenser?) was not "considerately written" (Cal. Carew MSS).

Dec. 31. Payment of £10 to Sp as secretary to Lord Grey as half year's salary (Concordatums).

1580–82. Various payments to bearers of despatches through Sp (Concordatums).

1580–86? Sp principally resident in and near Dublin. 1583–85, possibly at New Abbey.

1580–89. Writing of the FQ, I–III, partly in England, and partly in Ireland (Irish local color). "The ninth canto of the second book is the first passage that pretty certainly points to his being in Ireland; and all the rest was written in Ireland." (J. W. Hales, in Chambers Encycl.) See Sp's sonnet to Lord Grey, published with FQ:

"Rude rymes, the which a rustick Muse did weave
In savadge soyle, far from Parnasso Mount."

1581

Publication of the second edition of the Sh Cal.

Mar. 11. Letter from Ireland certified by Sp (Calendar).

Mar. 16. Similarly.

Mar. 22. Sp appointed registrar or clerk in Chancery for faculties (Cal. of Fiants; Cat. Harl. MSS; Liber Munerum, Pt. II, 28–29 gives the date as Mar. 22, 1580).

Apr. 29. Paper certified by Sp at Cork (Calendar).

May 16. Sp appears in person in Court of Exchequer, Dublin (Memorandum Roll; Ferguson; Grosart, I, 142).

June 26. Payment to Sp of £10 as half year's salary as secretary (Concordatums).

June 29. Paper certified by Sp at Dublin (Calendar).

Oct. 19. Entry of payment to Col. John Zowche, per bill due to Edmond Spencer, £32.

Dec. 9. Conveyance of Enniscorthy by Sp to Rich. Synot (Cal. of Fiants). See below under Dec. 6, 1582.

1582

Lease of a house in Dublin (part of forfeited estate of John Eustace, Viscount Baltinglas) to Sp for six years.

Sp receives a custodiam of John Eustace's land of the Newland (Calendar).

Mar. 11. Bryskett appointed clerk of the Council of Munster (Liber Munerum). At what period Sp began to act as his deputy is uncertain—probably in 1587.

Mar. 14. Patent to Roland Cowyk as Clerk of Chancery for Faculties (Liber Munerum). Did Cowyk succeed Sp?

Aug. 24. Lease to Sp of New Abbey, etc., County Kildare (Cal. of Fiants; DNB states that for the next two years "he was officially described as 'of New Abbey,' where he seems to have often resided." See Cal. of Fiants for appointments of Sp in 1583 and 1584 as Commissioner of Musters in County Kildare).

Aug. 29. Paper (in Sp's hand?—"copia vera"), at Dublin (Cal. of Fiants).

Sept. Return of Lord Grey from Ireland. End of Sp's secretaryship.

> Did Sp return with Lord Grey from Ireland? (Cf. Keightley, Collier, Todd, etc.). Probability of occasional trips to England, 1582–89, and possibly later, although the records prove his main residence in Ireland, 1580–98.
>
> On his recall Lord Grey was directed to "leave thy sword" [the sword of office] with Adam Loftus, Abp of Dublin and Chancellor, and Sir Henry Wallop, "Theasaurer at Wars there" (14 July, 1582). The sword was delivered Aug. 31 (Liber Munerum, Pt. II, 3 f.).

Dec. 6. Lease to Sp of Enniscorthy, etc. for 21 years (Cal. of Fiants; DNB dates this lease July 15, 1581).

1583

May 12. Sp appointed one of the commissioners of Musters in County Kildare (Cal. of Fiants).

> In 1583 Sp with Bryskett near Dublin for three days (Discourse of Civil Life).
> 1583–85. Sp principally resident at New Abbey, County Kildare.

1584

July 4. Sp appointed one of the commissioners of musters in County Kildare (Cal. of Fiants).

1585. [No records?]

1586

Death of Sidney.

Publication of third edition of the Sh Cal.

> Mar. 4. Kilcolman "taken" by Mr. Read (Calendar). Possibly acting for Sp, who in May seems to claim the estate.
>
> June 27. Sp down for 3028 acres [=Kilcolman] in the Articles for the Undertakers. Uncertain when he settled there—probably in 1586, possibly not until 1589 (Calendar 1586–88, pp. 35, 42, 93; cf. Grosart, I, 150. See below.)

July 18. Sonnet to Harvey dated from Dublin (cf. Marginalia, 57.)

Dec. 5. "Edmundus Spenser, prebendary of Effin" reported, among others, as delinquent in the payment of his First Fruits (Calendar; cf. Mod. Philol., XIX, 406–10).

Writing of Astrophel at end of 1586, soon after death of Sidney (DNB, XVIII, 797)? See 1587.

Lands of the Earl of Desmond in Munster forfeited in 1586 and plans instituted to plant them with English colonists (the "Undertakers"). Sp doubtless in this enterprise at this date. Articles for the Undertakers receive the royal assent June 27 (DNB, XVIII, 798).

1587

Probable date of writing of Astrophel (year of entry of Bryskett's Mourning Muse of Thestylis. Fleay suggests c. 1591).

1588–98

Sp principally resident in Munster—at Kilcolman, Cork, etc. (On his life at Kilcolman cf. Grosart, I, 150 ff.).

1588

Death of Leicester.

Oct. 1, 1587—Mar. 31, 1588. Mention of Sp as serving as Bryskett's deputy as clerk of the Council of Munster (Cal. Carew MSS). Bryskett titular holder of the Office Mar. 11, 1582—Mar. 31, 1600; then succeeded by Richard Boyle (Liber Munerum, Pt. II, 187).

June 22. Arland Uscher clerk of the Chancery for faculties—succeeding Sp? (Liber Mun. II, 28–29).

1589–95

Quarrel and litigation with Lord Roche (DNB; Grosart, I, 530 ff.)

1589–90

Composition of various poems published in the Complaints volume, 1591—probably the V of W V, R of T, Muiop., etc.

1589

Visit of Raleigh.

May. Sp's answer to articles for examining lands "past" to the Undertakers. Particulars as to his Kilcolman estate. His patent soon to be issued (Cal.).

Oct. With Raleigh to England; in London, Nov. 1589 (Grosart, I, 155 f.). F. F. Covington, Jr., suggests that Sp's visits to England 1589 and 1595 were undertaken partly to secure English colonists for Kilcolman, as required under the articles.

Oct. 12. Suit of Lord Roche vs Sp, "Clerk of the Council in Munster," et al. (Cal.).

Oct. 29. Sp's holdings mentioned in a list of patents to the English Undertakers (Cal.).

Dec. 1. Entry of the FQ in the Stationer's Register (Arber).

1590

Publication of the FQ, I–III.

Various copies of the Muiop. (published with the Complaints, 1591) are dated 1590 (Grosart, I, 160 ff.).

Jan. 23, "1589" [=N.S. 1590?]. Date of Sp's letter to Raleigh with the FQ.

May 8. Mention of a certain Chichester serving as substitute for Sp "in his office of clerkship of Munster"—while Sp was in England? (Cal.).

Oct. 26. Patent of Kilcolman to Sp, with particulars (Cal. of Fiants).

Dec. 29. Entry of the Complaints (Arber).

Probable date of writing of T of M, Daphnaida, etc. in 1590 (Fleay, Collier). The first two of the Four Hymns probably written c. 1590 (Long).

Visit to Hampshire (Aubrey; accepted by Sélincourt and placed in summer of 1590).

Dec. 1. Marriage of "Edmundus Spencer et Maria Towerson" (Notes and Queries, Ser. IV, Vol. X, 244).

Return to Ireland after printing FQ, I–III (Collier).

1591

Publication of the Complaints and Daphnaida.

Publication of fourth edition of Sh Cal.

Sp mentioned, under Cork, as one of the Undertakers in Munster (Cal. Carew MSS).

Jan. 1, 1591. Dating of Ded. of Daphnaida, at London (possibly 1592 N.S.; but cf. Grosart, I, 166).

Feb. 25. Grant of pension of fifty pounds annually to Sp, and his assigns, for life (Patent Roll; Prior.).

Oct. 12. Entry of the Sh Cal (Arber).

Dec. 27. CCCHA dated from Kilcolman (a literary device? Cf. Long; but cf. Collier, I, pp. lxxii f.: that Sp. came to London in autumn of 1589, returned to Ireland after printing of FQ in 1590, there wrote CCCHA in 1591, afterwards revised).

Sp in 1591 possibly mourning the death of a first wife (Daphn. l. 64: "like wofulnesse"; cf. l. 37).

1591–94. Writing of CCCHA (Fleay; Collier; etc.). Writing of Amoretti. Some of the sonnets probably of earlier composition.

1591–96. Writing of FQ, IV–VI, mainly in Ireland.

1592

"In 1592 Spenser fell in love again" (DNB).

Sp in list of Undertakers who had paid their rent (Cal.).

List of Undertakers in Munster. Sp mentioned (Cal.).

Sonnet to Harvey, published with Harvey's Foure Letters.

May 1. Entry of the Axiochus (Arber).

Aug.–Sept. Undertakers absent from their estates and complained of. Sp inferentially among the number—in England? (Cal.). Return to Ireland.

Sept. 2. Sp's assignees of Enniscorthy (Ferguson).

Dec. 31. Sp's holdings and rents specified in a list of the Undertakers in Munster (Cal.).

1593

Lord Roche's petition in Chancery, Ireland, vs Sp (see 1594).

1594

Feb. 12. After Sp's appearance in person in court, Ireland, Lord Roche "was decreed possession" of disputed lands (Grosart, I, 531).

June 11. Sp's marriage (Epithal; the date disputed by Long). Sp's wife Elizabeth Boyle, a kinswoman of Richard Boyle. "Probably as his second wife" (T. J. Wise; Lismore Papers; see various refs. under "Life," "Marriage and Wife," etc.).

Nov. 19. Entry of Amoretti and Epithalamion, "written not long since by Edmund Spencer" (Arber).

Sp possibly gives up clerkship of Council of Munster in 1594 (DNB; but cf. Lismore Papers).

1595

.Publication of CCCHA.

Publication of Amoretti and Epithal.

At close of 1595 Sp in London (DNB; Grosart, I, 205).

1596

Publication of FQ, second ed. of I–III, first ed. of IV–VI.

Publication of Daphnaida, second edition (with Four Hymns).

Publication of the Foure Hymnes.

Publication of Prothalamion.

Jan. 20. Entry of FQ, IV–VI (Arber).

Sept. 1. Dedication of the Four Hymns from Greenwich. Sp "with the court at Greenwich" (DNB).

Nov. 12. Report by Robert Bowes from Edinburgh to Burghley of complaint of King James against Sp and the king's desire for Sp's punishment (Cal., Scotland).

Nov. 8. Sp attended wedding of Earl of Worcester's daughters (Prothal.; J. B. Fletcher).

Sp probably wrote the V of I in 1596 (published 1633). Certainly written between 1594–97. (See V of I, Globe ed. of Sp 660: Mention of Sir Wm. Russell, "the honorable gentellman that now governeth there." Russell was Lord Deputy in Ireland Aug. 1594 to May 1597.)

1597

Publication of Sh Cal, fifth edition.

c. 1597? Purchase by Sp of the lands of Renny, County Cork, for £200, as a provision for his son Peregrine (Welply).

Sp's return to Ireland.

Grant of rights in certain of his lands in County Cork by Sp to J. McHenry, c. 1597 (Cat. of Add. MSS—authenticity doubted by Collier and Grosart).

1598

Feb. 7. Sp's arrearages of rent (Ferguson).

Feb. 25. Reference to a book by Walter Quin answering the FQ, "whereat the king [James] is offended" (Cal., Scotland).

Apr. 14. Entry of the View of Ireland, "upon condicion that hee [Matthew Lownes] gett further aucthoritie before yt be prynted" (Arber).

Aug. 14. Outbreak of Tyrone's rebellion in Ireland (DNB; Grosart, I, 227 ff.).

Sept. 30. Letter from England (from the Queen and Privy Council?) urging the appointment of Sp as sheriff of Cork County (MacLir).

Oct. Tyrone's rebellion breaks out in Munster; the "spoiling" of Kilcolman. Sp fled to Cork; loss of an infant (Jonson).

Spenser, the newly appointed sheriff, "seems to have been taken completely unawares" (DNB—a questionable statement; cf. V of I).

Various documents describing the rebellion (Cal.)

Dec. 5. Report to Privy Council that the sheriff of Cork and most of the Undertakers with their families were placed in Cork at the beginning of the Munster rebellion (Cal.).

Dec. 7. The sheriff of Cork in Cork (Cal.).

Dec. 9. Despatch from Cork, "sent by the hand of Edmund Spenser, the poet" (Cal.).

Dec. 21. Despatch from Sir Thos. Norris "By the hand of Spenser" (cf. Letter from Norris of Jan. 24, 1599: "Since my last by Mr. Spenser"—Cal.).

Did Sp's family accompany him to England at this time? (Cf. Keightley; etc.)

1599

Jan. 17. Letter of John Chamberlain fixing date of Sp's death as Jan. 16, 1599, at Westminster (Grosart, I, 235; Marginalia, 226; but, contra, J. W. Hales in Chambers' Encycl. interprets Chamberlain's reference to be to Jan. 13).

Sp's burial in Westminster Abbey (Camden; Warner; etc.).

Feb. Letter of Nicholas Curteys to Sir Robert Cecil, referring to Sp's services as clerk of the Council of Munster, a man "not unknown to your Honour," and reference to "Edmund Spenser being lately deceased" (Cal.).

Sp's monument in Westminster Abbey (Grosart, I, 239-40; and various refs. under "Life, Gen'l").

For copies of verses possibly thrown into Sp's grave see Alabaster, H(R), Breton, Thynne.

Sp's "poverty" and death from "lack of bread," after his flight from Ireland (Jonson, Camden, Johnston, etc.).

Undated; and after Spenser's death

Suit in Chancery by "Edmond Spenser and others" vs Matthew. "Personal matters" (Cal. of Proc. in Chancery).

Petition in Chancery by Lord Roche vs Sp. Certiorari granted (Archaeologia: dated 1593?; cf. Grosart).

Mar. 29, 1601. Mention of Sp as "late clerk of the Council" of Munster, and that he "was a servitor of the realm" (Cal. Carew MS).

1611. Mention of the "seigniory" of Kilcolman granted to "Edmond Spencer" (Cal. Carew MSS).

See also Cromwell, etc., etc.

Topics concerning Spenser's Life

The canon of Sp's life is still very uncertain, and the critical student must scan sharply many of the statements in even the most reputable biographies. Thus the Index and Epitome volume of the Dictionary of National Biography, p. 1228, makes the following statements in regard to Sp which at best are conjectural or require qualification: That his father was John Spenser; his birth in East Smithfield; derivation of the family from Lancashire; the dialect of the Sh Cal Lancastrian; that Harvey introduced him to Leicester and Sidney; the Areopagus "club"; Rosalind a yeoman's daughter; EK = Edward Kirke; "enthusiastic" reception of the Sh Cal; acquisition of Kilcolman in 1588; Astrophel written in 1586;- return to Kilcolman in 1591; death in poverty; the portraits.

Much of the life doubtless must remain ingenious conjecture, but the framework needs remodelling and the background needs to be repainted. The biographical material in Sp's own writings is doubtless the most significant of the sources for the life; considerable progress has been made in interpreting it. But certainty in relation to most of it can never be possible. High probability, however, in relation to much of it may be attained.

Various topics in relation to the life need further investigation. Thus, for example, the following may be suggested:

1. Spenser's "Poverty." Has been often adverted to. See under "Life, Gen'l," and esp. Todd's ed. of Sp, I, pp. cxxix ff. Note l. 8 of sonnet 74 of the Amoretti: "That honour and large richesse to me lent." Is this merely an acknowledgment of the pension? May it not also refer to Kilcolman and other grants in Ireland?
2. The Litigation with Lord Roche.
3. Spenser's Tenure of the office of clerk of the Council of Munster. His duties and its functions.

And see further topics suggested by the present writer in Studies in Philology, XIX (1922), 238–43; and in Mod. Philol., XIX (1922), 405–19.

THE CHIEF LIVES OF SPENSER

1607 Camden, William, Britannia.
1615 Camden, William, Annales (under "1598").
    Cf. also Camden's Remains (1605).
1633 Ware, Sir James, in Preface to his edition of Spenser's View of Ireland.
1639 Ware, Sir James, De Scriptoribus Hiberniae.
1662 Fuller, Thos., Worthies of England.
1669–96 Aubrey, John, Lives.

1675 Phillips, Edward, Theatrum Poetarum.

1679 Anon., Life of Spenser, with edition of Sp's Works.

1684 Winstanley, Wm., England's Worthies.

1715 Hughes, John, Life, prefixed to his edition of Sp's Works.

1732 Ball, John, Dissertatio de Vita Spenseri et Scriptis. With Bathurst's Latin translation of the Sh Cal.

1751 Birch, Thos., Life, with his ed. of Sp.

1753 Cibber, Theophilus (Robt. Shiels?), Lives of the Poets.

1758 Anon., Life, with Church's ed. of FQ.

1758 Upton, John, Life, with his ed. of FQ.

1763 Biographia Britannica.

1802 Ritson, Joseph, Bibliographica Poetica, pp. 343–49.

1805 Todd, H. J., Life, with his ed. of Sp's Works.

1806 Aikin, John, Life, with his ed. of Sp's Works.

1825 Robinson, Geo., Life, with ed. of Sp's Works.

1839 Mitford, John, Life, with ed. of Sp's Works.

1845 Craik, G. L., Spenser and his Poetry.

1847 Hart, J. S., Essay on Life and Writings. N.Y., 1847.

1855 Child, F. J., Life, with his ed. of Sp's Works. Boston, 1855.

1861 Cooper, Charles H., and Thompson, Athenae Cantabrigienses.

1862 Collier, J. P., Life, with his ed. of Sp's Works.

1869–97 Hales, J. W., Memoir, with Globe ed. of Sp's Works.

1879 Church, R. W., Spenser (Eng. Men of Letters).

1882 Grosart, A.B., Life, Vol. I of his ed. of Sp's Works.

1887 Minto, W., Life, in Encycl. Brit., XXII.

1897 Herford, C. H., with his ed. of the Sh Cal.

1897 Hales, J. W., in Chambers' Encyclopedia.

1898 Hales, J. W., and Sidney Lee, Life, in Dict. Natl. Biog. LIII (XVIII).

189– Fletcher, J. B., Life, in Encyclopedia Americana.

1908 Dodge, R. E. N., Life, with his ed. of Sp's Works. Boston, 1908.

1912 de Selincourt, Ernest, Introduction to ed. of Sp's Minor Poems (on the Works, only).

1912 de Sélincourt, in his one-volume ed. of Sp. Oxford, 1912.

Early material on Sp's Life (scattered) is to be found in numerous other sources. See especially references on Harvey's Marginalia; Drummond's Conversations with Ben Jonson; Fuller's Worthies; Robert Johnston's Hist. Rerum Brit.; Bryskett's Discourse; Camden, Ware, etc. See, below, references on the Life of Spenser.

MISCELLANEOUS AND GENERAL REFERENCES ON THE LIFE

See below, under "Works" references on the View of Ireland; "Spenser and Shakespeare"; under "Various Topics" see references on "Portraits," "Autograph," "Poet Laureate," etc.

For the historical background of Sp's life see generally Froude's History of England; the Cambridge History; A. F. Pollard, History of England, 1547–1603, Lond. 1915, esp. 433 (Plantation of Munster), 434, 445–46, ch. xxii (The Conquest of Ireland), and App. I (Authorities); Arthur D. Innes, England under the Tudors, Lond. 1905, esp. chs. xvi–xxviii.

BIOGRAPHICAL MATERIAL IN SPENSER'S WORKS:

E. de Sélincourt, especially (Introd. to his one-volume Oxford ed. of Sp, 1912) has utilized and interpreted the biographical material in Sp's works—"the pictures of his own life that are scattered about his verse." See pp. xiv ff. on the Sh Cal "as veiled autobiography."

See generally Whitman's Subject Index to Spenser, 224 ("Spenser"). In a general sense all of Sp's writings, like those of most poets, have autobiographical value and abound in self-revelation. But scattered through most of them are specific personal references, sometimes explicit, but more often tantalizingly vague and cryptic. Much of the commentary on Sp is devoted to the attempted elucidation of these. For convenience of reference some of the more significant of these are here listed. See also personal references listed under separate headings elsewhere, e.g., "Lost Works," "Sources," "Circle," "Spenser and Sidney," etc.

Sh Cal, E.K's Epistle (early love affairs); June, Oct. (poetic aim and theory; prelude to FQ; see also T of M); July (Bp. of Rochester); Oct. (autobiographical); Dec. (autobiographical, possibly, although it closely follows Marot; note the additions *not* in Marot; see its refs. to his tutor Wrenock and to Rosalind).

R of T, Ded. (visit to England, 1590).

MHT, ll. 890 ff. (Sp's experiences after graduating).

CCCHA is the most autobiographical of Sp's poems—"a verse diary." Cf. Ded.—"agreeing with the truth in circumstance and matter." See esp. the question of date, and ll. 20 ("thy turning backe") 24, 36, 93 (Sp's reason for living in Ireland), 113 (Buttevant), 183 ff., 272 ff. (the course of the passage over), 290, 293, 298 (place of the recital), 314 ff. (the state of Ireland); ref. to Sh Cal in the opening lines.

Amoretti, published with the Epithalamion, and although in parts possibly written much earlier, intended to be taken as treating generally the same subject—Sp's later love story. Largely autobiographical in spite of convention and imitation. Note Publisher's Ded. ("in his absence," etc.); on the date see sonnets 4, 19, 22, 60, 62, 68; see also 33 (personal, on the FQ, and Bryskett), 38, 50, 52, 60, 61, etc. for personal touches; 62 (written at the moment); 65, l. 4; 66, 69 (personal in spite of the borrowings), 72 (inner life), 74 (the three Elizabeths), 80 (autobiographic; on the FQ).

Epithalamion, esp. the opening lines; see also ll. 12 (reference to the Complaints volume?), 39, 56 (on the identification of the bride), 60–61, 167, 429 (envoy), 264 (date of wedding). Note many points of connection with and recurrence to the Amoretti.

Four Hymns: Dedication, date; No. I, ll. 151 ff. (Elizabeth or Rosalind?), 298–304 (written before his marriage?); No. II, l. 90; No. III, ll. 11 ff. (ref. to Sh Cal or to lost works?); No. IV, ll. 291 ff. (inner life in poet's latter days).

Prothalamion: esp. stanza 1, ll. 5–11 (cf. MHT, ll. 905–18), and stanzas 8 and 9.

Astrophel, passim.

FQ, I, Introd. stanzas (ref. to Sh Cal?); I, iii. 1 (Sp at court; the woman worshiper); I, ix, 4 (cf. Hunter, Chorus Vatum, IV, 473); I, ix, 17; I, x, 42, l. 9; I, xii, 1; II, Introd. stanzas; III, Introd. stanzas; III, ix, 1, 2; IV, Introd. stanzas (Burleigh; "my looser rimes"); IV, i, 42; IV, x, 1, 2; IV, xi, 34; IV, xi, 40 ff. (Irish rivers, etc.); V, passim (on Ireland, Grey's government, etc.; see esp. V, xii, 26 ff.); VI, Introd. stanzas; VI, ix, 35, 41 ff.; VI, x, passim (ref. to Epithal.; see 25, ref. to Sp's bride); VI, xii, 1, 40, 41; VII (Mutability) vi, 36 ff., 40 (ref. to CCCHA); VII, vii, 1. See the Letter to Raleigh, passim.

View of Ireland. (References to pages of Grosart's ed. of Sp, IX). The View of Ireland abounds in personal (autobiographical) references. Of course, as it is a dialogue, there is a certain amount of dramatic disguise and the interlocutors may not always speak unequivocally for Sp. But as it was a sort of informal state-paper and presentation of a proposed policy for Ireland, representing the best views of certain men of experience in Ireland (cf. p. 255), and as its appeal was to those in authority in England, it doubtless kept very close to facts as Sp saw them. Irenaeus is obviously his mouthpiece. There are numerous quasi-personal phrases, e.g., 47 ("I have often observed"), 50 ("I can witness"), 59 ("as oftentimes I have seen them"). See also at pp. 87, 101, 119, 122, 132, 155, 157, 159, 160, 172, 179, 188, 189, 195, 196, 201, 225, 226.

The more important autobiographical passages are at pp. 31 (written in England), 38 (personal knowledge of northern Ireland?),

39 (Lord Grey in Ireland; and so passim, esp. 164 ff.), 43, 45, 79 (possible reference to the travels of Irenaeus-Spenser, perhaps in 1579), 104 (Munster; cf. 161–62, etc.), 116 (on poetry and poets—cf. Letter to Raleigh), 132 (Sp and the religious calling—cf. 242), 132–34 (the good in Catholicism—cf. 243–44), 141–45 (guarded reprehension of the policy of some Lord Deputies of Ireland after, and before, Grey; ref. to Essex?), 147 (Sp forewarned, c. 1596, of the coming cataclysm in Ireland—cf. 173 ff.; 208), 150 (date of writing, "this last year"; = ?), 154 (Map of Ireland consulted), 155 ("I see and have often proved"—the words of a Deputy's secretary), 159 (Sp's experience of Desmond's rebellion), 164 (ref. to Sir Henry Sidney?), 166–68 (Sp present at massacre at Smerwick), 169 ff. (Sp out of sympathy with Sir John Perrott—Lord Deputy 1584–88), 181 (commendation of Sir Wm. Russell—Lord Deputy 1594–97); 183 ("I am no martial man"—but cf. language of letter recommending Sp as sheriff of Cork), 183 (the voice of Lord Grey's secretary), 192 (comment on the "plot" of the Munster undertakers—cf. 206 ff.), 220 (Sp on Lord Roche), 251, 252 (ref. to Essex?), 253 (written in England—"here"), 254, 255, 256 (hint of another book on Ireland by Sp, to follow).

Sp evidently saw that the old policies in Ireland were failing and so seizes the opportunity again to propose those of Grey. Perhaps the subsequent appointment of Sp as sheriff of Cork was a belated (and too late) recognition of the value of the recommendations of the V of I—cf. 184–85 on the delinquencies of the new officials sent over from England and the need of using old and experienced men.

The Spenser-Harvey Letters (references to Grosart, IX) are full of biographical material. See esp. Sp's letter of 5 Oct. 1579, pp. 262 ("intermitted the uttering of my writings"; ref. to Sidney and Leicester and benefits received by Sp—"some sweetness that I have already tasted"), 262 (a work of Sp's "being made in honor of a private personage unknown"—a woman; Sp's dependence on Harvey's advice), 263 ("my late being with her Majesty"—cf. 264 on "my next going to the Court"; Sp "in some use of familiarity" with Sidney and Dyer; their Areopagus, etc.; Sp's "Slumber" and other "pamphlets" intended to Dyer; Ascham), 264 (E. K.; this letter written 15 Oct. at Westminster, and 16 Oct., yet dated 5 Oct. 1579; his letters to be imparted only to Preston, Still, etc.), 265 (Specimens of Sp's "iambics"—to Rosalind?), 266 (this a farewell letter; Sp about to travel), 266–70 (Latin verses by Sp. He is soon to sail to Gallic lands, about to visit the Caucasus, the Alps, the Pyrenees, Babylon—perhaps under Leicester's tutelage, with an English mission to the Near East—; Sp a "new poet," and a youth with some genius; Harvey the confidant of his love-affairs), 270

(hopes to start next week, sent and maintained by "my Lord," i.e.
Leicester?; has promised to write Sidney who "so promised to do
again").
Letter of April, 1580, pp. 272 (Sp has tried English hexameters; the
rules of English quantity given him by Sidney, originally devised
by Drant, enlarged by Sidney, "and augmented with my observations"), 274 (Lost Works; his plans for poems; debt to Holinshed;
at work on the Faerie Queene).

The Academy, Lond., LVI (1899), 67, "Spenser's Tercentenary."
Rejects the idea of the starved, abused, and obscure Sp; notes on
King street, Westminster, and Sp's abode there during his last days:
a quarter then in good repute; his school, portraits, etc.

Add. MSS 25079–83, Brit. Mus. Vol. I = Letters and papers
chiefly to and from Sir John Spencer of Althorp, relating to
the musters in the county of Northampton. Nothing about
Sp. Remaining vols. cover 1600–47.

ACKERMANN, RICHARD [publisher only?]. History of the Uni-
versity of Cambridge [by W. Combe and F. Shoberl?].
Lond. 1815. 2v. illus. I, 51–80:
Pembroke Hall, with views. Brief sketch of Sp at p. 74 (copy in
Bost. Pub. Lib.).

ALLEN, THOS. A New History of London. Lond. 1839, IV, 119:
Sp's monument of 1778, with the inscription ("born in London in
1553, and died in 1598," etc.).

ALLIBONE, S. A. Dictionary of English Literature, Phila. 1899,
II, 2202–8:
The life; chronological catalogue of works (in order of publication);
numerous citations of "critical opinions."

Anthologia Hibernica. Dublin, 1793, I, 189:
A descendant of Sp at Drogheda possessing an original portrait of
Sp and valuable records.

Archaeologia, XXI (1827), 551–53:
Gives the text of two Bills in Chancery, from the Rolls Office at Dublin:
(1) Petition of Lord Roche: that Sp had recently [no date given]
sued Roche for three plowlands of Shanballymore; prays for a certiorari to remove the case into the Lord Chancellor's Court. "A
Certiorary graunted ad Dublin Canc."
(2) Petition of Sylvanus Spencer: that his father, Edmond Spencer,
was seized of the fee of "Kyllcolemane," "and dyvers other lands

and tenements in the County of Corck"; Sylvanus = the heir, but
these lands have come into the hands of Roger Seckerstone and the
petitioner's mother, "which they iniustly detayneth"; prays for
relief in Chancery. Date of no. 2 probably 1602–3. Cf. Grosart's
ed. of Sp, I, 157, 531.

ARCHDALL, MERVYN, and P. F. MORAN. Monasticon Hibernicum, Dublin, 1873–76. 3 v. illus. Orig. ed. 1786.
"History of Religious Houses in Ireland." See for place-names,
etc. See II, 289 on New Abbey and the lease to Sp; this in 1620 in
possession of Sir Henry Harrington. Vol. III not pub'd?

AUBREY, JOHN (1626–97). Lives of Eminent Men. Lond. 1813,
II, 541:
Anecdotes of Sp of doubtful authenticity; that Sp was an acquaintance of Sir Erasmus Dryden; Rosalind a kinswoman of the latter;
"Spenser's chamber" at Sir Erasmus Dryden's, where MS of stanzas
of FQ were found; as to Sp's person; that Sp lived for a time in Hampshire (on the authority of Samuel Woodford, the poet); Sp a friend of
Abp. Ussher; inscription on Sp's tomb. II, 553: Of the first meeting
of Sp and Sidney.

AUBREY, JOHN. Brief Lives, ed. A. Clark, Oxford, 1898: II,
232–33, 248.

BAGWELL, RICHARD. Ireland under the Tudors, Lond. 1885–90.
Vol. III, chs. xxxvi–xlvii, cover the period of Sp's life in Ireland.
See esp. 75, 198–99, 439, 457–58 (Sp and his friends in Ireland), etc.
See the index.

BAKER, THOS. Letters on Spenser. In European Magazine,
XIII (1788), 237–38:
Date of birth; competition with Andrews; Sp and Grindal.

BENNETT, GEO. History of Bandon. Cork, 1862. 4 ff.:
The project of the undertakers.

Biographia Britannica. Lond. 1747–66. VI, 3802–14:
The conventional "life," corrected in places and reworked. In-
ordinately padded with footnotes; the edition of 1777–93, by Kippis is
incomplete and does not extend to "S."

BIRCH, THOS. Life of Sp, with his ed. of Sp. Lond. 1751. I,
pp. i–xxxvii:
Sp's birth, London, c. 1553; story of rivalry with Andrews for fellowship at Cambridge an error; the trip abroad c. 1579; repeats some of
the old anecdotes, but mostly based on the material in Sp's writings.

BOAS, MRS. FREDERICK. In Shakspere's England. N.Y. 1904. Ch. xii:
> A popularizing sketch.

"Bodleian Letters." Title cited in Cooper's Athenae Cantabrig. See Aubrey, John.

BROUGHAM, HENRY, LORD. Cabinet Portrait Gallery of British Worthies. Lond. 1845, 6 v. IV, 135–60:
> An independently written short life. See 140–42 on Edmund Spencer the bearer of despatches from France, 1569; 144–47 on Rosalind; etc.

BRUCE, J. D. Edmund Spenser. In Warner's Library of the World's Best Literature. N.Y. 1897. XXXV, 13751–55:
> An excellent short sketch.

BRYSKETT, LODOWICK. A Discourse of Civill-Life. London, for William Apsley, 1606. Also London, for E. Blount, 1606. 279 pp. "Written to Arthur Lord Grey" (died 1593).
> Of first rate interest. Mention of Spenser at pp. 6, 25–29, 163, 271–72, 273, 275, 278, etc. Cf. 270–78 with FQ, III, vi. At the end occurs this passage: "This (loe) is as much as mine author hath discoursed vpon this subiect, which I haue Englished for my exercise in both languages, and haue at your intreaties communicated vnto you: I will not say, being betrayed by M. *Spencer*, but surely cunningly thrust in, to take vp this taske, whereby he might shift himselfe from that trouble."
>
> Cf. Harman's Edmund Spenser, ch. xx; Grosart's Sp, I, 148–49, 500–508. Todd's ed. of Sp, 1805, I, p. lvi; J. W. Draper in the Colonnade, N.Y. 1922, 41–42.
>
> Cf. Mary A. Scott, Elizabethan Translations from the Italian. Bost. 1916, 476–78 (that it is from the Italian of Giraldi Cinthio, i.e. his Tre Dialoghi della Vita Civile, published with his Hecatommithi, 1565; a French translation of this by G. Chappuys appeared in Paris in 1583 as Dialogues philosophiques, italiens-français, touchant la vie civile).
>
> Copies of Bryskett's Discourse are in the Harvard Library (also of the Dialoghi, 1574), the Huntington Library, and (a photostat) in the Newberry Library, Chicago.

BUCK, P. M. New Facts concerning the Life of Edmund Spenser. In Mod. Lang. Notes, XIX (1904), 237–38:
> Sp's life 1582–89; in Dublin 1586; documents newly cited.

DOCUMENT OF AUGUST 29, 1582, IN PUBLIC RECORD OFFICE, LONDON, SHOWING
SPENSER'S SIGNATURE

BUTLER, WM. F. T. Confiscations in Irish History. Dublin, 1917, 138–39:
A very general account of Irish grants to Sp and his family.

C., J. Biographical Sketches of Persons Remarkable in Local History: Edmund Spenser. In Journal of Cork Hist. and Arch. Soc., III (1894), 89–100; based on Gibson's Hist. of Cork.

Calendar of Proceedings in Chancery in the Reign of Queen Elizabeth. Lond. 1829–32. 3 v. III, 4 (S.s. 1.):
"Edmond Spencer and others" vs. Thomas, Emily and John Matthew. Performance of Trust. "Personal Matters." (Qu. Is this the poet?)

Calendars: see also Historical MSS Com. Reports, below.

Calendars of State Papers relating to Ireland. Henry VIII, Edward VI, Mary, and Elizabeth. Lond. 1860–1903. Volumes covering dates as below.

1574–85

191: Pelham's brother Spenser; similarly 233, 238; 292: Letter of Mar. 11, 1581, from Ireland, "certified" by Sp (cf. Grosart's Sp, I, 147); similarly 293 (March 16, 1581), 303 (other papers certified by Sp; one "under the hand of Spenser," Apr. 29, 1581, at Cork), 381 (May 17, 1582; certified by Sp at Dublin, June 29), 393 ("copia vera, Exr. Ed. Spenser," to which is added in another hand "Secretary to the L. Grey, L. Deputy here," Aug. 29, 1582, Dublin). See reproduction.[1]

345: 1582, in a list of "Lands and Goods of the rebels given by the Lord Deputy," "the lease of a house in Dublin belonging to Baltinglas for six years to come unto Edmund Spenser, one of the Lord Deputy's secretaries, valued at 5 l."; also Sp has a custodiam of John Eustace's land of the Newland (on "custodiams" of escheated lands cf. Lodge's Desiderata Curiosa, 75).

Cf. A. F. Pollard, Hist. of Engl., 1547–1603. Lond. 1910. 433: the attainder of Baltinglas, Apr.-May, 1586.

533: as to fortifying a castle of "Kilcoman."

And see the Preface, passim, esp. p. lxxvi on Sp at the Fort del Ore affair.

[1] Mr. H. R. Plomer writes: "I may point out that the words 'copia vera Edm. Spser' found on several documents at the Record Office do not imply that they were written by Spenser; as a fact, they are in several different hands and the words only mean, I suggest, that as chief secretary he had read the copies with the originals and found them correct."

1586–88

222: Dec. 8, 1586. "Collection of the arrearages of first fruits. These
contain the names of many of the clergy of the time, amongst others
. . . . Edmondus Spenser, prebendary of Effin."
Mr. H. R. Plomer supplies the following transcript from the original:
No. 18. A Booke of the proceedings againste the clergy of Ireland
vpon certen informaçons in the eschequor there. P. 698. Breuis
collectio quorundum arreragiorum primorum fructu*um* . . . .
debit ex deversis Dignitat ac promocion*ibus* spiritualibus infra-
script . . . .
P. 716. Limericen
Edmondus Spencer pre͞b. de Effin. iij *li*.
261: Letter of Irish Commissioners to Burleigh, Feb. 16, 1587: in the
course of the official survey of the lands of the Munster Undertakers Arthur Robyns, surveyor, has recently made a survey of
Kilcolman.

1588–92

131: March 4, 1588–89. "Mr. Reade hath taken Kilcolman being about
3000 acres, but what he hath done in it I know not." Cf. Grosart's
ed. of Sp, I, 150: as to Read, and date of first grant of Kilcolman.

Mr. H. R. Plomer cites a document of 4 Sept. 1587 in State Papers,
Ireland, Vol. 131.6 (PRO): that the manor of Kilcolman was assigned
by the Commissioners to "Andrewe Reade of Facombe, Co South-
ampton, gent."
198: May, 1589. The answer of Edmund Spenser, gent. to the articles
for examining attainted lands past to the undertakers. That he has
undertaken the peopling of a seigniory of 4000 acres allotted from the
undertakers, in which the castle and lands of Kilcolman and Rossack
were appointed unto him, but it is short 1000 acres of the 4000 due
him; his patent soon to be issued; four nobles rent on Ballingarragh
and 6/8 on Ballingfoynigh chargeable; but six households of English
people on his land, but others have promised to come. "Autograph,
p. 1." Cf. Grosart's ed. of Sp, I, 152 ff. on the Undertakers.
247: Oct. 12, 1589. Suit of Lord Roche to the queen against Edmond
Spenser, Clerk of the Council in Munster, and others; that Sp had
seized Lord Roche's land, despoiled his tenants, beaten his bailifs,
etc. Counter complaint against Lord Roche, who has imprisoned
Sp's men; and other details of their quarrel. "Autograph, with
endorsement by Edmond Spenser." (Lord Roche was on the Irish
side, and Sp's acts would probably be regarded by the English as
permitted to an undertaker put in possession of forfeited lands); cf.
Grosart's ed. of Sp, I, 156, 530 ff.

258: Oct. 29, 1589: "Mr. Edmond Spenser hath by particular 4000 acres." (In a list of patents to the English undertakers.)

341: Richard Whyte to Burghley, May 8, 1590: on evil conditions in Ireland; that many English in office there are papists. "In the begining of last Lent Sir Thomas Norreys, in Limerick, came to the Lord's Table, but not one of his gentlemen came thither except one Chitester [Chichester], substitute to Mr. Spenser in his office of clerkship of Munster."

Note: The seat of the Council of Munster was then at Limerick. Chichester was apparently serving as Sp's locum tenens during the latter's absence in England. See references to a Chichester, in Munster, in Cal. of Fiants, Elizabeth, Nos. 1205, 2128, 2803, 5261, 5407, 5496, 5954.

1592–96

56: Dec. 31, 1592: List of the undertakers in Munster: "Cork, Edmund Spenser hath of rentable lands the number of 3028 acres, *redditus inde per annum a festo Michaelis*, 1591, *pro tribus annis*, 8 l. 13 s. 9 d., *et a festo Michaelis*, 1594, *per annum, exinde imperpetuum* 17 l. 7 s. 6 1/2 d. Chief rents 1 l. 13 s. 4 d."

57: 1592. List of undertakers who have paid their rents to the exchequer: "Cork, Edmund Spenser, 5 l. 15 s. 10 d. at Easter, and Cork, Edmund Spenser, 3 l. 19 s. 6 d." at Michaelmas.

58: Spenser "absent" [from his estate and from Cork,—in England?] Aug.–Sept., 1592, and suspected, with others, of not having well "performed the plot of the habitation."

60: 1592. A similar list. "Mr. Edmund Spenser hath by particular only 4000 acres, the rent 22 l."

1598–99

280 f.: Official Report of the Rebellion of Oct. 1598, by Sir Thos. Norris, to the English Privy Council.

288: "A Note of the spoils committed and of the towns burned, in the barony of Buttevant . . . . 15 Oct. 1598." (Including Kilcolman?).

300: Justice Saxey's account, Oct. 26, 1598, of Tyrone's massacres (wherein, doubtless, Kilcolman was despoiled).

316 ff. "A discourse . . . by William Weever [probably a friend of Sp's] touching the proceedings of the rebels in Munster" (Oct. 1598): The defection of Sir Thos. Norris and consequent panic of the English, Oct. 7 and following; etc.

319 ff.: Oct. 1598. From a MS history of the time (1598): "The spoil of Kilcolman" ["vivid account of the insurrection; it must have reached Kilcolman between Oct. 11 and 17. Spenser not named among those who behaved badly, though Norris and Lyon were so named."—Edith Rickert]. That the Lord Lieutenant left a strong

garrison at Kilmallock; the rebels had burned Buttevant; the Lord Lieutenant in Cork 17 Oct. 1598; the wealthier English took refuge in the walled towns; flight of Sir Thos. Norris, Bp. Lyons, Justice Saxey, etc. Cf. 325, 330 f., 415 ff., and passim.

398: Dec. 7, 1598: Captains Thos. Southwell and Timothy Cottrell to the Privy Council: The sheriff of the County of Cork [Spenser? Cork was allowed *two* sheriffs], with the most part of the Undertakers, their wives and children, placed in Cork "at the beginning of the Munster rebellion" [but was the spoil of Kilcolman at "the beginning"?]. "There they yet remain" (Dec. 8, 1598).
The "Sheriff of Cork" was in Cork, Dec. 7, 1598 [was this Sp? When did he leave for England? Cf. Grosart's Sp, I, 230].

401: Despatch of Dec. 9, 1598, Cork, "sent by the hand of Edmund Spenser, the poet."

414: Cork, Dec. 21, 1598, Despatch from Sir Thos. Norreys to the Privy Council. Previous despatch sent by Spenser. Norris' despatch is given at pp. 396–401, endorsed "Received at Whitehall 24 Dec.," 1598.

431: A MS of the View of Ireland, in P.R.O.

431–33: "A briefe note of Ireland. Endorsed:" "A briefe discourse of Ireland by Spencer," 10 pp. Synopsis and quotations. Not the View of Ireland. Printed in Grosart's ed. of Sp, I, 537–55.

467: Letter of Sir Thos. Norreys to Sir Robert Cecil, Jan. 24, 1598–99, Cork: "Since my last by Mr. Spenser."

484: Letter of Nicholas Curteys to Sir Robert Cecil, Feb. 1598–99. Curteys has served "in that poor and troublesome place of clerk of the Council of Munster," held "upon the trust of Lodowick Bryskett and Edmund Spenser (men not unknown to your Honour)." Refers to "Edmund Spenser being lately deceased, the mean and witness of our mutual trust and confidence."

1600

242: Effin, near Kilmallock.

Calendars 1574–85.

Not noticed in the Calendar, 1574–85, the following entry appears in the State Papers, Ireland, Vol. 97. 17 (1) (At the Public Record Office. Transcript supplied by Mr. H. R. Plomer): A note of all suche monye as hath been paid and imprested by Sir Henry Wallopp Knight Threasurer at Warres in Ireland to sundrye Captaines serving in the said province [Munster] betwene the fyrst of September 1579 and the laste of August 1582, as hereafter vppon everye captaines head particularlye as sett down appereth, viz.

John Zowche esquier ⎱ xixth October 1581, per bill due
Collonell in Mounster ⎰ to Edmond Spencer
xxxij *li.*

Calendars, 1592–96.

Mr. H. R. Plomer supplies the following transcript of an entry in the State Papers, Ireland, Vol. 168, No. 10 (1), not noticed in the Calendars:

An abstract of the orders made before us the Comyssioners in Mounster in Somer 1592. The Originalls, pleadings, evidences, & other *pro*ceadings are at large recorded in the exchequer at Dublin. Com. Cork. Nic*ho*las Shynan pl.* [*Sometimes known as McShane & sometimes as Shane Barry.]

Edmond Spencer deft. for Ardadam a plowe land & Killoyenesie, half a plowe land, Balliellice a plo: lande, & Ardgilbert di plo: land.

The p*ts* tytle ys by discents from his auncestors. The defend*t* saith they were *p*cells of S*r* John of Desmondes landes, viz. *p*cell of Kilcolman and Rosacke to w*ch* her Ma*tie* is intitled.

After long pleadings, the parties for the dificulties of their tytles, especiallie consistinge uppon the true mearinge of the Townes, were contented to have it referred to an indifferent Iurie, to be impannelled by the Sherif of the Countie of Corke, who retorned a *p*sentment of a Iurie on the behalf of the defend*t*. Whereupon yt was ordered u*p*pon consideraci*on* of the said Inquiries, that the p*t* shall recover Ardgilbert and Balliellice, and that he his heires and assignes shall enioy theim against the defend*t*, untill better matter appeare, and that the defend*t* shall contynue the possession of Kilmeneasie against the p*t* untill better tytle shalbe made for him. Ellemocane where yt was *p*sented, that Wi*llm* Shenan did infeoffe Thomas Butler of Ardadam, the said Thomas his sonne Theobald Butler, did for his father assent and agree, that the p*t* shold recover the same notw*th*standinge anie such feoffement. W*ch* *p*cell of Ardadam ys likewise ordered the p*t* shall recover untill better matter appeare for her Ma*tie* or for the defend*t*. And for that Balliellice ys passed to the defend*t* at one plowe land, and Ardadam, at the rate of a plowe land: the defend*t* ys abated the rent of two plo: landes, viz after the rate of 28 plowe landes to a Seignorie of xij*m* [12,000] acres, and after the rate of a C [100] marks to a seignorie of xij*m* [12,000] acres in the Countie of Corke. W*ch* abatem*t* ys tyll Mich*is* 1594. 47s. 6d. and after for ever the s*ome* of 4*li.* 15s. sterlinge.

Calendar of Fiants in the Public Records in Ireland. In Reports of the Deputy Keeper. Dublin, 1869+ See index in App. to 21st and 22nd Reports.

Fiants: Elizabeth

No. 3694: Grant, 22 March, 1580–81, to Edmund Spenser, gent., secretary of the deputy, of the office of registrar or clerk in Chancery,

for faculties under the statue 28 Hen. VIII. To hold during good
behaviour, with the fees belonging to the office.—Given free from the
Seale in respect he ys Secretarie to the right honorable the Lord
Deputie. Cf. Catalogue of Harl. MSS.

Note: The Statute referred to, I take it, is not the *English*
Statute of 28 Henry VIII (see below), but that passed by the Irish
Parliament in 1537.

Cf. the Statutes at Large passed in the Parliaments held in Ireland
from the Third Year of Edward the Second, A.D. 1310, to the Twenty-
sixth Year of George the Third, A.D. 1786 inclusive. Published by
Authority. Dublin, 1786. Folio. ch. xix (1537), pp. 142 ff.,
"The Act of Faculties": Recital of conditions; licenses, faculties,
etc. not to be granted from Rome, but hereafter by the Abp. of Canterbury or his deputies subject to the approval of the Crown; dispensations where the tax to Rome amounted to four pounds to be confirmed
under the Great Seal and enrolled in Chancery, and others also, if
so wished, on payment of five shillings.

The Archbishop to have power to ordain a clerk to write and register
all licenses; the Crown also to ordain "one sufficient clerke, being
learned in the course of chancery" to inroll all confirmations of such
licenses; both clerks to sign all such licenses; also to register the same.
Two books of the "taxes" of such licenses to be kept, one with the
Archbishop's clerk, the other "with the clerke of the chauncerie"
appointed by the Crown. Complicated provisions as to fees: If the
tax be £4 or over, two thirds to be "perceived by the said clerke
of the chauncerie" to the use of the Crown and the Lord Chancellor,
and "to the use of the said clerke," one-third to the clerk of the
Archbishop,—i.e. three-fourths of this two-thirds to the Crown, the
remaining one-fourth to be divided again into three parts, of which
the Chancellor shall have two parts, and the clerk of the Chancery
the third part for his pains. Similar provisions as to the Archbishop
and his clerk. Provisions if the tax be less than four pounds. Exceptions allowing other bishops to issue certain licenses. Miscellaneous
provisions.

This act extends not only to England but to the King's other domin-
ions, including Ireland. Commissioners for ecclesiastical jurisdiction granting faculties to have the same authority as the Archbishop
of Canterbury. Cf. Liber Munerum Publicorum Hiberniae, Pt. VI,
7 ff. for a digest of this statute.

The English act of 28 Henry VIII is to be found in The Statutes at
Large, I Richard III to 31 Henry VIII, ed. Danby Pickering. Cambridge, 1763, IV, 443 ff. (Cap. xvi): Provisions similar to the above,

except as to fees, clerks, etc. No provision for extending the act to Ireland.

Professors Floyd R. Mechem and James P. Hall, and Mr. H. S. Oakley have kindly assisted me in finding the English acts. Other editions of the Statutes fail to give this act. Professor Mechem also has called my attention to a somewhat similar act of 25 Henry VIII. Cf. The Statutes at Large, ed. Pickering, IV, 296 ff.

The Act of 28 Henry VIII is described by C. L. Falkiner, Essays relating to Ireland, Lond. 1909. p. 13 *n.* The statement that it provides for faculties to be obtained under the seal of the Archbishop of *Dublin* is probably an inference from the Irish act. For the statement that with this office was united the cognate office of Registrar of Ecclesiastical Appeals I do not know the authority. Is this latter office that of "Clerk of Decrees and Recognizances," asserted to have been held by Sp. by Hardiman, Grosart and other writers? If so, the statement does not seem to be borne out by the lists of public officers in Ireland, *temp.* Elizabeth, given in the Liber Munerum Publicorum Hiberniae.

On the subject of "faculties" and the clerk in chancery for faculties see Encyclopedia of the Laws of England, Lond. 1907, VI, 1–2, on "Faculty, and Court of Faculties." Cf. also the Laws of England, by the Earl of Halsbury, Lond. 1910, XI, 540, "Faculty Cases."

It does not appear that Sp was a clerk of a court of law or equity. The "Court of Faculties," in English ecclesiastical law, was not a court for the trial or hearing of cases, but a sort of commission or advisory council for the archbishop. Sp's duties probably were merely those of a registrar for licenses and dispensations (= "faculties") issued under the authority of the primate, or his deputy in Ireland.

Qu. Was this office in Sp's case a mere sinecure ("a deputy allowed")?

Cf. F. I. Carpenter, in Mod. Philol., XIX (1922), 413–15.

Cf. Cottonian MS, Titus, B. XII, No. 89 (Brit. Mus.). "Concerning the instruccions delivered for passing facultyes, within this realm of Ireland":

Recites what "dispensacions" are reserved to the Archbishop of Canterbury, those of tax less than £4 "being committed to the Commissioners in Ireland." Other exceptions. Permits for (clerical) non-residence are reserved to the Archbishop.

Cf. Cottonian MS, Titus, B. XIII, fol. 263 ff. Dated 20 Dec. 1578:

Notes contents of letters patent granted Geo. Ackworth and Robert Garvey [commissioners of faculties in Ireland] under act of

the Parliament in Dublin 10 May, 28 Henry VIII, and 12 Jan.,
Eliz., ii. All holders of ecclesiastical benefices and dignities to exhibit
their titles; the commissioners to hear all suits; to exercise probate
jurisdiction in Ireland, acting for the Archbishop of Canterbury;
to impose fines, take recognizances, etc. Comments by Garvey follow. There also follows "A Note of such proffittes as came to the
Q's Ma*tie* by the execuc*i*on of the Commission for faculties in Ireland
An*o* 1577 (xv Dec. 1578)". . . . ."Fees for dispensac*i*ons paid to
Ldowyck Briskett, Clerke of the Chauncerie for Faculties to the Q's
onlie use since the beginninge of Easter terme 1577, till the beginninge
of Michaelmas terme 1578, as appeareth by his acquittances remain-
inge with Rowland Cowycke gent. register of faculties . . . . lxxxviij
li. xiiij *s.* sterl."

Cf. Fiant 2996, Eliz. 1576–77, for appointment of Ackworth and
Garvey as commissioners of Faculties.

Cf. H. Wood, Guide to Records of Ireland, Dublin, 1919, p. 58, on
duties of Clerk of the Faculties.

On the "faculties" generally see the various Calendars of State
Papers, Ireland, the indexes, s.v.

No. 3785: Lease, under commission, 15 July, 1581, to Edmund Spenser,
gent., of the site of the house of friars of Enescortie, with appurtenances; the manor of Enescortie, a ruinous castle, land, and a weir
there; lands of Garrane, Killkenane, Loughwertie, Barrickerowe
and Ballinepark, and the customs of boards, timber, laths, boats
bearing victuals, lodges during the fair, and things sold there, and
fishings belonging to the manor, and all other appurtenances as well
within the Morroes country as without. To hold for 21 years. Rent
£13. 6s. 4d. Maintaining one English horseman.—6 December, xxiv
(1582). Cf. Grosart's Sp, I, 146; Cf. Collier's ed. of Sp, I, p. xlix.

No. 3969: Lease, under commission, 15 July, xxii, to Edmund
Spenser, gent., of the site of the house of friars called the New Abbey,
Co. Kildare, with appurtenances; also an old waste town adjoining,
and its appurtenances, in the queen's disposition by the rebellion
of James Eustace. To hold for 21 years. Rent £3. Provisions as
in No. 2954 ["Provided that he shall not alien to any except they be
English both by father and mother, or born in the Pale; and shall
not charge coyne or livery."]. 24 Aug. xxiv (1582).

No. 5381: Lease under Commission, 17 Feb.; xxx, to Thomas Lambyn
gent.; the site of the house of friars called the Newe Abbey, co.
Kildare. (1 December, xxxii).

No. 5963: Grant of the estates recited in No. 3785, to Henry Wallop,
4 Nov. 1595. Recites lease to Edmund Spenser [No. 3785], conveyance from Sp to Rich. Synot, 9 Dec. 1581, and lease to Synot, No. 4092.

No. 5473: Grant to Edmund Spenser, gentleman, of the manor, castle, and lands of Kylcolman, Co. Cork, containing [recites the several ploughlands], amounting by measure to 3028 English acres; also a rent of 26s. 8d. due to the late lord ———— out of Ballyneg, and a rent of 6s. 8d., payable to the late traitor, Sir John of Desmond, out of Ballynloynigh, Co. Cork. To hold forever, in fee farm, by the name of 'Hap Hazard,' by fealty, in common socage. Rent £17. 7s. 6 2/3d. from 1594 (half only for the previous three years), and 33s. 4d. for the services of the free tenants. Also 1/2d. for each acre of waste land enclosed. If the lands are found by the survey to contain more than the estimated number of acres, grantee shall pay, 1 1/3d. for each English acre in excess. Power to impark 151 acres. Grantee to build houses for 24 families, of which one to be for himself, two for freeholders of 300 A., two for farmers of 400 A., and 11 for copyholders of 100 A. Other conditions usual in the grants to the undertakers in Munster, as in No. 5032 [payments due on alienation, free export of grain, discharge from all charges except those named in the grant, or those parliament may thereafter impose, penalties for non-fulfilment of conditions, forfeiture for alienation "to any being mere Irish," etc.]. 26 (Oct.), xxxii (1590). Cf. Collier's ed. of Sp, I, pp. lvii f. In the Lodge MSS, Pub. Record Office, Dublin.

No. 4150: Commission to Henry Cowley . . . . Edm. Spencer of New Abay (and others) . . . . to be commissioners of musters in the Co. of Kildare. 12 May, xxv (1583). Cf. Kildare, below.

No. 4464: Commission to Nich. White . . . . Hen. Cowley . . . . Edm. Spenser (and others), gentlemen, to take the muster in Co. Kildare . . . . according to the customs of the realm and the instructions of the lord deputy, 4 July, xxvi (1584). Cf. Catalogue of Cottonian MSS, Brit. Mus. Lond. 1802. Titus, B. XII, No. 75 (the commissioners for musters in Ireland), and No. 150 ("Orders of Council, concerning musters for Ireland").

No. 5535: In a grant of lands, 28 Feb. 1590–91, conveyance of a part of "Killcollman" [Is this Sp's Kilcolman?]. That it is "bounded by . . . . land of Viscount Fermoye [Lord Roche] on the east." That Sp and Lord Roche were adjacent neighbors. Confirmed by Jobson's MS Map of Cork (Trinity Coll., Dublin).

Calendar of the Carew MSS preserved . . . . at Lambeth. Ed. J. S. Brewer and Wm. Bullen. Lond. 1867–73.

1575-88

104: July 8, 1577. Sir Wm. Drury, President of Munster, to Leicester. His proceedings in Ireland. "I have sent to your L[ord] by this bearer a cast of falcons of the best eyrie in this province" [Possibly

Spenser was "this bearer"]; also relates the execution of Murrough
O'Brien July 1, 1577, (described in Sp's V of I, Globe ed., 636).

312: Letter of Justice Pelham to Lord Grey, Sept. 5, 1580: "Two letters
which I received of late, subscribed by you, were not so considerately
written by your secretary as I find by your own letters your Lop.
meant, and as in troth is due to the place of Justice (which unworthily
I hold) for the honour whereof it might have pleased him to have
made me a Lord one day, since I am to be unlorded the next day."

Note: The article on Pelham in the Dict. Nat'l Biog. assumes
that it is Spenser of whom Pelham complains. It is quite possibly
so; but Spenser was only *one* of Lord Grey's secretaries.

462: Book of the wages due the chief officers, and others, of the army
in Ireland, 1 Oct. 1587–31 March, 1588. Includes under "Munster":
"Lodouicke Briskett, clerk of the Council (at 20 l. ster. per annum),
13 l. 6s. 8d. (this is exercised by one Spenser, as deputy to the said
Briskett, to whom it was granted by patent, 6 Nov. 25 Eliz.)." Cf.
Grosart's Sp, I, 151; Collier's ed. of Sp, I, p. lvii.

Note: Did Sp serve as deputy before this mention of his tenure?
Bryskett was granted the clerkship 6 Nov. 1583. Soon after that
date Lord Ormonde in a letter states that Bryskett has sold his office
and gone to England (State Papers, Ireland, Vol. 107.49,—communi-
cated by H. R. Plomer). But Bryskett as appears above continues
to draw the salary. Did he sell the reversion of the office to Boyle?
(Cf. Lismore Papers, 2d. Ser., I, 19 ff.) And did Sp about this time,
c. 1584, begin to serve as Bryskett's deputy? Mr. Plomer points out
that it is apparent from Carew MS 625 (the copy of the Wages Book,
Oct. 1, 1587 to 31 March, 1583) that the statement "this is exercised by one Spenser as deputy to the said Bryskett" is an annota-
tion by William Sandes deputy for the Clerk of the Check. Sp might
long have been serving as deputy to Bryskett. The wages of the
office were £20 per ann. and "diette and table" (State Papers,
Ireland, Vol. 134.41; also Vol. 115.45).

Cf. p. 19, Carew to Burleigh, Feb. 1589, on lack of a clerk at Limerick.
Does this refer to the Clerk of the Council of Munster?

1589–1600

61: List of names of the undertakers in Munster, 1591. Under *Cork*
"Edmond Spencer."

1601–3

35: Letter of Privy Council to Sir G. Carew, Mar. 29, 1601. Encloses
a petition in behalf of "the wife and children of Edmond Spencer,
late clerk of the Council for that province (Munster) . . . . in regard
he was a servitor of the realm."

1603–24

256: In an abstract of Inquisitions taken in 1611 concerning the present state of the lands undertaken in Munster: "A fourth of the seigniory of Kilcolmaine granted to Edmond Spencer; the King's now tenant Silvanus Spencer." Notes on its then condition.

Calendar of Patent and Close Rolls of Chancery of Ireland, Henry VIII—Elizabeth, ed. Jas. Morrin. Dublin, 1861–63. 2 v. II, 90, 319: Enniscorthy.

Calendar of Ancient Records of Dublin, ed. Sir John T. Gilbert. Dublin, "by authority," 1889–1913. 16 v.

Sp's associates (Bryskett &c). Nothing on Sp.

Calendar of State Papers, Scotland, 1581–83. Lond. 1910.

521: Letter of James VI to Elizabeth, 2 July, 1583: "Postscript.— Madam, I have stayed Mr. Spencer upon the letter which is written with our own hand, which shall be ready within two days." (Collier, ed. of Sp, I, p. l suggests that Sp, after his supposed return to England with Lord Grey in 1582, was sent as envoy into Scotland, and is here referred to. But see next entry, p. 526).

526: Robert Bowes to Walsingham, July 9, 1583; this with others, to be sent "by the convoy of this bearer Mr. Richard Spencer," to whom the King has given his own letter.

546: Walsingham to Bowes, 21 July, 1583: the Queen has considered the letters "sent by Mr. Spencer" of the 9th and 13th.

Calendar of State Papers, relating to Scotland, 1589–1603, ed. M. J. Thorpe. Lond. 1858.

II, 723: Nov. 12, 1596. Robert Bowes, Edinburgh, to Lord Burghley "Great offence conceived by the King against Edmund Spenser, for publishing in print, in the 2nd part of the Fairy Queen, chapter 9, some dishonourable effects, as the King deemeth, against himself and his mother deceased. He [Bowes] has satisfied the King about the 'privilege' under which the book is published, yet he still desireth that Edmund Spenser, for his fault, may be duly tried and punished." Extract from Bowes' letter (transcript by Henry R. Plomer): Dated "At Edinb: the xij*th* of Novembr. 1596."

"The K[ing] hath conceaued great offence against Edward Spence publishing in prynte in the second book[1] p[ar]t of the Fairy Queene and ix*th* chapter some dishonorable effects (as the k. demeth thereof) against himself and his mother deceassed. He alledged that this booke was passed with previledge of her mats Commission[er]s for the veiwe and allowance of all wrytinges to be receaued into Printe.

[1] "Book" deleted in MS.

But therin I haue (I think) satisfyed him that it is not given out wth such p[ri]viledge: yet he still desyreth that Edward Spencer for his faulte, may be dewly tryed & punished."

signed Robert Bowes

Addressed to the right honorable his verie good L. the L. Burghley L. Thr[easur]er of England.

II, 747: Feb. 25, 1598. Geo. Nicolson to Sir Robert Cecill. A book, by Walter Quin, the Irishman, concerning the King's [James VI] title to England; Waldegrave's refusal to print it. Quin is also answering Spenser's book [The FQ, Duessa episode?] whereat the King is offended.

The following transcript of a part of this letter, from the Public Record Office, is supplied by Mr. Henry R. Plomer:

Dated "at Edenborough the 25th of February 1597" [=1598]: "Mr. Davyd Fowlis in the K[ing's] name and in great hast hathe pressed Robert Walgrave the K[ing's] printer to print a booke in Latyn made by Walter Quin the Irishman & corrected by Monseur D'Amon, concerning the K[ing's] title to England, that it may be dispersed to forrayne Princes: But Robert Walgrave deferred to do it vntill the Actes of Perliam[e]nt almost don should be ended. And with great grief and sorrow I assure yor honor told me thereof: lamenting his hard fortune, that ether he must printe it, stayenge here, or be vndon, and he feares quarrelled for his life if he refuse it, and printing it greve his conscience, offend her Majestie & vtterly loose his contry: allmost weping, and wishing that for avoyding of this he might have libertie to returne to his owne contrye; w[hi]ch being granted to him he wold returne and leave all here to themselues to printe as they coulde. Of w[hi]ch I have thought it my dutie to aduertise yor honor, that you may take what course herein you please, w[hi]ch vpon yor honors warrant to him shalbe secretly and suerly obeyed. Quyn is also answering Spencers booke whereat the K[ing] was offended."

Camden, William. Reges, Reginae, Nobiles, et Alii in Ecclesia . . . . Westmonasterii Sepulti . . . . Lond. 1606. 70:

"Edmundus Spencer Londinensis, Anglicorum Poetarum nostri seculi facilè princeps, quod eius poemata fauentibus Musis & victuro genio conscripta comprobant. Obijt immatura morte anno salutis 1598 & prope Galfredum Chaucerum conditur qui foelicissimè poesin Anglicis literis primus illustrauit. In quem haec scripta sunt Epitaphia:

Hic prope Chaucerum situs est Spenserius, illi
Proximus ingenio, proximus vt tumulo.

Hic prope Chaucerum Spensere Poeta poetam
Conderis, & versu, quàm tumulo proprior.
Anglica te viuo vixit, plausitque Poesis;
Nunc moritura timet, te moriente, mori."
Copy in Newberry Lib. Cf. E. Fenton, below.

CAMDEN, WM. Britannia, 1607.

Under "Middlesex," on famous persons buried in Westminster
Abbey. Also under "Northamptonshire," p. 376, on the noble family
of the Spencers.

Nothing in eds. of 1586 and 1587.

See Engl. translation, 1722, I, 388.

See Britannia, ed. E. Gibson, Lond. 1695.

319: "Geoffrey Chaucer, who being Prince of the English Poets, ought
not to be pass'd by; as neither Edmund Spenser, who of all the
English Poets came nearest him in a happy genius and a rich vein of
Poetry."

See Britannia, ed. R. Gough, Lond. 1806, II, 84.

CAMDEN, WM. Annales Rerum Anglicanarum et Hibernicarum
regnante Elizabetha. Lond. 1615, 1627.

Ed. of 1615, p. 171: Nec illa praeter Burghleium modo dictum plures
quam tres, et ex eruditissimorum quidem numero non minores quam
fama feruntur. . . . . Tertius, Edm. Spenserus, patria Londinensis,
Cantabrigiensis etiam Academiae alumnus, Musis adeo arridentibus
natus vt omnes Anglicos superioris aeui Poëtas, ne Chaucero quidem
conciue excepto, superaret. Sed peculiari Poetis fato semper cum
paupertate conflictatus, etsi Greio Hiberniae proregi fuerit ab epis-
tolis. Vix enim secessum et scribendi otium nactus, cum à rebellibus
è laribus eiectus et bonis spoliatus, in Angliam inops reversus, statim
expirauit, et Westmonasterii prope Chaucerum impensis Comitatis
Essesciae inhumatus, Poetis funus ducentibus, flebilibus carminibus
et calamis in tumulum conjectis.

English translation, 1635, etc. Ed. of 1688, Bk. IV, 564–65: Death
of Spenser, among distinguished Englishmen who died in 1598 [1599
N.S.]; Sp's great repute; esteemed one of the learned Englishmen of
his time; his struggle with poverty; Secretary to Grey ("ab epis-
tolis"); his death and burial.

CAMDEN, WM. Remains concerning Britain. Lond. 1870.

(Library of the Old Authors.) Editions 1605, 1614, 1623,
1629, etc.

51 (Sp the English Lucan), 344, 427 (laudatory verses on Sp under the
section on "Epitaphs").

CARGILL, ALEX. An Old-time Irish Secretary. In Westminster Review, CLXV (1906), 249–54:

A study of Sp "the man of affairs" in Ireland, especially as revealed in the View of Ireland. Superficial.

CARLISLE, NICHOLAS. Topographical Dictionary of Ireland, Lond. 1810.

For place-names. See on Effin, Enniscorthy, etc.

CARTWRIGHT, J. J. New Facts about Edmund Spenser. In the Academy, VI (1874), 8–9:

Nowell's benefactions to Sp at Merchant Taylors School. Of the Spensers connected with this School. John Spenser the poet's father? Gifts on 7th July, 1569 to "Edmunde Spenser" at Burnley in Lancashire. The Lancashire question discussed.

Catalogue of Additions to the Manuscripts in the British Museum. Lond. 1875+.

Nos. 25,079–25,083: "Letters, papers, and household accounts" of the Spencer family of Althorp, 1522–1656. Qu. If there may not be found some reference to Sp therein? Not found, after examination by H. R. Plomer.

No. 22,022: MS View of Ireland, 1596: "It contains passages which do not appear in the printed editions" [i.e. up to 1875, the date of this catalogue].

No. 19,869: Sp's grant of rights in lands in Co. Cork to J. McHenry, c. 1597. "With autogr. signature." Cf. Collier's ed. of Sp, I, pp. ciii–iv: doubts the authenticity of the document and of the signature.

No. 23,089, ff. 115–34: Notes on Spenser's life and works by G. Vertue, 1731.

No. 24,503, f. 75: Notes on passages in Sp's works by Joseph Hunter, 19th Cent.

Catalogue of the Harleian Manuscripts in the British Museum. Lond. 1808.

I, 136 (No. 286, item 152): Sp's appointment as sheriff of Cork, 30 Sept. 1598.

I, 405 (No. 677.25): MS of MHT.

II, 355 (No. 1932.1): MSS of the View of Ireland; 682 (No. 2393); MS Poem on Edward the Second. "The author perhaps might have been Mr. Edmund Spenser."

III, 447 (No. 6908.1): MS (17th cent. ?) of two of Sp's sonnets; another (1596) of nine of Sp's minor poems.

III, 529 (No. 7388): MS of V of I.

Mr. H. R. Plomer supplies this transcript from Harl. MS 4107: "Edmunde Spencer Register or Clerke in the Chauncerie of the faculties within the kingdome of Ireland qua*m* diu se bene gesserit. A depu[ty] all[owed]. canc. 22° die Marcii 23 Eliz."

Catalogue of the Manuscripts in Gonville and Caius College. By M. R. James. Cambr., 1907.

I, 217: No. 188, a 16th cent. MS of the View of Ireland.

Catalogi Cod. MSS, Bibl. Bodl. Partis Quintae. Oxon. 1862.

B. 478: MS of View of Ireland, 1596.

CAULFIELD, RICHARD. Council Book of the Corporation of Youghal. Guildford, Surrey, 1878.

"From 1610," etc., with map of Youghal, temp. Eliz. See pp. xxi f. View and description of Raleigh's house, and further Raleigh records. Cf. Grosart's Sp, I, 198. (Copy in Bost. Pub. Lib.)

CHALMERS, GEORGE. Supplemental Apology for the Believers in the Shakespeare Papers. Lond. 1799, 21–37:

Upon the life and writings of Spenser. Chalmers' unsuccessful search for Sp's baptism in the London parish registers, and for Sp's connection with the noble family of Spencers in the College of Arms, etc.; verification of the Sp records at Cambridge; the pension; vain search for Sp's will at Doctors Commons. Cf. Collier's ed. of Sp, I, p. xv *n*, xvii ff.

CHAMBERLAIN, JOHN. Letters, ed. Sarah Williams. Lond. (Camden Soc.), 1861, 41:

In letter of 17 Jan. 1598 [1599]: "Spencer, our principall poet, comming lately out of Ireland, died at Westminster on Satterday last."

CHURCH's ed. of the FQ. Lond. 1758. Anonymous Life of Sp prefixed.

Pp. xiv–xviii: Lady Carey and her sisters; xviii–ix: Sp's "North country" possibly Northamptonshire; xxi: Sp's journey to the continent; xxx–xxxii: the date of CCCHA, and Sp's being in England; xxxiii–xxxvii: Sp's marriage, etc.; xxxviii: the View of Ireland written in England; xl: that Ware's testimony as to the loss of Bks. VII–XII of the FQ is trustworthy; Sp's death in 1599; xlv–xlviii: Sp's monument.

CHURTON, RALPH. Life of Alex Nowell. Ox. 1809.

Brother of Robert and of Laurence Nowell. His Lancashire connections. Nothing on Sp.

CIBBER, THEOPHILUS. The Lives of the Poets of Great Britain and Ireland. Lond. 1753.

I, 91–106: the traditional account, with some new criticisms; based on Hughes. Sp's "poetical magic," exempt from "the rules."

CLARK, J. W., and ARTHUR GRAY, eds. Old Plans of Cambridge, 1574 to 1798. Cambr. 1921.

Bird's eye views of Cambridge, 1574, 1575, and 1592. Plan (by John Hamond) reproduced with explanations. See 43–46 on Pembroke Hall. See Sec. 7 of the Plan for plat of the Hall.

COLEMAN, JAS. Biographical Sketches of Persons Remarkable in Local History. In Journal Cork Hist. and Arch. Soc., III (1894), 89–100: "Edmund Spenser."

A compilation, informed with Irish prejudice.

COLLIER, JOHN PAYNE. Life of Shakespeare, prefixed to his ed. of Shakespeare. Lond. 1858.

I, 92: "Willy"=Shakespeare; 94–96: that Sp once resided in Warwickshire (on authority of the "muster-book of Warwickshire" in State-paper office); Sp born before 1553; addressed by Turbervile; 105–7: Aëtion=Shakespeare.

COLLIER, J. P. Bibliog. Account. . . . Lond. 1865.

I, 380–81: Gives Harvey's inscription in the copy of Howleglas presented by Sp. See Harvey Marginalia.

COLLIER, J. P. Chaucer's Monument; Spenser's Death. In Gentleman's Magazine, 1850, II, 485–87:

Mention of Sp's burial in Warner's Albion's England, ed. of 1606; Sp's monument; Sp's death-date.

COLLIER, J. P. Life of Sp, in his ed. of Sp. Lond. 1862. I, pp. ix–clxxviii, with an Index to the Life.

Collier's Life must be used with caution because of his reputation for literary forgeries. Accepts 1552 as year of Sp's birth; that he spent his boyhood in Warwickshire; theory of an early marriage (1587) and a daughter Florence—since discredited (Collier suffers from the delusion that there was only one *Edmund* Spenser in the poet's time); discusses the mooted points in Sp's Life, at times dogmatically. A biography of interest. Should be consulted.

Cf. Grosart's Sp, I, 238 n. T. R. Lounsbury, Studies in Chaucer, I, 29: on Collier's error as to Sp's supposed daughter Florence (born in London, 1587) and Sp's supposed residence in London then.

COMBE, W.   See R. Ackermann, above.

Concordatums, Book of.   In State Papers of Ireland, Elizabeth, in Public Record Office, London.   Cited in Grosart's ed. of Sp, I, 147.

Note: Wood's Guide to the Public Records of Ireland, p. 198, defines *Concordatum* as "a special fund at the disposal of the Lord Lieutenant and Council for payment of extraordinary expenditure." Grosart and the DNB state that Sp in 1582 received for "rewards" from this fund £162. Mr. H. R. Plomer sends me the following transcripts of this record, from which it appears that instead of being "rewards" to Sp the sums were paid over to Sp for rewards to messengers. The last entry of £20 per annum, however, was apparently for Sp's personal account, but possibly for expense-account rather than salary. The inference, however, is that Sp was officially a secretary and not merely private or personal secretary to Grey.

Transcript, State Papers, Ireland, Elizabeth, Vol. 97, pp. 22–33: A Certificate of all suche Concordat as is alredie paid by S*r*. Henrye Wallopp, knight Treasurer at warres there *wch* hath comd to his handes in the times of the Governments of S*r* Wi*llm* Drurye and Sir Wi*llm* Pelham knights late lord Justices and also in the time of the Lord Greye, Lor Deputie of the said Realme viz betwene the fyrst of September 1579 and the last of August 1582 et annis D*ni*.

p. 32.   Edmond Spencer for rewards to messengers, viz.

vltimo September 1580	xvij *li*
12 December	1580	xxv *li* ij *s* v*d*
28 March	1581	lii *li* iiij *s* x*d*
10 July	1581	lxij *li* xvj *s* vj*d*
9 November	1581	lvij *li* v *s* vj*d*
10 February	1581 [1582] lxv *li* xix *s* vj*d*
12 April	1582	xlvj *li* x *s* v*d*
24 June	1582	l *li* ix *s* x*d*
and 24 Augt	1582	liij *li* vj *s* ij*d*

in all as by several concordats appereth the sum of £[430–10–2*d*].

p. 32, verso.   Necessaries for secretaries and clerks attending the Lo: Deputye & Counsail viz. to Edmond Spencer ultimo Decr. 1580 x *li* et 26 Junij 1581 x *li*=xx *li* yr [£20 a year].

In State Papers, Ireland, Elizabeth, Vol. 92, 20 (1) appears the following: Edmond Spencer for Rewards by him payd to messengers at sundrie times, viz:

Ultimo Septembris 1580 by concordatum	£ 12.15
xij Decembris	1580 p*er* concordatum	18.16.10
xxviij March	1581	"	39. 3. 8
x Iune	1581	"	47. 2. 8
ix Nov*r*	1581	"	42.19. 2
In all	£160.17. 4

Cf. F. I. Carpenter, in Mod. Philol., XIX (1922), 415-16.
In the same document (vol. 92.20(1)) appear also the following
entries:
Lodwick Briskett clerk of the Counsail for the fees of his office,
after vij *li* x *s. p* ann. and for his allowaunce of paper p*ar*chment and
yncke w*th* ingrossinge of wrytings and records concerninge the state
after xl *li* ster*ling p* ann. viz. for two whole yeres ending xij Maj 1581.
as by concordatum xij *mo* Maij 1581 appereth. {xx xv *li*. [i.e. £95] ster.
                                                 {iiij
Edmonde Spençer, Secretarye to the Lord Deputie for his allowaunce of paper, yncke and p*ar*chment due to him for one whole yere
endinge xxiiij*to* Iunii 1581 as by two Concordat appereth.   xv *li*[£15]
ster.
Tymothie Reynoldes Secretarye to the Lord Deputie, for penne,
ynck, and paper due to him for one half yere endinge vltimo Decembris
1581, as by Concordat*um* dated seconde Ianuarye 1581. appereth
vij *li*. x*s* [£7.10] ster.
Sum*me* of the Allowaunces }
to Secretarye aforesayd   } cxvij. x*s* [£117.10] ster.

COOPER, CHARLES H., and THOMPSON COOPER. Athenae
Cantabrigienses. Cambr. 1858–1913.
II, 258-67: A carefully compiled (1861) life of Sp; the entry of payment
to Edmonde Spencer, 18 Oct. 1569, for bringing letters to the queen
from the English ambassador in France; the story of Sp's unsuccessful competition for a fellowship with Lancelot Andrewes is an error;
259, 264: on the Lost Works; lists forty works by Sp, including the
Lost Works, the translation of Axiochus, and Brittain's Ida. A
short bibliography appended.

COTTON, HENRY. Fasti Ecclesiae Hibernicae. Dublin, 1851–
78. 6 v. (copy in Harv. Lib.).
Lists of holders of ecclesiastical offices, arranged by sees and dates.
I (Munster), 422-24, list of prebendaries of Effin,—incumbents 1546
to 1610 do not appear.

COVINGTON, F. F., Jr., of the University of Texas, is writing a
Dissertation on Spenser in Ireland.

COX, SIR RICHARD. Hibernia Anglicana. Lond. 1689–90. 2 v.
(Copy in Bost. Pub. Lib., and in Newberry Lib.)
I, 310-456: "The Reign of Elizabeth": much on Sp's associates; 392,
list of the undertakers.

CRAIK, G. L. Spenser and his Poetry. Lond. 1845. Passim.
III, 139: the pension. One of the best studies of Sp's life.

CROKER, T. CROFTON. Historical Illustrations of Kilmallock
[Lond. 1840]. No letter press. Seven plates. No. 2 =
Plan of Kilmallock in time of James I.

CROKER, T. CROFTON. Researches in the South of Ireland.
Lond. 1824. 73, 108–12: Kilcolman; the portrait, etc.

CROMWELL, OLIVER. Letter of 27 Mar. 1657. In Thos. Carlyle,
Letters and Speeches of Oliver Cromwell, ed. S. C. Lomas.
Lond. 1904. III, 489–90:
A brief note by Carlyle and the Letter of Cromwell on the case of
Wm. Spenser, the poet's grandson. That Wm. Spenser received by
inheritance the poet's "estate in lands in the Barony of Fermoy and
County of Cork"; "his grandfather was that Edmund Spenser who by
his writings touching the reduction of the Irish to civility brought on
him the odium of that nation, and for those works, and his other good
services Queen Elizabeth conferred on him that estate"; "his grandfather, for whose eminent deserts and services to the Commonwealth
that estate was first given to him."

CUNINGHAM, GRANVILLE C. The Dates of Spenser's Birth and
Death. In Baconiana, Lond., XI (1913), 153–59:
On the dates 1510–96 on the early monument; that they are not to
be summarily rejected.

CUNNINGHAM, PETER. Extracts from the Accounts of the
Revels. Lond. (Shakespeare Soc.), 1853.
P. xxx: From Office Books of the Treasurers of the Chamber, temp.
Q. Eliz.: "Payde upon a bill signed by Mr. Secretarye dated at
Wyndsor xviij° Octobris, 1569, to Edmonde Spencer that brought
lres to the Quenes Matie from Sir Henrye Norrys knighte her Mats
Embassador in Fraunce beinge then at Towars in the sayde Realme,
for his charges the some of vjli xiijs iiijd over and besydes ixli
prested to hym by Sir Henrye Norrys—vjli xiijs iiijd."
Cunningham comments: "There is no difficulty, I presume, in sup-
posing that the poet went abroad in a Cambridge vacation, and
returned, carrying letters to the court from Sir Henry Norrys."

CURRY, JOHN. Historical and Critical Review of the Civil Wars
in Ireland. Dublin, 1775.
Quotes from the V of I. Unimportant.

CUSACK, MARY F. History of the City and County of Cork. Dublin, 1875. 560:
Sp sheriff of Cork; 316–17, 489.

DART, JOHN. Westmonasterium, or the History and Antiquities of the Abbey Church of St. Peters Westminster. Lond. (1723). 2 v. folio.
I, 75–76: Cites Camden's epitaph on Sp; brief discussion of the early monument.

Dictionary of National Biography, XVIII (London, 1909), 792–806: "Edmund Spenser" (by J. W. Hales and Sidney Lee).
Dates "1552?–99." A careful treatment and the standard source for most of the subsequent short biographies of Sp. Errs occasionally in the uncritical acceptance of statements about Sp as facts which are at best conjectural. Cites sources of information frequently, but almost as frequently omits so to cite them. Accepts the Lancashire theory, etc. Important.

DINGLEY, THOS. History from Marble. Printed [facsimile] from MS. Camden Soc. 1867, Vols. 94, 97. Pp. 471–72.
The inscription on Sp's tomb ("borne in London in the yeare 1516 [1510?]: and died in the yeare 1598"), and the Latin epitaph.

DRAPER, JOHN W. Spenserian Biography; a Note on the Vagaries of Scholarship. In The Colonnade (Year Book of the Andiron Club of New York City), 1922. 35–46.
A résumé of the course of discussion of some of the prominent topics relating to Sp, esp. the life, and esp. in recent years. Covers the question of biographical material in the Muiop., the Amoretti, Sh Cal, and the Lancashire question, the Areopagus, Bryskett's Discourse, the Lost Works, Sp's Puritanism, etc. Of interest.

DRAPER, J. W. Dr. Grosart's Rosalind. In Journal of Eng. and Germ. Philology, XXI (1922), 675–79:
A review of the Rosalind theories and the Lancashire question; evidence from Sp's rhymes (phonological) against the theory.

DRUMMOND, WM. Notes of Ben Jonson's Conversations (in 1619). See Jonson, Ben, below.

Dublin Review, XVII (1844), 415–47:
A pro-Irish study of Sp as a politician in Ireland.

Dublin University Magazine, LVIII (1861), 131–44: "Edmond Spenser, the State Papers."

Evidence (new in 1861) from MS and other sources. Sketch based on Craik's Life of Spenser; that Sp was in Ireland 1576–77 (evidence from the V of I); his leases of Enniscorthy Castle and of New Ross; custodiam of Newlands, etc.; his success and ability as a politician (officeholder); thrift and worldly success; the grant of Kilcolman; feud with Lord Roche; relations with Raleigh; the grievance of King James of Scotland against Sp; his last days; his state papers, in MS, unpublished. An important study.

Dublin University Mag. See S. Hayman, below.

DUNHAM, SAMUEL A. Eminent Literary and Scientific Men of Great Britain. Lond. 1836. I, 312–51:

Life of Sp. A solid piece of work, but out of date.

DUNLOP, ROBERT. "Sir William Pelham." In Dict. Natl. Biog. N.Y. 1909. XV, 700–702:

Pelham "offended at the lack of courtesy shown to him by the deputy's secretary, Edmund Spenser."

DUNLOP, R. In Cambridge Mod. Hist., III (1905), 599–601:

The Plantation of Munster and the undertakers.

DUNLOP, R. Short History of Ireland. Oxford. Clarendon Press (in press).

Mr. Dunlop has also written a longer history of Ireland, to appear in two volumes, illustrated.

EACHARD, LAURENCE. An Exact Description of Ireland. Lond. 1691.

With five maps. On Irish topography. Maps show Kilcolman, Enniscorthy, etc.

Edinburgh Review, "Spenser in Ireland" [by C. L. Falkiner], CCI (1905), 164–88:

A study of the influence of Ireland on Sp's poetry; and of Sp's life in Ireland. Intelligent examination of the evidence, with new light on many points. Two periods of residence, 1580–88 and 1588+, differently reflected in his poetry. Spenser's various holdings of land and offices; local color in his poetry; long residence in or near Dublin during first period; 1588+ in Munster. Noteworthy. See Falkiner, C. L., below.

EINSTEIN, LEWIS.   A Notice of Spencer.   In Athenaeum, 1900, II, 57:
> Cites a contemporary notice of Sp in Harl. MS 4107, f. 56, in a list of English officials in Ireland. It mentions Sp under 22 March, 1581, as "Register or Clerk in the Chancery of the faculties within the kingdom of Ireland, quamdiu se bene gesserit,"—a deputy allowed. See "Catalogue," above.

European Mag.   See Baker, Thos., above.

European Magazine, XIII (1788), 237-38:
> Correction of the story of the Andrews-Spenser competition for a fellowship; the story that Sp wrote Puttenham's Art of English Poetry.

F.   Spenser at Pendle Forest: In (Walford's) Antiquarian and Bibliographer.   Lond., V (1884), 229-37:
> Assumes Sp's residence in Lancashire at time of writing the Sh Cal, but finds more of Kent than of the north in the poem; nor is its language like the dialect of Lancashire.

F.   Spenser's Lancashire Home.   In Notes and Queries, 9th Ser., III (1899), 481-83:
> Argues for Sp's stay in the north, at Hurstwood, in Lancashire; on the Spensers of Hurstwood.

[FALKINER, C. L.]   Spenser in Ireland.   In Edinb. Review, CCI (1905), 164-88.
> A review of recent books including Grosart's ed. of Spenser. See Edinburgh Review, above.

FALKINER, C. L.   Essays relating to Ireland.   Lond. 1909, 3-31:
> "Spenser in Ireland" (see above); the new facts on Sp's life brought to light; of Grosart's contributions; studies Sp's Irish environment and its influence; that Sp was in Ireland in 1577 as Sir Henry Sidney's private secretary; Sp's duties as Clerk of the Chancery; acquaintance with Abp. Ussher; two periods of his life in Ireland, (1) 1580-88, mostly in Dublin, (2) 1588-98, in Munster; "topographical allusiveness" of the FQ examined; Sp's wife. Important.

FENTON, E.   Observations on some of Mr. Waller's Poems.   In Works of Edmund Waller.   Lond. 1729, pp. xxix-xxx:
> Entries from the University Register, Cambridge: that Sp "a Sizer (Quadrantarius) of Pembroke-Hall was matriculated on the 20th of May 1569; took the Degree of Batchelor of Arts 1572/3; and proceeded Master of Arts 1576." Therefore born about 1553; the story

of the second six books of the FQ a fiction; errors arising from his epitaph; this monument first set up thirty years after Sp's death by "Stone, who was master-mason to King Charles I." Stone's diary, in the possession of Mr. Vertue, maker of the illustrations to this ed. of Waller, cited as follows:

"I allso mad a monement for Mer Spencer the Poett, and set it up at Westmester, for which the Contes of Dorsett payed me 40 l." [Walpole dates this 1620]; that Stone designed the inscription; hence its blunders; Camden's Latin phrases about Sp's death intended as part of a guide to Westminster, not as a monumental inscription; the Latin verses appended to Camden's description "probably selected from those that were written by the Poets who attended his funeral,"—"being servile imitations of Cardinal Bembo's Epitaphs on Sannazarius and the immortal Painter of Urbino."

FERGUSON, JAMES F. Memorials of Spenser the Poet, and his Descendants, from the Public Records of Ireland. In Gentleman's Magazine, 1855, II, 605–9:

Extracts from the records: Sp's appearance in person in the Court of Exchequer, Dublin, 6 May, 1581; lease to Sp of New Abbey, Kildare, forfeited 24 Aug. 1582 [but cf. Cal. of Fiants], for non-payment of rent for seven and one-half years (Qu. Sp not the original recipient of the lease in 1575?); grant of Kilcolman, 6 Oct. 1590, and its terms; 2 Sept. 1592, Sp's assignees of the manor of Enniscorthie; 7 Feb. 1597 (1598?) arrearages of rent of "Mr. Spencer" on the abbey of Buttevant (cf. mention of Buttevant in CCCHA); other entries as to Sp's heirs (Silvanus, Peregrine, etc.); of the sale by Sp of the monastery of St. Augustine's, New Ross. Important records.

Cf. also Journal of Cork Hist. and Arch. Soc., XIV (1908), 39–43: abridgement of the above.

FITZGERALD, LORD WALTER. New Abbey of Kilcullen. In Journal of Co. Kildare Archaeological Soc. Dublin, 1902. III, 301–17:

History of Kilcolman; Sp's possession of it. Qu. Kilcullen not = Kilcolman?

FLETCHER, J. B. Spenser. Reprinted from the Encyclopedia Americana. N.Y. (1904–8), XIV.

The best brief account of its date (6 pp. double columns). Denies Sp's connection with Lancashire and the setting of the Sh Cal there. Elaborates Sp's imitation of the Pléiade movement. Arguments for a recasting by 1590 of the 1579 plan of the FQ. Sp's sources in Tyndale and Calvin.

FLETCHER, PHINEAS. The Purple Island, 1633. Canto **I**, stanzas 19–21:
> The crosses of Sp's life.
> "Poorly, poor man, he liv'd; poorly, poor man, he died." Of Essex's help in the end, and Burleigh's enmity.

FLORIO, JOHN. See under "Criticism to 1651" (on the relations of Sp and Leicester).

FOX, A. W. Edmund Spenser the Poet's Poet. In Trans. Burnley Lit. and Sci. Club, XX–XXI (1905), 97–101:
> A general essay; for the Lancashire theory (C.S.N.).

FRERE, W. H. The English Church in the Reigns of Elizabeth and James I, 1558–1625. Lond. 1904.
> Esp. chs. vii ("Grappling with Puritanism"), and xi ("Grindal's Failure").

FULLER, THOMAS. The History of the Worthies of England (1662). Ed. P. A. Nuttall. Lond. 1840. II, 379–80:
> A very brief notice; follows Camden. The story of Elizabeth's gift to Sp of a hundred pounds and Burghley's objection ("then give him what is reason"), and Sp's rhymed petition therefor. His epitaph.

FULLER, THOS. Abel Redevivus, Lond. 1651. Repr. ed. W. Nichols. Lond. (Wm. Tegg), 1867, 2 v. II, 156–79:
> "Life of Lancelot Andrews." Andrews a pupil of Mulcaster. Does not mention the story of Sp's failure to receive a fellowship at Cambridge in competition with Andrews, but does relate that of the similar rivalship of Andrews and Thos. Dove.

GALLWEY, T. See The Monitor, below.

GARNETT, RICHARD, and EDMUND GOSSE. English Literature, an Illustrated Record. N.Y. 1903–4. II, ch. iii:
> With illustrations of Merchant Taylors School, Spenser (portrait), Pembroke College, Sp's handwriting, etc.

Gentleman's Magazine, XXXI (1761), 221.
> "New Anecdotes of Spencer and Shakespeare." Old stuff!

Gentleman's Mag. Various notes on Sp and his life.
> XLVIII (1778), 387: "Monuments to the memory of Spencer and Gray were opened in Westminster Abbey."
> LXII (1792), 135: Restoration of Sp's monument in 1778, etc.
> LXX (1800), ii, 1127: local allusions in Sp; 1269.
> LXXXVIII (1818), i, 224: Kilcolman, Buttevant, portraits of Sp; ii, 577: Kilcolman.

Gentleman's Mag. 1864, I, 725–32:

> "The Public Records of Ireland." Defects in the Calendars of the Rolls in Ireland, 1861–62, omitting many entries on Sp, Bryskett, etc.

GIBSON, C. B. History of Cork. Lond. 1861. I, 254:

> Sp at Smerwick; ch. xvi; "The Poet Spenser,"—a review of Sp's career in Ireland and of the View of Ireland; see pp. 308–9 for documents on Sp's Irish holdings; Sp's descendants.

[GILBERT, J. T.] On the History, Position, and Treatment of the Public Records of Ireland. Lond. 1864. 2d. ed.

> A reprint, revised, of his art. in Dublin Review, CIV, of his "Record Revelations," and his "Record Revelations Resumed."
>
> Attacks preceding Calendars of State Papers in Ireland. Gives as example of omissions (pp. 137 ff.) various grants to Sp, Bryskett, etc. [now in the "Fiants"]. Quotes them in full, i.e. Grant 24 Aug. of 24 Eliz. of lease of New Abbey (described in detail); Grant, 1581, of lease of Enniscorthy; Grant of Kilcolman, 26 Oct. 1591, including the "chief rents forfeited by the late Lord of Thetmore, and the late Traitor, Sir John of Desmond." Of value.

GILBERT, SIR JOHN T. See also Calendar of Dublin.

GILFILLAN, G. Life of Sp prefixed to Vol. II of his ed. of Sp. Lond. 1859, p. vi:

> The three Spensers (1) bringing letters from Sir Henry Norris to the Queen, (2) addressed by Turbervile from Russia, (3) author of verses in the Theater of Worldlings—all in 1569.
> xi ff. The Rosalind question; xix–xx: Sp's marriage.
> xxi: that King James wrote to Burghley against Sp.

GLASENAPP, G. In Herrig's Archiv, CXII (1904), 392–94:

> Sp and Smithfield; traces of youthful memories in his works.

GOLLANCZ, I. Spenseriana. In Proceedings of the British Academy, 1907–8. 99–105:

> Sp's own copy of the FQ in Gollancz's possession; marginalia in it: a variant version of sonnet I of the Amoretti, interpreted by G. as inscription-verses addressed to Elizabeth Boyle on presentation of this copy to her; signature and holographs; G. promises an edition of these documents (it is still eagerly awaited). Some of Harvey's marginalia and the "Ex dono Edmundi Spenseri, Episcopi Roffensis Secretarii, 1578" inscription; its bearing on the Sh Cal. On the variations in copies of the first ed. of the FQ. The "calling in" of MHT. Important.

Also in Archiv. f. d. Studium d. neueren Spr. u. Lit., CXLI (1921),
138–43.   Cf. Mod. Philol., XI, 96.
Similarly the Athenaeum, No. 4180, 7 Dec. 1907, p. 732; The Times,
Lond. 28 Nov. 1907.

GREENLAW, EDWIN. Spenser and the Earl of Leicester. In
Pub. Mod. Lang. Asso., XXV (1910), 535–61:
   An attempt to expound Sp's relations to contemporary political
   intrigues (Leicester, Burleigh, etc.), c. 1579. That Leicester sacrificed
   Sp in a political exigency.
           Cf. P. W. Long in Pub. Mod. Lang. Asso., XXXI, 720 ff.

GRIERSON, H. J. C. In Mod. Lang. Rev., XVII (1922), 409–11:
on Sp and Leicester.

GROSART, A. B. Ed. of Sp, priv. print, 1882, I.
   Valuable for its collection of evidence, much of which, however,
   requires careful scrutiny and question. See esp. 36: copies of entries
   relating to Sp in record books of Pembroke Hall, sickness allowances,
   1570–76; 531: Documents in Roche's suit vs Sp, from the originals in
   Rolls Office. Important.

HALES, J. W. Folia Litteraria. Lond. 1893. 155–61:
   "Spenseriana" (from the Academy, Nov. 28, 1874): Sp at Merchant
   Taylors School; in Lancashire; who was Rosalind; etc.

HALES, J. W. In the Athenaeum, 1897, I, 415:
   That the Prothalamion was written in 1596, as it alludes to Essex's
   expedition to Cadiz in that year. Essex "was back at home, and
   Spenser was one of his guests, when the 'Prothalamion' was written."

HALES, J. W. See Dict. Natl. Biog., above.

HALES, J. W. In Chambers' Encyclopedia. Lond. 1897,
IX, 625–27:
   A sketch of the life. Some statements questionable. To be con-
   sulted.

HALPIN, N. J. On Certain Passages in the Life of Edmund
Spenser. In Proceedings of the Royal Irish Academy, IV
(1850), 445–51:
   That Rosalind = Rose Daniel, sister of Samuel Daniel, later married
   to John Florio (= Menalcas); that Sp's wife (proved by anagram) =
   Elizabeth Nagle, or Nangle. Cf. Sp ed. Grosart, I, 197.

HARDIMAN, JAS. Irish Minstrelsy. Lond. 1831. I, 319 n.:
   Quotations from original records on Sp's life; Sp's offices in Ireland,
   etc. Important.

HARDIMAN, JAS. Inquisitionum . . . . Cancellariae Hiberniae . . . . Repertorium. "By command," 1826. 2 v.

Irish Court of Chancery records. Vast detail about persons and places of Sp's time in Ireland. E.g. see "Dublin" No. 4 on Jas. Eustace; "Kildare" No. 4 mentions Newland; much on forfeited lands, etc. Arranged by counties; index for each.

HARVEY, GABRIEL. Letter Book (1573–80), ed. E. J. L. Scott. Camden Soc., 1884, 58–88:

Letters from Harvey to Sp 1579, 1580; are fuller of Harvey than of Sp, but nevertheless important for Sp's life. Cf. 89, 101: The name *Immerito* taken by Sp, "since a certayn chaunce befallen unto him,— a secrett not to be revealid."

HARVEY, GABRIEL. Works, ed Grosart. Huth. Lib. 1884.

I, 1–150 passim; also 180, 191, 212, 218, 234, 244, 252, 266. II, 24, 50, 83, 266.

See under "Spenser and Harvey."

Professor Gordon J. Laing has kindly supplied the following translation of the Latin passages in the Harvey-Spenser Letters which are the most important for the study of Sp's life;

I, 25: "Heus mi tu," etc. "Listen, my fine fusser, mighty chaser of the calico, universal lover extraordinary, consider, I beg you, the end which awaits the whole bunch of woman-haters. . . . . I shall then be content to appeal to your own learned experience, whether it be or be not too true: . . . . which I am in the habit of saying, which you yourself sometimes say, and men of experience say daily: Love is bitterness: Nor is Love a god, as they say, but bitterness and error and whatever else is generally added along this line as a result of experience; and cleverly, as it seems to me, did Agrippa emend that title of Ovid 'The Art of Love' and rightly called it 'The Art of Harlotry.' Another has aptly compared lovers to alchemists who dream charming dreams of mountains and fountains of gold and silver, but meanwhile are almost blinded and even suffocated by the frightful fumes of the charcoal; and he said that besides that well-known paradise of Adam, there was another one—a wonderful paradise of fools and lovers: the former was for the truly happy, the latter for those whose happiness was a matter of fancy and frenzy. But I shall discuss these matters elsewhere, perhaps in fuller detail."

27: "De quibus ipsis," etc. "On these very things and all the other equipment of the master traveller (and especially in regard to that divine herb of Homer—the Gods call it moly—with which Mercury fortified his beloved Ulysses against all Circe's potions, spells, drugs, and diseases) I shall, I hope, shortly speak to you in person and, as my custom is, far more copiously, perhaps also somewhat more subtly than usual and more like a statesman and man of affairs. In the meantime you will be content with three syllables: Fare you well."

38: "Multum vale," etc. "Warmest of greetings to you, Westminster, April 2, 1580. But, blessings on you! my sweetheart sends you sincerest expressions of devotion; she has been wondering for a long time why you have sent no reply to her letter. Look out or this may be fatal to you. It will certainly be so to me, nor will you, I think, get off scott-free. Good-bye a second time and as often as you like."

39: "Veruntamen," etc. "Nevertheless I follow you only, but I shall never catch up with you."

99: "Cuiusmòdi," etc. "Do, I beg you, except with me (and I am bound by a solemn oath and vow to give up the cup of love and at the very first opportunity to drain the cup of law)—do, I repeat, bid farewell to nonsense and trifling songs of this kind (which, nevertheless, I believe, will seem to you one of the things that cannot be done); I shall say nothing more. Farewell. From my place, April 23d."

Possibly, with other punctuation, the passage may refer to Spenser's draining the cup of law. But the punctuation of the original (the Huntington Library copy) is as in Grosart's reprint.

107: "Sed amabo te," etc. "But, blessings on you! I shall reply to your sweetheart's letter on the very first day I can with care. Meanwhile convey to her as many exquisite greetings and salutations as she has hairs, half-gold, half-silver, half-gemmy on her pretty little head. What would you? By your own Venus she is another dear little Rosalind; and not another but the same Hobbinol (with your kind permission as before) loves her deeply. O my mistress Immerita, my most charming Lady Collin Clout, countless greetings to you and farewell."

Translated also in Grosart's ed. of Sp, I, 125–28.

HASSENCAMP, R. History of Ireland, trans. E. A. Robinson. Lond. 1888, 22–31:

Brief sketch of Irish history in Sp's time.

HAWES, ROBERT. The History of Framlingham in the County of Suffolk, including brief notices of the Masters and Fellows of Pembroke Hall in Cambridge . . . . Woodbridge, 1798. 208–88:

Chs. ix–x: Best account of Sp's college (J.D.B.).

[HAYMAN, SAMUEL.] Spenser's Irish Residence. In Dublin Univ. Mag., XXII (1843), 538–57:
> Discursive remarks on Irish local color in the FQ, and on Sp's life in Ireland.

HAYMAN, S. The Handbook for Youghal. Youghal 1852. (Copy in N.Y. Pub. Lib.).
> Account of St. Mary's Church (where possibly Sp was married); of Richard Boyle; of Raleigh's house.

HAZLITT, W. C. Shakespeare, Himself and his Work. Lond. 1912. 116 n.:
> That a tract given by Sp to Harvey and seen by Hazlitt proves that Sp in 1578 was secretary to Dr. Young, Bishop of Rochester, "as Harvey tells us on the title." Cf. 150, 420.

HEARNE, THOMAS. Reliquiae Hernianae [1731], ed. P. Bliss. Lond. 1869 (Libr. of Old Authors). III, 71:
> The entry from Stone's MS as to erecting a monument to Sp at the expense of the Countess of Dorset (c. 1619); that Sp was born 1550.

The Hibernian Magazine. Dublin, 1782, 401–3:
> A perfunctory Life.

HIGGINSON, J. J. Spenser's Shepherd's Calender in Relation to Contemporary Affairs. N.Y. 1912.
> A new study of Sp's life to 1580. See passim for the background at Cambridge, esp. 29 ff., 282 ff., 314–19 (Sp's life abroad, c. 1578). Important contributions, but need critical scrutiny in parts and some correction. Cf. E. Greenlaw in Studies in Philology, XI, 1–25; G. C. Moore Smith in Mod. Lang. Review, IX, 394–98; Geo. Saintsbury in Englische Studien, XLVII, 91–92: P. W. Long in Journal Eng. and Germ. Philology, XIII, 344–50; Anon. (J. D. Bruce) in the N.Y. Nation, XCV (1912), 486: That H. "has defined accurately the relations of the poet to Sidney and Leicester," and that Leicester had nothing to do with Sp's appointment as secretary to Lord Grey.

Historical Account of the English Poets. See Jacobs, G., below.

Historical Manuscripts Commission, Reports. Lond. 1870+ IV, 411–12:
> The Towneley MSS, and the payments of the executors of Robert Nowell; the proof of Sp's education at Merchant Taylors School. Cf. p. xvi: suggests that John Spenser was the poet's father; that it was on the nomination of Archdeacon Watts that Sp was passed from Merchant Taylors School to Pembroke Hall (cf. 407).

406 ff: The entries cited and discussed.

613–14: Recantation of the theory that John Spenser was the poet's father.

IX, 362a: MS Book of Latin Epigrams by Thos. Porter, 1614 (MS of Earl of Leicester,—in 1884); one on Sp.

471b: Letter of Alex. Pope ("Spencer had ever been a favorite Poet to me.")

XII, App. pt. ix, 123: A MS of the View of Ireland, dated 1597, in Library of J. H. Gurney (in 1891).

XV, App., pt. iii, 295: In "a table to the redd counsell books, Dublin," index of an "Order for Edmonde Spencer against the lord Roche." The Salisbury MSS. Pt. XI (1906).

95: "Mrs. Spencer" (Sp's widow).

Pt. XIII (1915), 343 ff. List of the Undertakers, June 27, 1587.

HOGAN, EDMUND, ed. Description of Ireland . . . . in anno 1598 . . . . from a MS in Clongowes-Wood College. Dublin, 1878. 169:

That Cork had two sheriffs. See passim for Sp's Associates; also for place-names (index; e.g. Enniscorthy = Sir Henry Wallop's in 1598; Newland; etc.).

HOWITT, WM. Homes of the Poets. Lond. 1847. I, 13–39:

Sketch of Sp's life, based mainly on Craik. Mostly an account of Kilcolman, based on Dublin Univ. Mag. of Nov. 1843 and on Howitt's own visit there. An agreeable essay.

HUME, MARTIN A. S. The Great Lord Burghley. Lond. 1906 [1898].

For the hist. background. Sp is quoted, but not cited in the index.

HUNTER, JOSEPH. Chorus Vatum. Addit. MS 24490 in British Museum. (Photostat copy in Newberry Library, Chicago.)

III, 189: On Van der Noodt; 599: on Bryskett's Discourse.

IV, 443–74: Sp genealogy; evidence for Sp's connection with the noble family of Spencers; an Edmund Spenser in London, 1541; other Spensers in London. Cf. 470.

450: Notes on Sp's life; "Hollar is reported by Oldys to have said that Spenser was born in East Smithfield near the Tower . . . . Oldys preserved it in his notes on Winstanley in the Bodleian"; 454: dedication of the Four Hymns in 1596 "from Greenwich," "is perhaps the origin of the tradition that he lived at one time in Kent."

456–57: The date of Sp's death; the first monument.

461–62: Sp's descendants; "Mr. P. Cunningham told me that he had found in the Parish Register of St. Clement Danes the baptism of a Florence dau. of Edmund Spencer"; etc.

468: "Is there any probability in the conjecture that Edward Kelley may be the E. K.? He wrote in verse. He was born in 1555."

472–73: That Sp was "acquainted with the Welsh border country, if he did not once himself reside there." Instances Daphnaida and FQ, I, ix, 4.

HUTTON, LAURENCE. Literary Landmarks of London. N.Y. 1900. 285–86:

The few brief facts about Sp's life in London.

[JACOB, GILES.] Historical Account of the . . . . English Poets. Lond. 1719. Ed. of 1724, I, 195–204: "Mr. Edmund Spenser":

Sketch ‧of the life, with the anecdotes; "in the year 1579 he was sent abroad by the Earl of Leicester"; brief criticism of the poems.

JOHNSTON, ROBERT. Historia Rerum Britannicarum. Amst. 1655. (Copy in Harvard Library; also in Newberry Lib.)

249: "1598: Annus & hic abstulit, apud Anglos, maximum hujus aetatis Ornamentum, Edmundum Spenserum, Londini in tenui re natum; qui omnes superioris Seculi Poëtas Anglicos longè superavit; & ad declinandam Paupertatem, in *Hiberniam*, cum *Graio Prorege* secessit; ut per Otium ac Requiem, *Apollini & Musis* operam daret; ubi à Praedonibus *Laribus* ejectus, & Bonis spoliatus, Inops in Angliam redijt; & Mestitia rebus humanis exemptus, in Vestmonasterij Coenobio sepultus est, apud *Chaucerum*, impensis *Essexiae Comitis;* quia, ut Creditur, in *Cecilium Quaestorem* acriter invehitur, in *Fabula Hubartae Vetulae."* Marginal note= "Mother Hubert's tale."
Cf. Hunter's Chorus Vatum, IV, 450.

JONES, WALTER A. Doneraile and Vicinity. In Journal Cork Hist. and Arch. Soc., VII (1901), 238–42:

Kilcolman; brief life of Sp; etc.

JONSON, BEN. Conversations with Drummond, in 1619. In Works of J., ed. Gifford and Cunningham. Lond. n.d. (c. 1872).

III, 478: "That the Irish having rob'd Spenser's goods and burnt his house and a little child new born, he and his wyfe escaped; and after, he died for lake of bread in King Street, and refused 20 pieces sent to him by my Lord of Essex, and said, He was sorrie he had no time to spend them."
Jonson's copy of Sp's Works is noticed in Allibone, II, 2204.
Cf. Todd's ed. of Sp, 1805, I, pp. cxxxv–vii.

JOYCE, P. W. Irish Names of Places. Dublin, 1870–1913.

> I, 303: "There are in Ireland seven parishes, and more than twenty townlands (including Spenser's residence in Cork) called Kilcolman (Colman's church)." Qu. None other with a castle?

KEEPE, Henry. Monumenta Westmonasteriensia. Lond. 1682. (Copy in Harvard Library.)

> 46: Sp's tomb in 1682; comment on Sp; 208: inscription on Sp's tomb.

KEIGHTLEY, THOMAS. On the Life of Edmund Spenser. In Fraser's Magazine, LX (1859), 410–22:

> Additions and corrections to earlier biographies, esp. Todd and Craik; the Spenser family; date and place of birth (c. 1551); Sp after leaving Cambridge; trip to the continent, 1579–80; Rosalind (a purely ideal figure?); life in Ireland; that he did not return to England with Lord Grey in 1582; Kilcolman; Sp's sister; marriage; children; etc. Some of K's material seems to have been neglected by later biographers. To be consulted. Cf. Notes and Queries, Ser. III, Vol. IV (1863), 197.

KEIGHTLEY, T. Irish Rivers named in the "Faerie Queen." In Notes and Queries, Ser. IV, Vol. IV (1869), 169–70:

> Annotations on FQ, IV; some points in Sp's life; that he left his family behind when he fled from Ireland in 1598.

KEIGHTLEY, T. Spenser, the Poet of Ireland. In Notes and Queries, Ser. IV, Vol. VII (1871), 317–18:

> Irish local color in Sp's poetry.

KEIGHTLEY, T. Spenser's Irish Residence. In Dublin University Magazine, XXII (1843), 538–57:

> A general essay: 544: that Pollente, in FQ = Earl of Desmond; discussion of FQ, V; 546 f. on the plantation of Munster; effect on the poet of his Irish residence; his Irish rivers.

KEIGHTLEY, T. Edmund Spenser, his Life and Poetry. In British Quarterly Review, XXII (1855), 368–412.

> A general discussion. Of value. See 385 ff. on Sp's relations to Burghley and Leicester; 389 f. on the effect of the grant of Kilcolman and the pension.

KERR, ALEX. England in the Age of Spenser. In the Western, St. Louis, N.S., V (1879), 535–41.

> Negligible. Cf. Grosart, I, 6.

Kerry Magazine, No. 5, 1854. "The Antiquities of Tralee."

> P. 67 describes the state of the Desmond Palatinate. Passim are references to the V of I. Unimportant.

Kildare County Archaeol. Soc. Journals, 1891+
> Generally worth study, esp. for place-names, etc. See II (1896–99), 48 ff. on "The Pale"; 253 ff. the office of Sheriff, ₃sp. in Kildare (in 1583 the sheriff was Redmond Brymgham or Bermingham who, with others [incl. Sp]·had a commission of muster). See VIII (1915–17), 251 ff. on Kilcullen.

KILLEN, W. D. Ecclesiastical History of Ireland. Lond. 1875. 2 v.
> Various citations from V of I. See Bk. III, chs. iii–v on the state of the Church in Ireland, temp. Eliz.

KING, ALICE. A Cluster of Lives. Lond. 1874. 117–36:
> Brief biography of Sp. Unimportant.

KNIGHT, CHARLES. Biography, or Third Division of "The English Cyclopedia." Lond. 1867. V, 634–36.
> A perfunctory sketch.

LEE, SIDNEY. Great Englishmen of the Sixteenth Century. Lond. 1904. Ch. v, "Edmund Spenser."
> A summary of his life and works taken chronologically. A popular treatment; not critical.

LELAND, THOS. History of Ireland. Lond. 1773. II, Bk. IV, chs. i–v:
> Ireland under Elizabeth. Sp not in index (but see II, 283 n.).

Letters of Spencer Family. See Add. MSS, above.

LEWIS, SAMUEL. Topographical Dictionary of Ireland. Lond. 1837. I, 596:
> On Effin; 602: on Enniscorthy; that the estates were given by Queen Elizabeth to John Travers, who conveyed them to Sp; 477, on Doneraile; II, 84, on New Abbey.

Liber Munerum Publicorum Hiberniae, or the Establishments of Ireland, 1152–1827, being the Report of Rowley Lascelles, extracted from the Records. "By Command." 1824. Indexed in Ninth Report of the Deputy Keeper of Public Records in Ireland. Dublin, 1877. Appendix, pp. 21–58.
> Important for Sp's official life in Ireland. See Pt. II, 3: "Chief Governors—Eliz."; 13: Lord Chancellors; 23: "Six Clerks in Chancery" (held by Christopher Berford, 1578–1613); 28–29: "Clerks of the Decrees and Recognizances" (gives the incumbents only from 1605+. The office probably instituted in 1605).

29: "Registers or Clerks of the Chancery for the Faculties." "Institution of the Office"—i.e. first incumbent = "Lewis Briskett, Gent., Clerk of the P. Council—Patent Apr. 11, 1577 . . . . Fiant, 19 Eliz." Followed by "Edmund Spenser, Gent. (Sec'y to the L.D. Gray)—Briskett—Patent, Mar. 22, 1580 [sic] . . . . Fiant, 23." Patent, 14 Mar. 1582 to Roland Cowyk, "being now aged." "That he shall have and enjoy the same several offices in that our realm of Ireland [i.e. as exist in England, viz. "Clerk of our Chancery . . . . for . . . . matters and causes of Faculties," also "our sole Register for all manner of Appeales Ecclesiastical made to us into our Chancery], and be our Clerk of our Chancery there for the Faculties, and our sole Register for all manner of Appeales Ecclesiastical . . . . in as ample manner as either our officers do use and exercise those severall offices here in England . . . ." "and also the office of our Register of our late and new created Prerogative Court Ecclesiastical in Ireland" (established 1 Mar. 1580). Note: Sp was allowed a deputy. Was his office a sinecure? Did Cowyk act as his deputy "for the Faculties," but holding the office of "sole Register" for Appeals? Two incumbents seem to be contemplated by the statute (see above). Two entries follow: "Arland Uscher, Gent.—vice Spenser—Patent June 22, 1588—Fiant, 30."

"Thomas Say, Gent.—Cowyk deceased—Patent, Oct. 2, 1598." (But cf. Fiants, Eliz. no. 5034.)

   Note: Grosart in his ed. of Sp, I, 150, enters Sp's resignation of the office of "Clerk of Decrees and Recognizances," 22 June 1588, and refers to "Liber Hiberniae." In Pt. II, p. 182 of this volume in the list of the Clerks of Recognizances, 1564-1635, Sp's name does not appear, but at p. 29 the entry above shows that Sp was succeeded as clerk of the Chancery for Faculties, *22 June, 1588*, by Arland Uscher. Did Sp ever hold the office of Clerk of Decrees and Recognizances? Is there any documented authority for the statement? Cf. Hardiman. Cf. Mod. Philol., XIX (1922), 413-15.

41: Lord High Treasurer of Court of Exchequer, Thos. Earl of Ormond, 1559-1603; Sir Henry Wallop, Vice Treasurer, 1579-98.

79: "Prerogative Court" pursuant to the "Act of Faculties" 28 Hen. VIII. Commission with power to grant faculties, 1568; soon revoked and given to Adam, Archbishop of Dublin and Dr. Ambrose Forth.

80: "Sole Register of Appeals or Provocations Spiritual." Rowland Cowyck, Gt.—Patent Mar. 14, 1582. Arland Uscher, Gt.—Cowyck deceased—Patent Sept. 7, 1587 [Uscher died 1599].
   Cf. Fiants, Eliz. no. 5034.

181: "High Commission for Ecclesiastical Causes" [not for "faculties"].

182: "Principal Registers and Clerks of the Acts and Recognizances entered into before the said Commissioners." [Sp not in the list.]

184: "The Presidency Court of the Province of Munster," i.e. a council "to determine the complaints of her subjects and to reduce them to the knowledge of God." (Becomes "the Council of Munster"?) Capt. Zouch appointed by Lord Grey in 1581 "Governor General of the Province," and Sir Warham St. Leger Commander in Chief. Sir John Norreis President, 1584. Sir Thos. Norreis his brother Vice President in his absence, 1587. On Sir John's death in 1597 Commissioners appointed, Sir Thos. Norreis Chief Governor (Commissioners: John Bp of Limerick, William Bp of Cork, Nicholas Walsh, Wm. Saxey, Chief Justice of the Province, Geo. Thorneton, Francis Barkley, and Hugh Cuffe); Norreis Lord President later.

186: Justices of Munster.

187: "Clerks of the Council, and Keepers of the Signet and of all Books, Rolls, Pleadings and other Records of the Presidency Court:"

L. Briskett of Maghmane, Co. of Wexford, Esq. Mar. 11, 1582. Patent Nov. 6, 1583. [Sp acted as his deputy 1588+. See Lismore Papers.]

Richard Boyle, Gent ("Briskett surrd 31st March, 1600"). Patent May 8, 1600.

Pt. III, 9: Quotes from Harl. MSS a letter to make Spenser sheriff of Corke ult. Sept. 1598.

The Counsell Booke for the Province of Munster, from 1601, is in the Harl. MSS.

19: Reference to Cottonian MSS, Titus B, XII, No. 89. "A paper concerning the instructions for passing faculties in Ireland." Mr. Henry R. Plomer reports that this is not the "instructions" but only a commentary on them. It appears from this paper that certain "faculties" or dispensations in Ireland were reserved to the Archbishop of Canterbury (e.g. dispensations for non-residence); others were to be authorized by "the commissioners in Ireland."

24: (p. 317 of MS). Instructions concerning the escheated lands in Munster, 1589 (cf. No. 614).

Pt. V, 37: Adam Loftus, Abp. of Dublin, 1567–1605.
58: Wm. Casey, Bp of Limerick, 1571–91.
66: Wm. Lyon, Bp of Cork, 1583–1618.
94: The Prebend of Effin attached to the chapter of Limerick (cf. 207 "Effin Preb.").

The Lismore Papers . . . . ed. A. B. Grosart, Priv. print. 1886–88. 10 vols. See index of 1st series in Vol. V; of 2d series in Vol. V, 184. The indexes are defective.

See *1st. ser.* I, Introd., pp. xiv ff.: Elizabeth Boyle; I, 8: second re-marriage of Sp's widow; 189: money owed Sp's widow by Boyle's wife, interest paid to Peregrine Spenser; similarly 205 and 212; 291: Sp's wedding; IV, 242–43: Sp's daughter.

2nd ser. I, p. xv: further on Elizabeth Boyle; I, 19 ff.: agreement between Bryskett and Boyle as to Sp's office of clerk of the Council of Munster, to protect Boyle against the claims of Sp's heirs: 21: reference Feb. 1599 to "Edmond Spenser gent. deceased"; II, 12: Sp's widow to Boyle, 22 Dec. 1615, acknowledging his favors to her, and about investing estate of her children; 139 f.: Peregrine Spenser to Boyle, 2 Oct., 1618, about Peregrine's necessities, his taking service as a gentleman usher, etc.; 237 f.: Sp's widow to Boyle, 1 Apr. 1620, from his "Poore Kines Woman"; 60: Sp's widow to Boyle, 19 Nov. 1616, endorsed "ffrom my Cozen Tynt," as to her son's education in Boyle's household; III, p. xii; IV, 75–76, 115.

Cf. Grosart's Sp, I, 198: text of lease, 3 May, 1606, Richard Boyle to Elizabeth Boyle, alias Seckerstone of Kilcoran.

Literature, Lond., V (1899), 102:
Merchant Taylors Guild to install a stained glass window in honor of Sp.

LONG, PERCY W.   In Mod. Lang. Review, VI (1911), 396–97:
The date of Sp's marriage still uncertain.

LONG, P. W.   In Mod. Lang. Review, XII (1917), 89:
Whether Sp were born in 1550.

LONG, P. W.   Spenser's Rosalind.   In Anglia, XXXI (1908), 72–104:
A new identification; Rosalind a real person; the previous attempts to localize and identify her analyzed; against the theory of Sp's connection with Lancashire; the dialect of the Sh Cal not Lancastrian; Grosart's arguments refuted. Suggests Rosalind = Elizabeth North (Eliza Nord), daughter of Thomas North.

LONG, P. W.   Spenser's Visit to the North of England.   In Mod. Lang. Notes, XXXII (1917), 58–59:
Re-examines the E.K. gloss to Sh Cal, Jan. and June, on which the theory of Sp's visit to the north has been based; finds the evidence insufficient. That Sp might have picked up northern dialect-words from the ushers at Merchant Taylors School, who were northern men.

LONG, P. W.   Review of Dodge's edition of Spenser.   In Mod. Lang. Review, IV (1909), 529–31:
The printer's prefatory allusion (in the Complaints volume) to Sp's "departure over sea" is to his departure for Ireland in 1580; that

Sp inspired this Preface; Sp did not leave London until after the publication of The Complaints.

LONG, P. W. Spenser and Lady Carey. In Mod. Lang. Review, III (1908), 257–67:
> Sp's marriage, etc. Cf. V, 273 ff.; VI, 390. Cf. Pub. Mod. Lang. Asso., XXXII, 306 ff.; also de Sélincourt's ed. of Sp's Minor Poems, p. xxiv n.; H. J. C. Grierson, above.

LONG, P. W. In Englische Studien, XLIV (1912), 263–66:
> On the dates of several of Sp's poems; of Sp in London, 1590–91; of the dating of CCCHA from Kilcolman; etc.

LONG, P. W. Spenser's Dating of "Colin Clout." In The Nation, N.Y., LXXXIII (Nov. 1, 1906), 368–69:
> CCCHA dated from Kilcolman 27 Dec. 1591, and Daphnaida from London 1 Jan. 1591: that Sp is not using old style in the former and new style in the latter, but that the dating from Kilcolman is a literary device, Sp being then really in London. A possible solution of a mystifying puzzle.

LONG, P. W. Spenser's Birth-date. In Mod. Lang. Notes, XXXI (1916), 178–80:
> Reasons for believing that Sp was born in 1550 rather than 1552.

LONG, P. W. Spenser and the Bishop of Rochester. In Pub. Mod. Lang. Asso., XXXI (1916), 713–35:
> Formative influence of Young and Grindal on Sp's early years. Of Sp and Leicester, the Spenser-Harvey Letters, etc.

LYSAGHT, SIDNEY. Kilcolman Castle. In the Antiquary, V (1882), 153–56:
> Description of the locality; Sp's residence there.

MACLIR, M. Spenser as High Sheriff of Cork County. In Journal Cork Hist. and Arch. Soc., VII (1901), 249–50:
> "Letter to make Edmond Spenser Sheriff of Cork County," 30 Sept. 1598, published from Harl. MS. Sp described as "being a man endowed with good knowledge in learning, and not unskillful or without experience in the service of the warrs." Quotes Index to Sp's Grant of lands, from the Calendar to the Fiants of Elizabeth, 20 Oct. 1590.

MACRAY, WM. D. Annals of the Bodleian Library. Ox. 1890. 122–23:
> Sp's copy of Howleglas, presented to Harvey; with the latter's inscription.

MALONE, EDMUND. In Prose Works of Dryden. Lond. 1800. Vol. I, Pt. I, 84:
> Sp's pension.

MANNINGHAM, JOHN. Diary. Lond. (Camden Soc.), 1868, 43:
> First record of the story of the pension from the Queen and Sp's doggerel verses. Cf. J. P. Collier, Hist. Eng. Dram. Poetry, Lond. 1879, I, 323 n.

Memoranda Roll, 21–24 Eliz. Quoted in Grosart's ed. of Sp, I, 142:
> That "Edmondus Spencer, generosus," serving Lord Grey, appeared in person in the Court of Exchequer, Dublin, May 6, 1581. Entry verified (Letter from Public Record Office of Ireland, 2 March, 1922).

MEYNELL, ALICE. Where the Faerie Queene was written. In Atlantic Monthly, CIII (1909), 250–54:
> A popular essay; presents nothing new.

MITCHEL, JOHN. Life of . . . . Hugh O'Neil, Earl of Tyrone. Dublin [1846]. Revised ed. 1868 (in N.Y. Pub. Lib.).

Monasticon Hibernicum. See Archdall, M.

The Monitor, Dublin, II (1879), 19–27 [by T. Gallwey]:
> A pro-Irish attack on the V of I; review of Sp's career in Ireland. Unimportant.

MOORE, COURTENAY. Spenser's Knowledge of the Neighbourhood of Mitchelstown. In Journal Cork Hist. and Arch. Soc., X (1904), 31–33:
> Irish rivers and local color in the FQ; "Spenser's oak"; accuracy of his descriptions. Cf. also pp. 133–34: P. W. Joyce on the identification of Sp's Irish rivers.

MORLEY, HENRY. Ireland under Elizabeth and James I. Lond. 1890. 19–26:
> Sp's life.

MORRIN, JAS. See Calendar of Patent Rolls, above.

MORYSON, FYNES. Itinerary, 1617. Repr. Glasgow, 1907. II, 173:
> Recites patent "In Corke" to Vane Beacher . . . . master Spencer, and others, of 88,037 acres; how the undertakers disposed of their lands.

MULCASTER, RICHARD. Positions . . . . Necessarie for the
Training up of Children. 1581. Repr. London. 1887.
>The ideals, and doubtless in large part the practice, of the master
>of the school where Sp was taught. See esp. 269 ff.: authors proposed
>for reading; the value of the poets.

MULLINGER, J. BASS. History of the University of Cambridge,
Lond. 1888.
>For the background of Sp's college life. See esp. ch. vii.

MURDIN, WM., ed. Collection of State Papers relating to . . . .
the Reign of Queen Elizabeth, from 1571–96. Lond. 1759.
>Continuation of the Collection of S. Haynes who goes to 1571 only.
>Valuable for Sp's times and contemporaries. No index.

NEALE, JOHN P., and E. W. BRAYLEY. Westminster Abbey.
Lond. 1823. II, 34:
>View of Poet's Corner; 263–64: the monument.

New International Encyclopedia. N.Y. 1920, 2d. ed., XXI
388–89:
>A brief conventional life of Sp.

Notes and Queries. Various notes on Sp and his life.
>See Ser. I, Vol. VII (1853), 303 (Sp in Lancashire), 362, 410;
>Vol. X (1854), 204–5.
>Ser. II, Vol. IX (1860), 420 (notes on Sp by Edward Harley, Earl of
>Oxford—d. 1741); Vol. XI (1861), 182–83 (Sp and the Spencers of
>Althorpe; notes on Sp by Wm. Oldys).
>Ser. III, Vol. IV (1863), 373 (Sp's sister Sarah); Vol. IX (1866), 366
>(Sp's daughter Florence and the Spensers of Lancashire); 113–14
>(Oliver Cromwell and Sp's grandson); Vol. XI (1867), 418 (Tur-
>bervile's "Spencer").
>Ser. IV, Vol. X (1872), 244 (entry of the marriage of "Edmundus
>Spencer et Maria Towerson," 1 Dec. 1590; other Edmund Spenser
>entries). Cf. p. 301.
>Ser. VI, Vol. X (1884), 329, 502 (the autograph).
>Ser. IX, Vol. IV (1899), 44 (Rosalind).
>Ser. XI, Vol. V (1912), 310, 417 (portrait, etc.).

NOWELL. The Spending of the Money of Robert Nowell.
Priv. print. 1877.
>Evidence that Sp attended Merchant Taylors School and was one
>of Nowell's beneficiaries (on Sp's going to Cambridge, 28 Apr. 1569);

other Spensers, from Lancashire, similar beneficiaries (corroborative evidence of Sp's connection with Lancashire ?).
Cf. Grosart's Sp, I, 13 ff.

Patent Roll, 33 Elizabeth. Part III, no. 1364. MS at Public Record Office, London. Sp's Pension.

Mr. H. R. Plomer supplies the following transcript of this document:
Regina. Om*n*ibus ad quos, etc salut*em*. Sciatis qd. nos p*r*o diu*e*rsis causis et consideraci*on*ibus nos ad p*re*sens sp*e*cialiter mouen*s* de gra*c*ia n*o*st*r*a sp*e*ciali ac ex c*er*ta sciencia et mere motu n*o*st*r*is dedimus et concessimus ac p*er* p*re*sentes p*r*o nob*is* heredibus et successoribus n*o*st*r*is damus et concedimu*s* dicto subdito n*o*st*r*o Edmundo Spencer quandam annuitatem siue annualem reddit*us* quinquaginta librar*um* legalis monete Anglie p*er* annum; Habend guadend et annuatim p*re*cipiend dict*is* anuitatis sive annualis reddit*is* p*re*fat*is* Edmundo Spencer et assignes suis a die dat*is* ha*r* literar*um* n*o*strar*um* patent*is* p*r*o t*er*mino vite naturalis eiusdem Edmundi de Thesauro n*o*st*r*o heredum et success*orum* n*o*str*orum* ad receptis saccarii n*o*st*r*i. Westm*onasterii* p*er* manus Thesaurar*is* et Camerar*is* nostri heredum et successor*um* nostror-*um* ib*idem* p*r*o tempore existen ad quatuor anni t*er*minos vide*l*icet ad festa Annunciaci*on*io be*ate* Marie virginis Nativitatis sa*nct*i Ioha*n*is Bapt*iste* sancti Michaelis Arch*angel*i et natalis d*o*mini per equales por-*tio*nes soluend mandantes et p*er*cipien dict*is* Thesaurar*is* et Camerar*is* dict*is* Saccarii n*o*st*r*i p*r*o tempore existen qu*o*d dict*is* Annuitatis siue annualis redditis p*re*fat*is* Edmundo Spencer in forma p*re*dict*is* soluant seu soloi faciant duran vita sua p*re*dicta Eo qu*o*d expressa menciõ &c. In cujus rei &c. T. R. apud Westm̄. xxv die Februarii p*r*o breve de priuato sigillo.

Patent Roll, 37 Eliz., membrane 32. MS in Public Record Office of Ireland.

"Grant of lands in Co. Wexford to Sir Henry Wallop in as ample a manner as Edmond Spencer or Richard Synnott held them" (Letter from Record Office, Mar. 2, 1922).

The Patrician, IV (1847), 126–27:

On Sp's estate of Renney, Co. Cork, and his residence there; "Spenser's Oak." Cf. Welply, W. H., below.

PEACHAM, H. Truth of our Times. 1638.

"The famous Spenser did never get any preferment in his life, save towards his latter end ḥe became a Clerk of the Council in Ireland, and dying in England he dyed but poore. When he lay sick the noble and patterne of true honor, Robert Earle of Essex sent him twenty pound, either to relieve or bury him." (From MS transcript by J. P. Collier in Harvard copy of his ed. of Sp, I, p. cxlv).

The Percy Anecdotes. Lond. 1823. X, 17:
> Anecdote as to Sp's submitting his FQ to the Earl of Southampton.

POOLE, HENRY. Westminster Abbey: a Study on Poets' Corner. In The Antiquary, Lond. IV (1881), 137–39:
> By the master-mason of the Abbey. Sp's tomb, its exact location; the south Transept perhaps once called "Spenser's Corner."

PRATT, HELEN M. Westminster Abbey. N.Y. 1914. 2 v. illus. I, 198–200:
> Sp's tomb. See also the Bibliog.

PRENDERGAST, JOHN P. Cromwellian Settlement of Ireland. Lond. 1870. 2d. ed. See index.
> Anti-Spenser, pro-Irish. The View of Ireland frequently cited. Pp. 116–17: Sp's grandson, William Spenser. Cf. Grosart's ed. of Sp, I, passim.

PRIOR, SIR JAMES. Life of Edmond Malone. Lond. 1860. 394:
> Quotes from Indexes at the Signet Office the entry of annuity of "50 £ per ann. to Edmund Spenser during life"; 402: date of birth. Cf. 446, 447.

Quarterly Review, CCVI (1907), 446:
> "Spenser, a practical politician, with the views afterwards called Cromwellian, and an excellent man of business."

[RAWLINSON, RICHARD.] History of Sir John Perrott. Lond. 1728.
> Affairs of Ireland, 1572–92.

Registers of the Parish Church of Burnley in the County of Lancaster. Rochdale, 1899. (Copy in Boston Pub. Lib., and in Newberry Lib.)
> The registers begin in 1562; many Spensers entered (see index) including numerous "Edmund Spensers."

The Returne from Parnassus, 1601. P. 84 of Macray's ed.
> "And yet for all this, unregarding soile
> Unlac't the line of his desired life,
> Denying mayntenance for his deare reliefe.
> Carelesse (ere) to prevent his exequy,
> Scarce deigning to shut up his dying eye."

RICHEY, ALEX. G. A Short History of the Irish People. Dublin, 1887.
> See chs. xvii–xx; 504 ff. on state of the Irish Church; 543 ff. on Plantation of Munster. A valuable work.

ROBINSON, C. J., ed. Register of Merchant Taylors School
. . . . 1562–1874. Lond. 1882–83.
> I, 1: mere entry of Sp's name, with citation of evidence drawn from
> Nowell's account-book.

ROSSETTI, WM. M. Lives of Famous Poets. Lond. 1878, 21–33.

Salisbury MSS. See Hist. MSS Commission, above.

SÉLINCOURT, E. DE. Introd. to his one-volume ed. of Sp, 1912.
Pp. vii–xl:
> The best short life; especially skilful and judicious in its utilization
> of the biographical material scattered through Sp's works.

SEWARD, WM. W. Topographia Hibernica. Dublin, 1795.
> For place-names, e.g. Enniscorthy, Kilcolman, New Abbey.

SEWARD, WM. W. The Hibernian Gazetteer. Dublin, 1789.
> With introd. on Irish antiquities. See for place-names.

Shakespeare Jahrbuch, XLI (1905), 288–89:
> The substance of documents given in Mod. Lang. Notes, XIX,
> 237, and in Herrig's Archiv, CXII, 392.

SHELLEY, HENRY C. Edmund Spenser: A Tercentenary Survey.
In The Outlook, N.Y., LXI (1899), 35–46:
> A good short study of Sp's career, with interesting photographic
> reproductions of the Althorpe portrait, of documents, etc.

SHELLEY, H. C. In Spenser's Footsteps. In his Literary
By-paths in Old England. Bost. 1906. 5–60:
> A study, with illustrations, of some localities associated with Sp. A
> fresh and agreeable study of the life.

SHIRLEY, EVELYN P., ed. Original Letters and Papers in Illus-
tration of the History of the Church in Ireland. Lond. 1851.
> Valuable, although all date before 1571. See on Loftus, on first
> fruits unpaid, etc.

SMITH, CHARLES. The Antient and Present State of . . . .
Cork. Dublin, 1750.
> I, 63: Sp's lands; 299: the country which Sp celebrates; 340–42:
> Kilcolman.
> II, 256, 260–62: Irish rivers in Sp.
> Also Repr. by Cork Hist. and Arch. Soc., 1893, I, 311–13; 345–46.

Spenser, Brief Note of Ireland. In Sp ed. Grosart, I, 537 ff.

Spenser: "A summary of the Life of Mr. Edmond Spenser" (with the Harvey-Spenser Letters). In Spenser's Works, 1679.

A1–[A4]: Birth (in 1510); the Andrewes fellowship competition; the Sidney-Cave-of-Despair story; death, in 1596, of "a broken heart"; etc.

STANLEY, ARTHUR P. Historical Memorials of Westminster Abbey. Lond. 1886. 6th ed. 252–53:

Sp's funeral; and monuments.

TANNER, THOS. Bibliotheca Britannico-Hibernica. Lond. 1748. 684:

A brief life of Sp: "Ei dom. Philip Sidney primus fuit Maecenas; et titulo poetae laureati a regina Elizabetha ornatus," etc. Cites as authorities Ware, Stow.

THOMAS, FRANCIS S. Historical Notes, 1509–1714. Lond. 1856. 1149, 1263.

Negligible.

TODD's ed. of Sp, 1805, I, pp. i–clxxiii; esp. cxxix: inscription dated 1598 on Sp's death.

TOWNSHEND, DOROTHEA. Life and Letters of the Great Earl of Cork. N.Y. 1904. 3; 8; 13:

Plight of the Munster refugees, 1598, etc. See index.

TURBERVILE, GEO. Epitaphes and Sonnettes, annexed to the Tragical histories . . . . sent to certaine his frends in England at his being in Moscouia. Anno. 1569. With Tragical Tales, 1587 (also 1576, etc.). Repr. Edinb. 1837.

Pp. 300 ("My Spencer"), 308, 309, 375 ("To Spencer"). The Christian name is not given. But Wood (Ath. Oxon. ed. Bliss, I, 627) identifies this "Spencer" with the poet, and Collier accepts the identification.

Cf. J. P. Collier, Bibliog. Account, II, 70, 453.

The Universal Magazine, XLIX (1771), 337–44, "Life of Spenser."

Unimportant.

UPTON, JOHN. Preface to his ed. of the FQ, 1758. I, pp. v–xlii:

Pp. v ff. Criticism of the Sp "traditions." Sketch of the Life.

xi *n*: "'Tis probable . . . . that the disappointment he met with from the university [receiving no fellowship] (like Milton's on a like occasion) made him lay aside all thoughts of taking orders."

VENN, JOHN. Grace Book Δ, Cambridge University 1542–89. Camb. 1910.

260, 290 (Sp's A.M. 26 June 1576), 542.

VENN, JOHN, and J. A. VENN. The Book of Matriculations and Degrees . . . . University of Cambridge, 1544–1659. Camb. 1913.

630: "Spensar, Edm., Pembroke. Sizar. Easter Term, 1569. A.B. 1572–73; A.M. 1576."

W., E. N. Spenser's Monument. In Notes and Queries, Ser. I, Vol. I (1850), 481–82:

The inscriptions on the monument quoted from Winstanley [= Camden] and from the 1679 ed. of Sp. Of the date of Sp's birth. Cf. Vol. III, 510: suggests 1550.

WALCOTT, MACKENZIE E. C. Westminster, Memorials of the City, etc. Westminster, 1849. 66–68:

Of Sp in Westminster after his flight from Ireland; Burghley his evil genius; the "rhyme-reason" story; "but no money for Spenser ever past out of the exchequer" [an error]; etc.

WALPOLE, CHARLES G. A Short History of Ireland. Lond. 1882.

140: Sp at Smerwick; 143: citation from the View of Ireland; 145–47: conditions for the undertakers in the plantation of Munster, 1586; result of the scheme.

WALPOLE, HORACE. Anecdotes of Painting. Lond. 1786, 4th ed. II, 45:

Gives the entry as to Sp's monument, quoted by E. Fenton in his ed. of Waller. See Fenton, above.

WARE, SIR JAMES. De Scriptoribus Hiberniae, Dublin, 1639. (Copy in Univ. of Chicago Library. See also Ware's Works, Dublin, 1745, II, Pt. II, 327, for a translation.)

Liber secundus, Cap. V, p. 137: "Edmundus Spenserus, patriā Londinensis & academiae Cantabrigiensis alumnus, Poëtarum Anglorum suae aetatis princeps, in Hiberniam primùm venit cum *Arthuro Domino Grey Barone de Wilton*, Hiberniae Prorege, cui fuit à Secretis. Obijt Westmonasterij an 1599. & ibidem in ecclesiā S. Petri, prope Chaucerum sepultus est. Scripsit Anglicè *Poemata varia*, quae excusa in uno volumine extant. Item prosa, per modum Dialogi, inter Eudoxum & Irenaeum, *De Statu Hiberniae, Lib. I.* Promisit etiam in eo libro se de antiquitatibus Hiberniae scripturum, sed an praestiterit nondum reperi, verisimile autem est morte praeventum non praestitisse." Cf. Trans. Bibliog. Soc., XV, 84.

WARE, SIR JAMES, ed. The Historie of Ireland, collected by Three Learned Authors. Dublin, 1633.

Preface: Brief sketch of Sp's life. Birth, college career, sec'y to Lord Grey; his Kilcolman estate. "There he finished the later part of that excellent poem of his *Faery Queene*, which was soone after unfortunately lost by the disorder and abuse of his servant, whom he had sent before him into England." "He deceased at Westminster in the yeare 1599 (others have it wrongly 1598)." Based partly on Camden. But Ware was a careful historian, conversant with Irish affairs (formerly secretary to Richard Boyle, etc). He criticizes the V of I. His marginal notes should not be overlooked.

WARNER, WM. Albion's England. Lond. 1612. Therewith "A Continuance of Albion's England. By the first Author, W. W. Lond. 1606." (Copy in Newberry Lib.)

Address "to the Reader":

> "The Musists, though themselues they please,
> Their Dotage els finds Meede nor Ease:
> Vouch't Spencer in that Ranke preferd,
> Per Accidens, only interr'd
> Nigh Venerable Chaucer, lost,
> Had not kinde Brigham reared him Cost,
> Found next the doore Church-outed neere,
> And yet a Knight, Arch-Lauriat heere."

Miss E. P. Hammond suggests that the last four lines refer to Chaucer (= "Knight" i.e. "Dan Chaucer," and "Arch-Lauriat"), and not to Sp. Cf. Collier's ed. of Sp, I, p. clxviii.

WEBB, ALFRED. Compendium of Irish Biography. Dublin, 1878. 486:

"Edmund Spenser." Negligible.

WELPLY, W. H. In Journal of Cork Hist. & Archaeol. Soc., XXVIII (1922), 22–34 ("to be continued").

Evidence from records of a suit by Peregrine Spenser in 1622 (in Pub. Record Office, Dublin) that before his death Sp purchased certain lands (Renny, Co. Cork) for £200, nearly completing the payment (afterwards completed by his widow's second husband, Roger Seckerstone), as a provision for Peregrine. [Kilcolman being destined to Sylvanus?]

Westminster Review, LXXXVII (N.S. XXXI) (1867), 133–50.
"Edmund Spenser." A review of various books on Sp. State of
literature before Sp. Sketch of the life; birth before 1552; opposes
theory of visit to Lancashire; that the verses in the Th. of W. are by Sp;
that he quarrelled with Dr. Perne at Cambridge; advantages for his
genius of his Irish isolation; connection of his life and poetry. Of
interest.

WHITE, JAMES G. Historical and Topographical Notes. Cork,
1913. See Index.
> 44: Arbitration in 1641 between Sir Wm. St. Leger and "William
> Spencer, gent., heir to his brother Edmund Spencer [grandson of the
> poet ?],—relative to the boundary of property at Kilcolman."
> 264–73: Sp portraits; details of the grant of Kilcolman to Sp; the
> quarrel with Lord Roche; records as to Elizabeth Boyle; views of
> Kilcolman castle; etc. Should be consulted.

WILKINSON, T. T. Edmund Spenser and the East Lancashire
Dialect. In Transactions Historic Soc'y Lancashire and
Cheshire, N.S. VII (1867), 87–102:
> For the Lancashire theory, following F. C. Spencer and Craik.
> Examines the dialect of Sh Cal to confirm the theory; list of words
> peculiar to the Hurstwood locality.

WILLS, JAMES. Lives of Illustrious Irishmen. Dublin, 1839–47.
Vol. II, Pt. II, 280–95:
> A conventional writing of the life, made popular by recital of most
> of the entertaining traditions and anecdotes about Sp. Stresses the
> Irish aspects of Sp's life.

WILSON, HARRY B. The History of Merchant Taylors School.
Lond. 1812–14.
> Pt. I, ch. i (The Masterships of Mulcaster, etc.), and Pt. II, ch. i (Of
> the principal Scholars, temp. Elizabeth). Sp's school, but Edmund
> Spenser is barely mentioned. Much evidence, however, has been
> brought to light since 1812–14. Cf. Pub. Mod. Lang. Asso., XXXI,
> 714.

WINSTANLEY, WILLIAM. England's Worthies. Lond. 1684
(1st ed. 1660). 224–27:
> "The Life of Mr. Edmond Spenser." Recites the story of the
> pension. These three pages are little but anecdotage. Cf. also 121–22:
> Sp on Chaucer.

WISE, T. J. in his ed. of the FQ, 1897. I, pp. lxxxv–vii:
> "Chronology of Edmund Spenser."

WOOD, ANTHONY À. Athenae Oxonienses, ed. P. Bliss. Lond. 1813 (1st ed. 1691–92). I, 627:

> On Turbervile's "Poems," "written to . . . . Edm. Spencer," etc.

WOOD, HERBERT. Guide to the Records deposited in the Public Record Office of Ireland. Dublin (The Stationery Office), 1919.

> Indications of documents possibly bearing on Sp, most of them (lamentably) probably destroyed in the Four Courts, 1922; others probably extant elsewhere. Gives an account of all the Irish records.

WRANGHAM, F., ed. British Plutarch. Lond. 1816. II, 155–76.
> Negligible.

WRIGHT, THOS., ed. Queen Elizabeth and her Times. Lond. 1838. II, 120–22:

> Letter from Sir Richard Bingham to the Earl of Leicester, 11 Nov. 1580, describing the taking of Smerwick—at which Sp and Raleigh were present.

YOUGHAL. See Hayman, above.

OTHER SPENSERS CONTEMPORARY WITH THE POET

There were at least five or six other Edmund Spensers, and of course innumerable Spensers and Spencers with other Christian names, in the last half of the sixteenth century. It would help to clear up various puzzles in the poet's life were the available information in regard to these to be assembled. References to Spensers are numerous in such sources as the Calendars of State Papers, the Reports of the Royal Historical Manuscripts Commission, the Parish Registers, County Histories, and other historical and genealogical sources.

See references under "Parents and Family," below.

For other Spensers in Ireland see references below under "Pelham's brother Spenser"; also, Calendar of State Papers, Ireland, 1574–85, p. 295: Richard Spenser, gent., Mar. 29, 1581 (Qu. If in Ireland?).

Twenty-sixth Report of the Deputy Keeper of Public Records in Ireland. Dublin, 1895. Appendix, p. 803: entry of will of John Spenser, Dublin, 1569.

Calendar of Fiants, Elizabeth, Nos. 1138, 3581, 5873 (William Spencer—In Ireland): No. 3645 (James Spenscer).

GROSART, A. B.   Ed. of Sp, I, 29 *n*, 403–7, and passim.

HALES, J. W.   Folia Literaria.   Lond. 1893, 161:
> Burial of an Edmund Spenser, 1577, in Burnley.

Historical Manuscripts Commission Reports.   Lond.   1870+
IV, 406 ff.
> Other Spensers of the period of Sp's youth connected with his school or the Merchant Taylors guild. Cf. 613–14: doubts that John Spencer, "free journeyman" of Merchant Taylors guild, was the poet's father; on various Spensers at Burnley, Lancashire, and Sp's connection therewith.

The Salisbury MSS, Pt. III (London, 1889), 260:
> R. Douglas to A. Douglas, June 1, 1587: that a certain Englishman, taken in Scotland, confessed to the king that he and others were suborned by my lords of Leicester, Huntington, Treasurer, and one Mr. Spenser, to kill his Majesty. The story discredited.

HUNTER, JOS.   Chorus Vatum.   Brit. Mus. MS.
> IV, 443–74, esp. 449: An Edmund Spenser in London 1541; other contemporary Spensers living in London; also 462.

The Lismore Papers, ed. A. B. Grosart, Priv. print, 1886–88, 2d ser., IV, 75, 115:
> An Edmund Spenser, not the poet.

Notes and Queries, Ser. IV, Vol. X (1872), 244, 301.

RYE, WALTER.   Possible East Anglian Descent of the Poet Spenser.   In Norfolk Archaeology, XIX (1916), Pt. II, 175–82:
> The Spensers of Lancashire; other Edmund Spensers c. 1550–1650.

SPENCER, F. C.   In Gentleman's Magazine, 1842, II, 138–43.

VENN, JOHN, and J. A. VENN.   Book of Matriculations . . . . Univ. of Cambridge, 1913.   630–31:
> List of various Spensers at Cambridge, 1544–1659.

WELPLY, W. H.   In Journal of Cork Hist. and Archaeol. Soc., XXVIII (1922), 28:
> Other Spensers in Ireland, 16th Cent.

On the fly leaf of F. I. C.'s copy of Spenser's Faerie Queene, 1609, is the signature, in a seventeenth century hand, of "Thomas Spencer, fellow of King Colledge in Camb."

PARENTS AND FAMILY: DESCENDANTS

See also references on "Spenser's Marriage; Spenser's Wife," below.

ABRAM, W. A. A Review of the Evidence on the suggested Relation of the Poet Spenser to the Clan of Spensers in the Burnley District. In Trans. Burnley Lit. and Sci. Club, IV (1887), 73–82 (Copy in N.Y. Pub. Lib.):

> In continuation of the researches of F. C. Spencer, etc.; much on the Spensers of Hurstwood; in confirmation of Grosart, etc.

Arber's Transcript of the Stationers' Register, I, 111 b:

> "John Spynser, the sonne of Rycharde Spenser of Eltham in the County of Kynte Taylour hath put hym self apprentes to Grace Cater Wedowe Cytizen and stacioner of London from the feaste of saynte Mygchell the archangell [29 September] in the yere of our Lorde god 1564 eighte yeres." Cf. The Spending of the Money of Robert Nowell, p. xx.

Athenaeum, XXXIX (1862), 73–76:

> Spenser's daughter Florence: Spenser's two marriages.

BETHAM, SIR WM. Ulster Knight of Arms. Genealogical Table of Spenser's Descendants. In Gentleman's Magazine, 1842, II, 140:

> "Compiled by me from the Records of Ireland," 1841; gives particulars as to Sp's descendants, wills, etc.; the sole authority for Sp's son "Laurence" and daughter "Catherine." Cf. The Patrician, V; cf. W. H. Welply, below.

BRADY, W. M. Clerical and Parochial Records of Cork, Cloyne, and Ross. Lond. 1864.

> I, 12, 43; 351: Peregrine Spenser (from G. L. Craik); II, 114, 260 ff.: as to James Spenser, Curate of Youghal in 1662; also of deed in 1600 ("Ferguson's MSS, I, 74") of lands in Munster to the use of Roger Seckerton and his wife [Spenser's widow], with remainder to Peregrine Spenser, etc., with rem. to the right heirs of Edmund Spenser forever. Particulars as to Sp's heirs: Sons=Sylvanus, Laurence (his will, 1653, makes a bequest to one "Bathurst"), Peregrine; their marriages and children.

BUCK, P. M., JR. In Mod. Lang. Notes, XXI (1906), 80–84.

Calendar of Proceedings in Chancery in the Reign of Queen Elizabeth, Lond. 1827–32. I, 279 (E. e. 5):

John Englishe vs Richard Spencer, and others. Claim by will.
Two messuages in the parish of St. Dunston in the East, late the estate
of Elizabeth Spencer Widow. [Qu. Is this the poet's mother?]

Calendar of the Carew MSS, 1601–3, p. 35:
> Petition, 1601, in behalf of Sp's wife and children. Cf. 1603–24,
> p. 256. Cf. Collier's ed. of Sp, I, p. clii.

CARTWRIGHT, J. J. In the Academy, VI (1874), 8–9.

CHALMERS, GEO. Supplemental Apology. Lond. 1799, 35:
> Sp's descendants (with documents). Cf. Todd's ed. of Sp, 1805, I,
> pp. cxlvii ff.

CRAIK, G. L. Spenser and his Poetry, III, 243–52.

Cromwell, Oliver, Letters and Speeches of, by Thos. Carlyle,
ed. S. C. Lomas. Lond. 1904, III, 489–90:
> Letter of Cromwell of 27 Mar. 1657, on the case of Wm. Spenser, the
> poet's grandson.

Dict. Natl. Biog., XVIII (1909).
> 793: A younger brother John [Qu. No proof that he was Sp's brother?]
> entered Merchant Taylors School Aug. 3, 1571 and went later to
> Pembroke Hall. Not the John Spenser, later the president of
> Corpus Christi, Oxford. A sister Sarah. (Cf. Grosart, I, 423–26.)
> 802: Sp's descendants; "The poet's second son, Lawrence, was styled
> of Bandon; his will was proved in 1654"; Sp's daughter Catherine.
> Cf. W. H. Welply, below.

FERGUSON, JAS. F. Memorials of Spenser. In Gentleman's
Magazine, 1855, II, 605–9:
> Various records as to Sp's heirs (Silvanus, Peregrine, etc.).

Gentleman's Magazine, 1842, II, 138; 1843, II, 114 (Sp's descendants).

GIBSON, C. B. History of Cork. Lond. 1861. I, 309.

GROSART, A. B. Ed. of Sp, I, pp. xii–lxiv:
> Mostly on the Lancashire Spensers, with documents; that Sp's
> father was John Spenser. 204.

HARDIMAN, JAS. Irish Minstrelsy. Lond. 1831. I, 319 n,
321 f.:
> Sp's descendants (with documents).

Historical Manuscripts Commission, Reports. Lond. 1870+
IV, 411–12.

Cf. p. xvi (suggestion that John Spenser was the poet's father).
613–14: doubts that John Spencer "free jorneyman" of Merchant
Taylors guild was the poet's father; that John Spenser, afterwards
President of Corpus Christi, Oxford, was at Merchant Taylors School
while Sp was there; possibly he was the son of the journeyman; on
various Spensers at Burnley, Lancashire, and Sp's connection therewith; were Edmund and Isabel (=Elizabeth) Spenser of Burnley the
poet's parents? Family ties between the Spensers and the Nowells
(Sp's benefactor).

Salisbury MSS, Pt. XI (1906), 95:
Among the undertakers listed in 1600–1601, "Mrs. Spenser"
[Spenser's widow].

HOWITT, WM. Homes of the Poets. Lond. 1847. I, 13–39.
Sp's descendants.

HUGHES, JOHN. In his ed. of Spenser, 1715. I, pp. xxi–ii;
Sp's descendants.

HUNTER, JOSEPH. Chorus Vatum, MS. (Photostat copy in
Newberry Library, Chicago.)
IV, 443 ff: Sp genealogy; evidence for Sp's connection with the
noble family of the Spencers. A common ancestor possible only in the
great-great-great grandfather of the Spencer ladies, about 1420. An
Edmund Spenser in London, 1541. Other contemporary Spensers
living in London; Sp's descendants.

I. (D. A. C. N.). In the Patrician. Lond., V (1848), 54–55:
Gives a "Pedigree of Spencer's Family"; Sp's sister "Sarah" and Sp's
descendants; chief authority as to Sp's sister; but finds no proof as to
"Lawrence" or "Catherine." See Betham, above.

JONES, WALTER A. In Journal Cork Hist. and Arch. Soc.,
VII (1901), 238–42.

Journal of Cork Hist. and Arch. Soc., XI (1905), 196: "Pedigree
of the Poet Spencer's Family."

KEIGHTLEY, THOS. In Fraser's Magazine, LX (1859), 410–22:
The branches of the Spenser family: Sp's sister; his children.

The Lismore Papers. Ed. A. B. Grosart, Priv. Print, 1886–88,
1st ser., I, Introd., pp. xiv ff.:
Evidence that Sp's wife was Elizabeth Boyle; IV, 242–43: Sp's
daughter; 2d ser., I, p. xv: further on Elizabeth Boyle; II, 139:
Peregrine Spenser.

LONG, P. W.   In Mod. Lang. Review, III (1908), 257–67:
> That Sp was married before the writing of the Epithalamion and wrote the Amoretti after his marriage.

LONG, P. W.   In Mod. Lang. Review, VI (1911), 396–97:
> The date of Spenser's marriage still uncertain.

The Patrician.   See I (D.A.C.N.), above.

PAYNE, JOHN T., and HENRY FOSS.   Bibliotheca Grenvilliana. Lond. 1842–48.
> Pt. II, 182: "England, Ireland and Wales. A Collection of cases of Grievances, etc. The case of William Spencer of Kilcolman . . . . grandson and heir to Edmond Spencer the poet . . . . 1605–1704. Fol. 2 vols."
> The case of William Spenser is relative to the forfeiture of his estate and his petition for its restoration.

PRENDERGAST, J. P.   See Life, General References.

RYE, WALTER.   Possible East Anglian Descent of the poet Spenser.   In Norfolk Archaeology, XIX (1916), Pt. II, 175–82:
> Against Grosart and the theory of Sp's Lancashire connections. The pedigree of the Spencers of Althorpe; the name Spenser, or Spencer, "common all over England"; the "Edmund Spenser" of Lancashire, 1564; other Edmund Spensers, c. 1550–1650; Sp's father John (?) Spenser of East Anglia (Suffolk).

SPENCER, F. C.   Locality of the Family of Edmund Spenser. In Gentleman's Magazine, 1842, II, 138–43:
> That Sp's family was of Lancashire origin, at Pendle Hill (on authority of descendants of Sp's sister, and of documents signed by Sp's son). Sp's descendants, a genealogical table, from the Dublin College of Arms; entries of various Spensers in church registers in Lancashire.
> Cf. Higginson, Spenser's Sh Cal, 290.
> Spencer's conclusion have been generally accepted by Craik, Collier, Church, Grosart, etc.

SPENCER, J. B. (and others).   Edmund Spenser, and Spensers, or Spencers, of Hurstwood.   In Notes and Queries, 1st ser., VII (Apr. 23, 1853), 410–11:
> Facts as to the Spenser family. Cf. 303, 362: Sp's living descendants; his sister.

TOWNSHEND, D.   The Great Earl of Cork.   N.Y. 1904.   69:
> Sp's daughter Katherine.

W. (O).   In Anthologia Hibernica, I (1793), 189–90:
> A descendant of Sp at Mallow, Ireland, with Sp documents.

WHITE, JAS. G.   Historical and Topographical Notes.   Cork,
1913.   44, 264–73:
> Sp's descendants.

WELPLY, W. H.   The Family and Descendants of Edmund
Spenser.   In Journal of Cork Hist. & Archaeol. Soc., XXVIII
(1922), 22–34:
> New evidence in confirmation of statement that Sp's wife was
> Elizabeth Boyle found in the record of a suit by Peregrine Spenser in
> 1622 (in P.R.O., Dublin); disputes the theory that Sp had a third son,
> Lawrence; Characterization of Elizabeth Boyle (Spenser-Tynte-
> Seckerstone); censures Betham's account of the Spenser pedigree as
> very inaccurate; traces later fortunes of Sp's descendants. (Article
> "to be continued.")   Important.

SPENSER'S MARRIAGE; SPENSER'S WIFE

See references on "Life, General," the Lismore Papers; on
"Parents and Family," etc.

Athenaeum, XXXIX (1862), 73–76:
> The question of Sp's two marriages.

COLLIER, J. P.   In his ed. of Sp, I, pp. xv ff.:
> Presents the view that Sp was married by 1587, on the basis of ar
> entry in that year at St. Clement Danes, London, of the birth of
> "Florenc Spenser, the daughter of Edmond."   Collier seems to have
> been unaware of the existence of other Edmund Spensers at this period;
> his theory has been generally discredited, chiefly because of the doubt
> whether Sp were in England c. 1586–87.   It is, however, not impossible.
> Cf. cxii, cli ff.   Cf. Lounsbury, Studies in Chaucer.

Dict. Natl. Biog., XVIII, 799:
> Sp's wife Elizabeth Boyle, "probably daughter of one James Boyle."
> Married 11 June, 1594, "either in the cathedral of St. Finbarr at Cork,
> or in St. Mary's Church, Youghal."

FALKINER, C. L.   Essays relating to Ireland.   Lond. 1909.
169.

GILFILLAN, G.   In his ed. of Sp's Works.   Edinb. 1859, II,
pp. xix–xx.

GROSART'S Sp, I, 190 ff.:

> Sp's wife = Elizabeth Boyle, a kinswoman of Richard Boyle,—with documents (for further proof see Lismore Papers); marriage 11 June, 1594 (from the Epithalamion).
>
> 555-71: Sp's descendants.

HALPINE, C. G.   Colin Clout and the Faery Queen.   In Atlantic Monthly, II (Nov. 1858), 674-88:

> The Rosalind question, and the question of who was Sp's wife; Elizabethan name-anagrams; Sp's wife = Elizabeth Nagle; the proof by anagrams.

HARMAN, E. G.   Edmund Spenser.   Lond. 1914, 374 ff.:

> Doubts the Elizabeth Boyle theory; argues that Sp was married long before 1594.   Cf. pp. 568-69.

RICKERT, EDITH.

> Miss Rickert communicates the following:
>
> "The house of Boyle's brother-in-law, Sir Richard Smith, stood on the estuary of the river that empties into the sea at Youghal,—practically the sea.   In view of this fact, Sonnet lxxv and a line in the Epithalamion (. . . . 'the sea that neighbours to her neare') suggest that Spenser's Elizabeth may have been married from Smith's house and in Youghal church, rather than in Cork Cathedral."

TODD'S ed. of Sp, 1805, I, pp. cxlii-clii.

TOWNSHEND, D.   The Great Earl of Cork.   N.Y. 1904.   8:

> On Elizabeth Boyle.

WELPLY, W. H.   See under "Parents and Family."

SPENSER'S CIRCLE, FRIENDS, PATRONS, ASSOCIATES AND ACQUAINTANCES

Spenser's contact with his contemporaries, definite or indefinite, was very extensive.   A partial list of those with whom it has been suggested, or with whom there is reason to believe, that he was in touch at one time or another would include:[1]

Wm. Alabaster	Richard Barnfield
Lancelot Andrewes	Wm. Basse
Bishop Aylmer (Morrell?)	Theo. Bathurst

[1] My original list has been considerably enlarged from a similar list compiled by Miss Edith Rickert.   See, on these names, Whitman's Subject Index, p. 20 (Authors mentioned by Spenser").   Note Sp's treatment of the theme of Friendship in FQ, IV.

Nathaniel Baxter
Henry Bosvil
Richard Boyle (Earl of Cork)
Nicholas Breton
Sir Henry Brouncker
Sir Valentine Browne
Giordano Bruno
Lodovic Bryskett (Thestylis)
Lord Burghley
Wm. Camden
Christopher Carleil
Lady Carey (Phillis)
Wm. Casey, Bp. of Limerick
Sir Thomas Challoner (Palin?)
John Chalkhill
Geo. Chapman
Chichester
Thos. Churchyard (Palaemon or Harpalus)
Lady Compton (Charillis)
Margaret Countess of Cumberland (Marian)
Roland Cowyck
Mary Countess of Pembroke (Clorinda)
Samuel Daniel
Sir John Davies
Nicholas Dawtrey
Capt. Edward Denny
Earl of Derby
Lady Derby (Amarillis)
Herbert Dering
Penelope Devereux, Lady Rich (Stella)
Sir Robt. Dillon

M. Dormer
Thos. Drant
Michael Drayton (Aetion?)
Sir Wm. Drury
Sir Edward Dyer
Queen Elizabeth
Earl of Essex
Geoffrey Fenton
Sir Edward Fitton
Charles Fitzgeffrey
John Florio
Abraham Fraunce (Corydon?)
Geo. Gascoigne
Henry Gilford
Arthur Golding (Palaemon)
Barnaby Googe
Sir Arthur Gorges (Alcyon)
Richard Greenham
Fulke Greville
Arthur Lord Grey (Artegal)
Abp. Grindal (Algrind)
Joseph Hall
Gabriel Harvey (Hobbinol)
Richard Harvey
Sir Wm. Herbert (d. 1586?)
Lady Douglas Howard (Daphne)
Wm. Hunnis
Wm. Jones
Ben Jonson
E[dward] K[irke] (Cuddy?)
Thos. Kyd (at Merchant Taylors School, 26 Oct. 1565 ff.)

Richard Langherne [Laugher]
Lord Leicester (Arthur, Lobbin)
Lewes Lewkenor
Thos. Lodge (Alcon)
Adam Loftus, Abp. of Dublin
Long, Bp. of Armagh (1584–89)
John Lyly
Wm. Lyon, Bp. of Cork
Richard Mulcaster
Thos. Nashe
Sir Robt. Needham
Sir John Norris [Norreys]
Sir Thos. Norris
Sir. Thos. North
Countess of Northampton (Mansilia)
Henry Peacham
George Peele (Palin)
Andrew Perne
Sir John Perrot (Satyrane?)
Wm. Peter
Thos. Preston
Geo. Puttenham
Sir Walter Raleigh (Timias, Shepherd of the Ocean)
Timothy Reynolds
Daniel Rogers
Matthew Roydon
Sir Wm. Russell (V of I, ed. Grosart, 181)
Lady Anne Russell
Thos. Sackville (Harpalus?)

Sir Warham St. Leger ["Senleger"]
Lady Mary Sidney (Urania)
Sir Philip Sidney (Astrophel, etc.)
Thos. Smith
Wm. Smith
The Spencers of Althorpe
Ferdinando Stanley, 5th Earl of Derby (Amyntas?)
Henry Stanley, 6th Earl of Derby (Aetion?)
Rich. Stanyhurst (Cf. V of I; Harvey Letters)
John Still
Lady Strange
John Stubbs
Richard Tarlton (Willy?)
John Travers (Sp's brother-in-law)
Geo. Turbervile
Abp. Ussher
Arland Ussher
Wm. Vallans
Jean Van Der Noodt
Sir Henry Wallop
Frances Walsingham, Lady Sidney
Sir Francis Walsingham (Meliboe)
Wm. Warner
Anne, Countess of Warwick (Theana)
Thos. Watson
Archdeacon Watts

Wm. Webbe

Geo. Whetstone, Jr.

Wm. Whitaker

Thos. Wilcox

John Young (Roffin; Master of Pembroke, and Bishop of Rochester)

Col. John Zouch

See "Verses Addressed to the Author," prefixed to the Faerie Queene. The following possible identifications of the unknown initials thereto subscribed are suggested by Miss Edith Rickert:

H.B.

Henry Bosvill (cf. Collins, Memorials of State, I, 81); Sir Henry Brouncker; Henry Bedingfield; Sir Henry Bagnall (served in Ireland); Hugh Beeston; Henry Boughton; Sir Henry Bromley (cf. Chamberlain's Letters).

W.L.

Wm. Lawson; Wm. Lee (at Cambridge, 1579); Wm. Leigh; Wm. Leighton; Wm. Lewin (at Cambridge, 1584 ff.); Wm. Lawes; Wm. Lombard (knew Camden); Wm. Lyon ("the best guess").

R.S.

Robt. Sackville (married Anne Spencer, 1592); Sir Richard Smyth (Boyle's brother-in-law); Robt. Sidney; Richard Stapleton (DNB, XVIII, 798).

See also Sp's "Verses" to various noblemen, etc. Also, passim, the Spenser-Harvey Letters; Bryskett's Discourse; C. H. Whitman, Subject Index to the Poems of Edmund Spenser, New Haven, 1918. See, below, references on "Spenser and Sidney," "Spenser and Harvey," "Spenser and Raleigh," "Parents and Family," "Colin Clouts Come Home Again," "Areopagus," etc.

Cf. Collier's ed. of Sp, I, 154 ff.

Ritson, Bibliographia Poetica. Lond. 1802, 201:

That a Wm. Evans wrote complimentary verses prefixed to the first ed. of the FQ beginning

"Amongst the Grecians brave Homer beareth the bell."

These verses are not found in the Newberry Library copy of the 1590 ed. of the FQ (collation complete), nor in the collation of the copy in the Church Collection.

REFERENCES

These references are a selected list merely. The list might be vastly extended.

See, in Sp's Works, Sh Cal. Oct., ll. 53 ff., and Nov., ll. 117 ff. (on Sp and Leicester); passim (on Kirk—"familiar acquaintance"); cf. Harvey-Sp correspondence; also on Grindal, and others of the Circle— see various identifications of the Shepherd names. Is "our pleasant Willy" of T of M the Willie of Aug.? Is he Sidney? Cf. Sept.,—possibly

Van der Noodt; see its Gloss: "by the names of other shepherds he covereth the persons of divers others his familiar friends and best acquaintance."

See R of T, Dedication, and ll. 316 ff. (Countess of Pembroke); ll. 183 ff., 491 ff. (Leicester); ll. 436 ff. (Walsingham); ll. 448 ff. (Burleigh).

VG, passim (Leicester).

T of M, Ded. (Lady Strange; "private bands of affinitie").

Muiop., Ded. (the Spencers, Burleigh, Leicester).

MHT (Leicester, Burleigh).

CCCHA: many of Sp's associates introduced; problem of the unidentified names—ll.175 (Marin), 330 (Corylas), 354 (Alexis), 458, etc. (Lucida) 482 (Melissa), 518 (Galathea), 526 (Neaera), 586 (Aglaura), etc.; ll. 380 ff. (associates in England, at court, etc.); note bearing of ll. 470 ff. on the Epithalamion; 512, reference to Daphnaida; 648, reference to the pension(?); 655 ff., his life in Ireland; 682 ff., reference to MHT (?). Note recapitulations from MHT, FQ, Four Hymnes, etc. and echoes of others (R of T, etc.). See passim for Irish place-names, for the Rosalind matter (esp. 905 ff.—Rosalind = one of high station, l. 938).

BAGWELL, R. Ireland under the Tudors. Lond. 1890, III, 456–58. (Bryskett, Baxter, Fenton, etc.)

BASSE, WM. See "Criticism before 1651."

BATHURST, THEO.
Cf. John Worthington's Diary, Chetham Soc. Pub., 1886, II, 345.

BAXTER, NATH.
Sidney's tutor, Warden of Youghal College, 1592–98, friend of Sir Thos. Norris. Cf. Brady, Records of Cork, II, 410 f., III, 21; Corser, Collectanea, II, 63, 75, 216 ff.

BIRCH, THOS. Memoirs of the Reign of Queen Elizabeth. Lond. 1754, II, 487–88:
Essex's patronage of Sp.

BOND, R. W. See "Lyly" below.

BOURNE, H. R. Fox. Sir Philip Sidney. N.Y. 1891. 195 ff.
Sp's relations with Sidney, Harvey, John Still, Thos. Preston, Leicester, Dyer, and Greville.

BOYLE, RICHARD.
Cf. Salisbury MSS, No. 13591, in Hist. MSS Com. Reports; Townshend, The Great Earl of Cork, 9-12; Grosart in his ed. of Sp, I, 198 (document showing connection of Boyle and Sp's widow).

BROWNE, SIR VALENTINE.

In Ireland; Boyle's brother-in-law; cf. Bagwell, Ireland under the Tudors, III, 126.

BRYDGES, SIR EGERTON. In Restituta. Lond. 1814,' III, 346–49:

Lord Grey; IV, 345: A MS elegy, in 1614, by Robt. Marston on Thomas Lord Grey, refers to patronage of Sp by Arthur Lord Grey:

"Whose infant Muse, succor'd by thy faire wing.
Had leave to thrive, and thriving learn'd to sing."

BRYSKETT, L. Discourse of Civil Life. Lond. 1606.

Cf. Arthur Collins, Letters and Memorials of State, Lond. 1746, I, 211, 261 f., 265. Also references to Calendars of State Papers, Ireland, under "Life, General References."

Mr. H. R. Plomer is investigating the life of Bryskett, especially his points of connection with Sp, and expects soon to publish his results. Bryskett was sent with Justice Dowdall to treat with Tirlogh in August 1581. Sp succeeded Bryskett as Clerk of the Faculties and later as Clerk of the Council of Munster. Bryskett's letters (very briefly noted in the Calendars) throw much light on the state of Ireland and on questions of England policy. Mr. Plomer hopes to throw new light on Bryskett's Discourse in its bearing on the lives of Spenser and of Bryskett.

Calendar of State Papers, Ireland, 1574–85. 345:

A list of "Lands and Goods of the rebels given by the Lord Deputy," mostly to those of Grey's entourage and so doubtless known to Sp.

CARLEILL, CHR. (1551 ?–93).

Cf. Harvey Letter Book, 63, 75.

CHALKHILL, JOHN. Thealma and Clearchus. Lond. 1683.

The title-page states that the author was "an acquaintant and friend of Edmund Spenser."

CHICHESTER.

Cf. Cal. State Papers, Ireland, 1588–92, 341. Perhaps the Sir Arthur Chichester who later (1604–13) became Lord Deputy of Ireland, and whose MS copy of the V of I is noted in Cat. of Add. MSS (No. 22,022).

COLLIER, J. P. Ed. of Sp, I, pp. cx, cxvii (and index, pp. clxix ff.).

COLLINS, A. Peerage of England. Lond. 1812. I, 386–87:

The Spencers of Althorpe.

Concordatums, Book of. See under "Life, General References," above.

In addition to the names there cited Mr. Henry R. Plomer lists the following as appearing in that document (Vol. 97, pp. 22–37) "who were in all probability friends and associates of Edmund Spenser," viz. Edward Waterhouse, Geoffrey Fenton ("principall Secretary"), Michaell Briskett, Gervase Markham, Sir Nicholas Bagnall Knight Marshall, Sir William Gerrard late Lo. Chancellor, Barnaby Rich, William Grey comptroller of Ld Deputys house, William Dearinge, Treas. to Ld Deputy, Jordan Roche, Patrick St. Leger, Nathaniel Dillon (mentioned among the Secretaries to the Lord Deputy in 1580; in the earlier entries mentioned as Deputy for the Clerk of the Council).

COOPER, C. H., and THOMPSON. Edward Kirke. In Notes and Queries, Ser. II, Vol. IX (1860), 42:

Further particulars about Edward Kirke, sizar at Pembroke Hall, Nov. 1571; E. K. not Edward King; etc.

COOPER, J. H. MS Letter of, inserted in J. P. Collier's copy of his ed. of Sp, in the Harvard Lib.

I, p. xxxiv: On the career of Edward Kirke; purchase of "a sheperds calendar" for two shillings by his patron in 1583.

DENNY, CAPT. EDWARD (afterwards Sir Edward).

One of the undertakers; a commander under Grey and employed as envoy by Grey, Sir John Perrot, the Queen, etc.; friend of Sidney; cousin of Zouche; friend of Treasurer Wallop; received escheated lands, 1582; etc. See Calendars of State Papers, Ireland, 1574–85, 1586–88, 1588–92, 1592–96, 1599–1600, 1600 (see indexes).

Dict. Natl. Biog., XVIII, 794.

DRURY, SIR WM.

Cf. Collins, Memorials of State, I, 74 ff., 85 ff., 95, 108, 119, 122 f.

ELTON, O. Modern Studies. Lond. 1907. 1–36 ("Giordano Bruno in England").

EMERSON, O. F. Spenser, Lady Carey, and the *Complaints* Volume. In Pub. Mod. Lang. Asso., XXXII (1917), 306–22:
Supplements Dr. Long's study of the subject.

ERSKINE, J. In Pub. Mod. Lang. Asso., XXX (1915), 831–50:
On Bryskett and Sp.

FALKINER, C. L. Essays relating to Ireland. Lond. 1909. 13.
Sp's acquaintance with Archbishop Ussher.

FENTON, GEOFFREY.

    Cf. Townshend, The Great Earl of Cork, 2 (at Smerwick); 3 (associated with Bryskett); 33 f. (Boyle's father-in-law).
See "Sources, General," under "Fenton."

FITTON, SIR EDWARD.

    President of Munster to 1586. Cf. Newdigate, Gossip from a Muniment Room, 3.

FLEAY, F. G. Guide to Chaucer and Spenser. Lond. 1877. Pt. II, ch. iii.

    List of poets contemporaneous with Sp.

FLETCHER, J. B. Spenser and "E. K." In Mod. Lang. Notes, XV (1900), 330–32:

    That Sp and E.K. jointly wrote the annotations to the Sh Cal.

FRAUNCE, ABRAHAM. Victoria, ed. G. C. Moore Smith. Louvain (Materialien, Vol. XIV), 1906. Introd.:

    For fullest account of Fraunce.

FRITH, I. Life of Giordano Bruno. Lond. 1887. Passim, esp. ch. v, "England, 1583–85." See p. 128.

GOOGE, BARNABY.

    Kinsman of Cecil; in Ireland in Sp's time.

GREENLAW, EDWIN. Spenser and the Earl of Leicester. In Pub. Mod. Lang. Asso., XXV (1910), 535–61:

    An attempt to expound Sp's relations to contemporary political intrigues (Leicester, Burleigh, etc.), c. 1579; that Leicester sacrificed Sp in a political exigency. Cf. Long in Pub. Mod. Lang. Asso., XXXI, 720 ff.

GREY, ARTHUR, LORD.

    Cf. A Commentary of the Services and Charges of William Lord Grey of Wilton, by his son Arthur Lord Grey, ed. Sir P. D. G. Edgerton. Lond. Camden Soc., 1847, pp. xviii f.: Patronage of Sp by Arthur Lord Grey.

EDMUND GRINDAL. The Remains of. Cambr. (Parker Soc.), 1843.

GROSART, A. B. In his ed. of Sp, I, 25 ff., 32–36, 62 ff., 142 ff., 162, 194 n., 203, 206, 218, 245 ff. Cf. pp. 118, 180, 317, 426 ff.

HERBERT, SIR WM.
> One of the undertakers. See Calendars of State Papers, Ireland, 1586–88, 1588–92 (see indexes).

HIGGINSON, J. J. Spenser's Shepherd's Calendar. N.Y. 1912. Ch. ii:
> On E.K. pp. 165–81; Perne, 181–84; Preston, 184–88; Greenham, 188–97; Thomas Wilcox, 197–203; Leicester, 231–32; Rogers, 316 *n*; Stubbs, 323.

HUNTER'S Chorus Vatum, IV, 450:
> "See for his contemporaries at College the list of fellows of Pembroke Hall printed with Leland's Collectanea, V, 401, and Fuller's Hist. of Cambridge"; 468 ("Friends of Spenser").

Liber Munerum Publicorum Hiberniae. 1824.
> Lists giving the names of most of the public officers in Ireland in Sp's time.

LONG, P. W. In Anglia, XXXI (1908), 72–104 (Spenser and Sir Thomas North).

LONG, P. W. Spenser and the Bishop of Rochester. In Pub. Mod. Lang. Asso., XXXI (1916), 713–35:
> Sp's relations to Dr. Young and to Grindal, probably dating from Sp's years at Merchant Taylors School; Young headmaster of Pembroke College during five of Spenser's years there; Sp Young's secretary, 1578; Spenser and Leicester.

LONG, P. W. Spenser and Lady Carey. In Mod. Lang. Review, III (1908), 257–67:
> Lady Carey in Sp's poetry.

LONG, P. W. In Englische Studien, XLII (1910), 53–60:
> Coridon = Watson; Meliboe = Walsingham; Calidore = Essex.

LONG, P. W. In Mod. Lang. Review, IX (1914), 457–62:
> Sp and Lady Carey.

LUCE, ALICE, ed. The Countess of Pembroke's Antonie. Weimar, 1897. Pp. 7–16:
> Literary circle of the Countess of Pembroke—Sp, Breton, Daniel, Davies, Fraunce, Howell, Watson, Barnes, Browne, etc.

LYLY, JOHN. Works, ed. Bond, 1902. I, 18–19:
> Relations of Sp and Lyly. Cf. 62–63, 74, 516; II, 256.

LYON, WM.

1582 Bp. of Ross; 1584 Bp. of Cork and Cloyne—united with Ross, 1587; to Ireland about 1570; Grey's chaplain, 1580; on various commissions in Munster; tradition that he married Spenser. Cf. Grosart in Lismore Papers, 1st ser., I, pp. xxii ff., 167, 291; Cal. of State Papers, Ireland, 1574-85, 1592-96, 1598-99, 1599-1600, 1600, 1603-6 (see indexes).

MACDONALD, GEORGE. England's Antiphon. Lond. 1874. ch. v:

"Spenser and his Friends": quotations, with light comment on Sp, Raleigh, Sidney, Greville, etc.

MACKAIL, J. W. The Springs of Helicon. Lond. 1909. 81 ff.

MALONE, E. In his ed. of Shakespeare, 1821. II, 172 *n*.

Ralph Rowley (of Pembroke Hall, Cambridge) "probably a friend of Spenser's"; 205 *n;* Edmund Scorie a godson of Spenser's?

MASSON, DAVID. Life of John Milton. Lond. 1881. I, 592-94:

On the Countess of Derby (Lady Strange) and Sp's allusions to her. Her literary circle.

MORLEY, HENRY. Engl. Writers, XI, 144:

Lancelot Andrewes in Sp's circle.

MORLEY, H. Hobbinol. In Fortnightly Review, N.S., V (1869), 274-83:

Gabriel Harvey as Sp's friend; apologia for Harvey.

NORRIS, SIR JOHN.

President of Munster, 1585; his brother Thomas in his place later; lived at Mallow, only a few miles from Kilcolman; friend of Leicester. Cf. Townshend, The Great Earl of Cork, 20 (Boyle, who succeeded Sp as Clerk of the Council of Munster, says "I attended my Lord President [Norris] in all his employments"—so Sp with Norris, earlier?).

PEACHAM, H. See "Works; Apocrypha," No. IX.

Pedantius, A Latin Comedy formerly acted in Trinity College, Cambridge, 1631 (acted circa 1580?). Repr. ed. G. C. Moore Smith. Louvain (Materialien, Vol. VIII), 1905.

A satire on Gabriel Harvey. The Introd. gives a full account of Harvey. Cf. p. xlv: that Leonidas, the pupil of Pedantius, represents Sp.

Quarterly Review, CXCVI (1902), 483 ff. (on Bruno).

RENWICK, W. L. Mulcaster and Du Bellay. In Mod. Lang. Rev., XVII (1922), 282–87.

SÉLINCOURT, E. DE. Introd. to his one-volume Oxford ed. of Sp. Pp. xxiii f.:
> Sp and Grey; xxv ff.: Sp's circle in Ireland, Raleigh, the subjects of the dedicatory sonnets of the FQ; Sp's "unswerving loyalty to his friends."

SMITH, G. C. MOORE, ed. Gabriel Harvey's Marginalia. Stratford, 1913. 274:
> Bruno and the Sidney group. Refers to translation of the Cena de la Ceneri in Frith's Life of Bruno.

SMITH, G. C. MOORE. Spenser and Mulcaster. In Mod. Lang. Review, VIII (1913), 368:
> Wrenock (in Sh Cal, Dec.) = Mulcaster. Their relations.

SMITH, WM. See under "Criticism before 1651."

SPAMPANATO, V. Vita di Giordano Bruno. Messina, 1921. Vol. I, ch. ix.
> "Soggiorno a Parigi e a Londra." Best account of Bruno's residence in London. Thoroughly documented (J. D. B.).

UNDERHILL, J. G. Spanish Literature in the England of the Tudors. N.Y. 1899. 269 ff.

USSHER, ABP. JAMES. Whole Works. Dublin, 1864. 17 vols.
> The elaborate index-volume does not show any reference to Sp.

WALLOP, SIR HENRY.
> Cf. Arthur Collins, Peerage of England. Lond. 1779. 5th ed., V, 72–83: Sir Henry Wallop, his career in Ireland, 1580–99. See p. 77: Elizabeth's grant of the Abbey of Enniscorthy to Sp, and transfers to Synot, and to Wallop.

WATSON, FOSTER. Richard Mulcaster and his "Elementarie." In the Educational Times, XLVI (Jan. 1, 1893), 12–17.
> A few remarks (p. 14) on Mulcaster as Sp's "schoolmaster"; a few traces of possible influence.

YOUNG, JOHN (1534 ?–1605).
> Bp. of Rochester, etc. See Dict. Natl. Biog.; Cooper's Athen. Cantabrig. (and its references); Gabriel Harvey's Letter Book (Camden Soc. Pub.); Calendars of State Papers, Domestic, 1547–80, and later volumes (see indexes); etc.

SPENSER AND SIDNEY

See "Astrophel"; also references under "Areopagus."

Do Sidney's sonnets 6 and 28 refer to Sp?

For allusions to Sidney in Sp's poems see Whitman's Subject Index to Spenser, 218.

See Whitman Subject Index, on "Astrophel," "Sidney."

See esp. Sh Cal, April, Gloss; Envoy; July and Nov. (refs. to Kent); July, Gloss (Bp. of Rochester and Sidney; cf. Sept. l. 196, and Gloss).

R of T, Ded. (Sidney = Sp's "Patron"), and ll. 281 ff., 589 ff.

CCCHA, ll. 451 ff., 457.

Astrophel, passim; also Bryskett's Pastorall Aeglogue (therewith), l. 142.

FQ, VI, passim, esp. VI, i, 2–3; VI, ii, 3; VI, ix, 41 ff. (Sidney's participation in the pastoral vein and association with Sp therein).

Spenser-Harvey Letters, passim.

BASKERVILL, C. R.   In Pub. Mod. Lang. Asso., XXVIII (1913), 308 n.

BAXTER, N.   See under "Criticism before 1651."

BIRCH, THOS.   Life of Sp, with his ed. of Sp, 1751, I, pp. vii–ix.

BOURNE, H. R. Fox.   Sir Philip Sidney, N.Y. 1891.   195–208.
   Sp's relations with Sidney; Sp's literary influence on Sidney, etc.

BUCK, P. M., JR.   In Mod. Lang. Notes, XXI (Mar. 1906), 80–84.

"C," etc.   In Notes and Queries, Ser. III, Vol. IV (1863), 21–22, 65–66, 101–3 (Cf. 140, 150, 197, 236, 283).

CHURCH, R.   In his ed. of the FQ, 1758, I, 23.

COLLIER, J. P.   In his ed. of Sp, 1862, I.   See index.

Dict. Natl. Biog., XVIII, 795: "close intimacy."

FULTON, EDW.   Spenser, Sidney and the Areopagus.   In Mod. Lang. Notes, XXXI (1916), 372–74:
   That the club of the Areopagus was not an historic fact, but disputes Long's estimate (Anglia, XXXVIII, 173 ff.) that Sp and Sidney were not on fairly intimate terms.

GREENLAW, EDWIN.   Sidney's *Arcadia* as an Example of Elizabethan Allegory.   In Kittredge Anniversary Papers.   Bost. 1913, pp. 327–37:
   The Elizabethan conception of allegory in Sidney and Sp.   The Arcadia "a prose counterpart of the *Faerie Queene*."

GREENLAW, EDWIN. Shakespeare's Pastorals. In Studies in Philology, XIII (1916), 122–54:
Influence of Sidney on Sp.

GROSART'S ed. of Sp, I, 443–56.

HIGGINSON, J. J. Spenser's Shepherd's Calendar. N.Y. 1912. 243–57:
Sidney in Sp's writings. Cf. 280.

LOFTIE, REV. WM. Edmund Spenser at Penshurst. In A. Lang, Poets' Country. Lond. 1907. 313–24:
That Sp visited Sidney at Penshurst before 1579, the scenery of the locality being reflected in the Sh Cal.

LONG, P. W. Spenser and Sidney. In Anglia, XXXVIII (1914), 173–93:
That Sp was but slightly acquainted with Sidney, and the Areopagus was "a mere figure of speech"; the evidence closely examined; growth of the tradition of the Spenser-Sidney intimacy from Edward Phillips (1675) down; Sidney's influence on Sp.

MASTERMAN, PHILIP. In Spenser, Poet. Works. Bost. 1839. I, pp. x–xi.

PHILLIPS, EDWARD. Theatrum Poetarum Anglicanorum, (1675). Repr. Canterbury, 1900. 148–54:
Sidney's influence on Spenser.

Quarterly Review, CXCVI (1902), 441–45.

SÉLINCOURT, E. DE. Introd. to his one-volume Oxford ed. of Sp. Pp. xii ff.:
Their relationship not one of close personal intimacy; but "Spenser's love for Sidney was probably the deepest formative influence upon his life and character."

TODD'S ed. of Sp, 1805, I, p. clxix n.

TYTLER, PATRICK, F. Life of Raleigh. Edinb. 1833, 113–21.

WALLACE, MALCOLM W. Life of Sir Philip Sidney. Cambr. 1915. 107:
Reasons for believing that the acquaintance of Sp and Sidney "dated from their Cambridge days." 228–31: Relations of Sp and Sidney; discredits the story of Sp's visit to Penshurst and the Areopagus-club legend. "We simply know that Sidney and Dyer had Spenser 'in some use of familiarity.'" Cf. p. 256.

THE AREOPAGUS

See also references on "Spenser and Sidney," above.

BERLI, HANS.   Gabriel Harvey, der Dichterfreund und Kritiker. Zurich, 1913.   88–93.

BOURNE, H. R. Fox.   Sir Philip Sidney.   N. Y. 1891.   200:
The Areopagus. This passage "chiefly responsible for the rise of the Areopagus legend" (Mod. Lang. Notes, XXXI, 372).

BULLEN, A. H., ed.   Davison's Poetical Rhapsody.   Lond. 1890, I, p. lxxv.

Dict. Natl. Biog., XVIII, 795: "a literary club"; meetings at Leicester House, 1578–79.

DRAPER, J. W.   In the Colonnade.   N.Y. 1922.   41:
Résumé of the discussion on the Areopagus question.

FLETCHER, J. B.   Areopagus and Pléiade.   In Journal of Germanic Philology, II (1899).   429–53:
Proof of the existence of "an English group of literary reformers" . . . . . "itself a conscious following of the French group." Their literary doctrines. A helpful analysis and comparison of Sp and the French poets of the Pléiade.

GOSSE, E.   Sir Philip Sidney.   In Contemporary Review, L (1886), 642–43.

HARVEY, GABRIEL.   Three Letters, 1580.   In H's Works. ed. Grosart, I, 1 ff.

HIGGINSON, J. J.   Spenser's Shepherd's Calendar.   N.Y. 1912. 257–86:
Examination of various theories as to this "club," (composed of Spenser, Sidney, Dyer, Greville, Harvey, Kirke, Drant, and Leicester); points of difference between Sidney and Sp.

LEE, SIDNEY.   In Cambridge Mod. Hist., III (1905), 368–69:
The Areopagus "club."

MACINTIRE, ELIZ. J.   French Influence on the Beginnings of English Classicism.   In Pub. Mod. Lang. Asso., XXVI (1911), 496–527:
French origins of Areopagite critical ideas; Sp's critical theories and their French prototypes (512 ff.).

McKerrow, R. B. In Mod. Lang. Quarterly, IV (1901), 172–80; V (1902), 149 ff.:
Discusses the Areopagus movement and Sp's classical versifying.

Maynadier, H. The Areopagus of Sidney and Spenser. In Mod. Lang. Review, IV (1909), 289–301:
Questions the view (of Grosart, Symonds, etc.) that the Areopagus was a formally organized body. Analsyis of all early references to it.

Morley, H. Engl. Writers, IX, 74 ff.

Schelling, F. E. Poetic and Verse Criticism. Phila. 1891. 24 ff., 92.

Schelling, F. E. The Queen's Progress. Bost. 1904. 96 ff.

Smith, G. C. Moore, ed. Gabriel Harvey's Marginalia. Stratford, 1913. 274:
Bruno's account of the meetings of Sidney, Greville, and Dyer = the best evidence of the existence of this club.

Smith, G. Gregory, ed. Elizabethan Critical Essays. Oxford, 1904. I, pp. l ff. Cf. 372 ff.

Spingarn, J. E. Literary Criticism in the Renaissance. N.Y. 1899. 300 ff.

Stone, W. J. Classical Metres in English. Lond. 1899. 120, 126:
Sp and classical versifying.

Symonds, J. A. Life of Sidney. N.Y. n.d. (1886). 79:
"A little academy, formed apparently upon the Italian model."

Upham, A. H. French Influence in English Literature. N.Y. 1908. Ch. ii: "The Areopagus Group."

SPENSER AND HARVEY

See Whitman, Subject Index, 112, 119 ("Hobbinol"). See esp. Sh Cal, June, Sept. (Gloss), etc.; CCCHA, passim; Sp's sonnet to H in the "Four Letters"; the Spenser-Harvey Letters, passim.

Athenaeum, XXXIX (1862), 73–76.

Berli, Hans. Gabriel Harvey, der Dichterfreund und Kritiker. Zurich, 1913. 57–60:
The Sp-Harvey letters; 104–9: Sp and Harvey.

Collier, J. P. Spenser and Gabriel Harvey. In Athenaeum, XLII (1863), 533:
Harvey marginalia.

COOPER, C. H., and THOMPSON. In Notes and Queries, Ser. II, Vol. IX (1860), 42:
> Harvey a Fellow of Pembroke and probably tutor of Sp and Kirke.

GROSART'S ed. of Sp, I, 37 ff., 71–72, 125 ff.

HARVEY, GABRIEL. Marginalia, ed. G. C. Moore Smith, Stratford-upon-Avon, 1913.
> Of high importance. See the Introd., passim. Sp is mentioned by Harvey at pp. 122, 161, 162, 168, 169, 170, 173, 226, 231, 232, 233. Cf. pp. 281, 290; also 57 ff. (little evidence of meetings or correspondence between Harvey and Spenser after 1586, save a possible meeting in 1590). Pp. 23, 82, 173 (books given Harvey by Sp).

HARVEY, GABRIEL. Letter Book (1573–1580), ed. J. L. Scott. Lond. (Camden Soc.), 1884. Passim.

HARVEY, GABRIEL. Works, ed. A. B. Grosart. Huth Lib. 1884. 3 vols. Passim.

LONG, P. W. In Pub. Mod. Lang. Asso., XXXI (1916), 713–35.

Notes and Queries, Ser. II, Vol. IV (1857), 322.

SAINTSBURY, GEO. A History of Criticism. N.Y. 1902, II, 165–68:
> On Sp and Harvey, artificial versifying, etc. A mere summary.

SÉLINCOURT, E. DE. Introd. to his one-volume ed. of Sp, 1921. Pp. ix–xi.

WOODWARD, PARKER. In Baconiana. Lond. N.S. IX (1901), 118–24.

WOODWARD, P. Tudor Problems. Lond. 1912. 141–45:
> On the Sp-Harvey correspondence.

SPENSER AND RALEIGH

See CCCHA, passim; FQ, II, Introd., stanza 2; III, Introd., stanzas 4, 5; IV, xi, 22; VI, v, 12 ff.

"C." In Notes and Queries, Ser. III, Vol. IV (1863), 21–22, 65–66, 101–3. (Various: see 140, 150, 197, 236, 283.)

CANNING, A. S. G. Literary Influence in British History. Lond. 1904. Ch. v; "Spenser and Raleigh."

EDWARDS, EDWARD.　Life of Sir Walter Raleigh.　Lond. 1868.
I, 120–29:
>Raleigh's visit to Sp; relations of Sp and Raleigh.

GROSART'S ed. of Sp, I, 155 ff.

HENNESSY, SIR JOHN POPE.　Raleigh in Ireland.　Lond. 1883.
>Passim, esp. 114–16, "Spenser and Raleigh." Cf. 72–73. Cf. Grosart's ed. of Sp, I, 137 ff., 479 ff.

HOLINSHED.　Chronicle, Hooker's Appendix:
>Account of Raleigh in Ireland.

NELMES, THOS. E.　Kilcolman, or Raleigh's Visit to Spenser.
N.Y. 1875.　Verse, with brief introd. and notes.

Quarterly Review, CLXVIII (1899), 491–93.

ST. JOHN, JAS. A.　Life of Raleigh.　Lond. 1868.　I, ch. xi:
>The visit to Sp.

SÉLINCOURT, E. DE.　Introd. to his one-volume Oxford ed. of
Sp.　Pp. xxvii f.

SÉLINCOURT, HUGH DE.　Great Raleigh.　Lond. 1908.　Ch. ix.
>"Raleigh and Spenser." Of Raleigh at Youghal and the meetings with Sp; nature of Raleigh's influence on Sp. Cf. pp. 120–21.

TAYLOR, H. O.　Thought and Expression in the Sixteenth
Century.　N.Y. 1920.　II, 210 ff.

TYTLER, PATRICK F.　Life of Sir Walter Raleigh.　Edinb. 1833.
27, 30:
>Sp and Raleigh at Smerwick. 68 ff.: Irish estates of Sp and Raleigh. 113–21: Raleigh's visit to Sp; Raleigh's part in the FQ; their literary relations and those of Sidney and Sp.

PELHAM'S "BROTHER" SPENSER

The references in the Calendars of State Papers, cited below, to Justice Pelham and his "brother Spenser," indexed in the Calendars under "Edmund Spenser," at first sight furnish a puzzle. They indicate that this "Spenser" in 1579 and 1580 was alternately in England and Ireland as the bearer of despatches and in charge of some of Pelham's affairs. This puzzle seems to be cleared up by the references in the Calendar of the Carew MSS, which reveal that Pelham's "brother Spenser" was a certain James Spenser, not Edmund.

Calendar of State Papers, Ireland, 1574–85.

Pp. 191, 233, 238 (Mention of "Spenser" as "brother" of Lord Justice Pelham, July 17, 1580), 214 (Wallop's "letter of March 6 [1580] by James Spenser").

Calendar of the Carew MSS preserved . . . . at Lambeth, ed. J. S. Brewer and Wm. Bullen. Lond. 1867–73.

1575–88. P. 269:

Petition by Pelham, "sent by Mr. Spencer," to the Privy Council, July 9, 1580 [Lord Grey became Deputy in Ireland, in Aug. 1580] in behalf of his "brother Spencer," long employed in the North as Master of the Ordnance. Ed's note: "James Spencer was appointed Master of the Ordnance in the north of England in Nov. or Dec. 1569."

180: Again, Dec. 6, 1579, Pelham's "brother Spencer." Ed's note: "James Spencer? . . . . It has been supposed that this was Edmund Spenser, the poet." Cf. pp. 266, 267, 274, 276, 277, 283.

1589–1600: Pp. 395, 405, 406, 481, 498, 499.

1601–3: Pp. 16, 24: Further on James Spenser.

Catalogue of Western Manuscripts, British Museum. Lond. 1921. 13 B 1, f. 214:

"Letter from his brother-in-law Sir W. Pelham" on behalf of James Spenser.

COLLIER's ed. of Sp, I, p. 1 *n*.

TODD's ed. of Sp 1805, I, p. xlviii *n*.

SPENSERIAN PLACE-NAMES

See Whitman's Subject Index, s.v. "English Rivers," "Irish Rivers," etc. For general topography and modern names see the Ordnance Survey Maps of England and of Ireland; also Philips Handy Atlas of the Counties of Ireland, Lond. (c. 1892); etc.

For older names, etc., see "Maps of Ireland" under "Works, View of Ireland," below; also "Life, General References," esp. entries in Calendars, etc.; see R. Dunlop's Map of Ireland in the Time of Spenser, in Poole's Historical Atlas; Jas. Hardiman ed., Inquisitionum in Officio Rotulorum Cancellariae Hiberniae asservatarum Repertorium, Dublin, 1826–29, indexes, for innumerable Irish place-names. The Spenserian place-names in Ireland have been but slightly studied.

III
THE WORKS

III. THE WORKS

INTRODUCTORY

Spenser's works include

One allegorical verse romance or "epic" (FQ).

One pastoral, including political allegory, fables, lyrics, etc. (Sh Cal); pastoral setting appears in several other poems.

Four translations (VG; R of R; Bellay's Visions; Petrarch's Visions); translated passages appear in other poems.

Three elegies (R of T; Astrophel; Daphnaida).

One "Complaint" (T of M).

One verse satire, fable (MHT).

One mock heroic (Muiop.).

One emblem-poem (Visions of WV).

One verse-diary, pastoral (CCCHA).

One sonnet sequence (Amoretti).

Two marriage hymns (Epithal. and Prothal.).

Four platonic hymns.

One prose dialogue, political.

The completest collation of early editions of Sp is to be found in Geo. W. Cole's Catalogue of Books . . . . of the Library of E. D. Church. N.Y. 1909. This library is now a part of the Huntington Library at San Gabriel (Pasadena), California. See Nos. 650–64. No. 650 gives collation and description of the Theatre of Worldlings, with references to other bibliographical authorities; also a sketch of Sp's life.

The Church Collection (Huntington) contains nearly all of the first editions of Sp's works. Collation given of each, with bibliog. references and indication of location of other copies, and literary discussion.

See also for collations, Sélincourt's and Smith's ed. of Sp. Cf. Grosart's ed. of Sp for reproductions of title-pages, partial collations, etc.

ALLIBONE, S. A. Dict. of Engl. Lit. Phila., 1899, II, 2202–8:
Gives a "chronological catalogue" of Sp's works.

British Museum Catalogue.
Gives a list, nearly complete, of editions of Spenser; also of many books about Sp.

Dict. Natl. Biog., XVIII, 804:
> Gives a list of original editions of Sp in English libraries.

The Harvard University Bulletin, No. 12, for collations.

TODD's ed. of Sp, I, pp. clxxv ff.: on various editions.

The Grolier Club, Catalogue of an Exhibition of the Original Editions of the Works of Spenser. N.Y. 1899.

DE RICCI, SEYMOUR. The Book Collector's Guide. Phila. and N.Y. 1921, 546–48.

Edmund Spenser, a Bibliography (Brooklyn, 1893–94). Pratt Inst. Lib. School. Lectures on Gen. Lit., No. 39, pp. 420–23.
> Unimportant.

HUNTER, JOSEPH. Chorus Vatum, IV, 463 ff.

COLLIER, J. P. The Bridgewater Catalogue. Lond. 1837.
> 291: Description of the Complaints volume of 1591; 292: the Four Hymns volume of 1596.

GREG, W. W. Catalogue of Books presented by Edw. Capell to Trinity College, Cambridge. Cambr. 1903.
> 144–50: Various early editions of Sp analytically described; see esp. description of eds. of 1611 and 1617.

ALMACK, EDWARD. Fine Old Bindings, with other interesting Miscellanea in Edward Almack's Library. Lond. 1913. 124 ff.:
> Description of a copy of the FQ of 1590, formerly in Gabriel Harvey's possession; an earlier impression than any other copy extant; with variants and MS notes (Harvey's?) = textual emendations.

EDITIONS OF SPENSER: A SELECTED LIST

I. COLLECTIONS

Complete Works, Poetical Works, editions of the Faerie Queene before 1700, and separate works, editions before 1700.

A. In Spenser's Lifetime

A Theatre . . . . [of] Voluptuous Worldlings . . . . Devised by S. Iohn vander Noodt. Lond., By Henry Bynneman. 1569.
> Copy in Brit. Mus.; in Cornell Univ. Lib.; in Huntington Lib. "Epigrams" begin Bj, verso; "Sonets" begin B viii, recto.

The Shepheardes Calender. Lond. By Hugh Singleton, 1579.
First edition. Copy in Brit. Mus.; Huntington Lib., etc.

Three proper, and wittie, familiar Letters; lately passed between
two Universitie men . . . .

Two otner, very commendable Letters, of the same mens writing.
Lond. H. Bynneman, 1580.
Copy ("unique"?) in Brit. Mus.
A copy of the "Three Letters" is in the Huntington Library. It is
imperfect, lacking leaves F. ij. and F. iij, or pages 43–46 (supplied in
photostat facsimile from the B.M. copy—imperfection not noted in
the Huth catalogue, where this copy is described). Copy in Bodleian
(Malone Coll.).

The Shepheardes Calender, Lond. T. East for John Harrison
the younger, 1581.
The second edition. Copies (see DNB); in Huntington Lib.;
in Bodl. (Malone Coll.); etc.

The Shepheardes Calender. Lond. Iohn Wolfe, for Iohn Harrison the yonger, 1586.
Copies (see DNB); Huntington Lib.

The Faerie Queene. Disposed into twelve books . . . .
Lond. for William Ponsonbie, 1590. Books I–III.
First edition. Copies of the two issues in the Huntington Lib.
Copies also in various other public collections (Yale, Harvard, New-
berry Lib., etc.).

Muiopotmos. Lond. 1590.
Copy, separate, in N.Y. Pub. Lib. No separate ed. in Brit. Mus.
catalogue.

Complaints. Containing sundrie small Poemes of the Worlds
Vanitie . . . . by Ed. Sp. London. Imprinted for William
Ponsonbie, 1591.
Copies in Boston Pub. Lib.; Harvard Lib.; Yale Lib.; Lib. of
Elizabethan Club, Yale; Cornell Lib.; Huntington Lib.; Newberry
Lib.; Bodleian (Malone Coll.).
Contents: (1) Ruines of Time; (2) Teares of the Muses; (3) Virgil's
Gnat; (4) Prosopopoia, or Mother Hubberds Tale; (5) The Ruines of
Rome, by Bellay; (6) Muiopotmos, or The Tale of the Butterflie;
(7) Visions of the Worlds vanitie; (8) Bellayes visions; (9) Petrarches
visions.

A-Z, in fours, 92 leaves. Nos. 2, 4, 6 have separate title-pages and are sometimes found as separate publications (in Huntington, Boston, etc.). Note in Brit. Mus. catalogue: "Without pagination. Several of the Poems have special title-pages. The register is continuous. Pt. 4 [pt. 6 in some copies] containing Muiopotmos is dated 1590." B.M. copy has MS notes.

Daphnaida. An Elegie upon the death of the noble and vertuous Douglas Howard . . . . by Ed. Sp. London, for William Ponsonby, 1591.

Copies in Boston Pub. Lib. (also ed. of 1596), Harvard (ed. of 1596), Huntington, etc.

Prosopopoia, or Mother Hubberd's Tale. By Edm. Sp. Lond. 1591.

Part of the Complaints volume.

The Shepheards Calender. London, J. Windet for Iohn Harrison the Yonger . . . . 1591.

Copies in Brit. Mus.; Huntington.

Sonnet to Harvey (written 1586), published with Harvey's Foure Letters, 1592.

Colin Clouts Come home againe. London . . . . for William Ponsonbie, 1595.

With Astrophel.

A-K, in fours; 40 leaves. CCCHA=A-E$_2$; Astrophel=E$_3$-K$_4$. With running page-heads "Colin Clouts come home againe." Copies in Bost. Pub. Lib.; Harvard; Huntington; Lib. of Congress; Lib. of Elizabethan Club, Yale; Newberry Lib.; Bodleian (Malone).

Amoretti and Epithalamion. Written not long since by Edmunde Spenser. [London] for William Ponsonby. 1595.

Copy in Brit. Museum; Huntington; Bodleian (Malone); etc.

Daphnaida. 1596.

In Huntington; Boston; Bodleian (Malone); etc.

Fowre Hymnes, made by Edm. Spenser. London . . . . for William Ponsonby. 1596.

With Daphnaida.

Copies in Boston Pub. Lib.; Harvard; Huntington; Bodleian (Malone).

Prothalamion or A Spousall Verse made by Edm. Spenser . . . .
London . . . . for William Ponsonby, 1596.

> Copies in Boston Pub. Lib.; Lib. of Elizabethan Club, Yale; Hunt-
> ington Lib.; Bodleian (Malone).
> Not licensed, and therefore privately printed (Grosart).

The Faerie Queene. Disposed into twelue bookes, Fashioning
XII. Morall vertues. *With* The Second Part of the Faerie
Queene. Containing the Fourth, Fifth, and Sixth Bookes,
by Ed. Spenser. Imprinted at London for William Ponsonby. 1596. 2 vols.

> (ii)+590; and (ii)+518 pp.
> Copies in Brit. Mus. (four copies, with some variations); Hunting-
> ington; Yale; Harvard; Newberry Lib.; etc.

The Shepheards Calender. London. T. Creede for Iohn Harrison the yonger . . . . 1597.

> The last edition in Sp's lifetime.
> Copies in Harvard; Huntington Lib.; Yale; Brit. Mus. ("With
> . . . . a Latin version in MS by Bathurst.") Mr. H. R. Plomer writes:
> "There are two interleaved copies of this edition in the British Museum
> . . . . with a Latin version added in several handwritings. The
> text of this Latin version is clearly that of Theodore Bathurst (though
> it differs materially in places from the printed text of 1653), who was a
> student at the same college as Spenser. I have asked Dr. W. W.
> Greg's opinion and he puts forward the suggestion that Bathurst may
> have once owned these copies and had had his Latin version transcribed
> into them for presentation to his friends. Unfortunately there is no
> example of Bathurst's writing in the British Museum so that there is
> no possibility of comparison, and while it would be rash to say that the
> various hands are Elizabethan, it is quite possible that they might be,
> or at any rate of the time of James I." (But see the similar copies
> at Cambridge.)

B. After Spenser's Death

The Faerie Queene. . . . . Printed by H. L. for Mathew
Lownes. Lond. 1609. Folio.

> The first folio ed. of the FQ. The first edition of the Cantos of
> Mutability. Copies in Harvard; Yale; the Newberry Lib.; the Univ.
> of Chicago; etc.

Cf. J. C. Smith's ed. of the FQ, I, pp. xvii–xx: not edited by Harvey, as Todd conjectured; its editor "did not belong to the generation of Harvey and Spenser"; discusses its emendations of the text.

The Faerie Queen: The Shepheards Calendar: Together with the other Works of England's Arch-Poët, Edm. Spenser: Collected into one Volume; and carefully corrected. . . . . H. L. for M. Lownes [London] 1611.

The first folio of the collected works. It has been conjectured that Lownes the publisher was the editor of this volume.

Copies in Harvard; Yale; Newberry Lib.; etc.

The contents:

Title-page, 1 leaf

Ded. to Queen Elizabeth, 1 leaf

The Faerie Queene, text, pp. 1–363

The Author's Letter, 4 pp.

Verses by W. R., Hobbynoll, R. S., H. B., W. L., and Ignoto. 2 pp.

Introductory Sonnets, 8 pp.

Shepherds Calendar, Title and Introd. material, 10 pp.; the text, pp. 1–56.

MHT (Title page dated 1613), pp. 1–16.

CCCHA (title page, undated) as running head; together with Astrophel, Thestylis (at B₃), etc. unnumbered. 26 pp.

Prothalamion (title page "1611"). Text 2 pp.

Amoretti and Epithalamion (title page "1611"). Text of Amoretti, 14 pp. Epithalamion (separate title page "1611"). Text, 4 pp.

Foure Hymnes (title page "1611"). Ded. and text, 14 pp.

Daphnaida (title page "1611"). Ded. and text, 8 pp.

Complaints (title page "1611"). Ded. and text, 10 pp.

Teares of the Muses (title page "1611"). Ded. and text, 9 pp.

Virgil's Gnat. Ded. and text, 7 pp.

Ruins of Rome. Text, 6 pp.

Muiopotmos (title page "1611"). Ded. and text, 9 pp.

Visions of the World's Vanitie. 2½ pp.

Visions of Bellay. Parts of 3 pp.

Visions of Petrarch. 2 pp.

(Collation of F.I.C.'s copy. Copies vary.)

Cf. J. C. Smith's ed. of FQ, I, pp. xxi–ii; Grosart's ed. of Sp, I, 183–84.

Prosopopoia, or Mother Hubberd's Tale. By Edm. Sp. Lond. 1613.

Copy in Brit. Mus. with MS notes by Thos. Warton.

The Faerie Queen: The Shepheards Calendar: Together with the other Works of England's Arch-Poët, Edm. Spenser . . . . Mathew Lownes [Lond.] 1617.

> The second folio of the collected works.
> The edition of 1611 with new title-page.
> Copies in Harvard; etc. The Brit. Mus. copy has MS notes by Thos. Warton.

The View of Ireland. In Sir James Ware, ed., The Historie of Ireland, collected by Three Learned Authors. Dublin, 1633.

> The first edition. Copies in Newberry Lib.; Huntington; etc. Separate title-page for Spenser (occasionally found as a separate book):
> A View of the State of Ireland, Written dialogue-wise betweene Eudoxus and Irenaeus, By Edmund Spenser Esq. in the yeare 1596. . . . . Dublin, 1633. See Ware's Preface; also his Annotations. The text is followed by (8 pp., unpaged): "Certaine verses of Mr. Edm. Spenser's" (FQ, IV, xi, and verses "Out of the Seventh Book of the Faerie Queene, Cant. vi"); also certain of Sp's dedicatory sonnets, etc. The preface states that the View is printed from a MS copy from the Library of Abp. Ussher. Reprinted in the 1679 ed. of Sp and in numerous modern eds. of Sp.
> Mr. George Watson Cole, Librarian, informs me that the Huntington Library has the following:
> 1. Two Histories of Ireland, by Campion and Hanmer; View of the State of Ireland, by Spenser.
> 2. The Historie of Ireland: collected by Hanmer, Campion and Spenser (The View of Ireland being identical with the above).
> 3. Spencer's View of the State of Ireland, bound separately. All of 1633. The title-pages of 1 and 2 differ. Spenser's View of Ireland in 1 and 2 has a new series of signature-marks and has separate pagination and title-page, and "appears to have been so printed that it might be separately issued. . . . . There were certainly two issues of the whole work and there may have been two of Spenser's View of the State of Ireland." Cf. Sayle, 6047–50.

Calendarium Pastorale . . . . Latino carmine donatae a Theodoro Bathurst. Lond. 1653.

> With the English Text.

The Works of that Famous English Poet, Mr. Edmond Spenser. . . . . London, 1679. Folio.

> With a brief "Life," Brittain's Ida, the View of Ireland, "By Edmund Spenser, Esq.; in the year 1596," and Bathurst's Latin

version of the Sh Cal. Copies in Brit. Mus. (with MS notes by T. Tyrwhitt); Yale; etc.

Cf. DNB, XVIII, 805: that this edition "is believed to have been partly edited by Dryden."

Cf. G. C. Cuningham, under "Gen'l Criticism."

See below, under "Faerie Queene," for editions after 1700.

The Works, Ed. John Hughes. Lond. 1715. 5 Vols.

I, pp. i–xxii, Life; xxv–lvii, Essay on Allegorical Poetry, etc.; lviii–xcvi, Remarks on the Fairy Queen; xcvii–cxiii, Remarks on the Shepherds Calendar; etc.

II, 542–46: prints, for the first time, both endings of FQ, III.

VI, prints Britain's Ida, The View of Ireland, Bathurst's Latin version of the Sh Cal, and the Spenser-Harvey corrrespondence.

The text is modernized.

Cf. Disraeli, Amenities of Literature, II, "The Faery Queen"; on the merits of Hughes's criticism.

Works. Lond. 1750. 6 vols.

A reprint of Hughes's ed. of 1715, slightly revised. Copy in the British Mus. has MS notes by J. Mitford.

Poetical Works. In Bell's Poets of Great Britain. 1778. Vols. XV–XXII.

Based on Hughes and Upton.

*Poetical Works, from the Text of Upton. 8 vols. 1787.

Poetical Works. In Anderson's Poets of Great Britain. 1792–93. Vol. II.

Poetical Works . . . . with a Preface . . . . by J. Aikin. Lond. 1802. 6 vols. Aikin's ed. of Johnson's Poets.

Works, with the principal Illustrations [i.e. Annotations, etc.] of the various commentators, Ed. H. J. Todd. Lond. 1805. 8 vols.

Long the standard variorum edition. Still valuable and to be consulted.

Cf. Robt. Southey in The Annual Review, IV (1806), 544–55: a sympathetic review; some of the notes are of interest.

The Critical Review, Ser. III, Vol. VII (1806), 411–16.

The British Critic, XXVII (1806), 139–48. Favorable.

The Anti-Jacobin Review, XXV (1807), 1–12.

Edinb. Review, VII (1806), 203–17 (by Sir Walter Scott).

Collier's ed. of Sp, I, pp. ix ff.

*Poetical Works. Aikin's ed., with plates by Stothard. Lond. 1806. 8 vols.

Poetical Works. Lond. 1810. 6 vols.
With a preface, biographical and critical, by J. Aikin.
I, pp. i–xlviii, Life and Criticism. Unimportant.
V, 337–60, prints Britain's Ida.

Poems [with Life by Chalmers]. Lond. 1810.
In Chalmers' English Poets, III.

Poetical Works [with Aikin's Life, etc.]. Lond. 1819. 2 vols.

Poems. In British Poets, Chiswick, 1822. Vols. VI–XII.
I, pp. v–xxvi, Life by R. A. Davenport.

*Poetical Works. Lond. 1825 (Pickering). 5 vols.

Poetical Works [with Life by J. Mitford]. Lond. 1839. Aldine
ed. of the British Poets. Vols. XXXIX–XLIII.
I, pp. vii–viii: Four sonnets on Sp by J. M.; ix–lxxiv: Life. Of
slight interest; cf. xxxv–viii, on later lost books of the FQ.

Poetical Works, ed. G. S. Hillard, with introductory observations
on the Faerie Queene and notes by the editor. Bost. 1839.
5 vols.
First American edition. Essay on the Life and Writings by Philip
Masterman. Also 1848.

*Works, with observations on his life and writings [by J. C.].
Lond. 1840.

*Poetical Works. With introductory observations, and Aikin's
Life. Lond. 1842. 5 vols.

*Poetical Works, with Masterman's Life, etc. 1845. 5 vols.

*Works [with Todd's Life, etc.]. Lond. (Moxon), 1850.

Poetical Works . . . . with notes, original and selected, by F. J.
Child. Bost. 1855. 5 vols. Frequently reprinted.
Ed. of 1880: I, pp. vii–lxxiii, Life—in 1855 a freshly worked
study, carefully documented and reasoned. Still of value. Cf.
Westminster Review, N.S., XXXI (1867), 133–50; Collier's ed. of
Sp, I, pp. ix ff.

*Works [Todd's ed. in one vol.]. Lond. 1856. Also 1869, etc.

Poetical Works, with Memoir and Critical Dissertations, by the Rev. G. Gilfillan. Edinb. 1859. 5 vols. Also 1865, etc.

Text modernized.

I, pp. v–xviii, "Introduction to the Faerie Queene," its general scope, allusions, etc.

II, pp. v–xxii, Life. III, pp. v–xxii, The Genius and Poetry of Spenser; the dream-quality of his poetry; Sp and Bunyan; Sp and Shelley.

V, p. iii: omits the Ruins of Rome, etc., as proved by "external and internal evidence . . . . not to be the production of Spenser's pen." The evidence for this statement is not recited.

Works. Phila. (W. P. Hazard), 1857.

With Prefatory Observation by J. C. (In N.Y. Pub. Lib.)

Poetical Works. Phila. (J. B. Smith & Co.) 1860.

Reprint of Hillard's ed. (In N.Y. Pub. Lib.)

Poetical Works, ed. J. Payne Collier. Lond. 1862. 5 vols. and later reprints (abridged).

With Life, Notes (variorum and original), and Glossary. Reprints Britain's Ida, although rejecting Sp's authorship. To be consulted.

Cf. Westm. Review, N.S., XXXI (1867), 133–50; Athenaeum, XXXIX (1862), 73–76.

*Poetical Works [with Collier's Life]. Aldine British Poets, 1866.

Complete Works, ed. R. Morris and J. W. Hales. Lond. 1869.

Globe edition. Frequently reprinted. Revised 1897.

Memoir by J. W. Hales; Appendix of textual emendations; Glossary. A standard edition.

*Poetical Works [with Gilfillan's Memoir, etc.]. The text edited by C. C. Clarke. Lond. 1876–77. 5 vols. Cassell's Library ed. of the British Poets.

*Poetical Works. With Memoir, notes, etc. Lond. 1880. Chandos Classics.

Complete Works in Verse and Prose, with Life by A. B. Grosart, Essays, etc. Priv. print. 1882–84. 9 vols.

A valuable but disappointing limited edition. Never completed.

Complete Works, with an Introduction by W. P. Trent. N.Y. 1903.

Complete Poetical Works. Bost. 1908. "Cambridge Edition."
Ed. by R. E. N. Dodge. Preface, Introductions, Notes, Glossary,
Index to first lines. A standard one-volume edition.
Cf. Nation, N.Y., LXXXVI, 351; Jahrb. d. Shakespeare Gesellsch.
XLVI (1910), 336–38; Mod. Lang. Review, IV, 529.

Poetical Works. Ox. 1909–10.
Vols. I, II, The Faerie Queene, ed. J. C. Smith; Vol. III,
The Minor Poems, ed. E. de Sélincourt.
Little apparatus. Special attention to the text; that of the FQ
"founded upon a fresh collation of the Quartos of 1590 and 1596 and
the folio of 1609," but based on 1596.
I, pp. vii–ix: Sp's "mistakes" in the FQ; ix ff., on the date, order, and
method of composition (some statements too dogmatic, e.g., as to
the Epithalamion Thamesis); xv–xxii, basis of the text, variant read-
ings in various copies.
Indispensable for the textual study of Sp.
Cf. Athenaeum, 1911, p. 156; Mod. Lang. Review, V, 370–74; VII,
114; Engl. Studien, XLIV, 260; Anglia, Beiblatt, XXII (1911),
41–44; Mod. Lang. Notes, XXX, 123–25; The Nation, N.Y.,
LXXXIX (1909), 183; Literarisches Centralblatt, LXII (1911)
307; Deutsche Literaturzeitung, XXXI (1910), 356; Jahrb. d
Shakespeare Gesellsch., XLVI (1910), 336–38.

Poetical Works. Ed. J. C. Smith and E. de Sélincourt. Ox.
1912. Oxford Editions of Standard Authors.
The one-volume Oxford edition.
Life by Sélincourt.
Cf. Mod. Lang. Review, X, 111–12.

II. The Faerie Queene, Editions after 1700

See, above, I, "Complete Works," etc., for editions before 1700.

The Faerie Queene, with an exact Collation of the two original
Editions . . . . to which are now added a new Life of the
Author [by Dr. T. Birch] . . . . Lond. 1751. 3 vols.

The Faerie Queene. Ed. Ralph Church. Lond. 1758. 4 vols.
Attempts to rectify the text (see Preface). With annotations.
Cf. The Critical Review, VII (1759), 103–6: a favorable review—
with some bits of criticism (by O. Goldsmith); The Monthly Review,
XX (1759), 566–68.

The Faerie Queene. A New Edition with a Glossary, and Notes explanatory and critical by John Upton. Lond. 1758. 2 vols.

> I, pp. v–xlii, Preface; followed by Glossary; II, 329–666, Notes.
> The Brit. Mus. copy has further MS notes by Upton.
> Cf. The Critical Review, VIII (1759), 245–46; The Monthly Review, XX (1759), 566–68.

The Fairy Queen. With a Glossary. Lond. (Tonson) 1758. 2 vols. Illus.

> Based on Hughes's ed. With Life. Quotes his "Remarks," pp. xiii–xxxii. The rest is text and glossary.

The Faerie Queene. Lond. 1841. Also 1853.

The Faerie Queene, and Epithalamion. Lond. 1853. 1865, etc. With brief memoir by "T. A. B."

The Faerie Queene . . . . ed. T. J. Wise. Lond. 1895–97. 6 vols.

> With Preface by the Editor. Text based on ed. of 1590 for Books I–III, and on 1596 for IV–VI. Bibliographical account of these editions and of variant copies. Collations. I, pp. lxxxv ff., "Chronology."

The Faerie Queene, with an Introduction by John W. Hales. Lond. (Dent & Co.), 1897. 3 vols.

The Faerie Queene, ed. Kate M. Warren. Lond. 1897–1900 6 vols.

> Edited from the editions of 1590 and 1596. With Introd., Notes, and Glossary.
> Cf. Anglia, Beiblatt, XI, 294; Englische Studien, XXX, 296–98.

The Faerie Queene, ed. Geo. Newnes. Lond. [1905]. 2 vols. (Thin Paper Classics).

> The text merely—with two portraits. Cf. Athenaeum, 1909, II, 90.

The Faerie Queene, ed. J. C. Smith. Ox. 1909. 2 vols.

> See above, "Collected Editions."

III. FAERIE QUEENE, EDITIONS OF SEPARATE BOOKS, AND SELECTIONS

Faery Queene. Book I, ed. G. W. Kitchin. Ox. 1867 (Clarendon Press).

> Frequently reprinted. Revised, 1897.
> Introduction, Notes, and Glossary.

Book II, 1887.
>   With similar apparatus. Later reprints. Both useful.

The Canterbury Tales and the Faerie Queene. Edinb. 1870,
1872, etc. Ed. D. L. Purves.
>   Selections, with a brief Life.

*The First Six Cantos of the First Book of Spenser's Faery
Queene. With explanatory, illustrative, and grammatical
notes. . . . . By J. Hunter. Lond. 1870.

*Faerie Queene. Book I. With Life, and Notes [by J. S. Keltie].
Lond. 1871. (Chamber's English Classics.)

Faerie Queene. Book I. Ed. H. M. Percival. Lond. 1893.
>   Good introd. and full apparatus of notes.
>   Cf. Saturday Review, LXXV (1893), 492: A piquant and jocular
>   notice.

Faerie Queene, Britomart; Selections from Spenser's Faery
Queene, Books III, IV, and V. Ed. Mary E. Litchfield.
Boston (Athenaeum Press), 1896.
>   With Introd. and footnotes.

The Faerie Queene. Book I. Ed. with [Introd.], Notes and
Glossary, by W. H. Hill. Lond. 1897. (Univ. Tutorial
Series.)

Faery Queene. Book I. Ed. W. H. Hudson. Lond. n.d.
(19—). (Temple Series.)
>   With Introd., Notes, and Glossary. Cf. Athenaeum, No. 3983,
>   p. 267.

*Faerie Queene. Book I. Ed. W. Keith Leask. Lond.
(Blackie), 1902.

Selections from the Faerie Queene, ed. with Notes and Introduction by John Erskine. N.Y. (Longmans), 1905.

The Faerie Queene, Book I, ed. with introduction, notes, and
suggestions for study, by Martha Hale Shackford. Bost.
[1905]. Cf. Anglia, Beiblatt, XXI, 335.

*The Faerie Queene, Book I, ed. G. A. Wauchope. N.Y. 1907.
>   With introd. and notes

The Faerie Queene, Book V. Ed. with introduction and notes
by S. E. Winbolt. Lond. 1914.
>   A school edition.

The Faerie Queene.   Book II.   Ed. Lilian Winstanley.   Cambr.
1914.

> The Introd. (pp. xviii–li) has an elaborate study of the sources of
> this book, mediaeval, classical, and Italian; and (pp. li–lxxii), an essay
> on "Spenser and Aristotle" (Sp's ethical scheme=based on Aristotle).

Book I.   Cambr. 1915.

> The Introd. (pp. viii–xliii) is a thorough study of the "Historical
> Allegory of Book I"; the "Notes" are supplementary. Pp. xliii–lxxx,
> "Sources of Book I."
> Both frequently reprinted.   Important studies.
> Cf. Mod. Lang. Notes, XXXI (1916), 189–91.

The Faerie Queene, Book V . . . . ed. with Introduction and
Notes by A. B. Gough.   Ox. 1918.

> The notes are full.   See pp. l–li (Table of "Historical Events alluded
> to in Book V").
> Cf. Studies in Philology, XVII, 254.

*The Faerie Queene, Book I, ed. C. L. Thomson.   Lond. 19—?
(H. Marshall).

IV. Faerie Queene, Paraphrases

See also "Pseudo-Spenser;" "Faerie Queene, General Criticism," below.

See DNB, XVIII, 805, for a list of paraphrases.

Spencer Redivivus, containing the First Book of the Fairy Queen,
his essential Design preserv'd, but his obsolete Language and
manner of Verse totally laid aside.   Deliver'd in Heroick
Numbers.   Lond. 1687.

> The Preface is of interest: that Sp's language was unintelligible in
> 1687; against the stanza; Sp's powers of invention praised.
> The opening lines:

>> "A worthy knight was riding on the plain,
>>   In armour clad, which richly did contain
>>   The gallant marks of many battels fought,
>>   Tho' he before no martial habit sought."

> Cf. Lounsbury's Chaucer, III, 155; Sp ed. Todd, I, p. clxxix.

*Spenser's Fairy Queen attempted in Blank Verse.   Lond. 1774.

> Cf. The Monthly Review, LII (1775), 111–13.

Prince Arthur, An Allegorical Romance. The Story from
   Spenser. Lond. 1779. 2 vols.
   A prose paraphrase. Cf. The Monthly Review, LX (1779), 324.

The Tatler, No. 194 (July 6, 1710).
   "Transproses" FQ, IV, x.

PEABODY, Mrs. Holiness or the Legend of St. George. Bost.
   1836.
   A prose paraphrase of FQ, I, with a short appendix of interpretative
   notes.

TOWRY, M. H. Spenser for Children. Lond. 1885.

The Legend of the Knight of the Red Cross or of Holinesse.
   Lond. 1871.

Y (R.A.), The Story of the Red Cross Knight from Spenser's
   Fairy Queen. Lond. 1887.

RABBETH, J. E. The Story of Spenser's Faerie Queene. Lond.
   1887.
   Prose paraphrase.

MACLEHOSE, SOPHIA H. Tales from Spenser chosen from the
   Faerie Queene. N.Y. 1890.

EDWARDSON, E. The Courteous Knight and other Tales.
   Borrowed from Spenser and Malory. Edinb. 1899. Illus.

ROYDE-SMITH, N. G. Una and the Red Cross Knight and other
   Tales from Spenser's Faery Queene. Lond. 1905.

MACLEOD, MARY. Stories from the Faerie Queene . . . .
   with Introduction by John W. Hales. N.Y. 1905.

*WILSON, C. D. The Faery Queene, Book I. Rewritten in
   simple language. Chicago, 1906.

BROOKS, EDW., ed. The Story of the Faerie Queene. Phila.
   1908. Illus.
   A prose paraphrase of episodes in the FQ, with Introduction.

CHURCH, A. J. The Faery Queen and her Knights: Stories
   retold from Edmund Spenser. N.Y. 1909.

GRACE, R. W. Tales from Spenser. Lond. 1909.
   Prose paraphrase. The Epilogue discusses the FQ.

*DAWSON, LAWRENCE H. Stories from the Faerie Queene, retold from Spenser. Lond. 1910.

V. MINOR POEMS, ETC.

See also below, "Selections, Miscellaneous." See above, "Collections," for editions of the Minor Poems before 1700.
Professor J. S. Bolton, University of Syracuse, N.Y., has in preparation an edition of The Complaints.

Dispersed Poems . . . . now first collected. Lond. 1792.

Complaints. N.Y. 1888 (Cassell's Nat'l Lib.)

Daphnaida and other Poems. Lond. 1889 (Cassell's Nat'l. Lib.)

Amoretti. N.Y. (Laurel Press), 1901.
No apparatus (copy in N.Y. Pub. Lib.).

Prothalamion and Epithalamion. Bost. 1902.

Epithalamion and Amoretti. Lond. (Bumpus), 1903.

Amoretti and Epithalamion. In Elizabethan Sonnets . . . . with Introd. by Sidney Lee. Lond. 1904. 2 v.
II, 213–60, The Text; I, pp. xcii–ix: Lee on the Sonnets and their sources.

*Sonnets and Poems. Selected. With biographical introduction by H. Bennet. Lond. 1906. (Carlton Classics.)

Minor Poems, ed. by Ernest de Sélincourt. Ox. 1910.
A text based on the editions in Sp's lifetime, collated with the Folio of 1611. The Introd. discusses the value of these editions in the case of each poem. Also discusses the dates of the poems in certain doubtful cases. Sound and judicious. Appendix II characterizes the chief editions of Sp from 1617 to 1884, from the point of view of the text. Valuable.
Cf. G. C. Macaulay in Mod. Lang. Review, VII, 114–17; P. W. Long in Engl. Studien, XLIV, 260–66; The Spectator, CVI (1911), 186; Jahrbuch der Shakespeare-Gesellsch., XLVII (1911), 367–68; Deutsche Literaturzeitung, XXXII (1911), 2594; Lit. Centralblatt, LXII (1911), 204–5.

Amoretti: Spenser's Amoretti set to music by Dr. Greene. Lond. for Jno. Walsh [174–].

Astrophel. Reprinted from the ed. of 1595. In Arber's English Garner. Lond. 1877, I, 249–96.

Epithalamion. With illustrations by G. W. Edwards. N.Y. 1895.

Epithalamion. Essex House Press, 1901.

Epithalamion and Amoretti. Lond. (Bumpus), 1903.

The Fowre Hymnes. Ed. by Lilian Winstanley. Cambr. 1907.
> With Introd. and Notes: Sp's Platonism, with reference to Plato's Symposium and Phaedrus, Ficino's Commentarium in Convivium, and Bruno's Gli Heroici Furori.
> Cf. Athenaeum, Apr. 4, 1908, 413; The Nation, N.Y., LXXXVIII, 90.

Letters: The Spenser-Harvey Letters. In G. G. Smith, Elizabethan Critical Essays. Ox. 1904, I, 87–126.
> Cf. the Notes, pp. 372–80. Also in Haslewood's Ancient Critical Essays, Lond. 1815, II; in Grosart's ed. of the Works of Gabriel Harvey, I, 1–108; and in various editions of Sp.

*Mother Hubberd's Tale of the Fox and Ape. Selected from the Works of Edmund Spenser. Lond. 1784 (Brit. Mus. Cat.)
> Cf. Monthly Review, LXXI (1785), 228.

The Shepherds' Calendar.
> The Brit. Mus. Catalogue enters an edition, with Bathurst's Latin version, "London, 1633." This is a misprint for 1653 (verified by H. R. Plomer).

Calendarium Pastorale . . . . Latino carmine donata a Theo. Bathurst. Lond. n.d. (1732).
> Original ed. 1653.
> English and Latin texts. Also in Hughes's ed. of Sp, 1715, Vol. VI (the Latin text); and in other eds. of Sp. For the significance of the seventeenth century Latin versions of English poems, such as this, see Mackail, Springs of Helicon, 143: "The testing of these English poems by a certain classical standard."
> Cf. Censura Literaria, III (1815), 179–93.

The Shepheardes Calendar. Edition of 1579 in facsimile. Ed. with Introd. by H. O. Sommer. Lond. 1890.
> The Introd. lists the various early editions; discusses "E.K."

The Shepherd's Calendar. N.Y. n.d. (Cassell's Nat'l. Lib.)

The Shepherd's Calendar. Song from the January Eclogue, Set to Music by Helen A. Clarke. Bost. 1892.

The Shepheards Calender.   Ed. C. H. Herford.   Lond. 1895.

>   The best edition.   With its apparatus (now needing some revision),
> supplemented by Higginson's work on the Sh Cal (used with caution)
> the student is well equipped.   Cf. Academy, XLVIII, 315.

The Shepheardes Calender.   Ed. F. S. Ellis.   Kelmscott Press,
1896.

The Sheperdes Calender.   Illus. by Walter Crane.   N.Y. 1897.

The View of Ireland.

>   First ed. Dublin, 1633; was reprinted at Dublin 1763, etc. Also
> in A Collection of Tracts . . . . illustrative . . . . of Ireland, Dublin,
> 1860, I; in Ancient Irish Histories, Dublin, 1809, I; in H. Morley, Ire-
> land under Elizabeth and James I, Lond. 1890.   (See the Introd., esp.
> pp. 13–14, 19–26); etc.
>
> For MSS of the View see above, "Life, General References" (various
> "Catalogues"), and below, references on the "View of Ireland."

VI. SELECTIONS, ETC.

See above, preceding section; also "Faerie Queene, Paraphrases,"
"Faerie Queene, Selections."

Poems [Selected].   Ed. with an Essay, by R. Noel.   Lond. 1887
(Canterbury Poets.)

Love-Verse from the Minor Poems.   Ed. A. B. Grosart.   Chicago, n.d. [189–].   (The Elizabethan Lib.)

The Spenser Anthology, 1548–91.   Ed. E. Arber.   Lond. 1899.
Pp. 1–47, Selections from Sp.

Lyric Poems.   Ed. E. Rhys.   Lond. n.d.   (Lyric Poets Series.)

Poems, selected and with an Introduction by W. B. Yeats.
Lond. 1906.   (The Golden Poets.)

>   Cf. J. Bailey's Poets and Poetry, Ox. 1911, 45–54; The Spectator,
> XCVII (1906), 627.

VII. TRANSLATIONS

Cf. Encycl. Brit., 1911, XXV, 642a: "There is no complete translation of
it [the FQ] in any of the continental languages."

Sonnets, transl. by Joseph von Hammer [Eng. and German].
Vienna, 1814.

Il Cavaliero della Croce Rossa, o la Leggenda della Santita; poema in dodici canti; dall' inglese di Edmundo Spenser recato in verso italiano, detto ottava rima, da Tomaso Jacopo Mathias. Napoli, 1827.
>   Copy in Yale, and in N.Y. Pub. Lib., dated 1826 (with introd.)

La Mutabilità. Poema in due canti dell' Inglese recato in verso Italiano, detto ottava rima, da T. J. Mathias. Napoli, 1827.
>   With Introd. (in Italian), pp. i–x. Copies in Yale, and N.Y. Pub. Lib.

Fünf Gesänge der Feenkönigin. In freier metrischer Uebertragung, von C. G. Schwetschke. Halle, 1854. Also 1866 in Schwetschke's Ausgewählte Schriften.
>   Copy in Yale.

Amoretti d'Edmund Spenser. Traduit . . . . par F. Henry. Paris, 1913.
>   With Introd., dealing with Sp's relations to Desportes, etc.

Calendarium Pastorale. See above.

L' "Epithalame" d'Edmund Spenser traduit en verse français. In Revue de Littérature Comparée, I (1921), 398–415.

*MARTELLI, G. B. La vergine Una: canti dodici di Edmondo Spenser, poeta inglese del sec. decimosesto. Milan, 1831.
>   "Tr. FQ, I, in ottava rima" (J. B. Fletcher).

VIII. PSEUDO-SPENSER

A selection of those purporting to be by Sp, excluding the obvious imitations. See also below, "Works, Apocrypha." For later imitations claiming (by a transparent literary device) to be *by* Sp see section "Criticism, etc." Cf. Todd's ed. of Sp, I, pp. clxxix ff., "Alterations of Spenser."

[*JEGON, ROBERT?]. A Supplement of the Faery Queene, in three Bookes. MS (c. 1635) in Univ. of Cambridge Lib.

The Faerie Leveller: or King Charles his Leveller descried, and deciphered in Queene Elizabeth's Dayes. By her Poet Laureat, Edmond Spenser, in his unparaleled Poeme, entituled, The Faerie Qveene, A lively representation of our times. Lond. 1648.

CROXALL, S. An Original Canto of Spencer . . . . now made public by Nestor Ironside, Esq. 1713. Repr. in facsimile, N.Y. (A. H. Nason), 1912.

Another Original Canto of Spencer . . . . 1714.

[WEST, GILBERT?]. A Canto of the Fairy Queen written by Spenser. Never before published. Lond. 1739.

[UPTON, JOHN?]. Spenser's Fairy Queen, A New Canto. Lond. 1747.

THE WORKS: GENERAL REFERENCES

See also "Minor Poems."

ARBER, E. Transcript of the Registers of the Company of Stationers of London, 1554–1640. Birmingham, 1875–94.
> I, 183 b, July 1569–July 1570. The Theatre of Worldlings.
> II, 164 b, 5 Dec., 1579. The Sh Cal.
>> 170, 30 June, 1580. The Three Letters.
>> For other literature concerning the earthquake of 1580 see 167 b ff.
>> 173 b, 29 Oct., 1580. The Sh Cal.
>> 251 b, 1 Dec., 1589. The Faerie Queene.
>> 268 b, 29 Dec., 1590. The Complaintes.
>> 271 b, 7 Mar., 1591. The Sh Cal.
>> 280 b, 12 Oct., 1591. The Sh Cal.
>> 287 b, 1 May, 1592. Axiochus.
>> 315, 19 Nov., 1594. Amoretti and Epithalamion, "written not longe since by Edmund Spencer."
> III, 7, 20, Jan., 1596. The FQ; books IV–VI.
>> 34 a, Apr. 14, 1598. The View of Ireland.
>> 113, 3 Sept., 1604: transfer of the FQ; similarly 115 b.
> I have not examined the Transcripts after June, 1605 (III, 125 b).

DIBDIN, T. F. The Library Companion. Lond. 1824. II, 693–94:
> The order of appearance of Sp's works (pp. 701–2 of ed. of 1825).

Harvard Library Bulletin, No. 12, June 1, 1879. 323–24:
> List of early eds. of Sp in Harvard Library, Boston Pub. Lib. and Mass. Hist. Soc.

LONG, P. W. In Mod. Lang. Review, XII (1917), 87:
> On the order of arrangement of the Works.

Nichol's Literary Anecdotes. Lond. 1812.
> I, 653: An edition of "Spenser's Works, by subscription," 1747, by Dr. Thos. Morell. Apparently never published.

OSGOOD, C. G. A Concordance to the Poems of Edmund Spenser. Washington (Carnegie Institution), 1915.
> Of first-rate importance. Indispensable for the thorough study of Sp.
>
> Preface: p. xii: on the chronology of the works; p. xiii: list of the works in suggested chronological order.
>
> Cf. Dodge's ed. of Sp, whose order Osgood, on final consideration, would prefer.

[RITSON, JOS.]. Bibliographia Poetica. Lond. 1802. 343-49:
> Mainly a brief list of early editions of Sp.

LOST WORKS

Referred to in (1) Printer's Preface to the Complaints, 1591; (2) Sh Cal Oct., Argument, cf. ll. 122-24, and Gloss.; June, Gloss.; Nov., Gloss.; (3) Sp's Letter to Harvey, 5 Oct. 1579; (4) Sp to Harvey, "Quarto nonas Aprilis, 1580"; (5) Harvey to Sp, "nono Calendas Maias," 1580; (6) Amoretti, Sonnet 80, on later books of FQ. Possibly also in Hymn of Heavenly Love, ll. 11-14.

    I. Ecclesiastes, mentioned in 1
    II. Canticum Canticorum, translated, mentioned in 1
    III. A Senights Slumber, mentioned in 1 and 3
    IV. The Hell of Lovers, mentioned in 1
    V. His Purgatorie, mentioned in 1
    VI. The Dying Pellican, mentioned in 1, 4, and 5
    VII. The Hours of the Lord, mentioned in 1
    VIII. The Sacrifice of a Sinner, mentioned in 1
    IX. The Seven Psalmes, mentioned in 1
    X. His Dreams, mentioned in 2, 4, and 5
    XI. His Legends, mentioned in 2
    XII. His Court of Cupid (cf. FQ, VI, vii, 32 ff.), mentioned in 2
    XIII. Moschus his Idyllion of Wandering Love (see the Letters), mentioned in 2 (March)
    XIV. The English Poet, mentioned in 2 (Oct.)
    XV. Slumber (perhaps No. III), mentioned in 3
    XVI. Epithalamion Thamesis, mentioned in 4, and 5
    XVII. Nine Comedies, "whereunto . . . . you give the names of the Nine Muses," mentioned in 5
XVIII. "Sonnets," mentioned in 2

XIX. Pageants, mentioned in 2
XX. Stemmata Dudleiana, mentioned in 3, and 4
XXI. Later books of the FQ (see Ware, below), mentioned in 6
XXII. On the Antiquities of Ireland. A treatise promised in the last line of the V of I, but probably never written (cf. Ware).

REFERENCES ON THE LOST WORKS

The British Critic, XXVII (1806), 139–48:
> A review of Todd's ed. Accepts the testimony of Ware and Stradling that later books of the FQ were written (now lost).

BIRCH, THOS. In his ed. of Sp 1751, I, pp. xxiii–v:
> Accepts and defends Ware's story of the loss of Bks. VII–XII of the FQ.

BRUCE, J. D. In Mod. Lang. Notes, XXVII (1912), 183–85.

BUCK, PHILO M., JR. Add. MS 34064 and Spenser's *Ruins of Time* and *Mother Hubberd's Tale*. In Mod. Lang. Notes, XXII (1907), 41–46:
> The MS (of c. 1596) described; a short poem ascribed to Sp therein (spurious), printed; other selections from Sp, with variant readings. The MS probably derives, not from the 1591 printed text, but from an anterior MS version. Conjectures that two "sonnets," therefrom reproduced, may be part of Sp's Dying Pellican. (Very doubtful; they have nothing of the accent of Sp in his known works.)

BUCK, P. M., JR. Spenser's Lost Poems. In Pub. Mod. Lang. Asso., XXIII (1908), 80–99:
> Lists twenty-one "lost" works, from the sources listed above, and also those ascribed to Sp "by tradition" (i.e. Books VII–XIII of the FQ, and the translation of the Greek dialogue "by Axiochus"); discusses the question of the reappearance of most of these works in altered form or under other titles; political reasons for their suppression and subsequent reappearance.
> Cf. Shakespeare-Jahrbuch, XLVI (1910), 203–4. See H. E. Sandison, below.

CHILD, F. J. In his ed. of Sp, I, pp. xvi–xx.

COLLIER, J. P. In his ed. of Sp, I, pp. xlii ff., lxxv ff., cxxxii, cxxxviii, cxxxix ff., cxlviii.

COOPER, C. H. and T. Athenae Cantab. Cambr. 1858–1913. II, 259, 264.

CRAIK, G. L. Spenser and his Poetry, I, 21–31.

Dict. Natl. Biog., XVIII, 795.

DRAPER, J. W. In The Colonnade. N.Y. 1922. 43.

FLETCHER, J. B. In Journal of Germ. Philology, II, 429 ff.
Esp. on the English Poet.

GROSART'S ed. of Sp, I, 94–99.

HARTLIB, S. Letter of Jan. 1, 1660. In John Worthington's
Diary. Chetham Soc. 1847.
I, 259: "I shall long to have your promises about the renowned Spenser,
and shall very willingly make search after any pieces of his, as well
in Ireland as in England." Cf. pp. 271, 279.

HUNTER, Chorus Vatum, IV, 466–67.

JUSSERAND, J. J. Hist. litt. du peuple Anglais. II, 387.

MAYER, C. La Reine des Fées. Paris, 1860. 22 ff.

OSGOOD, C. G. Spenser's English Rivers. Yale Univ. Press, 1920.
105–8: On the Epithalamion Thamesis; represented in FQ, IV, xi, only
in the part dealing with English rivers, and that imperfectly.
Also in Trans. Conn. Acad. of Arts and Sciences, XXIII (1920), 65–108.

SANDISON, HELEN E. Spenser's "Lost" Works. In Pub. of
Mod. Lang. Asso., XXV (1910), 134–51:
In answer to Buck's theory.

SCHELLING, F. E. Spenser's Lost Work "The English Poete."
In Mod. Lang. Notes, V (1890), 273–76.

SÉLINCOURT, E. DE. Introd. to his one-volume Oxford ed. of
Sp. Pp. xx–xxi.

STRADLING, JOHN. Epigrammatum Libri quatuor. Lond. 1607.
Quoted in Brydges Restituta, IV (1816), 146 f.
Several references to Sp, including the following:
"Ad Edm. Spencer eximium poëtam, de exemplaribus suis quibusdam
manuscriptis, ab Hibernicis exlegibus igne crematis, in Hibernica
defectione.

> Ingenii tantum noram tibi flumen, ut ipsum
>   Absumi flammis non potuisse putem.
> Flumen at ingenii partim tibi sorbuit ignis:
>   Qualis, qui flumen devoret, ignis erat ?
> Sylvestris populus sylvestres injicit ignes:
>   Talibus obsistunt flumina nulla pyris."

Translation by Professor Paul Shorey:

To Edm. Spencer, distinguished poet, concerning some manuscript copies of his, burned by the Irish outlaws in the Irish rebellion.

"I knew that you had such a river of genius, that I could not deem it possible that it could be consumed by the flames. But the fire did destroy the river of your genius in part. What manner of fire was it that destroys a river? A rude sylvan people hurls upon you sylvan brands. No rivers can resist such a pyre."

Allusion doubtless to the supposedly lost later books of the FQ. Does Stradling's allusion antedate Camden's? Cf. Todd's ed. of Sp, 1805, I, p. cxx.

TODD's ed. of Sp, 1805, I, pp. vii ff.; lxx ff. (and notes); cxv-cxxi (on lost books of FQ—cf. clxxi); clviii *n* (Sp the author of Puttenham's Art of Eng. Poetry?).

TOWRY, M. H. A Note on Spenser's Twenty Lost Works. In The Bibliographer, Lond., I (1882), 129–30:

A list, with rehearsal of what is known and what is conjectured. That perhaps the sonnets in the Th. of W. are the lost Dreams; of which there may have been an edition of 1580 with E K's notes. But these sonnets hardly meet Harvey's characterization of the Dreams ("above the reach and compass of a common scholar's capacity").

VALLANS, W. Tale of Two Swannes, 1590. Repr. in Leland's Itinerary, ed. Hearne. Ox. 1769.

V, pp. viii–xiv: Gives the text of Vallans' Poem. Vallans' preface urges "those worthie Poets, who have written 'Epithalamion Thamesis' to publish the same. I have seen it in Latin verse, in my judgment well done, but the author, I know not for what reason, doth suppresse it. That which is written in English, though long since it was promised, yet it is not perfourmed. So as it seemeth, some unhappy Star envieth the sight of so good a work" . . . . etc. Cf. Brydges Restituta, IV, 446.

WARE, SIR JAS. Historie of Ireland. Dublin, 1633.

Preface: "There [at Kilcolman, or Cork] hee finished the later part of that excellent poém of his *Faery Queene*, which was soone after unfortunately lost by the disorder and abuse of his servant, whom he had sent before him into England."

(Ware was in a position to know the facts.) Cf. Amoretti, sonnet 80, l. 7.

WEBBE, WM.   A Discourse of English Poetrie, 1586.   Repr. ed.
Arber.   Lond. 1870.
> 23, 36: Important early mention of some of the Lost Works, "in ye
> close custodie of certaine his freends" (The English Poet, Dreames,
> Legends, Court of Cupid, "with other").

WORTHINGTON, JOHN.   The Diary and Correspondence, ed.
Jas. Crossley.   Chetham Soc. 1847–86.
> I, 261–63: A list of Sp's Lost Works.   See 259, 271, 279, on the efforts
> of Worthington and Hartlib to recover these works.   Cf. II, 76, 86,
> 345.

APOCRYPHA

See also "Pseudo-Spenser," above.
> In the case of Shakespeare almost every work of his time signed "W.S."
> has been ascribed to him, whether confidently or doubtfully.   Some-
> thing of the same sort is now happening in the case of Spenser.
>   Note, however, that the recorded list of names in "E.S." of the
> last half of the sixteenth century is comparatively limited.   See
> Dict. Natl. Biog. and Cat. of Brit. Mus.   The following are note-
> worthy: Sir Edwin Sandys, Edward Sharpham, Sir Edward Stafford,
> Sir Edward Stradling.   Less probable are: Sir Edward Sackville,
> Edwin Sandys, senior, Sir Edward Saunders, Edmund Scambler,
> Edward Seymour, Sir Edmund Sheffield, Edward Simpson, Edmund
> Snape, Edward Squire, Sir Edward Stanhope, Edward Stanley, Esmé
> Stuart.   See also "S(E)," The Discoverie of the Knights of the
> Post, 1597.
> By a few the verses in the Theatre of Worldlings would be classed among
> the Apocrypha.   I accept them as Spenser's.

COOPER, C. H. and T.   Athenae Cantab.   Cambr. 1858–1913.
> II, 259, 264: Lists forty works by Sp, incl. the lost works, the transla-
> tion of Axiochus, and Britain's Ida.

Dispersed Poems . . . . now first collected.   In Waldron's
Literary Museum, 1792.
>   Includes Sp's verses in the Spenser-Harvey Letters, in Nennio's
> Treatise of Nobility, in the Historie of George Castriot, in Lewkenor's
> Venice, a couplet inscribed in a book belonging to the Earl of Cork,
> attributed to Sp, verses "by Spencer" in the Chorus Poetarum, 1674,
> and a sonnet signed "E. S.," prefixed to Peacham's Minerva Britanna,
> 1612.   See below.

MANNINGHAM, JOHN.   Diary.   Camden Soc. 1868.   43:
> The doggerel verses about his pension, ascribed to Sp.

[NEVE, PHILIP.]   Cursory Remarks on some of the Ancient English Poets.   Lond. 1789.
> 22-25: On various Sp Apocrypha, e.g. Britain's Ida, and "An Iambicke Elegie, called 'Love's Embassy' in Davison's Poetical Rhapsody, 1602" [=from the Harvey-Spenser Letters].

I. BRITAIN'S IDA

First appeared as "Brittain's Ida, written by that Renowned Poet Edmund Spencer," Lond. 1628.
> The publisher, Thomas Walkley, in the Epistle tells us: "I am certainly assured, by the ablest and most knowing men, that it must be a worke of *Spencer's*."
> Cf. Cambr. Hist. Eng. Lit., IV, 165.

GROSART, A. B.   In his ed. of Phineas Fletcher's Poems, 1869, I, 4-48:
> "Who wrote Brittain's Ida?"   (Also separately, 1869).   A summary of critical opinion on the authorship.   Concludes for Fletcher.

CORY, H. E.   Spenser, The School of the Fletchers, and Milton. Univ. of Cal., 1912.   330-31.

II. THE AXIOCHUS

The Axiochus (pseudo-Platonic dialogue), "translated by Spenser."
> No mention of this occurs in Hughes's ed. of Sp in 1715, or in earlier eds. of Sp.   In Upton's ed. of Sp, 1758, however, it is ascribed to Sp.

Cambr. Hist. Eng. Lit., IV, 439:
> Entry of "Axiochus on the Shortness and Uncertainty of Life."
> "Attributed to Plato, translated by Edm. Spencer."

P. DE MORNAY.   Six Excellent Treatises, 1607.
> Contains a translation of the Axiochus, probably the one in question.   Copy in the Newberry Library.   I plan to reprint this text.

ARBER'S Transcript, II, 287 b.
> "Cutberd Burbee.   Entred for his Copie vnder the hande of master *Watkins Axiochus of Plato* . . . . vjd."   1 May, 1592.

III. The Doleful Lay of Clorinda

LONG, P. W. Spenseriana, The Lay of Clorinda. In Mod.
Lang. Notes, XXXI (1916), 79–82:
Confirming Sélincourt's theory that Sp wrote the Lay in the name of
the Countess of Pembroke.

HARMAN'S Edmund Spenser, 351 ff.:
Written for the Countess of Pembroke by Sp.

OSGOOD, C. G. The Doleful Lay of Clorinda. In Mod. Lang.
Notes, XXXV (1920), 90–96:
Agrees with Sélincourt and Long that this poem is by Sp; parallel-
isms with his works cited.

SÉLINCOURT. Introd. to his one-volume Oxford ed. of Sp,
P. xxxv *n*.

IV. Discourse of Civill Life

Sir A. W. Ward in the Cambr. Hist. Engl. Lit., VII, 211 *n* tries to
add to Sp's Apocrypha by attributing to Sp The Discourse of Civill
Life, by Bryskett (pub. 1606, but probably written before 1593). See
ref. to Bryskett under "Life, General References," above. The
concluding words of the book, there quoted, may have suggested the
idea.

V. The Mourning Muse of Thestylis

ARBER'S Transcript, II, 220 b, 22 Aug. 1587.
"John Woulfe Receaved of him for pryntinge *the mourninge muses of
Lod.[ovick] Bryskett vpon the Deathe of the moste noble Sir* PHILLIP
SYDNEY *knight* &c. allowed vnder bothe the wardens handes. . . . .
vj*d*."

COLLIER, J. P. Poetical Decameron. Edinb. 1820. I, 97 ff.

MUSTARD, W. P. Lodowick Bryskett and Bernardo Tasso.
In Amer. Journal of Philology, XXXV (1914), 192–99:
That the Mourning Muse of Thestylis is a paraphrase of Tasso's
Selva nella Morte del Signor Aluigi da Gonzaga, with some help from
Virgil. Similarly of A Pastorall Aeglogue upon the Death of Sir
Phillip Sidney,—from Tasso's Alcippo. Cf. also XXIX (1908), 4–5.

VI. Edward II

Edward II, A MS Poem on.
Conjecturally assigned to Sp in the Catalogue of the Harleian MSS.
Lond. 1808, II, 682.

VII. S., E. DE REBUS GESTIS BRITANNIAE

S., E. De rebus gestis Britanniae commentarioli tres. Ad
. . . . Henricum Broncarem. Londini. . . . . Henrici Bin-
neman. n.d. (c. 1570, acc. to B. M. Cat.; probably c. 1582).

Attributed to Sp in C. E. Sayle's Cat. of Early Engl. Printed Books
in the Univ. Library, Cambridge.

Mr. F. H. Jenkinson, Librarian of the Univ. Library, Cambridge,
writes: "The attribution of this little book to Edmund Spenser rests
on the evidence of the book itself, which seems to me almost conclusive."
Copies are in the University Library, Cambridge, the British Museum,
and the Newberry Library, Chicago.

There are four editions in the B. M.

1. London [1570?]
2. Hamburgi, apud Theodosium Wolderum, 1598.
3. Ambergae, Typis Johannis Schonfield, 1603.
4. Oxoniae. Excudebat Leonard Lichfield Impensis Matthiae Hunt, 1640.

The book is both history and description. It sketches British history,
Books I and II to the conquest, Book III since the Conquest, under
the titles of the successive monarchs, to Elizabeth. There are two
pages on the reign of Elizabeth, mentioning the plague ("usque eo,
vt Londini, 8. minus mensium spatio, 23660. homines consumpti
perierint"). On the concluding page there is a reference to the
History of Polydore Vergil, suggesting that the book may be partly
based upon that source. The first two books include some of the
material introduced into FQ, II, x, but there are significant omissions
and differences.

Cf. Calendar of State Papers, Ireland, 1598–99. 467: Sir Henry
Brouncker in Ireland.

Liber Munerum, Pt. II, 184: Brouncker President of the Council of
Munster, 1603.

F. I. Carpenter, in The Manly Anniversary Volume (forthcoming,
1923).

VIII. A DIALOGUE ON IRELAND

A MS among the Irish State Papers of 1598, in the Public Record
Office, London. Photostat copy in the Newberry Library, Chicago.

The interlocutors are Peregyn and Silvyn (Peregrine and Sylvanus, the
names of Spenser's sons). On the MS is written "by Thos. Wilson,"
whom Bagwell guesses to be "a stalking horse" for Edmund Spenser.

BAGWELL. Ireland under the Tudors, III, 302 *n*.

HARMAN. Edmund Spenser, 566–68.

Calendar of State Papers, Ireland, 1598–99.   505–7:
> Description and synopsis of the above ("State Papers. Ireland.
> Elizabeth, Vol. 203, No. 119").

IX. COMMENDATORY VERSES

Commendatory Verses, prefixed to Henry Peacham's Minerva
Britanna, Lond. 1612, at B₄, signed, "E. S.," and headed
"To Master Henry Peacham, A Vision upon this his
Minerva":

> "Methought I saw in dead of silent night
> A goodly Citie all to cinders turned,
> Upon whose ruines sate a Nymphe in white,
> Rending her haire of wiry gold, who mourned
> Or for the fall of that faire Citie burned,
> Or some deare Love, whose death so made her sad,
> That since no ioye in worldly thing she had.
> This was that Genius of that auntient Troy,
> In her owne ashes buried long agoe;
> So grieu'd to see that Britaine should enioy
> Her Pallas, whom she held and honour'd so:
> And now no little memorie could show
> To eternize her, since she did infuse
> Her Enthean soule, into this English Muse."

If this be not by Spenser, it is a most astonishingly versisimilar imitation of him.

X. VERSES IN THE CHORUS POETARUM

Verses in the Chorus Poetarum, by the Duke of Buckingham
and others, ed. Chas. Gildon.   Lond. 1694.   172–73:

> "By Spencer," beginning:
> > "Phillis is both blithe and young"

—so obviously *not* by Spenser that it might be better relegated to the
"Pseudo-Spenser" section.

XI. A POEM

A Poem of 26 lines, beginning

> "From the heavnes there hath descended,"

in Brit. Mus. Add. MS 34064, and there ascribed to Sp. Cf. Buck,
P. M., Jr., in Mod. Lang. Notes, XXII (1907), 41–46: Prints the
poem in full.

XII. Various Scattered Verses

Sir James Ware, Historie of Ireland, 1633. Sig. L 2 (after p. 120) quotes as translated by Sp in a book belonging to Richard Boyle, Earl of Cork:

"Nulla dies pereat, pereat pars nulla diei,
Ne tu sic pereas, ut periere dies."

"Let no day passe, passe no part of the day,
Lest thou do passe, as dayes do passe away."

Also quotes as by Sp verses written upon the same Earl's lute:

"Whilst vitall sapp did make me spring,
And leafe and bough did flourish brave,
I then was dumbe and could not sing,
Ne had the voice which now I have:
But when the axe my life did end,
The Muses nine this voice did send.
E. S."

("As Ware was in Cork's service—cf. Lismore Papers, Index—he should have known whether these verses were genuine"—Edith Rickert.)

In general see also:

LITHGOW, R. A. D.   The Paradise of Dainty Devises, 1576.   In Trans. Royal Soc. of Lit., 2d Ser., XVII (1895), 66:
On poems in it signed "E. S."

COLLIER, J. P., in his ed. of Sp, I, p. civ:
Refers to the entry in the Stationer's Register, 25 Oct. 1593 of *A Memoriall of the Life and Death of Lorde Graye of Wilton,*—"by E. Spenser" interlined and afterwards struck out.   Never published, and now lost?   Cf. Arber's Transcripts, II, 302: does not mention the interlineation.

Was this possibly a preliminary study for the V of I?

See "Scattered Verses," below.

SOURCES IN GENERAL, READING, SPENSER'S LIBRARY, ETC.

References to titles dealing mainly with the Faerie Queene are not included.

See also, below, "Spenser and Chaucer," "Spenser and Dante," "Spenser and Shakespeare," "Spenser and Platonism," "Faerie Queene, Sources"; and under each work.

There are numerous references to his reading in Sp. See Whitman's Subject Index, "Authors Mentioned by Spenser." See esp. Sh Cal, Epistle Dedicatory; April, Argument; June; Dec.; and passim; R of T (Mirror for Magistrates, Camden, Du Bellay).

Numerous references in View of Ireland, esp. (refs. to pages of Grosart's ed. of Sp, IX) 51 (Caesar—cf. 68–69), 66 (Buchanan—cf. 68–69, 90), 67 ff. (Irish chronicles), 68 (Strabo, etc., cf. 70, 78), 68 (Pompeius Mela—cf. 71), 68 (Tacitus—cf. 71), 78 (Diodorus Siculus—cf. 78, 84, 89, etc.), 82 (Olaus Magnus—cf. 93), 82 (Jo. Bohemius—cf. 99, 101, etc.), 84 (Herodotus—cf. 89), 84 (Virgil), 90 (Stanyhurst), 93 (Solinus), 94 (Herodianus), 94 (Plutarch), 95 (Lucian), 76 (Camden—cf. 96), 111 (Aristotle), 174 (Aesop), 217 (the English Chronicles—and passim), 254 (Machiavelli).

A partial list of the authors with whom Sp was evidently familiar would include:

Greek: Homer, Plato, Aristotle, Theocritus, Bion and Moschus, Lucian, Plutarch, Hesiod, Heliodorus, Herodotus.

Latin: Virgil, Ovid, Lucretius, Statius, Longus, Lucan, Cicero, Horace.

Italian: Ariosto, Tasso, Petrarch, Dante (?), Sannazaro, Mantuan, Boccaccio, Machiavelli, Poliziano, Ficino, Giraldi da Cinthio, Benivieni, Minturno, Doni, Piccolomini, Castiglione, Guicciardini.

French: Du Bellay, Marot, Ronsard, Du Bartas, Desportes, some of the old Romances, Bodin, Baïf.

English: Chaucer, Gower, Langland, Geoffrey of Monmouth, and other Chronicles, Hawes, Malory, Skelton, Sackville, Holinshed, Camden, Sidney, Dyer, Gascoigne, Raleigh, Watson, Chapman, Shakespeare, Hakluyt, the Metrical Romances. See CCCHA.

Miscellaneous: The Bible, The Arthurian Legends in various versions, The Seven Champions of Christendom, The Reynard Cycle, Ulenspiegel.

ALANUS DE INSULIS. De Planctu.

Cf. FQ, VII, vii, 9. Does Sp merely reproduce Chaucer's citation?

ALLEN, H. W. Introd. to his ed. of Celestina, trans. Jas. Mabbe. Lond. n.d., p. xxxviii:

The passage on Howleglass, given in Harvey's Marginalia, p. 23.

BORGHESI, P. Petrarch and his Influence on Engl. Lit. Bologna, 1906. 102–4.

COLLIER, J. P. Bibliographical and Critical Account of the Rarest Books in the Engl. Lang. Lond. 1865. See Index.

COLLINS, J. C. Ephemera Critica. N.Y. 1902. 120–21:
Influence of Plato and Aristotle on Sp.

CRANE, RONALD S. The Vogue of Guy of Warwick from the close of the Middle Ages to the Romantic Revival. In Pub. Mod. Lang. Asso., XXX (1915), 125–94:
Elizabethan criticism of the mediaeval romances; their vogue in Sp's time; contemporary reworkings of them.

*DAVIS, W. H. Castiglione and Spenser. 1908. MS Diss. Columbia Univ. Lib.

DE MOSS, W. F. See under "Faerie Queene: Sources."

DE VERE, AUBREY. In Great Thoughts, 4th Ser., VIII (1901), 219:
A note on Sp and Lucretius as moral teachers (H. R. P.)

Dict. Natl. Biog., XVIII, 794: Sp's reading. 803.

DODGE, R. E. N. A Sermon on Source-Hunting. In Mod. Philol., IX (1911). 214–16:
Discusses Upham's theory of Sp's borrowings from Du Bartas; their common sources; 217–19: Criticizes Nadal's theory of Sp's use of Chaucer in Muiopotmos; 219–22: On Lee's views on the Amoretti, sonnet 68, and of Desportes as its "source"; and of Kastner's theory of Desportes as the source of sonnet 48.

DODGE. See also under "Faerie Queene, Sources."

Edinb. Review, The Pléiade and the Elizabethans, CCV (1907), 353–79.
Cf. 370, Sp and Ronsard.

EINSTEIN, L. The Italian Renaissance in England. N.Y. 1902. 341 ff.:
Italian influence on Sp.

ELTON, O. Modern Studies. Lond. 1907. 1–36:
"Giordano Bruno in England"; cf. DeMoss, under "Faerie Queene, Sources."

FENTON, GEOFFREY.
Mr. Robert Dunlop formerly had in his possession a copy of Geoffrey Fenton's translation of Guicciardini's Wars of Italy [London, 1579 ?], "stamped on the binding in gold letters E. S." He writes: "You know that Fenton and Spenser were close friends and I can't help thinking that this may have been a presentation copy to the poet from the author" [i.e. translator]. See also Monophylo.

FLETCHER, J. B. Spenser. In Encycl. Americana.
> On Sp's sources in Tyndale and Calvin.

GALIMBERTI, ALICE. L'Ariosto Inglese. In Nuova Antologia,
4th Ser., CVI (Aug. 1, 1903), 407–18:
> Wherein Sp differs from Ariosto; Sp's relations to the Italian Renaissance; Sp and Sidney; FQ, VI, x, 2 = "l'illustrazione della Primavera botticelliana"; Sp the true representative of the influence of the Italian spirit on the English.

GREENLAW, E. The Influence of Machiavelli on Spenser. In
Mod. Philol., VII (1909), 187–202.

GRESWELL, W. P. Memoirs of Politianus, etc. Manchester,
1805.
> Discussion, with selections from the poems (with translations, notes, etc.) of Poliziano, Pico, Sannazaro, Bembo, etc.

GUICCIARDINI. See Fenton, above.

HARVEY, GABRIEL. Works, ed. Grosart, 1884. I, 137–40
(Letter to Sp):
> On books most read at the University [and all probably known to Sp]; as to Sp's interest in "all generall poyntes of governement, and the great archepollycyes of all ould and newe common welthes"; 180: that Sp was "one that could very wel abide Gascoignes Steele Glasse."

HARVEY, GABRIEL. Marginalia, ed. G. C. Moore Smith.
Stratford-upon-Avon, 1913.
> Important for the relations of Sp and Harvey, and its revelations as to Harvey's reading and intellectual interests, many of which Sp probably shared. See index for list of the authors cited. Of especial interest are Harvey's notes on Gascoignes Certayne Notes (168–70) with his discussion of literary principles, and on Speght's Chaucer (225–34); on Du Bartas see p. 161; etc. Cf. Mod. Lang. Review, XII, 218–21.

HARVEY, GABRIEL. Letter Book (1573–80), ed. J. L. Scott.
Camden Soc., 1884.
> 58–88: See esp. 67: for hint of Sp's interest in the theatre; 75: that Sp was responsible for the publishing of their letters; 78–80: their reading; 80: that Sp [Harvey?] studied law?

HAWES, STEPHEN.
> Cf. Saintsbury, Short Hist. Engl. Lit., 1898. 165.
> See also "Faerie Queene, Sources," Manly, etc., below.

HAZLITT, WM. Collected Works, ed. Waller and Glover.
Lond. 1904. X, 73–74:
Sp and Ariosto.

HERFORD, C. H. Studies in the Lit. Relations of England and
Germany in the Sixteenth Century. Cambr. 1886. 288:
Sp and Ulenspiegel.

HUGHES, M. Y. Some Aspects of the Relation of Edmund
Spenser's Poetry to Classical Literature. 1921. MS Diss.
in Harvard Lib.
Treats of Sp's relation to (1) Theocritus, Bion, and Moschus,
(2) Virgil (influence on Sh Cal and on FQ), and (3) Aristotle.

JULLEVILLE, PETIT DE. Histoire de la Langue et de la Littérature française. Paris, 1897.
In Vol. III (Seizième Siècle), chs. iii, iv and v, the literary history
of Sp's chief French sources and models may best be studied. See also
the bibliographies. Points of likeness with Sp's case and matters of
imitation by him may be noticed passim, throughout these chapters.
See esp. pp. 106, 108, 110, 128 ff., 156–58, 161, 166 (note the contrast),
194–96, etc.

JUSSERAND, J. J. Spenser's "Twelve Private Morall Vertues
as Aristotle hath devised." In Mod. Philol., III (1906),
373–83:
Discrepancies between Sp's list and Aristotle's; contemporary
treatises on the virtues; Sp's source in Piccolomini's Della Istitutione
morale, 1543; illustrated by Bryskett's Discourse. Cf. De Moss under
"Faerie Queene, Sources."

KERLIN, ROBT. T. Theocritus in English Literature. Lynch-
burg, Va. 1910. See index, esp. 16–22.

KOEPPEL, EMIL. Die englischen Tasso Uebersetzungen des
16t. Jahrhunderts. In Anglia, XI (1889), XII (1890), and
XIII (1891).
See XI, 341–62, "Edmund Spenser's Verhältniss zu Tasso": parallels
cited from FQ, Amoretti, and Britain's Ida.

LEE, SIDNEY. The French Renaissance in England. N.Y.
1910.
248: That Sp's practice of compound epithets derives from the Pléiade.
349–50: Sp's debt to Du Bartas.

LEE, VERNON [VIOLET PAGET]. Euphorion. 3d ed. Boston, n.d. [188–].

    275–76: Degeneration of the mediaeval epic cycles up to Sp. Cf. 316, 320.

    321 f.: Comparison of Boiardo and Sp.

    327–33: Sp and Tasso, the last of the school of Boiardo, compared; unreality of their world; their melancholy; contrasted with the Eliz. dramatists. The end of mediaeval romance with Tasso and Sp.

LISLE, WM. See "Criticism to 1650."

MACINTIRE, ELIZ. J. In Pub. Mod. Lang. Asso., XXVI (1911), 520–22:

    Sp and Ronsard, with parallels.

MACRAY, W. D. Annals of the Bodleian Library. 2d ed. Ox. 1890. 122–23.

    Sp's copy of Howleglas, with inscription in Gabriel Harvey's hand, Dec. 20, 1578, at London.

MAIBERGER, M. Studien über den Einfluss Frankreichs auf die Elisabethanische Literatur. Frankfurt, 1903.

Monophylo, drawne into English by Geffray Fenton. A Philosophical Discourse and Division of Loue. [Lond.] 1572.

    Photostat in the Newberry Library. Copies in Bodleian, and Huntington Libraries.

    A translation of Pasquier, Le Monophile, Paris 1554. Copy of ed. of 1566 in Newberry Lib.

MORLEY, H. Clement Marot and other Studies. Lond. 1871. See index.

MUSTARD, W. P. Later Echoes of the Greek Bucolic Poets. In Amer. Journal of Philology, XXX (1909), 245 ff.

    See pp. 246, 268, 273, 276, 280; also XXXIX (1918), 193 ff. See p. 197.

[NEVE, PHILIP.] Cursory Remarks on some of the Ancient English Poets. Lond. 1789. 17–25:

    Chiefly on Sp's sources. That "Spencer obscures himself by imitations."

NITCHIE, ELIZ. Vergil and the English Poets. N.Y. (Columbia Univ.), 1919.

    Ch. v: "Spenser and the English Renaissance."

OWEN, S. G. Ovid and Romance. In Eng. Lit. and the Classics. Ox. 1912. 183–85:
> Ovid's influence on Sp, with illustrations, and some details of his borrowings.

PADELFORD. See under "Faerie Queene, General."

PALGRAVE, F. T. Spenser in Relation to his Immediate Predecessors. In Grosart's ed. of Sp, IV, pp. ix–xxiii.

PASQUIER. See Monophylo, above.

Quarterly Review, XLVII (1832), 23:
> Sp's use of Hesiod.

Quarterly Review, CXCVI (1902), 483–508: Giordano Bruno in England.
> Bruno's relations with Fulke-Greville and Sidney; no evidence that B. knew Sp; 503 ff., on "intellectual contact between Bruno and Spenser"; what they have in common; the parallels perhaps accidental; that possibly Sp knew Bruno's Speccio; comparison of it with the FQ, and especially the Cantos of Mutability. A valuable short study.

RENWICK, W. L. In Mod. Lang. Review, XVII (1922), 1–16:
> Sp's debt to the Pléiade in matters of diction; also XVII (1922), 282–87, on Sp's debt to Mulcaster and the Pléiade.

RIEDNER, W. Spensers Belesenheit. I Theil: Die Bibel und das klassische Altertum. Leipzig, 1908.

RUUTZ-REES, CAROLINE. Some Notes of Gabriel Harvey's in. Hoby's Translation of Castiglione's *Courtier*. In Pub. Mod. Lang. Asso., XXV (1910), 608–39:
> Interesting Harvey marginalia. See 620 ff. on Harvey's books and reading.

SANDYS, JOHN E. A History of Classical Scholarship. Cambr. 1906–8. 2d ed. I, 376–77:
> Dionysius the Areopagite the source of Sp's "trinall triplicities."

SAWTELLE, ALICE E. The Sources of Spenser's Classical Mythology. N.Y. 1896.
> A convenient dictionary of the subject, with additions to the material of the annotations in the preceding editions of Sp. Some topics elaborately developed, e.g. Gardens of Adonis, Arachne, Cupid, etc. Could be carried farther. Cf. C. G. Osgood, The Classical Mythology of Milton's English Poems, N.Y. 1900, p. xx *n:* on Sp's mythology.

SÉLINCOURT, E. DE. Introd. to his one-volume Oxford ed. of Sp, pp. viii f.:
> Sp's reading at school and college; xvii.

TOWRY, M. H. Spenser and Boccaccio. In the Bibliographer, Lond. V (1884), 120:
> That Boccaccio's Genealogia and Natalis Comes were the sources of Sp's mythology. E.g. cf. "Demogorgon" in Sp and in Boccaccio.

TUCKER, THOS. G. The Foreign Debt of English Literature. Lond. 1907. See index.
> A very general treatment. Adds nothing new on Sp's sources.

UNDERHILL, J. G. Spanish Literature in the England of the Tudors. N.Y. 1899.
> See index, and esp. 273–75: Sp's use of Lazarillo de Tormes, etc.

UPHAM, A. H. French Influence in English Literature. N.Y. 1908. Pp. 25–33, 38, 44–46, 57, 66–69, 120–21, 139, 167–69, 199–200, 449, 506–18.

VIANEY, JOSEPH. Le Pétrarquisme en France au 16e Siècle. Paris, 1909.
> Study of Sp's French models in the Petrarchan tradition, esp. Marot, Du Bellay, etc.

WARTON, THOS. Observations on the Fairy Queen. Lond. 1807.

WARTON, THOS. Hist. Eng. Poetry, ed. W. C. Hazlitt, IV, 177.

WHITMAN. Subject Index, 20, 188.

WINBOLT, S. E. Spenser and his Poetry. Lond. 1912.
> 23 ff. Sp's reading; 70 ff. Sp's debt to Ovid; and passim.

WINSTANLEY, LILIAN, in her ed. of The Fowre Hymnes, Introd. and Notes. See also under "Faerie Queene, Sources."

SPENSER AND CHAUCER

See Whitman, Subject-Index, "Chaucer."

See esp. MHT, Daphnaida, Muiopotmos, FQ, IV, ii, 32 ff.; VI, iii, 1; VII, vii, 9; V of I (Grosart's ed.), 112, 233.

See also under "Versification."

BROWNING, ELIZABETH BARRETT.   The Greek Christian Poets and the English Poets.   Lond. 1863.   134 ff.
>   Sp and Chaucer compared.

Edinburgh Review, XXV (1815), 59 ff.

GREENLAW, E.   In Pub. Mod. Lang. Asso., XXVI (1911), 419–51.

GREG, W. W.   Pastoral Poetry.   Lond. 1906.   95.

GROSART'S ed. of Sp, I, 78 ff.

HALES, J. W.   Introd. to Snell's Age of Transition.   Lond. 1905.   II, pp. viii–x:
>   Relation of Sp to Chaucer, very briefly touched.   Negligible.

HAZLITT, WM.   Lectures on the English Poets, 1818.   Lect. II: "Chaucer and Spenser."

HERFORD, C. H.   In Academy, L (1896), 28.

LEGOUIS, E.   See under "Versification."

LOUNSBURY, T. R.   Studies in Chaucer.   N.Y. 1892.
>   III, 42–46: Profound influence of Chaucer on Sp in "language and literary methods"; Sp's direct obligations to Chaucer outlined.
>   54–57: Sp's conception of Chaucer's language and verse.

NADAL, T. W.   Chaucer's Influence on Spenser.   MS Dissertation, 1909.
>   In Harvard Library.   Pub. in part as "Spenser's Daphnaida and Chaucer's Book of the Duchess," in Pub. Mod. Lang. Asso., XXIII (1908), 646–61, and as "Spenser's Miuopotmos in Relation to Chaucer's 'Sir Thopas' and 'The Nun's Priest's Tale'" in Pub. Mod. Lang. Asso., XXV (1910), 640–56.

PALMER, G. H.   Formative Types in English Poetry.   Bost. 1918.   65 ff.

ROSENTHAL, BRUNO.   Spenser's Verhaeltniss zu Chaucer.   Berlin and Kiel, 1911.   Diss.
>   Schematic; superficial.

SAINTSBURY, GEO.   In Cambr. Hist. Eng. Lit., II, 165, 184.
>   That Sp did not misunderstand Chaucer's verse.

SÉLINCOURT, E. DE.   Introd. to his one-volume Oxford ed. of Sp.   Pp. xvii f., xxxii, xxxiv, lxi–lxii:
>   Judicious appraisal of Sp's debt to Chaucer.

SPEGHT, THOS.   Life of Chaucer, prefixed to ed. of C's Workes, 1602. ciij*b*.

> Cites commendations of Chaucer by men of learning, including "two of the purest and best writers of our daies, the one for Prose, the other for Verse, M. *Ascham*, and M. *Spenser*." And refers to Sp's praise of Chaucer as Tityrus in Sh Cal and to Sp's continuation of the Squire's Tale in the FQ; etc.

SPURGEON, CAROLINE F. E.   Chaucer devant la critique. Paris, 1911.

> See index, esp. pp. 29, 30.

SPURGEON, CAROLINE F. E.   Five Hundred Years of Chaucer Criticism and Allusion, 1357–1900.   Lond. (Chaucer Soc. Pub.), 1914. 2v.   No index.

> See Pt. I, pp. 118, 132–34, 161 for Sp's Chaucer allusions.

WHITMAN, C. H.   Subject Index to Spenser.   New Haven, 1918. 49.

WINSTANLEY, LILIAN, in her ed. of FQ, I, pp. liv–lix.

SPENSER AND DANTE

KOEPPEL, E.   Dante in der englischen Litt. des 16 Jahrh.   In Zeitschrift für vergleichende Litteraturgeschichte, III (1890), 449–51:

> Thinks it very doubtful whether we can trace Dante's direct influence on Sp; and that Plumptre is too bold in so doing.

KUHNS, OSCAR.   Dante and the English Poets from Chaucer to Tennyson.   N.Y. 1904, 58–70:

> As to the influence of Dante on Sp; that the evidence is very doubtful.

LOWELL, J. R.   Essay on Spenser.   In his Writings, Bost. 1891, IV.

Notes and Queries, Ser. VIII, Vol. I (1892), 333, 439; Ser. XI, Vol. IV (1911), 447, 515; Vol. V (1912), 33.

PLUMPTRE, E. H.   The Commedia and Canzoniere of Dante . . . . a new Translation.   Lond. 1886–88.

> II, 358: Finds points of likeness in the dedicatory epistles of both poets, and in the multiple allegory.

> II, 428–29: Discusses the probable knowledge of Dante by Sp.

TOYNBEE, PAGET. Dante in English Literature. Lond. 1909.

> I, pp. xx–xxi: Sp's debt to Dante an open question, but in spite of Lowell's opinion to the contrary it is difficult to trace a connection. The parallelisms alleged are probably mere coincidences.

> I, 80–82: Further as to Sp's knowledge of Dante, with list of alleged parallel passages. Cf. 309–15, 598–600, 609; II, 126, 132, etc., where the opinions of Upton, Todd, Aikin, Leigh Hunt, etc., are quoted.

TOYNBEE, PAGET. Britain's Tribute to Dante in Literature and Art. Lond. 1921. 8.
Negligible.

SPENSER AND SHAKESPEARE

See also references on Tears of the Muses ("Willy"), and CCCHA ("Aëtion"), below.

> In Shakespeare: see Mid. N. Dream, I, i; V (possible allusion to Sp); Hen. VIII, II, ii ("bold bad man"; cf. FQ, I, i, 9); Much Ado (cf. FQ, II, iv); Winters' Tale (cf. FQ, VI, ix, xii); Sonnets.

CHALMERS, GEO. Supplemental Apology for the Believers in the Shakespeare-Papers. Lond. 1799. Pp. 21–37, 38 ff., 270 n.

COLLIER's ed. of Sp, I, pp. x–xi, lxxx.

DE MONTMORENCY, J. E. G. The "Other Poet" of Shakespeare's Sonnets. In Contemporary Review, CI (June, 1912), 885–89:

> Shakespeare's Sonnets an allegory, and Sp = the rival poet; Aëtion = Shakespeare; evidence of relations between the two poets.

ERSKINE, J. The Eliz. Lyric. N.Y. 1903. 171.

GREENLAW, EDWIN. Shakespeare's Pastorals. In Studies in Philology, XIII (1916), 122–54:

> Influence of Sidney's Arcadia and of Sp on As You Like It, on Cymbeline, and on Winter's Tale. Shakespeare's "pastoralism" and Spenser's.

GROSART, A. B., in his ed. of Sp, I, 82, 91 ff., 182, 184, 351; IV, p. lxxxiii.

HAZLITT, W. C. Shakespeare, Himself and his Work. Lond. 1912. Pp. 52, 288.

HERMAN, E. Shakespeare und Spenser. In his Drei Shake-speare-Studien, Erlangen (1879).
> II, 455–92: On the relations between Mid. N. Dream and Tears of Muses. 492–525: "Spensers 'pleasant Willy' und Aëtion."

LE FRANC, ABEL. Sous le masque de Shakespeare. Paris, 1918. 2 v. I, ch. iii:
> "Spenser et Shakespeare; L'Énigme d'Aëtion." Also 221 ff.: That "Willy" is not Shakespeare.

The London Magazine, IV (1821), 265–68: On Spenser's Supposed Acquaintance with Shakespeare.
> A notice of Malone's Shakespeare, esp. the parts on Sp. Reasons for believing that Aetion is not Shakespeare, but is Sackville.

MADDEN, DODGSON H. Shakespeare and his Fellows. N.Y. 1916. 12–53:
> "Edmund Spenser." That Aëtion=Shakespeare; of their relations. An elaborate structure, based on thin conjecture.

Notes and Queries, Ser. VI, Vol. X (1884), 274, 390, 455; Vol. XI (1885), 72, 417; Ser. X, Vol. I (1904), 204:
> Rosalind, Colin, and William in Sh Cal and in As You Like It.

PAGE, THOS. Spenser and Shakespeare. Their Lives and Literary Work. Lond. n.d.
> A superficial pamphlet. Does not treat of their relations.

PALGRAVE, F. T. In Grosart's ed. of Sp, IV, pp. lxxxiii f.

RUSHTON, WM. L. Shakespeare illustrated by old Authors. The Second Part. Lond. 1868. Passim.

WOODWARD, PARKER. Euphues the Peripatician. Lond. 1907.
> 50 ff.: Parallelisms in Sp and Shakespeare.

SPENSER AND PLATONISM

See also "Four Hymns," "Amoretti."

BEMBO. Gli Asolani.
> A possible source.

BUCK, P. M., JR. Platonism in Spenser. Paper read by title before Mod. Lang. Asso. Cf. Pub. Mod. Lang. Asso., XXV (1910), Proceedings, p. xlii.

CASTIGLIONE. Il Cortegiano.

COLLINS, J. C. Ephemera Critica. N.Y. 1902, 120–21.

COURTHOPE, W. J.   Hist. Eng. Poetry, II, 240–42.

CRANE, THOS. F.   Italian Customs of the Sixteenth Century.
New Haven, 1920.
> For the Italian treatment of the theme of Platonic love.

FLETCHER, J. B.   In Eng. Graduates' Record.   Columbia Univ.
1905.   72 ff.

HARRISON, J. S.   Platonism in English Poetry of the Sixteenth
and Seventeenth Centuries.   N.Y. 1903.   See index.

KERR, W. A. R.   The Pléiade and Platonism.   In Mod. Philol.,
V (1908), 407–21:
> Platonism in some of Sp's "sources."   Cf. Pub. Mod. Lang. Asso.,
> XIX (1904), 33–63.

*NOBILI.   Trattato dell' Amore Humano (ed. Pasolini, Rome, 1895).

SCHROEDER, KURT.   Platonismus in der engl. Renaissance vor
und bei Lyly.   Berlin, 1907.   Diss.
> An attempt to supplement Harrison's Platonism in Eng. Poetry by
> a study of Platonism in Eng. Prose before Spenser, esp. in Colet,
> Erasmus, and More.

STEWART, J. A.   Platonism in English Poetry.   In Engl. Lit.
and the Classics.   Ox. 1912.   25–48.
> On the platonism of Wordsworth, Coleridge, and Shelley, with
> passing reference to Sp.

*TASSO.   Notes, and Conclusioni.

VARCHI, Benedetto.   Lezzioni.
> Copy of ed. of 1561 in Newberry Lib.

WINSTANLEY, LILIAN.
> In her ed. of FQ, I, pp. lix–lxvi.

WINSTANLEY, LILIAN.
> In her ed. of The Fowre Hymnes, Introd. and notes.

PUBLISHERS AND PRINTERS

ARBER.   Transcripts, passim.   See under "Works, General
References."

COLLIER, J. P.   In his ed. of Sp, I, pp. liii *n*, lxxi (Ponsonby).

GROSART'S ed. of Sp, I, pp. lx f. (Singleton).

McKerrow, R. B. ed., Dictionary of Printers and Booksellers in England . . . . 1557–1640. Lond. (Bibliog. Soc.), 1910:
    See Henry Bynneman, Humphrey Lownes, Matthew Lownes, William Ponsonby, Hugh Singleton.

Sheavyn, Phoebe. The Literary Profession in the Elizabethan Age. Manchester, 1909.
    67: On Ponsonby; 157 n.

Smith, D. Nichol. Authors and Patrons. In Shakespeare's England. Ox. 1916. II, 183–84:
    That Sp received nothing for his writings. Cf. 185, 191 ff.: Sp's Patrons, Burghley, Sidney, etc.

Transactions Bibliog. Soc., London, IV (1898), 124–25:
    On Humphrey Lownes as publisher of the 1611 ed. of FQ; typographical peculiarities of this edition.

PICTORIAL ILLUSTRATIONS

The Bookman, N.Y., XV (1902), 144–45:
    Extract from FQ, II, xii, with full-page illustration.

Birch's ed. of FQ.
    Illus. by 32 plates, after designs by W. Kent.

Dawson, L. H. Stories from the Faerie Queene. Lond. 1910.
    Illus. by Gertrude D. Hammond.

Epithalamion, with illustrations by G. W. Edwards. N.Y. 1895

Faerie Queene and Epithalamion. Lond, 1853, etc.
    Illus. by E. Corbould.

The Faerie Queene. Lond. (Dent & Co.), 1897.
    "Pictured and decorated" by L. Fairfax Muckley.

Grace, R. W. Tales from Spenser.
    Illustrations [twelve] by Helen Kück. Lond. 1909.

Hughes, J. Ed. of Sp's Works, 1715.
    Illustrated.

The Legend of the Knight of the Red Crosse. . . . . Lond. 1871.
    Illus. with twelve drawings by C. M. B. Morrell.

Macleod, Mary. Stories from the Faerie Queene. Lond. [1897].
    Drawings by A. G. Walker.

Notes and Queries, Ser. III, Vol. IV (1863), 150, 236.

Poetical Works, ed. Aikin, 1806.
Plates by Stothard.

Prothalamion and Epithalamion.
Illus. by Edwin Blashfield. Bost. 1902.

ROSSETTI, W. M. Life of John Keats. Lond. 1887. 55:
A painting of the Cave of Despair, by Severn.

ROSSETTI, W. M. Dante Gabriel Rossetti, his Family Letters.
Lond. 1895, II, 12, 13.

ROYDE-SMITH, N. G. Una and the Red Cross Knight. Lond.
1905.
Illus. by T. H. Robinson.

The Shepherdes Calender, illus. by Walter Crane. N.Y. 1897.

The Shepheardes Calendar. Kelmscott Press, 1896.
Illus. by A. J. Gaskin.

TOWRY, M. H. Spenser for Children . . . . with illustrations in
colours by Walter J. Morgan. Lond. 1885.

UPTON, JOHN. In his ed. of the FQ, 1758, I, p. xl.

WILSON, C. D. The Faery Queene, Book I, rewritten. Chicago,
1906.
"Decorated by Ralph Fletcher Seymour."

WISE, T. J. ed. The Faerie Queene.
Pictured by Walter Crane. . Lond. 1897.

FAERIE QUEENE, GENERAL REFERENCES

See also "Versification, the Spenserian Stanza."

*ALTENBURG, ——. The Beauties of Spenser, or an Analytical
Survey of Spenser's Faerie Queene. Krossen, 1865. Progr.

BACKE, W. Essay on Spenser and his Fairy Queen, especially
with regard to the Language. Stralsund, 1872. Progr.

BASCOM, JOHN. Philosophy of Engl. Lit. N.Y. 1895. 108–10.
Esp. on the allegory.

BAYNE, RONALD. "Masque and Pastoral," being ch. xiii of Vol. VI of the Cambridge Hist. of Eng. Lit., Cambr. 1910. 330, 335-36:
> On "the relation of Spenser's art to the masque"; the masque element in the FQ. Sp's influence on Jonson and other writers of masques.

BIRCH, THOS. In his ed. of Sp, 1751, I, The Life, pp. xxxvi-vii.

BRAND, JOHN. Observations on Popular Antiquities . . . . ed. Sir Henry Ellis. Lond. 1849. II, 476-508:
> A review of the literature on "Fairy Mythology"; 499: that Sp "was contented with the fairies of romance," and not those of popular tradition followed by Shakespeare.

BRIE, FRIEDRICH. Sidney's Arcadia: eine Studie zur englischen Renaissance. Strassburg, 1918. (Quellen und Forschungen, CXXIV.) 32-37:
> Comparison of the Arcadia and the FQ as two contemporary efforts to depict the Cortegiano ideal (J. D. B.).

British Quarterly Review, XXII (1855), 400-12.

BUCK, P. M., JR. On the Political Allegory in "The Faerie Queene." Lincoln (Nebraska Univ. Studies, XI), 1911. 159-92:
> An attempt at further interpretation of the several books in their order in this aspect; e.g., Book III = "the allegory of Elizabeth's courtships."

BUCKLEY, W. E. Preface to Reprint of Thos. Edwards' Cephalus and Procris, 1595 (Roxburgh Club, 1882). Pp. xviii ff.:
> On the name "Artegal" (FQ, Bk. V).

Bulletin Metropolitan Museum of Art, New York, VIII (1913), 118-23:
> "The Armor of Sir James Scudamore."
> That this Sir James Scudamore is referred to in the FQ; his armor now in this museum. Illustrated. Cf. Masson's Life of Milton, I, 749.

BUTTERWORTH, WALTER. Symbol and Allegory in Spenser. In Manchester Quarterly, XXI (1902), 229-43.
> Very general and thin.

C., The Faerie Queene Unveiled. In Notes and Queries, Ser.
III, Vol. IV (1863), 21–22, 65–66, 101–3 (cf. 140, 150, 197,
236, 283).
> Points in common in FQ and Sidney's Arcadia; interpretation of
> the allegory of the FQ; etc. (Ingenious but uncertain conjectures.)
> Cf. Higginson, Spenser's Sh Cal, 222.

C., J. H. Brief Notes on the FQ. In Notes and Queries, Ser. I,
Vol. III (1851), 369.

CAËTANI-LOVATELLI, E. Antike Denkmäler und Gebräuche.
. . . . Leipzig, 1896. 57–65:
> "Die Adonisgarten." The classical myth, symbolizing death and
> birth.

CARPENTER, F. I. Spenser's Cave of Despair. In Mod. Lang.
Notes, XII (1897), 257–73:
> Theme of Bk. I, canto ix of the FQ compared with its prototypes;
> Sp's immediate source for this episode in the Mirror for Magistrates;
> later imitations and analogues, esp. in Tennyson's Two Voices.

Catalogue of MSS in University Library, Cambridge.
> Ee iii. 53: A MS continuation of the FQ in three books, c. 1632. Cf.
> Hunter, Chor. Vat., IV, 459.

Chamber's Journal, XV (1851), 19–22. "The Fairy Queen."
> Entered in certain bibliographies under "Spenser." Actually deals
> with C. Perrault, and not on Sp.

Chambers' Repository, Edinb., V (1854), No. 40.
> "Spirit of the Fairy Queen." Extracts, with general comment.

CHURCH, RALPH. Ed. of FQ, 1758. Anon. Life of Sp prefixed,
I, pp. i–xi:
> Discusses the text, and preceding editions; xxiv: FQ partly written
> in England, but mostly in Ireland.

CHURCH, R. W. Spenser (Eng. Men of Letters), chs. iv–vi.
> Good general treatment.

CLARK, ELLEN U. Another Aspect of the "Faerie Queene."
In Andover Review, XIV (1890), 609–20:
> In answer to Pancoast (q.v.). Sp's real aim and ideals; nature of
> his moral power and appeal; his symbolic pictures. A suggestive bit
> of sympathetic appreciation.

COLERIDGE, CHRISTABEL R.   Finger Posts in Faery Land.   In
  Monthly Packet, London, II (1891), 102–9, 223–29, 342–49,
  462–69, 584–92, 698–704:
    Popularizing, expository essays, with running synopsis of the FQ.

COLLIER, J. P.   In his ed. of Sp, I, pp. xliii ff., lx ff., cxix ff.

COOK, A. S.   The Amazonian Type in Poetry.   In Mod. Lang.
  Notes, V (1890), 321–28.
    Discusses this type in the FQ, and its sources.

COOK, A. S.   Spenser's Faerie Queene, I, i, 6.   In Mod. Lang.
  Notes, XXII (1907), 208–9: textual notes.

COURTHOPE, W. J.   Hist. Eng. Poetry.   Lond. 1897+.
    II, 239 ff.: Allegory of FQ; 245–49: Design of the FQ; 256–82:
  its unity, sources in Ariosto, structure, style, verse, diction.
    III (1903), 2: Gloriana (Elizabeth) as a center of interest. Cf. 141.

COURTHOPE, W. J.   In Cambr. Hist. Eng. Lit., III, 228–38.

CRAIK, G. L.   Hist. Eng. Lit.   Lond. 1861.   I, 503–20.

CRAIK, G. L.   Spenser and his Poetry.   Lond. 1845.
    Good general treatment.

CREIGHTON, M.   The Age of Elizabeth.   N.Y. 1891.   217–18.

CROMPTON, JAMES.   Spenser's "Faerie Queene"; its Place and
  Influence in Literature.   In Manchester Quarterly, I (1882),
  219–43:
    Slight and sketchy. Cf. 237–39: Sp and Bunyan; 239–43:
  Milton's debt to Sp.

CROTHERS, SAMUEL M.   Among Friends.   Bost. 1910.   236–53:
    On the FQ as a "Romance of Ethics." Slight but suggestive.

CUTTELL, JOHN.   Spenser's "Fairie Queen."   In Great Thoughts,
  VIII (1901), 283 ff.
    Negligible.

DELATTRE, FLORIS.   English Fairy Poetry.   Lond. and Paris,
  1912.   80–91:
    Fairy mythology subordinate in Sp's design,—a "mere literary
  device"—but a part of the charm of the poem.

DE MONTMORENCY, J. E. G.   The Red Cross Knight.   In
  Contemporary Review, CVII (1915), 659–63.
    Negligible.

DE MOSS, W. F. Spenser's Twelve Moral Virtues "according to Aristotle." In Mod. Philol., XVI (1918), 23–38, and 245–70:
> Criticizes Jusserand's arguments. Sp and Aristotle's Ethics, points of agreement; Sp not indebted to Bryskett's Discourse.

DE VERE, A. Essays chiefly on Poetry. I, 86 ff.:
> On FQ, III, vi.

DIGBY, SIR KENELM. Observations on the 22nd. Stanza in the 9th Canto of the 2nd Book of Spenser's Fairy Queen. Lond. 1644.
> Quoted in various eds. of Sp.

DISRAELI, I. Amenities of Literature. N.Y. 1870.
> II, Sections on "Spenser," "The Faery Queen," and "Allegory." Slight and superficial. But note comment on Sp's imagery: "This diffusion . . . . often raises the illusion of revery, till we seem startled by reality"; "the charm of his diffusion."

DIXON, W. M. Epic and Heroic Poetry. Lond. 1912. See index. Ch. viii: "The Romantic Epic: Spenser."
> Excellent general criticism of the FQ; 155–57, on Sp as a painter's poet; 161: "A picture-book of the spiritual life"; 169: Sp "the greatest colourist among English Poets." Comprehensive assessment of the qualities of the FQ and of Sp the poet. Judicious reply to criticisms adverse to Sp.

DODGE, R. E. N. The Well of Life and the Tree of Life. In Mod. Philol., VI (1909), 191–96:
> Allegory of Bk. I, canto xi interpreted.

DOWDEN, E. Elizabethan Psychology. In Atlantic Monthly, C (1907), 388–99.
> Cf. 391 on FQ, II, ix, 22; and passim, on Sp's psychology.

DRAPER, J. W. Narrative Technique of the Faerie Queene. To appear in Pub. Mod. Lang. Asso.
> Narrative plan of FQ does not mainly follow the Orlando Furioso; points of difference; entrance *in medias res*, and making a separate knight the hero of each book, etc., rather from Italian criticism of the century and from Malory. Italian sources of the epic theory of the Letter to Raleigh.

Edinb. Review, CLXI (1885), 142–76.

ERSKINE, J. The Virtue of Friendship in the Faerie Queene.
In Pub. Mod. Lang. Asso., XXX (1915), 831–50:
The Renaissance friendship-theme as treated by Sp, esp. in FQ, IV;
Sp and Bryskett's Discourse; that Sp knew Giraldi's Tre Dialoghi,
Bryskett's original, and utilized them; friendship treated as a moral
virtue by both; FQ, IV treats its theme by incidents illustrating the
evils which flow from the lack of friendship; its plan studied.

FALKINER, C. L. Essays rel. to Ireland. Lond. 1909. 3–31:
"Topographical allusiveness" of the FQ examined; much more
prominent in Books IV–VI.

FLEAY, F. G. Guide to Chaucer and Spenser, 97–99.

FRAUNCE, A. Arcadian Rhetorike, 1588.
Quotes the (then unpublished) Faerie Queene.

GAYLEY, C. M., and B. P. KURTZ. Methods and Materials of
Lit. Crit. Bost. 1920. II, 744–45:
The FQ as a literary epic ("Romantic epos"); questions suggested
for investigation.

Gentleman's Magazine, XXXII (1762), 266–68:
"Some account of . . . . Gothic Chivalry; with critical Remarks
on Spencer and Tasso."

Gentleman's Magazine, 1819, I, 318–20:
Critique of the FQ.

GLASENAPP, G. Zur Vorgeschichte der Allegorie in Edm.
Spenser's "Faerie Queene." Berlin, 1904. Diss.

[GILMAN, S.] The Faery Queene of Spenser. In North Amer.
Review, V (1817), 301–9.

GLOVER, TERROT R. Poets and Puritan. Lond. 1915. 1–33:
On the FQ and its purpose to fashion a gentleman or noble person
in virtuous and gentle discipline.

GOLLANCZ, I. In Proceedings of Brit. Academy, 1907–8.
99–105:
Variations in copies of first ed. of FQ.

GOSSE, E. A Short History of Mod. Eng. Lit. Lond. 1898.
82–86:
Excellent condensed statement of the historical position of the FQ;
its Celtic atmosphere; a clever page of aesthetic appreciation.

GOUGH, A. B. Who was Spenser's Bon Font? In Mod. Lang. Review, XII (1917), 140–45:
> On FQ, V, ix, 25, 26: Bon Font-Malfont = Ulpian Fulwell.

GREEN, J. R. History of the English People. N.Y. 1881. II, 461–67.

GREENE, HERBERT E. A Grouping of Figures of Speech. In Pub. Mod. Lang. Asso., VIII (1893), 432–50:
> For a definition of allegory.

GREENE, H. E. The Allegory as employed by Spenser, Bunyan, and Swift. In Pub. Mod. Lang. Asso., IV (1889), 145–93:
> The nature of allegory; allegory in earlier and Elizabethan literature.

GREENLAW, EDWIN. Sidney's Arcadia as an Example of Elizabethan Allegory. In Kittredge Anniversary Papers. Bost., 1913. 327–37:
> The Eliz. conception of allegory in Sidney and Sp. The Arcadia "a prose counterpart of the *Faerie Queene.*"

GREENLAW, E. In Studies in Philology, XVII (1920), 331 ff.:
> On FQ, III, vi (The Gardens of Adonis).

GREENLAW, E. In Mod. Philol., IX (1912), 347–70:
> An exposition of FQ, V and its political allegory. Accepted by Sélincourt (Introd. to his one-volume ed. of Sp, p. xlix *n*).

GREENLAW, E. Spenser's Fairy Mythology. In Studies in Philology, XV (1918), 105–22:
> Sources and analogues of the fairy material in the FQ; contemporary pageantry; "Celtic Faerie in Spenser"; "Faerie" in the historical allegory; use of the chronicles in the FQ. An introductory sketch. Suggestive.

GREENLAW, E. Review of Cory's Edmund Spenser. In Mod. Lang. Notes, XXXV (1920), 165–77:
> Correcting some of Cory's speculations about the FQ. Discusses Sp's method in allegory; and further of his political views, relations with Leicester, etc.; on the structure of the several books of the FQ; some of Sp's models in the Romances; his symbolism; justification of the structural and poetical quality of the later books of the FQ.

GREENLAW, E.   The Faerie Queene.   In Encyclopedia Americana.   N.Y. 1918 (revised edition), X, 708–10:
   Clear explanation of Sp's plan, and of the sources of the plan in contemporary critical ideas;   relation of the FQ to the Arthurian Romances;   its debt here greater than to the Italian sources;   its nationalistic inspiration and historical allegory;   its pervasive spirit of romance;   the stanza;   his pictures and pageants.

GRIMESTON, E.   A Generall Historie of the Netherlands.   Lond. 1609.   Bk. XIII:
   Contemporary accounts—which illustrate the FQ.

HAMANN, ALBERT.   An Essay on Spenser's Faery Queen. Berlin, 1888.   Progr.

HARMAN, E. G.   Edmund Spenser and the Impersonations of Francis Bacon.   Lond. 1914.   Chs. iii, xvii:
   "Baconian" interpretation of the FQ.   There are some scattered guesses that are worth looking into.

HARRISON, J. S.   Platonism in Eng. Poetry.   N.Y. 1903.   Ch. i:
   Treats of Holiness, Temperance, and Chastity as "Ideals of Christian Virtues" influenced by Platonism, with illustrations largely from Sp.   Platonism as a system of ethics absent from the later books of the FQ.   Sp's conception of Justice (Bk. V) especially is non-Platonic. 210–21: Platonic elements in the Cantos of Mutability.

HART, J. S.   Essay on the Life and Writings of Edmund Spenser, with a special exposition of the Fairy Queen.   N.Y. 1847.
   Negligible.

HAZLITT, W. C., ed.   Fairy Tales, Legends, and Romances illustrating Shakespeare and other early English writers. Lond. 1875.

HEISE, W.   Die Gleichnisse in E. Spenser's Faerie Queene und ihre Vorbilder.   Königsee, 1902.   Diss.

HICKEY, EMILY.   Sir Calidore; A Paper for Girls.   In Catholic World, XCIII (1911), 632–45.

HIGGINSON, J. J.   Spenser's Shepherd's Calender.   150 ff.

HINCKLEY, HENRY B.   In Mod. Lang. Notes, XXIV (1909), 125:
   On FQ, II, xi, 26.

HOFFMAN, MAX. Ueber die Allegorie in Spenser's Faerie Queene. Gleiwitz, 1887. Diss.

HOPE, CONSTANCE. Alma. A Study from Spenser. In the Month, XCVI (1900), 384–91:
A slight popular sketch of Sp's "philosophy of love." Negligible.

HOWARD, FRANK. The "Faerie Queene" Unveiled. In Notes and Queries, Ser. III, Vol. IV (1863), 21–22, 236–37, 283. Cf. 150–51.
On the historical allegory, esp. as to Sidney = Redcross Knight, and Essex = Prince Arthur.

HUGHES, M. Y. Spenser and Utopia. In Studies in Philology, XVII (1920), 132–46:
On FQ, V: Sp's class feeling and attitude towards "democracy."

HUGHES, M. Y. Spenser's "Blatant Beast." In Mod. Lang. Review, XIII (1918), 267–75:
Sp's figure of the Blatant Beast interpreted from contemporary literature and politics; the figure suggested by Plato; "Puritan" a term of reproach in Sp's day; Sp "never thought of himself as a Puritan."

HUME, DAVID. History of England, app. iii:
On the allegory.

HUNT, THEO. W. The "Faerie Queene,"—a Religious Romance. In Homiletic Review, XLVIII (1904), 98–102:
The FQ as "an allegory of the human soul"; seriousness of Sp's teaching by example; "this great Reformation poem; in line, in its ethical spirit, with the sermons and doctrinal discussions of the day"; opens the way for Milton.

HURD, RICHARD. Works. Lond. 1811. IV, 231 ff., esp. Letters vii, viii:
On unity of the FQ, etc.

INNES, A. D. England under the Tudors. Lond. 1905. 454:
The FQ gives "the Elizabethan spirit embodied in poetry," and is "necessary to a sympathetic understanding of the times."

JACK, A. A. Chaucer and Spenser. Glasgow, 1920. 180–244. Also ch. vii, on "The Faeries of Spenser."

JOHNSON, C. F. Forms of Eng. Poetry. N.Y. 1904. 354 ff.

[JORTIN, JOHN.] Remarks on Spenser's Poems. Lond. 1734.
Also in Jortin's Tracts. Lond. 1790, I, 54–306:
> Mainly notes on selected passages, with citation of parallels in
> classical authors.
> Cf. The Present State of the Republick of Letters, XIV (1734), 444–46:
> A notice of Jortin's Remarks.

[JORTIN, JOHN.] Remarks on Spenser—Additional Notes. In
his Tracts, 1790. I, 54–259.

JOYCE, P. W. Spenser's Irish Rivers. In Fraser's Magazine,
N.S., XVII (1878), 315–33:
> On the Irish rivers in Sp's poetry (FQ, IV, xi; Cantos of Mutability;
> CCCHA); Sp's truth to fact. Important for study of these passages.

JOYCE, P. W. On Spenser's Irish Rivers. In Proc. Royal
Irish Acad., X (1866–69), 1–12.
> Of various Irish place-names in Sp. Expanded in the preceding.

JOYCE, P. W. The Wonders of Ireland. Lond. 1911. 72–114:
> "Spenser's Irish Rivers." Reprinted from Fraser's Mag.

JUSSERAND, J. J. Hist. litt. du peuple Anglais. II, 414–44.

JUSSERAND, J. J. In Revue de Paris, 1 May 1903: 75 ff.

KEIGHTLEY, THOS. Irish Rivers named in the "Faerie Queen."
In Notes and Queries, Ser. IV, Vol. IV (1869), 169–70:
> Annotations on FQ, IV. Cf. Vol. VII (1871), 317–18.

KEIGHTLEY, THOS. Typographical Errors in the "Faerie
Queen." In Notes and Queries, Ser. IV, Vol. VII (1871),
383–84:
> Textual emendations.

KEIGHTLEY, THOS. Real Persons in the "Faerie Queen." In
Notes and Queries, Ser. IV, Vol. VII (1871), 49–50:
> Various identifications suggested. Cf. p. 176.

KEIGHTLEY, THOS. Allegory in the "Faerie Queen." In
Notes and Queries, Ser. IV, Vol. VII (1871), 1–2:
> That there is in fact only one allegory, that of Book I; interpreta-
> tion of Book I.

KEIGHTLEY, THOS. Plan of the "Faerie Queen." In Notes and Queries, Ser. IV, Vol. IV (1869), 211–12:
That the real arrangement was to be in four parts of three books each; the unwritten parts were to treat, Pt. III, of Constancy, Fortitude, Patience; Pt. IV, of Piety, Prudence, Wisdom; hints as to how these were to be worked out.

KEIGHTLEY, THOS. Fairy Mythology. Lond. 1860. 55–59:
"Spenser's Faerie Queene." Sp's use of the fairy land of "the romancers"; conjecture that Huon of Bordeaux was his principal authority; locus of the poem ("though it shadow forth England, it is distinct from it"); part of invention in Sp's fairy mythology; traces of popular tradition; but mainly "the Fairy-land and the Faeries of Spenser are those of romance."

KEIGHTLEY, THOS. In Dublin Univ. Mag., XXII (1843), 538–57:
544 ff.: Discussion of FQ, V.

KEIGHTLEY, THOS. In Brit. Quar. Review, XXII (1855), 400 ff.
General discussion of the FQ.

KEIGHTLEY, THOS. See under "Life, General."

KIRKLAND, MRS. C. M. Spenser and the Faery Queen. Lond. 1847.
Negligible.

KLEIN, J. L. Geschichte des englischen Dramas. Leipzig, 1876. II, 833–44:
On the allegory. A negative and rambling discussion.

KOEPPEL, E. In Archiv. f. d. Stud. d. n. Spr. u. Litt., XCV (1895), 164–68:
On the Blatant Beast; its French Source in the Chevalier Doré of 1541 (or Perceforest).

*KUHLEMEY. Critical Remarks on Edmund Spensers Faerie Queene. Elberfeld, 1870.

LITTLEDALE, H. Essays on Tennyson's Idylls of the King. Lond. 1893. 17:
Passages in the FQ giving the Arthurian story.

LITTLEDALE, H., and C. E. DOBLE. Spenser "Faerie Queene," I, ii, 18. In the Academy, Lond., XLV (1894), 310, 350.

LONG, P. W.   In Mod. Lang. Review, III (1908), 257–67:
> That Elizabeth, Lady Carey was the Amoret of the F.Q.

LONG, P. W.   Spenser's Sir Calidore.   In Englische Studien, XLII (1910), 53–60.
> On FQ, VI, x.   Accepts identifications of Coridon = Watson, Meliboe = Walsingham, but not Calidore = Sidney.   Argues Calidore = Essex; Essex married Walsingham's daughter, as Calidore marries Pastorella.   Cf. Sp's sonnet to Essex.   Makes out a plausible case; but what about Essex as the protagonist of Courtesy?   Cf. Sélincourt, Introd. to his ed. of Sp, p. liii n.

M., H.   Faerie Queene, II, ix, 22.   In Athenaeum, XXI (1848), 800.

MACKAIL, J. W.   The Springs of Helicon.   Lond. 1909.   85 ff.
> Should be an invaluable aid for the modern-minded reader in "getting at" the FQ.   The renaissance setting and qualities of the poem; 103 ff.: Appreciation of the FQ; its qualities and differentiae; not an "epic" (contra, see Gayley and Kurtz); the allegory; dream quality; an "interlaced series of masques"; the stanza (119–27); etc. Cf. Mod. Lang. Review, V, 114–18.

MARCH, FRANCIS A.   Method of Philological Study of the Eng. Lang.   N.Y. 1886.   74–87:
> Questions on Sp and the FQ, general and linguistic, analyzing in elaborate detail FQ, I, i, 1–5.

MAURICE, F. D.   Friendship of Books.   Lond. 1889.   Lect. viii:
> "Spenser's Faery Queene."   A popular lecture, discursive, and slight, but agreeable criticism.

MAYER, CARL.   La Reine des Fées . . . . étude litt. et historique.   Paris, 1860.   Diss.
> From the point of view of a partisan of sixteenth century Catholicism.   Superficial.   A few good observations; e.g.: "Il est un paysagiste des plus habiles, le meilleur poëte descriptif."

MINTO, WM.   In Encycl. Britannica, XXV (1911), 642a:
> A brief but helpful discussion of the relation of the allegory to the structure of the FQ.   Questionable, however, is the theory that "the world would probably never have divined that there was an allegory" were it not for the letter to Raleigh.

MINTO, WM.   Characteristics of English Poets.   Bost. 1889. Ch. iv.

MORLEY, HENRY. English Writers. Lond. 1891–95. IX, 324 ff.:
  Useful for its running synopsis of the FQ, canto by canto.

MORLEY, H. In Cassell's Lib. of Eng. Lit., "Illus. of Eng.
  Religion," 193 ff.:
  Allegory of FQ, I.

MUSTARD, W. P. Note on Spenser, FQ, V, v, 24. In Mod.
  Lang. Notes, XX (1905), 127.

NICHOLS, JOHN. The Progresses and Public Processions of
  Queen Elizabeth, 1788. 2 vols.
    Illustrations of the pageantry, personifications, and ceremonial
  literature aimed at the court taste, and suggestive of many of the
  features of the FQ. For example:
    II, Harvey's Gratulationes Valdinenses, 1578; Churchyard's
  Discourse of the Entertainment in Suffolk and Norfolk, 1578 (Figures
  of gods, and goddesses, personifications of Chastity, etc. The Queene
  of Fairies, etc.); The Honorable Entertainment at Elvetham, 1591
  ("Speech of the Fairy Quene").

Notes and Queries, Ser. VIII, Vol. IV (1893), 165, 215, 405, 472.
    On parallel passages in FQ and their sources in Tasso, Virgil, etc.;
  Sp's "well" of Helicon. Ser. IX, Vol. IX (1902), 28: As to a supposed
  MS supplement to the FQ in the Pub. Lib. at Cambridge.

Notes and Queries. Various Short Notes on FQ: Ser. I, Vol.
  VIII (1853), 367: the missing books; X (1854), 143: textual,
  from F.J.C.; 370; Ser. IV, Vol. VII (1871), 283; Ser. VII,
  Vol. VIII (1889), 186, 478; IX (1890), 55, 178; Ser. VIII,
  Vol. IX (1896), 228, 313; Ser. IX, Vol. II (1898), 167;
  Ser. X, Vol. VIII (1907), 105: mistakes in FQ; Ser. XII,
  Vol. IV (1918), 71, 226.

OSGOOD, CHARLES G. Spenser's English Rivers. In Trans.
  Conn. Academy, XXIII (1920), 65–108. Also Yale Univ.
  Press. 1920.
    Sp's pictorial art; the English rivers in FQ, IV, xi, identified;
  Sp's debt to Camden and Holinshed (Wm. Harrison), and to Saxton's
  maps, 1579; rivers in Ruins of Time, and FQ, III, iii, 7–14.

PADELFORD, F. M. The Political and Ecclesiastical Allegory
  of the First Book of the Faerie Queene. Bost. 1911.
    An extension of J. E. Whitney's interpretation of the historical
  allegory. Sp's position as a low Church Calvinist. Red Cross Knight

=Henry VIII, the lion=Cromwell, Sansloy=Gardiner, Sansfoy= Wolsey, Sansjoy=Pole, etc.; and canto xi depicts the concluding struggle under Elizabeth with the Catholics and Mary Queen of Scots (=Duessa), with application of the story in some detail to the events of contemporary history. Cf. R. E. N. Dodge in Jour. Eng. and Germ. Philol., XII (1913), 490–96; Winstanley's ed. of FQ, I, passim; Archiv f. d. Stud. d. neueren Spr., CXXVII (1911), 478–79.

PADELFORD, F. M. Spenser's Arraignment of the Anabaptists. In Journal of Eng. and Germ. Philology, XII (1913), 434–48:
An interpretation of FQ, V, ii; Sp's censure on communism and contemporary manifestations of it=an arraignment of the Anabaptists. Cf. Pub. Mod. Lang. Asso., XXXII (1917), 267–91.

PADELFORD, F. M. The Political, Economic and Social Views of Spenser. In Journal of Eng. and Germ. Philology, XIV (1915), 393–420:
Sp's theory of government and society; Sp and Bodin; his views on economic matters.

PADELFORD, F. M. The Women in Spenser's Allegory of Love. In Journal of Eng. and Germ. Philology, XVI (1917), 70–83:
The allegory of love in FQ, III, IV, and V; and exposition of the characters of Amoret, Belphoebe, Florimell, Radigund, and Britomart; Sp's philosophy of love.

PADELFORD, F. M. Talus: the Law. In Studies in Philology, XV (1918), 97–104:
Interpretation of the allegory of the Talus passages in FQ, V.

PADELFORD, F. M. The Virtue of Temperance in the Faerie Queene. In Studies in Philology, XVIII (1921), 334–46:
Supplementing De Moss's paper (see above), by a detailed analysis of Sp's treatment of the theme of temperance in the Legend of Sir Guyon; Sp's close following of Aristotle's ideas.

PANCOAST, H. S. One Aspect of Spenser's "Faerie Queene." In Andover Review, Oct. 1889, 372–85.

PATCH, H. R. Notes on Spenser and Chaucer. In Mod. Lang. Notes, XXXIII (1918), 177–80:
"Pageants of the rivers" in Sp and his contemporaries.

PATON, LUCY A. Studies in the Fairy Mythology of Arthurian Romance. Bost. 1903.
Sp barely referred to.

PECK, H. W. Spenser's *Faerie Queene* and the Student of To-Day. In Sewanee Review, XXIV (1916), 340–52:
> The allegorical as contrasted with the romance elements traced through the poem; its structural defects.

PHILPOT, WM. B. Certain Aspects of the Faery Queen and some of the other Poetry of Spenser. In Grosart's ed. of Sp, I, 340–72.
> Negligible.

*PORTER, MARY LOUISE. The Holy Wars in Mediaeval and Modern English Literature. 1921. MS Diss. in Cornell Univ. Lib.

POWELL, C. L. The Castle of the Body. In Studies in Philology, XVI (1919), 197–205:
> On FQ, III, ix. The allegory of the body in poetry before Sp; Sp's source in Du Bartas.

Quarterly Review, CV (1859), 431:
> On FQ, II, x, 10, "The Western Hogh"; that Sp perhaps visited there.

RAHILLY, T. A. Identification of the Hitherto Unknown River "Aubrian" of Spenser fame. In Journal of Cork Hist. and Arch. Soc., 2d Ser., XXII (1916), 49–56:
> On "Aubrian" in FQ, IV, xi, 41. That it is a small river, in part the boundary between Cork and Kerry, called Breanach; probability of a visit to it by Sp in 1580.

ROBIN, P. A. Spenser's House of Alma. In Mod. Lang. Review, VI (1911), 169–73:
> On FQ, II, ix: an attempt to interpret its allegory.

[RUSHTON, WM.] In Afternoon Lectures. London. 1863–69. I, 54 ff.
> The FQ as illustrating the struggle of romanticism vs. classicism; the question of unity; etc.

RUSKIN, JOHN. Stones of Venice, Vol. III. See index, and App. 2.
> Discusses, inter alia, Sp's system of the virtues and the vices and their treatment in mediaeval-renaissance poetry and art (in Vol. II, ch. viii); App. 2, "Theology of Spenser"; interprets the allegory of parts of FQ, I. Sympathetic.

SAINTSBURY, GEO.   In Traill's Social England. N.Y. 1894,
III, 514–16.

SCHLEGEL, F.   Lectures on the History of Literature.   Lond.
(Bohn Lib.), 1882.   273–74.

SCHMICK, H.   Spenser und seine Fairy Queen.   In Archiv. f. d.
Stud., XXIII (1858), 39–62.
   Negligible.

SCHOFIELD, W. H.   Chivalry in English Literature.   Chaucer,
Malory, Spenser, and Shakespeare.   Cambr. 1912.   142 ff.

SÉLINCOURT, E. DE.   Introd. to his one-volume Oxford ed. of
Sp.   Pp. xl–lxvii:
   A sound short treatment.   See p. lii *n:* List of identifications of
   characters in FQ.

SKEAT, WALTER W.   A Student's Pastime.   Oxford, 1896.   354:
   On FQ, I, i, 8, and Sp's "tree-list."

SPENCE, JOSEPH.   Polymetis.   Lond. 1747.   2d ed. 1755.
   Dialogue xix: "The Defects of our Modern Poets, in their Allegories: instanced from Spenser's Fairy Queen."   Three main defects:
   (1) mixture of heathen and Christian mythology, (2) misrepresenting
   the allegories of the ancients, (3) "something that is wrong in the allegories of his own invention."   These heads illustrated in detail.   The
   meticulous inquiry of a rather naïve purist whose sense of critical duty
   struggles with his natural delight in Sp.   If this list of Sp's faults
   "should prejudice you at all against so fine a writer, read almost any
   one of his entire Cantos, and it will reconcile you to him again."   And
   see passage at end of preceding Dialogue: Sp "a very great man,
   whose genius I respect . . . . the best allegorist, as I take it, among
   all modern poets."

SULLY, JAS.   Dreams as related to Literature.   In The Forum,
VII (1889), 68:
   The dream-like quality of the FQ.

TUCKWELL, WM.   Spenser.   Lond. 1906.   38–68.

TUELL, ANNE K.   The Original End of *Faerie Queene*, Book III.
In Mod. Lang. Notes, XXXVI (1921), 309–11.

UPTON, JOHN.   Remarks on the Action and History of the
Faerie Queene.   See Upton's ed., I, pp. xx ff.   Quoted in
Todd's ed. of Sp, II.   Cf. Cory, Critics of Spenser, 149–50.

UPTON, JOHN. A Letter concerning a New Edition of Spenser's Faerie Queene. Lond. 1751.
> Discusses the plan, allegory, sources in Ovid and Chaucer, etc.

VAN DAM, B. A. P., and C. STOFFEL. Chapters on Eng. Printing. Heidelberg (Angl. Forschungen), 1902. 7–9.
> Textual emendations to FQ and some of the minor poems.

WALKER, JOS. C. Hist. Memoirs of the Irish Bards. Dublin, 1818. Repr. 1876. 96 *n:*
> That the Sir Ferraugh of FQ, IV, ii, 4, derives from the Irish legendary hero Forroch or Ferragh. Cf. 136 *n.*

WARTON, THOS. Observations on the Fairy Queen. Lond. 1752. Repr. in Todd's ed. of Sp, II.
> The standard commentary of the Romantic School.

WHITNEY, J. E. The Continued Allegory in the First Book of the Faery Queene. In Trans. Amer. Philol. Asso., XIX (1888), 40–69. Cf. Padelford, above.

WHITNEY, LOIS. Spenser's Use of the Literature of Travel in the *Faerie Queene.* In Mod. Philol., XIX (1921), 143–62:
> Especially on the material used in FQ, II, xii, and other incidental references to voyages of sixteenth century seamen; that the prologue to the FQ, II, dates 1584 or later. Parallels between the Legend of St. Brandan and FQ, II, xii. Other sources in Celtic legend, in Lucian, and in Tasso.

WILSON, JOHN ("Christopher North"). In Blackwood's Magazine, XXXVI (1834), 408–30, 681–737; XXXVII (1835), 49–71, 540–56, 659–76.
> General discussion of the FQ. Sympathetic and suggestive. Romanticist.

FAERIE QUEENE: CANTOS OF MUTABILITY

See also "Faerie Queene, General References."

BRANDON, SAMUEL. The Virtuous Octavia, 1598. Repr. Malone Soc., 1909. ll. 895 ff.
> Close analogue to the Mutability cantos (Qu. Did Brandon know them in MS before 1598?).

COLLIER, J. P. In his ed. of Sp, I, pp. cxx–xxi, cxxxii.

DE MOSS, W. F. The Influence of Aristotle's "Politics" and "Ethics" on Spenser. Chicago, 1918. 49–64.

DE VERE, A. Essays chiefly on Poetry, I, 74 ff.

Edinburgh Review, CLXI (1885), 160–68; CCI (1905), 164–88.

ELTON, O. Modern Studies. Lond. 1907. 30 ff.:
Relation of the Mutability cantos to Bruno. Cf. Greenlaw in Studies in Philology, XVII, 336 *n*.

EVANS, S. A Lost Poem by Edmund Spenser. In Macmillan's Magazine, XLII (1880), 145–51:
That Sp considered the FQ completed with six books published in 1596; true meaning of the letter to Raleigh; the Cantos of Mutabilitie not intended as part of FQ; the last two stanzas really an envoy; a study of the cantos as a separate poem; intended as a refutation of Bruno; Sp's philosophy of nature. Should be consulted. Cf Trent's ed. of Sp, p. xii *n*.

FALKINER, C. L. Essays rel. to Ireland. Lond. 1909. 26–31.
Mutability cantos compared with the V of I.

FURNIVALL, F. J. Spenser's Last Lines. In the Academy, Lond., VII (1875), 325:
That the last stanza of FQ, VII, viii (Mutability) were perhaps Sp's last lines, written after his flight to England.

GREENLAW, E. In Studies in Philology, XVII (1920), 320–59.

GREENLAW, E. The Sources of Spenser's Religion of Nature. To appear in Studies in Philol., 1923.

JACK, A. A. Chaucer and Spenser, 241–44.

MACKAIL, J. W. The Springs of Helicon. 132–33. Cf. 192.

Quarterly Review, CXCVI (1902), 503 ff.

SÉLINCOURT. Introd. to his one-volume ed. of Sp. P. xxxviii.

TRENT, W. P. In his ed. of Sp. P. xii *n*.

WISE, T. J. In his ed. of the FQ, 1897. I, p. lxxix:
These cantos not a part of the FQ. "Possibly they form the only surviving portion of a second projected or attempted Epic."

FAERIE QUEENE, SOURCES

See also "Sources, General," "Spenser and Chaucer," "Spenser and Dante," "Spenser and Sidney," "Faerie Queene, General References."

See the notes in various annotated eds. of the FQ or of single books thereof.

Analogues, near or remote, of many features in the FQ are to be found in most of the Romances, prose and metrical, before Sp. See esp. Malory's Morte d'Arthur, Eger and Grime, Amis and Amiloun, William of Palerne, Sir Degoré, Beves of Hampton, Guy of Warwick, Sir Eglamour, Libeaus Desconus. Most of these features are more or less conventionalized in the Romances and it is difficult to prove Sp's indebtedness in particular points.

*AMADIS DE GAULE. Les Livres I à XII. Paris, 1540–56.
Cf. Brunet, Manuel du Libraire, Paris, 1860, I, 206 ff., for the various editions and translations of this romance. Sp probably knew the French version. A copy of Anthony Munday's translation, 1619, is in the Univ. of Chicago Library. See Robert Southey's translation, repr. in "Library of Old Authors," Lond. 1872.

AYRES, H. M. The *Faerie Queene* and *Amis and Amiloun*. In Mod. Lang. Notes, XXIII (1908), 177–80.

*BAIHOFEN. Die Sage von Tanaquil. Heidelberg, 1870.

BASKERVILL, C. R. The Genesis of Spenser's Queen of Faerie. In Mod. Philol., XVIII (1920), 49–54:
The idea of the Fairy Queen as a symbolic "head of ancient chivalry" = influenced by the Entertainment at Kenilworth in 1575; other contemporary uses of the idea.

BERDAN, JOHN M. Early Tudor Poetry. N.Y. 1920. 116:
The "foundations" of the FQ in early 16th cent. literature.

Blackwood's Magazine, XCIX (1866), 200–23:
Sp and Ariosto.

BLANCHARD, H. H. Italian Influence on the "Faerie Queene." MS Diss., 1921, Harvard Library.
A study of the Influence of Boiardo, Ariosto, Tasso, and Dante on Sp.

BOND, R. W. Ariosto. In Quarterly Review, CCVIII (1908), 139–43:
Sources of FQ in Ariosto and Tasso; general features of Sp's borrowings; a general discussion supplementing Dodge.

BRANDL, A.   In Paul's Grundriss der germ. Philologie.   Strassburg, 1893.   II, pt. i, 689:
> Elements of the FQ found in Hawes.

BRIGGS, W. D.   Spenser's "Faerie Queene," III, ii, and Boccaccio's "Fiammetta."   In Matzke Memorial Volume, Stanford Univ. Pub., 1911.   57–61:
> A suggested source; parallelisms pointed out.

BROADUS, E. K.   The Red Cross Knight and Lybeaus Desconus.   In Mod. Lang. Notes, XVIII (1903), 202–4:
> Points of similarity in the story of the Red Cross Knight and Una and the story of Lybeaus Desconus.

BRUCE, J. D.   Spenser's *Faerie Queene*, Book III, canto VI, st. 11 ff., and Moschus' Idyl, *Love the Runaway*.   In Mod. Lang. Notes, XXVII (1912), 183–85:
> That Sp's passage derives from Moschus through the Prologue to Tasso's "Aminta."

CAXTON, WM.   The Book of the Ordre of Chyvalry or Knyghthode, n.d. (1484).   Repr. ed. F. S. Ellis, 1892.
> Has been suggested as a "source" of the FQ; but Sp could have used it only in the most general way.

COOK, A. S.   The House of Sleep: A Study in Comparative Literature.   In Mod. Lang. Notes, V (1890), 9–21:
> Sources of FQ, I, i, 39–46, in Ariosto, Poliziano, Chaucer, Statius, Ovid, etc.

DEGUILEVILLE, GUILLAUME DE.   The Pilgrimage of the Life of Man, englisht by J. Lydgate, Ed. F. J. Furnivall, Lond. (EET Soc.), 1899–1904.   Cf. Pt. III, pp. lxxv ff.

DE MOSS, W. F.   The Influence of Aristotle's "Politics" and "Ethics" on Spenser.   Chicago, 1918.   "Reprinted in part from Mod. Philol., XVI."

DE MOSS, W. F.   Spenser's Twelve Moral Virtues "according to Aristotle."   In Mod. Philol., XVI (1918), 23–38, and 245–70:
> Criticizes Jusserand's arguments.   (See under "Sources, General.")   Sp and Aristotle's "Ethics," points of agreement; Sp not indebted to Bryskett's Discourse.

Dodge, R. E. N.   Spenser's Imitations from Ariosto.   In Pub. Mod. Lang. Asso., XII (1897), 151–204:

> A thorough analysis of Sp's debt to Ariosto.   Standard.

Dodge, R. E. N.   Spenser's Imitations from Ariosto: Addenda. In Pub. Mod. Lang. Asso., XXXV (1920), 91–92.

Dunlop, J. C.   History of Prose Fiction.   Lond. (Bohn's Lib.), 1888.   I, 260:

> That the romance of Arthur of Britany "suggested to Spenser the plan and outline of his Faery Queene"; 378: on Southey's view of Sp's source in the Amadis; 407: analogues of the self-propelling gondelay in FQ, II, vi.
>
> II, 21: Analogues of magic mirror in FQ, III, iii; 218: Sources of FQ, II, iv.

Edinb. Review, CLXI (1885), 168–76:

> Sp and Lucretius.

Fletcher, J. B.   Huon of Burdeux and the Faerie Queene.   In Journal of Germ. Philology, II (1898), 203–12:

> Parallels between the two works (some of them rather fanciful).

Fowler, Earle B.   Spenser and the Courts of Love.   Menasha, Wis. 1921.   Univ. of Chicago Diss.

> Influence of mediaeval allegory of the courts of love on the FQ, esp. in its settings, atmosphere and characters, studied in detail; sources of various episodes considered.

Geoffrey of Monmouth.   Cf. J. E. Sandys in Cambr. Hist. Eng. Lit., I, 168 ff.   Cf. 284.   Cf. Carrie A. Harper, below.

Gilbert, A. H.   Spenser's Imitations from Ariosto: Supplementary.   In Pub. Mod. Lang. Asso., XXXIV (1919), 225–32:

> Supplements Dodge's list of parallels; "Spenser's conclusions and transitions in the manner of Ariosto."

Greenlaw, E.   Spenser and Lucretius.   In Studies in Philology, XVII (1920), 439–64:

> Sp's debt to Lucretius; the sources of the Garden of Adonis passage (FQ, III, vi) and of the Cantos of Mutability in Lucretius as well as in Plato and Ovid.

GREENLAW, E.   In Studies in Philology, XIII (1916), 122–54:
> Influence of Sidney's Arcadia on the Pastorella-Calidore episode in FQ, VI; their common source in Daphnis and Chloe (Longus); Ariosto subordinate as a source; Greene not a source; Tasso only in small part.

GREENLAW, E.   The Influence of Machiavelli on Spenser.   In Mod. Philol., VII (1909), 187–202.   Cf. H. S. V. Jones, below.

HALL, EDGAR A.   Spenser and Two Old French Grail Romances. In Pub. Mod. Lang. Asso., XXVIII (1913), 539–54:
> Debt of FQ, VI, i–ii to the Perlesvaus and parts of the Conte du Graal.

HARPER, CARRIE A.   The Sources of the British Chronicle History in Spenser's Faerie Queene.   Phila. 1910.   Bryn Mawr Diss.
> Sources of FQ, II, x, and III, iii; incidentally also III, ix, and IV, ii. Basis=in Geoffrey of Monmouth; less in Holinshed; here and there elsewhere, esp. Warner, Camden, Gorboduc and the Mirror for Magistrates; that FQ, II, x was "first planned as a separate poem," and that "it was partly written before Spenser decided to include it in the Faerie Queene," and "is to be grouped with the early [lost] Epithalamion Thamesis."   A solid, careful, and intelligently planned study.
> Cf. R. E. N. Dodge in Journal Eng. and Germ. Philology, XI (1912), 289–91; G. C. Macaulay in Mod. Lang. Review, VII (1912), 279; Jahrb. d. Shakespeare Gesellschaft, XLVIII (1912), 348; Lit. Centralblatt, LXII (1911), 1153; Archiv (Herrig's), CXXVII (1911), 478; Engl. Studien, XLIV (1912), 403–8.

HOLINSHED.   Chronicles.   App.
> On Raleigh in Ireland; suggested by Dean Church as source of various incidents.

HOLME, JAS. W.   Italian Courtesy-Books of the Sixteenth Century.   In Mod. Lang. Review, V (1910), 145–66.   Cf. 502–4.

HOOLE, JOHN.   Preface to Translation of Orlando Furioso, 1783.   In Chalmers' Poets, XXI; see pp. 5, 12.
> Resemblance of Sp to Ariosto; disadvantages of allegory, in such poems.

Huon of Bordeaux (Lord Berner's version), ed. S. L. Lee.   Lond. (EET Soc.), 1882–87.

JONES, H. S. V.   Spenser's Defense of Lord Grey.   Univ. of Ill. 1919.
> Sources of Sp's political philosophy in FQ, V, and elsewhere, in Bodin and others.

KER, W. P.   Epic and Romance.   Lond. 1897.   392:
> That Sp's Red Cross Knight "is founded upon Malory's Gareth" in the Morte d'Arthur; and that his story in part resembles some of the adventures in Renaud de Beaujeu's Guinglain (= Gawain).

KOEPPEL, E.   Edmund Spenser's Verhältniss zu Tasso.   In Anglia, XI (1889), 341–62:
> Sp's debt to Tasso studied in detail; parallel passages cited.

KOEPPEL, E.   Spenser's Florimel und die Britomartis Sage des Antoninus Liberalis.   In Herrig's Archiv, CVII (1901), 394–96.

Libeaus Desconus.   Cf. J. W. H. Atkins in Cambr. Hist. Eng. Lit., I, 295.
> Cf. Broadus, E.K., above, and Phetzing, A. C., below.

LOWES, J. L.   Spenser and the *Mirour de l'Omme*.   In Pub. Mod. Lang. Asso., XXIX (1914), 388–452:
> That this poem of Gower's, discovered in 1895 in a single extant MS, was known to Sp.   Influence on FQ, I, iv (The Seven Deadly Sins); use also of the Confessio Amantis; traces of Gower in other passages of the FQ.   Qu: Do both Sp and Gower draw on common material?

MACARTHUR, J. R.   The Influence of Huon of Burdeux upon the Fairie Queene.   In Journal of Germ. Philology, IV (1902), 215–38:
> In part a reply to J. B. Fletcher's theory (see above).   Finds the influence of Huon on Sp only in minor details.

MACKAIL, J. W.   The Springs of Helicon.   92–94:
> Sp and Livy; 97–98: Sp's Greek sources.

MADDEN, SIR FREDERIC.   Introd. to his ed. of Syr Gawayne. Lond. (Bannatyne Club), 1839.   P. xli:
> Sp's debt to the Gawain romances.

MALORY'S Morte d'Arthur.
> Cf. J. W. Hales, Folia Literaria, 21–22.

MANLY, J. M. In Encycl. Britannica, IX (1910), 612 b:
That the FQ owes nothing to Hawes in general conception or in detail.

MAYER, C. La Reine des Fées. Paris, 1860. Ch. v.

MAYNADIER, H. The Arthur of the English Poets. Bost. 1907. Ch. xv. "Spenser."
Similarity of Sp's poetry to mediaeval romance in characters, incidents, names, etc.

MEAD, W. E., ed. Selections from Malory's Morte d'Arthur. Bost. 1901. Introduction, pp. xli–ii:
"A few passages [in the FQ] that suggest an acquaintance with Malory."

MURISON, WM. In Cambr. Hist. Eng. Lit., II (1908), 233–35:
Influence of Hawes on Sp estimated; points of resemblance listed, e.g., idea of discipline of the hero; chivalry in allegorical symbolism; symbolical armor, after St. Paul; similar allegorical figures, etc.

Notes and Queries, Ser. I, Vol. XI (1855), 121, 391; Ser. VIII, Vol. IV (1893), 165, 215.

NUTT, ALFRED. The Fairy Mythology of English Literature. In Folk Lore, VIII (1897), 29–53.

OEHNINGER, LUDWIG. Die Verbreitung der Koenigssagen der Historia Regum Britanniae von Geoffrey of Monmouth in der poetischen elisabethanischen Literatur. Muenchen, 1903. 98 ff.

OSGOOD, C. G. See "Faerie Queene, General."

PADELFORD, F. M. See "Faerie Queene, General."

PERRETT, W. The Story of King Lear, from Geoffrey of Monmouth to Shakespeare. Berlin, 1904. 90–92.

PHETZING, AMELIA C. The History of the Fair Unknown. MS Diss. (1920) in Univ. of Chicago Library.
Ch. vii deals with FQ, I and its sources in Libeaus Desconus and elsewhere.

POWELL, CHILTON L. English Domestic Relations, 1487–1653. N.Y., Columbia Univ. Press, 1917. Ch. iv:
The Domestic Conduct Book; and 187–89: Influence of the conduct books on FQ.

POWELL, C. L. See "Faerie Queene, General."

SACKVILLE, THOS. Induction to the Mirror for Magistrates. In Works, ed. Sackville-West. Lond. 1859.

This poem not only shows more dignity, elevation, and imaginative amplitude of style than anything in modern English poetry before Sp (and so influenced Sp), but also furnished closer models for Sp's method of Personification. See, e.g., stanzas 32 ff.

SAINTSBURY, GEO. Short Hist. Eng. Lit., 1898. 132 *n*.
Sp and Piers Plowman.

SANDYS, J. E. See Geoffrey of Monmouth, above.

SCHOEMBS, J. Ariosts Orlando Furioso in der engl. Litt. des Zeitalters der Elizabeth. Soden, 1898. Diss. 54–67:
Parallels between OF and FQ.

SÉLINCOURT, E. DE. Introd. to his one-volume Oxford ed. of Sp. Pp. lvi–lvii.

SIDNEY, PHILIP. The Countess of Pembrokes' Arcadia, 1590. (Written before 1586). Facsimile Reprint, ed. H. O. Sommer. Lond. 1891.

Possibly Sidney suggested to Sp the writing of the FQ. (See "W. L.'s" verses prefixed to the FQ). Sp probably knew the Arcadia in MS and was strongly influenced by it in a general way and also specifically, e.g., the name Pyrocles, the hair of the heroine falling about her face, the general atmosphere of an ideal world of mingled knights, ladies and shepherds, the complexity of incidents, certain points of style, etc. The influence appears especially in the last three books of the FQ (written after the publication of the Arcadia in 1590?); Book III of the Arcadia (combats and knight errantry) is quite in the vein of the FQ. The influence was probably reciprocal.

SKELTON, JOHN. The Bowge of Courte.

Probably gave Sp suggestions not only for his satire of the court, but also and more especially for his method of personification and for a few specific figures, e.g. see the description of Disdain (ll. 288 ff.), of Riot (ll. 344 ff.), etc. Cf. also Skelton's Colyn Cloute for the name, and the satire on the clergy, illiterate priests, Simony, etc.

SNELL, F. J. The Age of Transition. Lond. 1905. I, 120:
Anticipations of Sp in Hawes.

SOUTHEY, ROBT., ed. Palmerin of England. Lond. 1807. I pp. xlii–iv:
That Sp imitates Amadis of Greece.

VEGETIUS. L'art de cheualerie selon Vegece . . . . explicit le livre de droit d'armes . . . . 1488.

"L'ouvrage est moins une traduction de Végèce qu'un traité sur l'art de la guerre. . . . . On y trouve beaucoup de choses relatives à la chevalerie du moyen âge. On l'attribue à Jean de Meun" (Brunet, Manuel, V, 1111). At sig. 4a, col. 2, is a heading: "Icy sont declairés les douze vertus que vng noble homme et de noble couraige doibt auoir en son cueur." The twelve virtues are then described (in verse). They are: Noblesse, Foy, Feaulte, Honneur, Droicture, Prouesse, Amour, Courtoisie, Diligence, Nectete, Largesse, Sobresse (H.R.P.).

See Caxton's Translation "The Fayt of Armes and of Chyvalrye (1489). C. ascribes the work to Christine of Pisa. Cf. Todd's ed. of Sp, 1805, I, p. liv (Source of the "twelve virtues"). Copies of Caxton's translation in Huntington Lib. and in Library of J. P. Morgan.

Cf. Wm. Blades, Life and Typography of Caxton. Lond. 1863. II, 205 ff.

Cf. John Macfarlane, Antoine Vérard. Lond. (Bibliog. Soc.), 1900.

WALTHER, MARIE. Malory's Einfluss auf Spenser's Faerie Queene. Eisleben, n.d. (189–). Diss.

Superficial, but notes the more striking points of resemblance. See esp. 8 ff.: names of characters in common; and of places.

WHITNEY, LOIS. See "Faerie Queene, General."

WINSTANLEY, LILIAN. Introd. to her ed. of FQ, I, pp. xliii–lxxx; and her ed. of FQ, II, Introd., ch. iii:

Emphasizes and traces Sp's debt to the romances, esp. The Seven Champions, Bevis of Hampton, Huon of Bordeux; also The Court of Love poems; Chaucer; Classical Sources; Renaissance sources, incl. Ascham, Castiglione, and Vives.

Similarly her ed. of Book II, pp. xviii–li (Sources), and li–lxxii ("Spenser and Aristotle").

ZANDER, FRIEDRICH. Stephen Hawes "Passetyme of Pleasure" verglichen mit Edmund Spenser's "Faerie Queene," unter Berücksichtigung der allegorischen Dichtung in England. Ein Beitrag zur Quellenfrage der Faerie Queene. Rostock, 1905. Diss.

MINOR POEMS, COMPLAINTS, ETC.

The Complaints volume: "The poems were mostly earlier ones, revised, and were possibly published before. Of the 'Ruines of Rome' and 'Mother Hubberd's Tale' there is a MS extant decidedly varying from Ponsonby's text (Brit. Mus. Add. MS 34064)"—J. B. Fletcher. Cf. Mod. Lang. Notes, XXII (1907), 41–46.

BROWN, T. E.   In the New Review, XVI (1897), 393–404.

Catalogue of Books and MSS bequeathed by Francis Douce to the Bodleian Library.   Ox. 1840.
> MSS, p. 46, no. cclxxx, 4, 6, 7: MS copies of MHT, T of M, and V of P.

COLLIER, J. P.   In his ed. of Sp, I, pp. lxxiv ff.

COURTHOPE, W. J.   Hist. Eng. Poetry, III, p. xxxii.

CRAIK, G. L.   Spenser and his Poetry, III, sect. iv.

EMERSON, O. F.   Spenser, Lady Carey, and the Complaints Volume.   In Pub. Mod. Lang. Asso., XXXII (1917), 306–22:
> Supplements Long's study of the subject; plan of the volume; its typographical peculiarities.

FLETCHER, J. B.   Spenser's Earliest Translations.   In Journal of Eng. and Germ. Philology, XIII (1914), 305–8:
> Further notes supplementing Friedland (see below under "Theatre of Worldlings"). Of Ponsonby's part in the Complaints volume; does Sp use him as "a blind," as he did E.K.? The arrangement of the volume.

GAYLEY, C. M., and B. P. KURTZ.   Methods and Materials of Lit. Crit.   Bost. 1920.   II, 403:
> Sp's "Complaints"; analogues; they fall under the head of "The Elegy."

GROSART'S ed. of Sp, I, 175 ff.; III, 2 ff.

JORTIN, JOHN.   Tracts.   Lond. 1790.   I, 260–81:
> Annotations on some of the Minor Poems.

LEE, S.   The French Renaissance in Engl., 237:
> Origin of the title "Complaints" in Marot.

LONG, P. W.   See also under "Life, General References."

LONG, P. W.   In Englische Studien, XLIV (1912), 263–66:
> Date of the Complaints; and of Sp in Lond. 1590–91; dating of CCCHA "from Kilcolman"; date of Daphnaida.

PALGRAVE, F. T.   Essay on the Minor Poems of Spenser.   In Grosart's ed. of Sp, IV, pp. ix–cvii.

Retrospective Review, XII (1825), 142–65: "Spenser's Minor Poems."
> Superficial comment, with long extracts.

ROBINSON, RICHARD.   A Golden Mirror.   1589.   Copy in Brit. Museum.
> Poetical "Visions"; to be compared with Sp's; less emblematic, more mediaeval.

SCOTT, MARY A.   Eliz. Translations from the Italian.   Bost. 1916.   137–39:
> Italian sources of the Complaints.   Cf. Pub. Mod. Lang. Asso., XI (1896), 405–6.

SÉLINCOURT, in his ed. of Sp's Minor Poems.   Pp. xvi–xxi:
> The editions, MSS, etc.

SÉLINCOURT.   Introd. to his one-volume Oxford ed. of Sp. Pp. xxix ff.

SMITH, REED.   Allegory and its Use by Spenser in his Minor Poems.   MS Diss., 1909.   In Harvard Library.

AMORETTI

BERDAN, JOHN M.   Spenser's Amoretti.   MS read at Baltimore meeting of Mod. Lang. Asso., Dec. 1921.
> Discusses the tendency to seek French influence in the Amoretti and to explain them by giving a late date of composition; this is merely an assumption; Sp's inclination would be to resort to Italian rather than French material; a great variety of Italian models were accessible to him in the Italian anthologies.   Sonnet 30 imitates Cazza (in Rime Scelte, various editions from 1563 to 1590); imitations from the same anthology in sonnets 3, 18, 34, 73, 77, 81; Sonnet 57 is suggested from Rime Diverse, 2; 9 and 10 from 5; 48 and 58 from I Fiori.   These may not be distinct "sources," but are close analogues demonstrating the conventional nature of many of the Amoretti, suggesting question as to the integrity of the sequence.

BORGHESI, P.   Petrarch and his Influence on Engl. Lit.   Bologna, 1906.   102–4:
> Sp scarcely a Petrarchist, but has "much of the Platonism of Petrarch"; his poetry not Italian in its inner spirit, but his sonnets

"are Italian, or at least more or less Italianated"; inferiority of his sonnets; "he intellectuallizes his emotion so much that it is emotion no longer."

BORLAND, LOIS. In Mod. Philol., XI (1913), 132.

CHALMERS, GEO. Supplemental Apology. Lond. 1799. 21–39: That the Amoretti were addressed to Queen Elizabeth; the sonnets discussed; "written as an apology for the delay of the Faerie Queene."

CHURCH'S ed. of FQ, 1758, I, pp. xxxiii–vii.

COLLIER'S ed. of Sp, I, pp. cxi ff.

COOK, A. S. Five Spenserian Trifles. In Journal of Eng. and Germ. Philology, XVII (1918), 289–90: Suggested emendations to the text of the Amoretti.

CORSON, H. A Primer of Eng. Verse. Bost. 1892. 182–83: Versification of the Amoretti.

DENNIS, J. Studies in Eng. Lit. Lond. 1876. 405–8.

DESHLER, C. D. Afternoons with the Poets. N.Y. 1879. 46–60.

DRAPER, J. W. In the Colonnade, 1922. XIV, 37–38: Biographical material in Sp's sonnets.

ERSKINE, J. The Eliz. Lyric. 153–58: "The individual sonnets have not the merit of the series as a whole"; effect of the rhyme scheme; a true sequence; "the series is really but one poem"; special characteristics of the parts; the emphasis on Platonic beauty. 171: Debt of Shakespeare to Sp in the sonnets.

FLETCHER, J. B. Mr. Sidney Lee and Spenser's *Amoretti*. In Mod. Lang. Notes, XVIII (1903), 111–13: Criticism of Lee's theory that the "Idea" of the sonnets is the Platonic conception.

GOLLANCZ, I. In Proceedings of Brit. Academy, 1907–8. 99 ff. A variant version of sonnet 1.

GREENE, DR. MAURICE. Spenser's Amoretti set to Music. Lond. 1739, and 1775. Cf. Notes and Queries, Ser. IV, Vol. I (1868), .127.

GROSART'S ed. of Sp, I, 195 ff., 511–28.

HARMAN, E. G. Edmund Spenser. Ch. xiv: Queen Elizabeth the subject of the sonnets.

[HITCHCOCK, E. A.] Spenser's Colin Clouts Come Home Againe Explained. N.Y. 1866.
> The Amoretti interpreted as "hermetic studies."

HUNT, T. W. Spenser and Later Sonnet-writers. In Bibliotheca Sacra, LXVIII (1911), 264–67.
> Negligible.

JOHNSON, C. F. Forms of Eng. Poetry. 116–17.

KASTNER, L. E. Spenser's "Amoretti" and Desportes. In Mod. Lang. Review, IV (1908), 65–69:
> Sp borrows from Desportes rather than from Petrarch; parallels analyzed. Cf. III (1908), 271: Sp borrows little from Du Bellay. Cf. Mod. Philol., IX, 221.

KEIGHTLEY, T. In Brit. Quar. Review, XXII (1855), 395:
> The Amoretti not all addressed to Sp's wife.

KEIGHTLEY, THOS. In Fraser's Magazine, LX (1859), 419–20:
> Interpretation of Sp's love-story from the Amoretti.

KELLY, JAMES FITZMAURICE. History of Spanish Literature. N.Y. 1898. 186:
> A close analogue of Sonnet 81, in Francisco de la Torre; a common Italian source probable.

KELLY, J. F. Note on Three Sonnets. In Revue Hispanique, XIII (1905), 257–60:
> The same subject; the common Italian source found in Tasso.

LEE, SIDNEY. The French Renaissance in England. N.Y. 1910. 219–20:
> That the Cupid and the Bee epigrams printed with the Amoretti follow French versions (after Anacreon), of which six had appeared before 1573. "His version approaches far more closely to that of Ronsard or Baïf than to Anacreon's original Greek."
> 261–63: Sp does not borrow slavishly from French sources in his sonnets, yet "Desportes was clearly a dominant master of Spenser's sonneteering muse."

LEE, SIDNEY, ed. Elizabethan Sonnets. N.Y. n.d. I, pp. xxxiv–vii, xlviii, xcii–ix:
> Sp one of the parents of the Eliz. sonnets; analogues and models in continental sonnets; use of Bellay and Marot; his verse; source in Petrarch, Ronsard, etc.; autobiographical features.

LEE, SIDNEY. The Elizabethan Sonnet. In Cambr. Hist.
Eng. Lit. Cambr. 1909. III, 250–52:
  Sp's early sonnets; their French sources.
  257–60: The Amoretti, form, sources in Tasso, Ronsard, Desportes,
  etc.; leading motives traced to a common poetic stock; conceits; etc.
  Of value for its tracing of sources, but otherwise unenlightening.

LITTLEDALE, H. A Note on Spenser's "Amoretti." In Mod.
Lang. Review, VI (1911), 203:
  That sonnet 15 is borrowed from Desportes' Diane, I, xxxii.

LONG, P. W. In Mod. Lang. Review, III (1908), 257–67:
  That Sp wrote the Amoretti after his marriage; Elizabeth Lady
  Carey = the Elizabeth of the Amoretti.

LONG, P. W. See also under "Four Hymns."

LONG, P. W. Spenser's Sonnets "As Published." In Mod.
Lang. Review, VI (1911), 390–97:
  That the lady sung in the Amoretti is not the same as the lady of
  the Epithal.; the two poems not companion pieces. Cf. Mod. Lang.
  Review, IV, 256–67; V, 273–81.

LONG, P. W. Courtly Love in the Reign of Queen Elizabeth.
1906. MS Diss. in Harv. Lib. Pp. 185–89.

MACINTIRE, ELIZ. J. In Pub. Mod. Lang. Asso., XXVI (1911),
521 ff.
  Comparison of the Amoretti with Ronsard's Amours.

MORE, PAUL E. Shelburn Essays. N.Y. 1905. II, 1–19:
  "Elizabethan Sonnets." A review of S. Lee's Eliz. Sonnets, and a
  critical estimate of the Eliz. sonnet cycles.

PALGRAVE, F. T. In Grosart's ed. of Sp, IV, pp. lxxxvii–xcii.

Penn. Monthly, VI (1875), 739–48: "An Elizabethan Courtship."
  Discursive discussion of the sonnets as autobiographical material.
  Cf. Sp ed. Grosart, I, 195.

REED, E. B. English Lyrical Poetry. New Haven, 1912.
164–67.

SECCOMBE, T., and J. W. ALLEN. The Age of Shakespeare.
Lond. 1903. I, 22–24.

SÉLINCOURT in his ed. of Sp's Minor Poems, pp. xxiv–vi.

SÉLINCOURT. Introd. to his one-volume Oxford ed. of Sp, pp. xxxv ff.:
> That while they may contain some extraneous material "Spenser intended them to be regarded as addressed to his future wife."

SMITH, J. C. The Problem of Spenser's Sonnets. In Mod. Lang. Review, V (1910), 273–81:
> That the Amoretti and Epithal. are addressed to the same lady; disputes P. W. Long's theory of the relations of Sp and Lady Carey; parallels in the two poems. Cf. Mod. Lang. Rev., VI, 203.

TODD'S ed. of Sp, 1805, I, pp. cvii–cx.

WILSON, JOHN. In Blackwood's Magazine, XXXIV (1833), 848–49.

ZOCCO, IRENE. Petrarchismo e Petrarchisti in Inghilterra. Palermo, 1906. 89–95:
> Finds in Googe, Spenser, and Habington exceptions to the statement that the sonnets of the poets of the period are not based on real experience or emotion; notes Petrarchan echoes in the Amoretti, but minimizes the conventional elements therein; echoes of Watson in Sp; the originality of Sp's Petrarchistic poetry in his conception of woman; Sp's improvements on the sonnet-sequence commonplaces.

ASTROPHEL

See under "Spenser and Sidney."

COLLIER, J. P. In his ed. of Sp, I, pp. lv–vi; cx, cxxii.

ERSKINE, JOHN. The Elizabethan Lyric. N.Y. 1903. 187–89:
> "The general tone of this narrative-lyric is Greek and suggests the Homeric Hymns."

GROSART'S ed. of Sp, I, 209 ff.

HUGHES, M. Y. Relation of Spenser's Poetry to Classical Literature. Harv. Diss., MS. App. I.

KERLIN, R. T. Theocritus in Eng. Lit., 19:
> Its source in Theocritus.

PALGRAVE, F. T. In Grosart's ed. of Sp, IV, pp. ci–civ.

SHAFER, R. Spenser's Astrophel. In Mod. Lang. Notes, XXVIII (1913), 224–26:
> A study of its sources in Bion.

SHERMAN, S. P. In Pub. Mod. Lang. Asso., XXIV (1909), 285.

COLIN CLOUT'S COME HOME AGAIN

CHILD, F. J.   In his ed. of Sp, I, pp. xxxvi–vii.

CHURCH'S ed. of FQ, 1758, I, pp. xxx–ii:
> The date of CCCHA; and of Sp's being then in England.

COLLIER, J. P.   In his ed. of Sp, I, pp. lxxii–xciii (on the date); cxxi–ii.

COLLIER, J. P.   In his ed. of Shakespeare, 1858, I, 105–7.

COLLIER, J. P.   Hist. Eng. Dram. Poetry. Lond. 1879, II, 339 *n*.
> Palaemon = Alabaster, of whose verse he gives specimens.

COURTHOPE, W. J.   Hist. Eng. Poetry, III, 9 ff.

FLEAY, F. G.   Guide, 89–96.

FLETCHER, GILES.   Licia, 1593. Repr. in Miscellanies of the Fuller Worthies Lib., III, 1871.   Cf. 87:
> On the contrast between base love and true love—illustrating Sp's lore of love as expounded in CCCHA.

FRAUNCE, ABRAHAM [the "Corydon" of CCCHA].
> Fullest account of Fraunce in G. C. Moore Smith's Introd. to his ed. of Fraunce's Victoria. Louvain (Materialien, XIV), 1906. Cf. J. G. Underhill, Spanish Lit. in the England of the Tudors. N.Y. 1899. 269 ff.

GREG, W. W.   Pastoral Poetry. Lond. 1906.   98 ff.

GROSART'S ed. of Sp, I, 172 ff.

HARRISON, J. S.   Platonism in Eng. Poetry, 122.

HAZLITT, W. C.   Shakespear, Himself and his Work. Lond. 1912.   52, 288: "Aëtion."

[HITCHCOCK, E. A.]   Spenser's Colin Clout's Come Home Again Explained.   N.Y. 1866.
> The text given, with discursive commentary, moralizing the text and finding it to be a deep allegory of life. Fantastic. Reviewed in N.Y. Nation, II (1866), 182–83.

JOYCE, P. W.   In Fraser's Magazine, N.S. XVII (1878), 315–33.

JUSSERAND, J. J.   Hist. Litt. du peuple Anglais.   II, 388, 392.

LEE, SIDNEY.   Life of Shakespeare.   N.Y. 1898.   79–81.

LE FRANC, A. Sous le masque de Shakespeare. Paris, 1918.
I, ch. iii:

> That Amyntas is Ferdinando, Earl of Derby, and Aëtion is William Stanley his brother; the family arms bore an eagle. Full study of the Stanley family.

LONG, P. W. Courtly Love. Harv. Diss. P. 188.

LONG, P. W. Spenser's Dating of "Colin Clout." In The Nation, N.Y., LXXXIII (Nov. 1, 1906), 368–69:

> CCCHA dated from Kilcolman 27 Dec. 1591 and Daphnaida from London 1 Jan. 1591, explained as a literary device. Cf. Sélincourt, Introd. to his one-volume Oxford ed. of Sp, p. xxxi *n.*

LOONEY, J. T. "Shakespeare" Identified. Lond. 1920. 73:

> Aëtion not Shakespeare.

LOUNSBURY, THOS. R. Studies in Chaucer. N.Y. 1892.
III, 56:

> The imitations of Chaucer's verse in CCCHA.

MALONE, E. In his ed. of Shakespeare, 1821. II, 226–79:

> Analysis of the poem. The date (written 1594); the allusions: Harpalus = Churchyard; Coridon = Fraunce; Alcyon = Gorges; Palin (Palinode) = Peele; Alcon = Lodge; Palemon = Golding; so Alabaster, Daniel, Raleigh; Amyntas = Earl of Derby; Aëtion = Shakespeare; with copious particulars on these names as embodied in Sp's allusions.

MOFFATT, JAMES S. *Colin Clout's Come Home Again.* MS Diss. 1919. In Lib. of Univ. of North Carolina.

> The relation of the poem to pastoral and to court of love conventions; its relation to Breton's Pilgrimage to Paradise; new light on the Rosalind story in Sp's poetry (E.G.).

NASHE, THOMAS. Pierce Penilesse, 1592. In Nashe's Complete Works, ed. Grosart, 1883–84. II, 132–35:

> An address to "thrice noble Amintas," and blame of "heavenly Spencer" that "in that honourable Catalogue of our English *heroes*, which insueth the conclusion of thy famous Faerie Queene, thou wouldst let so speciall a Piller of Nobilitie passe unsaluted." Did this passage prompt Sp's praise of "Amintas" in CCCHA? (So Todd conjectures, in his ed. of Sp, I, p. xc.)
>
> Cf. McKerrow's ed. of Works of Nashe, IV, 151: That Amintas = Earl of Derby; gives no opinion as to Sp's response to Nashe's reproof, but prints the names of those who *are* "saluted" in the FQ.

NICHOLSON, B. Spenser's Harpalus. In Notes and Queries, Ser. V, Vol. I (1874), 323–24.
That Harpalus=Puttenham.

PALGRAVE, F. T. In Grosart's ed. of Sp, IV, pp. lxxix–lxxxvii.

ROBERTSON, J. M. Shakespeare and Chapman. Lond. 1917. 119:
Aëtion=Drayton.

ROLFE, W. J. A Life of William Shakespeare. Bost. 1901. 521:
"Aëtion"=Shakespeare.

SÉLINCOURT, in his ed. of Sp's Minor Poems. P. xxiii.

SÉLINCOURT. Introd. to his one-volume Oxford ed. of Sp. Pp. xxxi n:
Its date; Ponsonby's preface "a piece of intentional mystification"; xxxv: "In no other poem are we more keenly sensible of the subtle charm of Spenser's personality than in this graceful piece of idealized autobiography."

The Shakspere Allusion-Book. N.Y. and Lond. 1909. I, 1:
That "Aëtion"=Shakespeare; that Sp finished the first draft of this poem in Dec. 1591, and later amplified it.

STOPES, CHARLOTTE C. Thomas Edwards, Author of "Cephalus and Procris." In Mod. Lang. Review, XVI (1921), 220, 222:
"Amyntas"=Ferdinando Lord Strange; "Aëtion"=Edwards.

TODD's ed. of Sp, 1805, I, pp. lxxxix–cv.

WARD, A. W. Hist. Eng. Dram. Lit. Lond. 1899. I, 493.

DAPHNAIDA

COLLIER, J. P. In his ed. of Sp, I, pp. lxxxviii ff.; cxxv f.

ERSKINE, J. The Elizabethan Lyric. N.Y. 1903. 176–77:
"Not a strict elegy according to the Greek model"; order of themes haphazard, and no note of consolation.

GROSART's ed. of Sp, I, 166 ff.

LONG, P. W. Courtly Love. Harv. Diss. P. 188.

NADAL, THOS. W. Spenser's *Daphnaida* and Chaucer's *Book of the Duchess*. In Pub. Mod. Lang. Asso., XXIII (1908), 646–61:
> Chaucer's poem as Sp's model and source; parallelisms traced in detail. Cf. Shaks. Jahrb., XLVI (1910), 204.

PALGRAVE, F. T. In Grosart's ed. of Sp, IV, pp. lxxvi–viii.

SÉLINCOURT. In his ed. of Sp's Minor Poems. Pp. xxi–iii.

TODD'S ed. of Sp, 1805, I, pp. lxxxvii–ix.

WILSON, JOHN. In Blackwood's Magazine, XXXIV (1833), 843–48.

EPITHALAMION

See also references under "Amoretti," above.

CASE, R. H., ed. English Epithalamies. Lond. 1896.
> See Introd. for sketch of the history of the genre.

COLLIER, J. P. In his ed. of Sp, I, pp. cxvii–viii.

ERSKINE, J. The Elizabethan Lyric. N.Y. 1903. 16:
> Lyrical in quality, but in form an idyl or series of stanza-pictures. 189–93: "The complete poem is a series rather than an organic whole" [a very misleading statement if its structure be studied and its general effect recalled]; its combination of singing quality and of erudition, of conventional material and spontaneous effect; its external form.

HARMAN, E. G. Edmund Spenser. Ch. xiv:
> That the Epithal. does not celebrate Sp's marriage, but was written for an impending marriage of Queen Elizabeth.

HARRISON, J. S. Platonism in Eng. Poetry, 31–33.

JOHNSON, C. F. Forms of Eng. Poetry. N.Y. 1904. 149–52.

JUSSERAND. Hist. litt. du peuple Anglais, II, 393 ff.

LEGOUIS, ÉMILE. L'"Epithalame" d'Edmund Spenser traduit en vers français. In Revue de Littérature Comparée, I (1921), 398–415:
> With Introd. and brief notes: the Epithalamion in its class=unrivaled in the world's literature. The poem analyzed; local color in it. "Sa beauté est avant tout dans la largeur du rythme et la richesse de chaque tableau."

Long, P. W.   In Mod. Lang. Review, III (1908), 257–67:
> That Sp was married before the writing of the Epithal.

Long, P. W.   See also under "Amoretti."

Lowell, J. R.   The Old English Dramatists.   Bost., 1892.
29:
> "The whole metrical movement of the 'Epithalamion' recalls that of Petrarca's noble 'Spirto gentil.'"

Mackail, J. W.   The Springs of Helicon, 102–3.

Milner, Geo.   See under "Versification."

Notes and Queries, Ser. X, Vol. III (1905), 246:
> Its verse form; 412, 474.

Palgrave, F. T.   In Grosart's ed. of Sp, IV, pp. xciv–vi.

Sélincourt.   Introd. to his one-volume Oxford ed. of Sp.
Pp. xxxv–vi.

Tuckwell, W. M.   Spenser.   34–36.

Wilson, John.   In Blackwood's Magazine, XXXIV (1833),
849–52.

FOUR HYMNS

See also T of M, "Erato."

Bellay's Sonnet to Heavenly Beauty, 1550 (trans. in A. Lang, Ballads and Lyrics of Old France, 11).

Benivieni, G.   Canzone e sonnetti della amore e della belleza divina, 1500.
> See Translation in Thos. Stanley's History of Philosophy.   Lond. 1655.   Cf. J. B. Fletcher, below.

Böhme, T.   Spensers Literarisches Nachleben.   Berlin, 1909.
37.

Bruno, Giordano.   The Heroic Enthusiasts.   Trans. L. Williams.   Lond. 1887.
> Passim; the original is one of the "sources."

Buoni.   Problems of Beautie.   Trans. S. L.   Lond. 1606.
> Illustrates the current of contemporary ideas inspiring the Four Hymns.   Copy in Newberry Lib., and in Univ. of Chicago.

CASTIGLIONE, BALDASSARE. Il Cortegiano, trans. by Sir Thos. Hoby, as The Book of the Courtier, 1561. Repr. with Introd. by Walter Raleigh. Lond. 1900 (Tudor Translations).
> See especially 342–65: the Doctrine of Love and Beauty. Cf. Raleigh's Introd. pp. lxviii–lxxvii.

CAVALCANTI. Ode of Love. Trans. in Mod. Philol., VII, 423.

CHURCH'S ed. of FQ, 1758, I, p. xxxvii.

COLLIER, J. P. In his ed. of Sp, I, pp. cxxiv ff.

COURTHOPE, W. J. Hist. Eng. Poetry, II, 241.

COURTHOPE, W. J. In Cambr. Hist. Eng. Lit., III, 215–17:
> Mainly on the sources of the first two Hymns, in Plato through Ficino (a close and instructive comparison); 243–44: briefly on the later Hymns.

CRAWFORD, CHAS. Collectanea. First Series. Stratford on Avon, 1906. 45.

ELTON, O. Modern Studies. 323.

ERSKINE, J. The Elizabethan Lyric. N.Y. 1903. 193–95.

FICINO, MARSILIO. Commentarium in Convivium. With the first edition (Latin) of Plato, Florence (1483). Copy in Newberry Lib. Italian version as Sopra lo Amore over' Convito di Platone. Firenze, 1544.
> A general source book for Sp's ideas.

FLETCHER, J. B. A Study in Renaissance Mysticism: Spenser's "Fowre Hymns." In Pub. Mod. Lang. Asso., XXVI (1911), 452–75:
> An interpretation of the Four Hymns as examples of neo-Platonic mysticism; and especially of their relation to Benivieni. Real nature of the contrast between the two early Hymns and the two later ones. The doctrine of love in its several stages. Sources in the Italian neo-Platonists. Who was Sp's "Sapience." The mystic union with the Holy Ghost through heavenly beauty in heavenly love.

FLETCHER, J. B. Benivieni's "Ode of Love" and Spenser's "Fowre Hymns." In Mod. Philol., VIII (1911), 545–60:
> That Sp draws more from Benivieni than from Ficino and Bruno (as Miss Winstanley assumes) for his neo-Platonism and Calvinism. The Ode translated and reprinted and compared with Sp in detail.
> Reprinted, revised, in Fletcher's The Religion of Beauty in Woman. N.Y. 1911. 116–46.

GREENLAW, E.   In Studies in Philology, XVII (1920), 345 ff.:
    A study of Sp's cosmos and philosophy in the Hymns.

GROSART'S ed. of Sp, I, 78–82, 206–9.

*HARRIS, R.   Origin of the Doctrine of the Trinity.   Manchester.
1919.
    For the source of Sp's "Sapience" (J. W. D.).

HARRISON'S Platonism in Eng. Poetry.   Ch. ii:
    Platonic conception of Love and Beauty in Sp (and others); sources
in Ficino and Italian Platonism, with exhibition of parallelisms; Sp's
general theory of aesthetics (109 ff.).   "Spenser is first a Platonist and
then a Christian."

HEROET, A.   La Parfaicte Amye, 1542.   See his Oeuvres
Poétiques, ed. F. Gohin.   Paris (Soc. des Textes Franç.
Mod.), 1909.   Cf. S. Lee, French Renaissance in England,
114–15.

HOLME, J. W.   In Mod. Lang. Review, V (1910), 164:
    Guazzo as an analogue of the Hymns.

LONG, P. W.   The Date of Spenser's Earlier Hymns.   In Englische Studien, XLVII (1913), 197–208:
    A study of internal evidence bearing on the date and their place
in Sp's life; probably written c. 1590; their connection with the Amoretti and Teares of the Muses, of similar date.

OSGOOD, C. G.   Spenser's Sapience.   In Studies in Philology,
XIV (1917), 167–77:
    The figure of "Sapience" in the Hymn of Heavenly Beauty.
Various interpretations; sources in several biblical passages.   See R.
Harris, above.

PADELFORD, F. M.   Spenser's Fowre Hymnes.   In Journal of
Eng. and Germ. Philology, XIII (1914), 418–33:
    By way of modification of J. B. Fletcher's view of the Hymns, holds
that the two earlier hymns are "in accord with this neo-Platonic theory
of love," but the two later "are based upon Calvinistic doctrines that
are squarely opposed to it."   The neo-Platonic view expounded by
Castiglione contrasted with Sp's later views.   Analysis of the Hymns.
Platonic elements abundant in the last two hymns, but all "construed

to the satisfaction of Calvinism and disciplined to its creed." Sp's view of the function of love and woman's beauty, and treatment of the theme in the FQ.

PALGRAVE, F. T.   In Grosart's ed. of Sp, IV, pp. xcvii–c.

RALEIGH, W.   Introd. to Castiglione's Book of the Courtier. Lond. (Tudor Transl.), 1900.

SÉLINCOURT.   In his ed. of Sp's Minor Poems, p. xxvi.

SHELLEY's Hymn to Intellectual Beauty.

STANLEY, THOS.   History of Philosophy, 1656. Pt. V.

THOMAS, G.   Etude sur l'Expression de l'Amour Platonique dans la Poésie Italienne du moyen âge et de la Renaissance. Paris, 1892.
> Growth of the conception, esp. in Dante, Petrarch, Lorenzo de Medici, Ficino, and Michael Angelo.

WINSTANLEY, LILIAN, ed.   The Fowre Hymns.   Cambr. 1907. Introd.:
> Sp and Plato, ix–xxviii; infl. of Plato on FH, xxviii–lvii; infl. of Ficino and Bruno on the FH, lviii–lxxii.

WYNDHAM, GEO.   Introd. to his ed. of the Poems of Shakespeare, N.Y. n.d.   Pp. cxix–cxxi:
> That the "Hymne in Honour of Beautie does but versify the argument" of the fourth book of Hoby's Translation of Castiglione's Il Cortegiano (1561).

LETTERS

See also "Life: Spenser and Harvey"; "Areopagus."

BERLI, HANS.   Gabriel Harvey.   Zurich, 1913.   57–60.

GROSART's ed. of Sp, I, 131 ff.

HARVEY's Marginalia, ed. G. C. Moore Smith, 27 ff.

LONG, P. W.   In Pub. Mod. Lang. Asso., XXXI (1916), 713–35:
> In part a study of the Letters, and their problems.

TODD's Life of Sp in his ed. of Sp, 1805, I, pp. i ff.
> Where the Letters are utilized in part.

MOTHER HUBBERD'S TALE

The history of fable-literature before Sp may be studied in various works by Saint-Marc Girardin, Hervieux, du Méril, Keidel, C. Robert, etc. See esp. the last named ("Fables Inédites, etc.) on the French and Italian fabulists of the Sixteenth century.

ALDEN, R. M. The Rise of Formal Satire in England. Phila. 1899. 74–75:
> Nature of the satire in MHT: "the first satire of the period to appear in the decasyllabic couplet"; framework based on mediaeval beast-fables, not from classical sources; original and not on conventional lines of Eliz. satire.

BRATHWAITE, RICHARD. Strappado for the Divell, 1615. Ed. J. W. Ebsworth. Boston (England), 1878, 129 ff.

BUCK, P. M., JR. In Mod. Lang. Notes, XXII (1907), 41–46:
> Variant readings from a MS c. 1596.

BUCK, P. M., JR. In Pub. Mod. Lang. Asso., XXIII (1908), 83–84:

CAXTON, WM. The History of Reynard the Fox (1481). Repr. ed. Arber. Lond. 1895.

CHILD, F. J. In his ed. of Sp, I, p. xxxiv.

CHURCH'S ed. of FQ, 1758, I, pp. xxvi–ix.

CHURCH, R. W. Spenser, 108–15.

COLLIER, J. P. Poetical Decameron, I, 100.
> Whether MHT in an earlier form was "called in."

COLLIER, J. P. In his ed. of Sp, I, pp. lxxxi ff.

CRAIK, G. L. Hist. Eng. Lit., I, 495, 497–503.

DRYDEN. Hind and Panther, Pt. III, ll. 1–11.

Father Hubberd's Tale. In Middleton's Works, ed. Bullen, VIII, 47 ff. Cf. also I, Introd.

GOLLANCZ, I. In Proceedings of Brit. Academy, 1907–8, 99–105:
> The "calling in" of MHT.

GREENLAW, E. In Pub. Mod. Lang. Asso., XXV (1910), 535–61, esp. 545 ff.:
> The MHT and its political allegory explained; first version c. 1579; evidences of later re-working; Simier = the ape, Burghley = the fox,

Elizabeth = the lion; the poem "primarily a Chaucerian story based on the Renard cycle," with added political satire. Cf. Winstanley's ed. of FQ, Bk. I, p. ix.

GREENLAW, E. The Sources of Spenser's "Mother Hubberd's Tale." In Mod. Philol., II (1905), 411–32:
> Source not in Doni's Morall Philosophie as Grosart maintains, but is in the Renard the Fox cycle, the prologue being suggested by the Decameron.

GREENLAW, E. The Influence of Machiavelli on Spenser. In Mod. Philol., VII (1909), 187–202:
> On the sources of MHT. In Machiavelli. Cf. H. S. V. Jones, Spenser's Defense of Lord Grey: an answer to Greenlaw, denying Sp's sympathy with or dependence on Machiavelli.

GROSART'S ed. of Sp, I, 82–89, 178 ff.

HALES, J. W. Old Mother Hubbard. In the Athenaeum, 1883, I, 248:
> On folk-lore as to Mother Hubbard; possibly connected with St. Hubert.

HARVEY, GABRIEL. Works, ed. Grosart, 1884. I, 164 (from "Foure Letters," 1592):
> That "Mother Hubbard, in heat of choller . . . . wilfully over-shot her malcontented selfe. . . . ."
> 205: On the "invective and satyricall spirites" of the time, who "can tell parlous tales of beares and foxes as shrewdlye as mother Hubbard, for her life."

HIGGINSON'S Spenser's Shepherd's Calender. 90, 161 n, 321 ff.

JUSSERAND. Hist. litt. du peuple Anglais. II, 390.

JUSSERAND. In Revue de Paris. 1 May, 1903. 63.

KEIGHTLEY, T. In Brit. Quar. Review, XXII (1855), 385–89:
> Its quality as satire; its date (c. 1583–84); the ape = Earl of Oxford; etc.

LONG, P. W. In Pub. Mod. Lang. Asso., XXXI (1916), 725 ff.:
> MHT suggested by Dr. Young's Sermon, 1575, where is recited the fable motif.

LOUNSBURY, T. R. Studies in Chaucer. N.Y. 1892. III, 56:
> Imitations of Chaucer's verse in MHT.

MACINTIRE, ELIZ. J.   In Pub. Mod. Lang. Asso., XXVI (1911), 524–25.

NASHE, THOMAS.   Complete Works, ed. Grosart, Huth Lib. 1883–84.

 II, 106–9 (Pierce Penilesse, 1592): A fable partly in imitation of MHT.

 II, 212 (Strange Newes, 1593): Attacks Harvey for bringing in Mother Hubbard for an instance, and so doing a disservice to Sp. "Who publikely accusde or of late brought *Mother Hubbard* into question, that thou shouldst by rehearsall rekindle against him the sparkes of displeasure that were quenched?"

 II, 270: A similar allusion.

 III, 172: The phrase "Barnabe the bright."

PADELFORD, F. M.   In Mod. Philol., XI (1913), 100–102:

 On the date of MHT, 1577–79.

PALGRAVE, F. T.   In Grosart's ed. of Sp, IV, pp. lxvi–lxx.

Piers Plowman, B text, Passus VI, 108–44.

 Cf. MHT, ll. 250–90. Cf. ll. 350–75, etc. Cf. Plowman's Tale; Pierce Plowman's Crede, etc.

SCHOPPER, HARTMANN.   Speculum vitae aulicae. De admirabili Fallacia et Astutia Vulpeculae Reinikes Libri Quatuor. Nunc primùm ex idiomate Germanico latinitate donati . . . . Francof. 1579. (Epistola dated 1566; editions of 1567, etc.) Copy in Bost. Pub. Lib. English translation as The Crafty Courtier. Lond. 1706.

 Probably conveyed suggestions to Sp. See esp. Bk. II, ch. ix (the fox's meeting with the ape); Bk. III, chs. vii–ix (he cajoles the queen-lioness); Bk. IV, ch. x (he is made keeper of the great Seal and governs for the lion-king); and Bk. I (the fox's trial and condemnation).

SCOTT.   Philomythie.   See under "Criticism before 1651."

SÉLINCOURT.   Introd. to his one-volume Oxford ed. of Sp. Pp. xxii f., xxix f., xxxii f.

TODD's ed. of Sp, 1805, I, pp. lxxx–vii.

TUCKWELL's Spenser.   31–32.

MUIOPOTMOS

Böhme, T. Spenser's literarisches Nachleben. Berlin (Palaestra XCIII), 1911. 41–42.

Cory, H. E. Spenser, a Critical Study, 187–89.

Draper, John W. In The Colonnade. N.Y. 1922. XIV, 37:
A concise digest of recent discussion of the biographical material in the Muiopotmos (J. C. Smith, Nadal, Manly, Long, Lyons, Reed Smith, Emerson:—q.v.).

Emerson, O. F. In Pub. Mod. Lang. Asso., XXXII (1917), 306–22.

Grierson, H. J. C. Spenser's "Muiopotmos." In Mod. Lang. Review, XVII (1922), 409–11:
Controverts Long's theory that Lady Carey is shadowed in the Muiopotmos. Suggests that it is an allegory on the same theme as MHT, viz. the relations of Sp and Leicester.

Harman's Edmund Spenser. 179 ff.

Heywood, John. The Spider and the Fly. Repr. in part in J. M. Berdan, Early Tudor Poetry. N.Y. 1920. 103–15.

Long, P. W. Spenser's "Muiopotmos." In Mod. Lang. Review, IX (1914), 457–62:
That Clarion is Sp; the poem, after Renaissance conventions, a "complaint" of his ensnarement by Lady Carey. See Lyons, and Nadal, below.

Lyons, Jessie M. Spenser's Muiopotmos as an Allegory. In Pub. Mod. Lang. Asso., XXXI (1916), 90–113:
Controverts Nadal's theory. The poem, composed 1590, reflects the quarrel of Raleigh and Essex; Clarion=Raleigh (cf. Marinell in FQ, III, iv, and IV, xii); "the gay gardins"=The Court.

Nadal, T. W. Spenser's *Muiopotmos* in Relation to Chaucer's *Sir Thopas* and *The Nun's Priest's Tale*. In Pub. Mod. Lang. Asso., XXV (1910), 640–56:
That the Muiopotomos is not an allegory, but a pure mock-heroic after the model of the two poems of Chaucer named above, esp. the latter. See Long and Lyons, above; Dodge under "Sources, General."

Ovid. Metamorphoses=source of several passages.

SÉLINCOURT. Introd. to his one-volume Oxford ed. of Sp.
Pp. xxxiii–iv:
Against any allegorical interpretation.

SMITH, J. C. In Mod. Lang. Review, V (1910), 279 ff.

SMITH, REED. The Metamorphoses in *Muiopotmos*. In Mod.
Lang. Notes, XXVIII (1913), 82–85:
Its source and framework from Ovid; the poem not an allegòry;
influence of Chaucer.

TUELL, ANNE K. Note on Spenser's Clarion. In Mod. Lang.
Notes, XXXVI (1921), 182–83.

WILSON, JOHN. In Blackwood's Magazine, XXXIV (1833),
840–43.

PROTHALAMION

CHURCH'S ed. of FQ, 1758, I, pp. xxxvii–viii.

COLLIER'S ed. of Sp, I, pp. cxxvi ff.

ERSKINE, J. The Elizabethan Lyric. N.Y. 1903. 195–96:
Compared with the Epithal.; "complimentary rather than pas-
sionate in tone." "The pictures, in the same idyllic manner, are
carefully elaborated, and the carefulness is perceptible." Its structure narrative rather than lyric.

FLOWER, W., and others. Two Prothalamia. In Athenaeum,
1897. I, 378, 415–16, 446–47, 480–82, 510, 544, 577–78:
Of Vallans' poem "Tale of Two Swannes," 1590 (Repr. in Hearne's
ed. of Leland's Itinerary. Lond. 1711. V, p. viii) as a source of the
Prothalamion; this view controverted by J. W. Hales; 446: that both
draw from Leland's "Cygnea Cantio"; 447: that Vallans' poem dates
after 1608 (controverted p. 480, as it was entered 1590); 481: that
literary relations existed between Sp and Vallans (see p. 578). Cf.
Osgood, Spenser's English Rivers, 101.

HALES, J. W. In Athenaeum, 1897, I, 416:
The Prothal. written in 1596.

HALES, J. W. Longer English Poems. Lond. 1892. 203 ff.

MILNER, GEO. See under "Versification."

PALGRAVE, F. T. In Grosart's ed. of Sp, IV, p. ci.

TODD'S ed. of Spenser, VIII, 101 *n.*
Todd agrees with Warton that Sp uses Leland's Cygnea Cantio.

RUINS OF ROME

CHILD, F. J.   In his ed. of Sp, I, p. xxxiv.
> Child seems doubtful of Sp's authorship of the R of R.

GILFILLAN'S ed. of Sp, 1859, V, p. iii:
> Omits the R of R "as proved by external and internal evidence not to be the production of Spenser's pen."   The evidence not recited.

KOEPPEL, E.   In Engl. Studien, XV, 74 ff.

PALGRAVE, F. T.   In Grosart's ed. of Sp, IV, pp. lxxiii f.

RUINS OF TIME

Analogues: The Visions; The Ruins of Rome; Mirror for Magistrates; Lydgate's Fall of Princes; etc.

BUCK, P. M., JR.   In Mod. Lang. Notes, XXII (1907), 41–46:
> Variant readings from a contemporary MS.

CHILD'S ed. of Sp, I, pp. xxxi f.

COLLIER, J. P.   In his ed. of Sp, I, pp. lxxviii.

COLLIER, J. P.   Bibliog. Account, II, 496.

EMERSON, O. F.   In Pub. Mod. Lang. Asso., XXXII (1917), 306–22:
> The poem written 1590; etc.

ERSKINE, J.   The Elizabethan Lyric.   N.Y. 1903. 177–78.

FRIEDLAND, L. S.   Milton's *Lycidas* and Spenser's *Ruines of Time*.   In Mod. Lang. Notes, XXVII (1912), 246–50:
> That the elegiac parts of the Ruins of Time suggest Lycidas.

GROSART'S ed. of Sp, I, 181–84.

HALES, J. W.   Spenser and Verulam.   In Middlesex Notes and Queries.   Lond. 1896 (July).   127–34:
> That the R of T contains fragments of the Dreams and Pageants; written c. 1580, and revised before publication in 1591.

LUCE, ALICE, ed.   The Countess of Pembroke's Antonie.   Weimar, 1897.   7–16:
> Dedication to Lady Pembroke.   Cf. CCCHA, ll. 485–95, and Astrophel.

PALGRAVE, F. T.   In Grosart's ed. of Sp, IV, pp. lx–lxiii.

WEEVER, JOHN. Epigrammes, 1599. Repr. ed. R. B. McKerrow. Lond. 1911. 101 (cf. 123):
> That the Ruins of Time were "called in"—perhaps along with MHT in the same volume.

SHEPHERDS' CALENDAR

See also "Language, Archaisms"; for biographical material in Sh Cal see "Life, General References," introd. paragraphs.

Atlantic Monthly, "Colin Clout and the Faery Queen." II (1858), 674–88:
> The Rosalind question.

AUBREY, JOHN. Lives, ed. A. Clark. II, 232.
> On Rosalind.

BASKERVILL, C. R. The Early Fame of the Shepheards Calender. In Pub. Mod. Lang. Asso., XXVIII (1913), 291–313:
> Contests Greenlaw's view that the Sh Cal was little known until the publication of the FQ brought it into prominence; marshalls the evidence of its early influence.

BASKERVILL, C. R. Two Parallels to "Lycidas." In N.Y. Nation, XCI (1910), 546:
> Notes influence of the May eclogue on Lycidas; that Sp was influenced by Skelton's "Colin Clout."

BOURNE, H. R. FOX. Sir Philip Sidney. N.Y. 1891. 195–208:
> "Reminiscences" of the scenery of Penshurst in the Sh Cal.

BRUNNER, K. Die Dialektwörter in Spensers "Shepherds' Calender." In Archiv. f. d. Studium d. neuren Spr. u. Lit., CXXXII (1914), 401–4.

BUCK, P. M., JR. Notes on the *Shepherds' Calendar*. In Mod. Lang. Notes, XXI (1906), 80–84. Cf. Higginson, Spenser's Sh Cal, 235.

"C." In Notes and Queries, Ser. III, Vol. IV (1863), 21–22, 65–66, 101–3:
> Guesses as to Rosalind; that EK = Sp.

CALDERHEAD, I. G. In Defense of "E.K." In Mod. Lang. Notes, XXVII (1912), 74–75:
> Answers J. F. Royster's article in MLN, Jan. 1909, and justifies E.K.'s defense of Sp's archaisms.

Catalogue of MSS in the Library of Gonville and Caius College, Cambridge. Cambr. 1908. II, 627 (No. 595):

A MS transl. of the Sh Cal into Latin hexameter verse by John Dove, c. 1590. "This copy differs from one in the British Museum." Cf. Todd's ed. of Sp, I, p. xii. See below, "Pembroke College."

CHURCH, R. W. Spenser, ch. ii.

CLARKE, HELEN A. Musical Setting of part of the January eclogue. Repr. from Poet-Lore, 1892.

COLLIER, J. P. In his ed. of Sp, I, pp. xxxii:

The Sh Cal published 1580 N.S.; xxxvi ff.

COULTER, CORNELIA C. Two of E.K.'s Classical Allusions. In Mod. Lang. Notes, XXXV (1920), 55–56:

On Sh Cal, March, l. 16, and April, ll. 122–23.

COURTHOPE, W. J. Hist. Eng. Poetry. II, 242–45:

Its sources and hist. background; 249–56: Unity of the poem, the allegory, diction, verse, etc.

COURTHOPE, W. J. In Cambr. Hist. Eng. Lit., III, 219–28.

CRAIK, G. L. Hist. Eng. Lit., I, 487–94.

Dict. Natl. Biog., XVIII, 794 (Rosalind), 796.

DRAPER, J. W. The Glosses to Spenser's "Shepheardes Calendar." In Journal of Eng. and Germ. Philology, XVIII (1919), 556–74:

A study of the sources of Sp's diction in this poem; lists (1) words taken from Middle English writers, (2) from earlier sixteenth century writers, (3) new loan-words, etc.; that E.K. was helped by Sp; that many words in the Gloss are of northern origin, but not especially of Lancashire.

DRAPER, J. W. In The Colonnade. N.Y. 1922. XIV, 38–40:

Summary of recent discussion on the Rosalind question, the Lancashire theory, etc.

DRYDEN. Works, ed. Saintsbury. Edinb. 1882–93. XIII, 324–25. (Ded. of Transl. of Virgil, 1687):

The Sh Cal "not to be matched in any modern language"; its Doric diction.

EATON, H. A. The Pastoral Idea in English Poetry in the Sixteenth Century, 1900. MS Diss. in Harvard Lib.

>Ch. vi on the Sh Cal; ch. ix the Pastoral Eclogue between 1579 and 1603, whereunder of "The Eclogues chiefly influenced by the Shepherds' Calendar"; etc.

ERSKINE, J. The Eliz. Lyric. N.Y. 1903. 104–16:

>Lyric quality in the Sh Cal; its advance over preceding verse; study in detail of lyrics in the Sh Cal; "the careful design that all Spenser's lyrics show"; the versification; pastoral elegy in the November eclogue compared with analogues.

F. In (Walford's) Antiquarian Mag. and Bibliographer. Lond., V (1884), 229–37:

>Sh Cal written in Lancashire; its language; of Rosalind and Sp's rival Menalcas.

FLETCHER, J. B. "The Widdowes Daughter of the Glenne." In Mod. Lang. Notes, XXII (1907), 63:

>On E.K.'s Glosse to Sh Cal, April, l. 26, and the Rosalind question.

FLETCHER, J. B. Spenser, the Cosmopolitan Poet. In Eng. Grad. Record. Columbia Univ., 1905. 70–71:

>Sources of "Cuddies" theory of poetry in Oct. eclogue of Sh Cal traced to Minturno.

FLETCHER, J. B. Spenser and "E.K." In Mod. Lang. Notes, XV (1900), 330–31:

>That Sp and E.K. jointly wrote the annotations to the Sh Cal.

GAIRDNER, JAMES. The English Church in the Sixteenth Century. Lond. 1903.

>For the historical background of the ecclesiastical satire of the Sh Cal.

Gentleman's Magazine, 1867, I, 207–8, 501–2:

>As to Lancashire dialect in the Sh Cal, pro and con.

GOSSE, E. See Grosart, below.

GRAHAM, WALTER. Some Notes on Spenser and Bacon. In Mod. Lang. Notes, XXVIII (1913), 212–14:

>"Emblems" in the Sh Cal and their sources.

GREENE, E. B. An Essay on Pastoral Poetry. Prefixed to Fawkes' Theocritus, 1767. In Chalmers' Poets, XX, 168–69:

>Originality of Sp in pastoral; appropriateness of his style and matter.

GREENLAW, E. The Shepheards Calender. In Pub. Mod. Lang. Asso., XXVI (1911), 419–51:
>Its sources in Googe and in poems of the 16th century Chaucer Canon; its polemical and political purpose in the five "moral" eclogues, similar to that of the MHT.
>Nature of Chaucer's influence. Circumstances of the publication of the Sh Cal.
>Cf. Higginson, Spenser's Shepherd's Calender. App. A.

GREENLAW, E. The Shepheards Calender, II. In Studies in Philology (Univ. of N. Carolina), XI (1913), 1–25:
>Continuing his article above. Answers criticisms of Higginson and Baskervill. Discusses relations of Sp and Leicester. Further on the interpretation of the Feb. eclogue. Cf. Anglia, Beiblatt, XXXI (1920), 1.

GREEN, HENRY. Shakespeare and the Emblem Writers. Lond. 1870. 134–37:
>Emblems in the Sh Cal and Visions of Bellay.

GREG, W. W. Pastoral Poetry and Pastoral Drama. Lond. 1906. Ch. ii, sect. ii, Spenser; iii, Spenser's Immediate Followers.
>Historical importance of the Sh Cal; the archaisms; Chaucer's influence; 95–99: its prosody; later imitations.

GROSART'S ed. of Sp, I, 100–21, 442; II, passim; III, pp. ix ff. (Edmund Gosse's Essay on English Pastoral Poetry), xlix ff., lxxii ff. ("Who were Rosalind and Menalcas?"), cviii ff. (Edward Kirke); IV, pp. xxiv ff.

GUMMERE, F. B. Beowulf and English Verse. In Amer. Journal of Philology, VII (1886), 60–70:
>Versification of the Sh Cal.

[HALPINE, C. G.] Colin Clout and the Fairy Queen. In Atlantic Monthly, II (1858), 674 ff.
>The Rosalind question.

HALPIN, N. J. See "Life, General References."

HARMAN'S Edmund Spenser. 502 ff.:
>Rosalind = Mary Sidney.

HARVEY, G. Works, ed. Grosart, I, 90, 92.

HIGGINSON, J. J.　Spenser's Shepherd's Calender in Relation to
Contemporary Affairs.　N.Y. (Columbia Univ. Press), 1912.

This and Herford's ed. of the Sh Cal are the two most important
aids to the study of this poem.　Uses the material of contemporary
history extensively.　Closely reasoned, sometimes too credulously,
and many of the conclusions are conjectural, as the author admits.
Therefore must be used with caution.　Overemphasizes the satirical
elements in the Sh Cal at the expense of the literary.　That the Sh Cal
was in part composed at Cambridge, and extensively circulated in MS,
43, 203-31: the Rosalind question; the Feb., May, July and Sept
eclogues examined in detail; in Feb. the Fable of Oak and Brier refers
to fall of Duke of Norfolk; in May, Fable of Fox and Kid, the Kid =
the Puritans, Fox = high church party; in July, account of Bishop
Aylmer (Morrell); in Sept., argues "Roffy" is not Dr. Young, Bishop
of Rochester [but Sp was actually his secretary in 1578], but is the
Bishop of Ely; attacks theory of Grosart and others of Sp's sojourn in
Lancashire (289 ff.); that the "North Countrye" = Cambridge, "South
partes" = London; Sp's relations with Leicester (319 ff.).　Cf. above
under "Life, General References."

HOOPER, JAMES.　Spenser's Rosalind.　In Notes and Queries,
Ser. IX, Vol. IV (1899), 44-45:

Was Rosalind Rose Dynely?

JAMESON, MRS. ANNA B.　Memoirs of the Loves of the Poets.
Bost. 1894.　Ch. xiv: "Spenser's Rosalind and Spenser's
Elizabeth."

JUSSERAND.　Hist. litt. du peuple Anglais.　II, 398-414.

JUSSERAND.　In Revue de Paris, 1 May, 1903.　68-75.

The Kalender of Shepherdes, 1503, 1506.　Numerous subsequent editions, incl. 1559, c. 1560, c. 1580, and later (some
editions appearing as "The Shepheards Kalender," e.g
c. 1596, and 1611).　Repr. ed. H. O. Sommer.　Lond. 1892

A sort of popular almanac, encyclopedia of popular science, and
handbook of devotion.　Cf. Warton, Hist. Eng. Poetry, ed. W. C
Hazlitt.　Lond. 1871.　III, 155 f.

It suggested to Sp not only the title of the Sh Cal, but perhaps also
prompted him to help counteract the influence of this popular manual
"by a member of the Church of Rome in the interest of his church"
(Sommer), by the insertion of matter of Protestant doctrine and polemic

in his poem. Also not without influence of the same reverse sort on passages of the FQ, such as the pictures of the Seven Deadly Sins, the House of Holiness, the allegory of the human body, etc.

KEIGHTLEY, T. In Fraser's Magazine, LX (1859), 410–22:
Identifications in the Sh Cal.

KEIGHTLEY, T. In Brit. Quar. Review, XXII (1855), 377:
The Rosalind question.

KLUGE, F. Spenser's Shepheard's Calendar und Mantuan's Eclogen. In Anglia, III (1880), 266–74:
That Sp uses Mantuan as he does Marot; parallelisms studied in detail.

LEGOUIS, E. See under "Versification."

LOFTIE, WM. In A. Lang, Poets' Country. Lond. 1907. 313–24:
That the scenery of Penshurst appears in the Sh Cal.

LONG, P. W. Spenser's Rosalind. In Anglia, XXXI (1908), 72–104:
A new identification; Rosalind a real person; the previous attempts to localize her and identify her analyzed; against the theory of Sp's connection with Lancashire; the dialect of the Sh Cal not Lancastrian; Grosart's arguments refuted. Suggests Rosalind = Elizabeth North (Eliza Nord). Cf. Long, under "Life, General References."

LONG, P. W. The Name *Shepherds' Calendar*. In Archiv. f. d. Stud. d. n. Spr. u. Litt., CXXXI (1913), 429–30:
Current errors in the modern form of the title of Sp's poem and the theory on which they rest.

LONG, P. W. In Pub. Mod. Lang. Asso., XXXI (1916), 732 ff.
The Feb. eclogue and the application of the fable of the Oak and the Brier.

LONG, P. W. Spenser and the *Plowman's Tale*. In Mod. Lang. Notes, XXVIII (1913), 262:
An echo of this pseudo-Chaucerian poem in the Sh Cal.

LOONEY, J. T. "Shakespeare" Identified. Lond. 1920. 341 ff.:
The Sh Cal = "simply a series of burlesques upon prominent men of the day"; on the March eclogue and its parodies of the Earl of Oxford and of Sidney.

LOWELL, J. R. Works, IV, 300 ff.

MACKAIL, J. W.   The Springs of Helicon, 83–85.

MAIBERGER, M.   Studien über den Einfluss Frankreichs.   50 ff.

MALONE, E.   In his ed. of Shakespeare, 1821.   II, 214 *n.*
> On Sh Cal, Nov. "Dido"=an illegitimate daughter of Leicester;
> 217 *n*: "Rosalind"=Elisa Horden.

MORLEY, HENRY.   Clement Marot.   Lond. 1871.   I, 255–75;
II, 7, 20–32:
> On Marot and Sp's debt to him.

MORLEY, HENRY.   Hobbinol.   In Fortnightly Review, N.S.
V (1869), 274–83.
> On Gabriel Harvey.

MUSTARD, W. P.   E.K.'s Classical Allusions.   In Mod. Lang.
Notes, XXXIV (1919), 193–203:
> The allusions traced to their sources.

MUSTARD, W. P., ed.   The Eclogues of Baptista Mantuanus.
Baltimore, 1911.   Introd. and pp. 50, 134–36, 140, 142, 146:
> The debt of the Sh Cal to Mantuan.

MUSTARD, W. P.   Notes on The *Shepheardes Calender*.   In
Mod. Lang. Notes, XXXV (1920), 371–72:
> Some sources of the Sh Cal.

Notes and Queries, Ser. X, Vol. I (1904), 204:
> Rosalind, Colin, and William in Sh Cal and in As You Like It.

Notes and Queries.   Various short notes on the Sh Cal.
> Ser. I, Vol. IV (1851), 473: on verses in "June" omitted in folio
> eds.; X (1854), 204: on E.K.
> Ser. II, Vol. X (1860), 367, 435; Ser. III, Vol. IV (1863), 102
> E.K.=Sp; Rosalind=Rondelais, the poet's Muse; 197; Ser. V, Vol. VI
> (1876), 365: Sp's rival, Menalcas; Ser. VIII, Vol. IV (1893), 405: the
> "well" of Helicon; 472; Ser. XI, Vol. VII (1913), 150, 231; Ser. XII,
> Vol. IV (1918), 12, 138.

PADELFORD, F. M.   In Mod. Philology, XI (1913), 96–100:
> On the satire of the Sh Cal; composition of several of the eclogues
> in 1578; Roffyn=Bishop of Rochester.   Cf. 85 ff.

PAUL, FRANCIS.   "The Shepheards Calender."   In Amer.
Catholic Quar. Review, XLIII (1918), 167–69:
> Sh Cal and Sp briefly considered from the Catholic point of view

Pembroke College, Cambridge.

Mr. Ellis H. Minns, Librarian of Pembroke College, writes me that the College has a copy of the Sh Cal "with a translation into Latin verse made and written out by Spenser's friend Theodore Bathurst, sometime fellow." Qu. Whether Bathurst were a contemporary of Sp and his translation made in Sp's lifetime? The few data given about Bathurst in the Dict. Natl. Biog., etc. seem to be highly conjectural. Cf. the similar copy in the British Museum. See above under "Catalogue," etc.

PLESSOW, MAX. Geschichte der Fabeldichtung in England bis zu John Gay. Berlin (Palaestra, LII), 1906. Pp. xxiii–liv:

Fable literature in England before Sp. Pp. liv–vi: fables in Sp.

POPE, ALEX. Discourse on Pastoral Poetry. In Works, ed. Croker, etc. 1871, I, 257 ff. Cf. X, 508–9.

REISSERT, O. Bemerkungen über Spenser's Shepheards Calendar und die frühere Bukolik. In Anglia, IX (1886), 205–24:

Sources and models of the Sh Cal. Resemblances studied in detail.

RENWICK, W. L. The December "Embleme" of the "Shepheards Calender." In Mod. Lang. Review, XIV (1919), 415–16:

This emblem = Marot's *devise.*

ROYSTER, J. F. A Note on Spenser's Archaism and Cicero. In Mod. Lang. Notes, XXIV (1909), 30–31. Cf. I. G. Calderhead in M.L.N., XXXVII (1912), 74–75.

SÉLINCOURT. In his ed. of Sp's Minor Poems. Pp. vi–xvi.

SÉLINCOURT. Introd. to his one-volume Oxford ed. of Sp. Pp. xi, xiv:

Rosalind ("Human probability is all on the side of the sincerity of his attachment"); xiv ff.: E.K. = Edward Kirke; its sources, diction, and metre, etc.; p. l *n:* that Sp does not refer to Rosalind in the Mirabella episode in FQ, VI.

SMITH, G. C. MOORE. Spenser's "Shepherds Calendar," "November." In Mod. Lang. Review, II (1907), 346–47:

"Dido" = Ambrosia Sidney. Cf. Higginson on this attempted identification.

SMITH, JOHN J. Catalogue of the MSS in the Library of Gonville and Caius College. Cambr. 1849. 272:

MS version of the Sh Cal in Latin hexameters, c. 1590.

SOMMER, H. O. Englische Hirtendichtung. Marburg, 1888.
46–54.

SOMMER, H. O. Who was the Commentator of Spenser's "Shepherdes Calender"? In the Academy, Lond., XXXIV (1888),
171–72:
> That E.K.=Sp himself; accepts Uhlemann's conclusions. See
> below.

UHLEMANN, DR. Der Verfasser des Kommentars zu Spenser's
Shepherds Calendar. Hannover, 1888. Progr.
> Cf. H. O. Sommer in Englische Studien, XIV (1890), 149: Agrees
> with U. that "E.K."=Sp.

WEBBE, WM. Discourse of English Poetrie, 1586. Repr. ed.
Arber. Lond. 1870. 23, 35, 52, 59–61, 65, 81.

WHETSTONE, GEO. Poem on Death of Sidney (1587 or later).
Quoted in Collier's Poetical Decameron, I, 64–68:
> It attributes the authorship of the Sh Cal to Sidney.

WHITNEY, GEOFFREY. A Choice of Emblemes. Leyden, 1586.
Facsimile Repr. ed. H. Green. Lond. 1866. Pp. xvi, xvii,
lxvi–vii, 379:
> Compare emblems in Sh Cal and Visions of Bellay.

WILSON, JOHN. In Blackwood's Magazine, XXXIV (1833),
830 ff.

WINDSCHEID, KATHARINA. Die englische Hirtendichtung von
1579–1625. Halle, 1895. Diss. 7–9:
> The Sh Cal; 9 ff., its influence.

TEARS OF THE MUSES

BERLI, HANS. Gabriel Harvey. Zurich, 1913. 52–54:
> That Sp takes merely the title of the poem from Harvey's Musarum
> Lachrymae.

CHALMERS, GEO. Supplemental Apology. Lond. 1799. 270 n.
> "Willy" not Shakespeare, but Sidney.

CHILD, F. J. In his ed. of Sp, I, pp. xxxii–iii.

COLLIER, J. P. In his ed. of Sp, I, p. lxxix.

COLLIER, J. P. In his ed. of Shakespeare, 1858, I, 92.

COLLIER, J. P. Hist. Eng. Dram. Poetry. Lond. 1879. II, 338–41:
> That "Willy" is not Lyly.

Davison's Poetical Rhapsody, ed. Bullen, I, 67:
> "Willy." Cf. Meres' list for other Willies.

FEUILLERAT, A. John Lyly. Cambr. 1910. 225 *n*:
> Doubts that "Willy"=Lyly or Sidney.

FRAUNCE, A. Arcadian Rhetorike, 1588.
> Refers to "Willies Poems."

GABBETT, H. S. Spenser's "Pleasant Willy." In Athenaeum, LXVI (1875), 507–8:
> Discussion of the "Willy" passage in the Teares of the Muses, with a history of critical opinion on the point; inclines to Lyly.

GAYLEY, CHARLES M. Representative Eng. Comedies. N.Y. 1903. I, 405:
> That "Alcon"=Lodge (see "Alcon" in Lodge's Looking Glass for London, 1594).

GREENE, ROBT. Alphonsus, 1599. Prologue:
> The Muses appear; analogue.

GROSART's ed. of Sp, I, 89 ff., 185–89.

HARMAN's Edmund Spenser. 164 ff.

Gabrielis Harveii Rhetor . . . . Londini, H. Bynneman, 1577. Copy in Univ. of Chicago Library: contains also Smithus, vel Musarum Lachrymae, 1578.
> Harvey's poem on the death of Sir Thomas Smith probably suggested the title of Sp's Tears of the Muses. Each muse laments in turn, viz., Clio, Melpomene, Thalia (see for mention of Chaucer, etc.), Euterpe, Terpsichore, Erato, Calliope, Uranie, Polymneia (Sp's order).

HAZLITT, W. C. Shakespear Himself. Lond. 1912. 150:
> An early MS note in a copy of Sp, 1611, suggests that "Willy" = Tarlton.

LE FRANC, A. Sous le masque de Shakespeare. Paris, 1918. I, 221 ff.:
> "Willy"=William Stanley.

LONG, P. W. See under "Four Hymns."

LOONEY, J. T. "Shakespeare" Identified. Lond. 1920. 338–46:
> "Willy" not Shakespeare or Sidney, but the same as the "Willy" of Sh Cal, who is the Earl of Oxford.

LYLY, JOHN. Works, ed. Bond. Lond. 1902. I, 62–63:
> "Willy."

MACKAIL, J. W. The Springs of Helicon. 101.

MALONE'S ed. of Shakespeare, 1821. II, 167 ff.:
> The aptness of Sp's censure of the stage; guesses at the allusions; "Willy" not Shakespeare; "Willy"=Lyly; other Eliz. anagrams; the poem analyzed.

MASSON, D. Life of Milton, I, 592 ff.

PALGRAVE, F. T. In Grosart's ed. of Sp, IV, pp. lxiii–lxv.

Quarterly Review, CXV (1864), 435 *n:* that "Willy"=Sidney.

REUTER, W. Edmund Spenser's "The Tears of the Muses" considered as a document of the literary history of the time. Saarlouis, 1864.

ROLLINS, HYDER E. In Journal of Amer. Folk Lore, XXX (1917), 376–77:
> That "Willy"=Tarlton (see his ballad of Willie and Peggie, 1588).

ROWE, NICHOLAS. Life of Shakespear, 1709. Quoted in D. Nichol Smith, Eighteenth Century Essays on Shakespeare, Glasgow, 1903. 6–7:
> "Willy"=Shakespeare. Cf. 68–69: Lewis Theobald, contra.

SHAKESPEARE. Midsummer Night's Dream, V, i, 52.

The Shakspere Allusion Book. N.Y. and Lond. 1909. II, 461:
> That "Willy" is not Shakespeare; reasons for believing that "Willy"=Tarlton.

The Shirburn Ballads, 1585–1616. Andrew Clark, ed. Ox. 1907. 351:
> That "Willy"=Richard Tarlton.

STOPES, MRS. C. C. William Hunnis and the Revels of the Chapel Royal. Louvain. (Materialien, XXIX), 1910. 270:
> Suggests that "Willy"=Hunnis.

THEATRE OF WORLDLINGS

See also "Visions of Petrarch."

Athenaeum, XVIII (1845), 120, 150.

> Whether Sp did not translate the "sonnets" of Petrarch prefixed to the Theatre directly from the Italian rather than the French.

CORSER, T. Collectanea Anglo-Poetica. Chetham. Soc. Pub. 1860–83. Pt. X (1880), 312–19:

> A full account of the Van der Noodt "Theatre" of 1569: accepts Sp's authorship of the epigrams and sonnets.

DIBDIN, THOS. F. Typographical Antiquities. Lond. 1810. IV, 107–8:

> Description of the French version (1568) of the Th. of W.

FLETCHER, J. B. Spenser and the Theatre of Worldlings. In Mod. Lang. Notes, XIII (1898), 409–15:

> In answer to Koeppel. Holds that Sp is the author of the poems in the Theatre of Worldlings.

FLETCHER, J. B. Spenser's Earliest Translations. In Journal of Eng. and Germ. Philology, XIII (1914), 305–8.

FRIEDLAND, L. S. Spenser's Earliest Translations. In Journal of Eng. and Germ. Philology, XII (1913), 449–70:

> The question of Sp's authorship of the poems in the Theatre of Worldlings re-argued, with review of Koeppel, Fletcher, Dodge, etc. Accepts Sp's authorship.

Gedichten van Jonker Jan van der Noot. Met Inleiding en Aanteenkeningen van Albert Verwey. Amsterdam, 1895.

GROSART'S ed. of Sp, I, 15–28.

KOEPPEL, E. See "Visions of Petrarch."

NICHOLSON, B. See under "Visions of Petrarch," "Visions of Bellay."

Le Theatre auquel sont exposés . . . les inconveniens & miseres qui suiuent les mondains & vicieux. . . . . Par le Seigneur Iean Vander Noot. Londres, 1568.

> Copy in the Brit. Museum. Transcript of the "sonnets" therein by Henry R. Plomer, in the Newberry Library, Chicago.

Notes and Queries, Ser. VII, Vol. II (1886), 443. Cf. III, 262.

PLOMER, HENRY R.

Mr. Plomer writes me that there were two John Van der Noots living in England in the sixteenth century (Documents at the Record Office), and that Sp's Van der Noot was not the physician (who died in 1556), as Grosart states. Mr. A. W. Pollard suggests that Sp was introduced to Van der Noot the author of The Theatre by Bynneman, his publisher.

SÉLINCOURT. In his ed. of Sp's Minor Poems. Pp. xxvii–viii.

VERMEYLEN, AUG. Leven en Werken van Jonker Jan van der Noot. Antwerp, 1899.

THE VIEW OF IRELAND

See also refs. under "Life, General References," above, relating to Ireland; also for biographical material in the V of I; "Spenser and Raleigh"; cf. generally the FQ, Bk V.

The V of I is mainly based on Sp's observations and experience of some fifteen years in Ireland, and so in large measure is personal and in some measure is autobiographical. A considerable body of literature dealing with the state of Ireland in Spenser's time exists. For a selected list of the printed texts see references below. Much is still in MS form. See the various catalogues of MSS in English libraries. A striking example is to be found in the Catalogue of the Manuscripts in the Cottonian Library, deposited in the British Museum. Lond. 1802. I, p. 551: Titus, B. XII, especially Nos. 11, 21, 23, 27, 40, 56, 64, 75, 81, 105, 107, 110, 113, 118, 129, 134, 142, 144, etc. No. 129, "Part of a discourse on Irish affairs," possibly by Sir Philip Sidney, should be of especial interest. Many of these led up to and probably influenced Sp's View of Ireland. See mention of them in V of I, p. 1.

Anthologia Hibernica. Dublin, 1793. I, 189:

A MS of the V of I, dated 1595.

ARBER'S Transcript. Lond. 1876. III, 34a:

"xiiij Aprilis (1598). Mathewe Lownes. Entred for his Copie vnder the hand of master Warden man a booke intituled *A viewe of the present state of Ireland. Discoursed by waye of a Dialogue betwene Eudoxus and Irenius.* vppon Condicion that hee get further aucthoritie before yt be prynted. . . . . vj*d.*"

*BAGNALL. Slender Description of Ulster in 1586. Lond. 1854 (?).

BALE, JOHN. Vocacyon to the Bishoprick of Ossorie in Ireland, 1553. In Harleian Miscellany, 1810, VI, 437–64:
> Bale was made Bishop of Ossory in 1552. This is a highly colored account of his experiences there.

BIRCH, THOS. In his ed. of Sp, 1751, I, The Life, pp. xxv–vii.

BORDE, ANDREW. Fyrst Boke of the Introduction of Knowledge [1542]. Repr. E.E.T. Soc. Lond. 1870. Ch. iii:
> Of the Irish and their customs. See the notes.

A Briefe Note of Ireland (1598). By Spenser? In Sp, ed. Grosart, I, 537 ff.
> Compare its tenor and arguments with the V of I.

BUCHANAN, GEORGE. Rerum Scoticarum Historiae. In his Opera Omnia. Lugd. 1725, Vol. I.
> Probable source of various passages in the V of I. Mr. F. F. Covington, Jr., calls attention especially to Book II, chs. 1, 11, 13, 16, 17, 18, and Book IV, ch. 3. He also notes Camden and Holinshed as "sources" (Letter of Apr. 26, 1922).

C. In Notes and Queries, Ser. III, Vol. IV (1863), 237:
> That the reference at the end of the V of I is not to Essex, but to Raleigh.

Calendars, Ireland, 1598–99. 431:
> A MSS of the V of I in Pub. Record Office, London.

CAMPION, EDW. History of Ireland. MS in Trinity College, Cambridge, R. 7. 18. Dated 1571.

CANNING, A. S. G. Literary Influence in British History. Lond. 1904. Ch. v.

CARGILL, A. An Old-Time Irish Secretary. In Westminster Review, CLXV (1906), 249–54:
> Mainly on the V of I and Sp's political career in Ireland. Negligible.

Catalogue of MSS, Cambridge Univ. Lib. Cambr. 1856.
> I, 440, Dd. x. 60: A MS of the V of I. ("On f. 86 is 'Finis 1596,' and the cipher for E. Spenser.")
> I, 535, Dd. xiv. 28: Another MS of the V of I. ("At the end is 'Finis Anno. Dni 1590.'")

Catalogue of Add. MSS in Brit. Museum. London. 1875+
> No. 22,022: MS of V of I, 1596.

Catalogue of Harleian MSS in Brit. Mus. Lond. 1808.
> II, 355: MS of the V of I (No. 1932).
> III, 529: MS of the V of I (No. 7388).

Catalogue of MSS in Gonville and Caius Coll., by M. R. James. Cambr. 1908.
> I, 217, No. 188: a 16th cent. MS of the V of I.

Catalogue of MSS in Trinity Coll, Dublin. Dublin, 1900.
> "Spenser" does not appear in the index. Todd (ed. of Sp, I, cxxii *n*) cites a MS of the V of I in this library.

Catalogi Cod. MSS Bibl. Bodl., Partis Quintae, Oxon. 1862.
> B. 478: MS of V of I. See note.

Catalogue of MSS in Lambeth.
> There seems to be no entry of the Lambeth MS of the V of I in M. R. James Catalogue of the MSS in the Lambeth Palace Lib. Grosart states that he used this MS as the basis of the text in his edition.

CHURCH'S ed. of FQ, 1758, I, p. xxxviii:
> The V of I written in England.

CHURCHYARD, THOS. Generall Rehearsall of Warres. ("Churchyard's Choise.") Lond. 1579. (Copy in Newberry Library, Chicago.)
> Partly an account of wars and other affairs in Ireland in the time of Sir Henry Sidney (by a participant).
> Cf. Corser, Collectanea, IV, 366 ff. Cf. Grosart's Sp, I, 482 ff.

COLLIER, J. P. In his ed. of Sp, I, pp. cxxvii ff.

*COOPER, LAURA T. Spenser's Veue of the Present State of Ireland. An Introduction, with Notes on the first 55 pages in Grosart's edition. MS Diss., 1913. In Cornell Univ. Lib.

COOPER. Athenae Cantabrig., II, 550:
> MS of V of I; for other MSS see p. 263.

COVINGTON, F. F., JR. Elizabethan Notions of Ireland. In the Texas Review (Univ. of Texas), VI (1921), 222–46:
> See 227 ff. on the V of I and conditions in Ireland in Sp's time. A brief commentary on the V of I. Useful.

COVINGTON, F. F., JR. Another View of Spenser's Linguistics. In Studies in Philology, XIX (1922), 244–48:
> Correction of some statements in J. W. Draper's article in Mod. Philol., Jan. 1920 (see below); as to the text of the V of I.

Cox, Sir Richard. Hibernia Anglicana. Lond. 1689–90.
>I, "To the Reader"; 391–92; 310–456, on "The Reign of Elizabeth." Copy in the Harvard Lib., and in Newberry Lib.

Craik, G. L. Hist. Eng. Lit., I, 579.

Cromwell, Oliver. See "Life, General References."

Cusack, Mary F. An Illustrated History of Ireland. Kenmare Convent, 1876. 439–40.

Davies, Sir John. Discoverie of the State of Ireland, 1612. Repr. in Prose Works of D., ed. Grosart, 1876, Vol. I, 1–168.

De Moss, W. F. The Influence of Aristotle's "Politics" and "Ethics" on Spenser. Chicago, 1918. 65–68.

Derricke, John. Image of Ireland (in verse, 1578). Lond. 1581. Repr. in Somers' Tracts. Lond. 1809–15. I, 558–621:
>In part a sort of "allegorical" description of Ireland and of the native Irish; of the Irish rebels and Sir Henry Sidney's government of Ireland. Also Repr. ed. J. Small. Edinb. 1883. Cf. the notes in Small's ed. for comparisons with Sp's V of I.

The Description of Ireland and the State thereof as it is at this present. In Anno 1598. From MS, ed. E. Hogan. Dublin, 1878.
>P. xi: List of Descriptions of Ireland:
>1. Topographical Poems of O'Duggan and O'Heerin.
>2. MS Abbreviate of Ireland and Description of the Power of Irishmen, by Dean Nowell who died in 1576.
>3. Campion's, in 1575.
>4. Derricke's "Image of Ireland," 1581.
>5. Carew MSS, No. 635.
>6. Stanihurst's "Plaine and Perfect Description," 1586.
>7. A brief Description by Payne, in 1589.
>8. Dymmok's "Treatice of Ireland," circ. 1598.
>9. Camden's, in 1607; the best hitherto published.
>10. Barnaby Riche's "New Description of Ireland," in 1610.
>11. Moryson's, in 1617.
>Followed by: "Descriptions of Parts of Ireland"—some sixteen items.

Draper, J. W. Spenser's Linguistics in *The Present State of Ireland*. In Mod. Philol., XVII (1919), 471–86:
>Sp's knowledge of Irish lore narrow and imperfect. See Covington, F. F., Jr., above.

Desiderata Curiosa Hibernica. [John Lodge, ed.] Dublin, 1772.
> See Vol. I, passim, for contemporary papers illustrative of the state of Ireland, temp. Elizabeth.

Dublin Review, XVII (1844), 424 ff.   Cf. Grosart's Sp, I, 136 ff.

DUNHAM, S. A.   Lit. and Scientific Men, I, 327–34.

DUNLOP, R.   Sixteenth Century Maps of Ireland.   In Eng. Hist. Review, XX (1905), 309–37:
> Gives catalogue of maps in Brit. Mus., Pub. Record Office, Lib. of Trinity Coll., Dublin, etc.   Important.
> Cf. F. I. Carpenter, in Mod. Philol., XIX (1922), 4:6–18.   Photographs of several of the maps described by Dunlop are in the Library of Congress and the Newberry Lib.

DUNLOP, ROBERT.   Map of "Ireland from 1541 to 1653," with descriptive text.   In R. L. Poole, Historical Atlas of Modern Europe.   Ox. 1902.   No. xxxi.

DYMMOK, JOHN.   Treatise of Ireland (c. 1600).   Dublin (Irish Archaeol. Soc.), 1843.

Edinburgh Review, CCI (1905), 184–85.

ELTON, CHARLES I.   Origins of English History.   Lond. 1890. 2d. ed. rev. 157–58.

FALKINER, C. L.   Essays rel. to Ireland.   Lond. 1909.   26–31:
> Reality of the problem discussed in the V of I; compared with the Mutability cantos.

FROUDE, JAMES A.   History of England.   N.Y. 1890.
> For material illustrative of Sp's V of I see Vol. II, ch. viii; IV, parts of ch. xviii; VIII, chs. vii, ix; X, ch. xxiv; XI, ch. xxvii.

GILBERT, JOHN T., ed.   Facsimiles of National Manuscripts of Ireland.   Lond. 1882.   Pt. IV, i, pp. xv ff.:
> A Map of Ireland ("Hibernia. Insula . . . . 1567") by John Goughe.   In Pub. Rec. Office, Lond.   "Carefully drawn."

GREEN, ALICE STOPFORD.   The Making of Ireland and its Undoing.   Lond. 1908.   See index.

GREENLAW, E.   In Mod. Philol., VII (1909), 187–202:
> That the V of I follows the plan of Machiavelli's Prince.

GREENLAW, E. Spenser and British Imperialism. In Mod. Philol., IX (1912), 347–70:

Sp's political views; the Irish problem in the FQ and in the V of I; influence of Sidney and Raleigh on these opinions.

GROSART'S ed. of Sp, I, 139, 141, 216–17. See 230 ff.; 537–55:

Text of Sp's "Brief Note of Ireland"; IX, 9–10: on the MSS.

HAMILTON, LORD ERNEST. Elizabethan Ulster. Lond. n.d.

HARINGTON, SIR JOHN. A Short View of the State of Ireland, written in 1605. In Anecdota Bodleiana, No. 1. Ox. 1879.

The editor, W. D. Macray, calls attention to various points in which it illustrates the V of I.

HARMAN'S Edmund Spenser. Ch. xix:

A comparison of Sp's and Bacon's views on Ireland; pp. 550–51: on its date (1596); 557: the V of I founded on Sir Henry Sidney's despatches.

HARPER, CARRIE A. The Sources of Brit. Chron. Hist. in Spenser's FQ. Phila. 1910. 17–23:

Sp's sources in the V of I.

HARVEY, GABRIEL. Works ed. Grosart, 1884, I, 137–40.

HERBERT, SIR WM. Description of Munster, in Cal. of State Papers, Ireland, 1586–88, pp. 527–47.

Hist. MSS. Com. Reports, XII, Pt. ix, 123.

MS of V of I, dated 1597, in Lib. of J. H. Gurney.

HOGAN, EDMUND, ed. See above, "Description of Ireland."

HYDE, DOUGLAS. A Literary History of Ireland. Lond. 1910. 494–95.

JONES, H. S. V. Spenser's Defense of Lord Grey. Univ. of Ill. Studies in Lang. and Lit. 1919.

The political philosophy of the V of I and FQ, V; Sp's treatment of the Irish question explained from contemporary politics and current political philosophy; side lights from the State Papers, from Hooker, Harvey, Bacon, and the French political philosophers de l'Hôpital, de la Noue, and especially Bodin; close contact of Sp's circle (Sidney, Harvey, the Cambridge scholars, etc.) with these writers; Sp's debt to Bodin. A study of "literary environment" rather than of immediate literary sources; attempts a refutation of Greenlaw's theory of Sp's dependence upon Machiavelli; all that Greenlaw traces to Machiavelli Jones finds in Bodin. Cf. Das lit. Echo., 15 June 1921, p. 1144; Eng. Hist. Rev., XXXVI (1921), 306.

JOYCE, P. W. A Short History of Ireland. Lond. 1911. 6:
Approves Sp's opinion of the Irish bards; cf. 63, etc.

JUSSERAND, J. J. In Revue de Paris, 1 May, 1903, 66–67.

KEATING, GEOFFREY (c. 1570–1650). History of Ireland, ed.
with transl. by D. Comyn and others. Lond. 1902–14.
(Irish Texts Soc.) I, 3, 25–31, 65.

KILLEN, WM. D. The Ecclesiastical History of Ireland. Lond.
1875. I, 466–69. Cf. 426–28.

KING, J. Irish Bibliography. In his Irish Researches, No. 1. 1903.
Topical arrangement. Unimportant.

LEDWICH, EDW. Antiquities of Ireland. Dublin, 1793. Ed. of
1803. 21, 319:
References to the V of I, with praise of "the profound erudition of
Spenser"; corrects some of Sp's statements.

LEE, CAPT. THOMAS. A Brief Declaration of the Government
of Ireland, 1594 (Trinity Coll., Dublin, MS). In Desiderata
Curiosa Hibernica. Dublin, 1772. I, 87–150. Also in
J. Curry, Hist. and Crit. Review of Civil Wars of Ireland.
Dublin, 1775. App. I.

LEGGE, ROBT. Address to the Lord Treasurer (on civil and
judicial abuses in Ireland). Cf. Hist. MSS Com. Reports,
Cal. of Salisbury MSS, XIII, 359.

Liber Munerum . . . . Hiberniae.
Contains reference to much material illustrative of the V of I.
See Pt. III, 10, 11, 12, 13 ("The State of Ireland as it was left by Sir
Henry Sydney, 1571"), etc.; p. 19, No. 130 (A Discourse on Ireland),
p. 20, No. 75 ("Sir Henry Sidney's plot for the administration of Ireland,
1575"); see No. 111, and No. 196 (Report of the State of Ireland "de-
bated in council, Nov. 5, 1597")—and many other entries of similar tenor.

LITHGOW, WM. The Totall Discourse of the Rare Adventures
and Painefull Peregrinations . . . . 1632. Repr. Glasgow,
1906. 370–81:
Description of Ireland. Cf. Morgan's Phoenix Britannicus.
Lond. 1732. I, 212–16.

LODGE, JOHN, ed. Desiderata Curiosa Hibernica; or a Select
Collection of State Papers. Dublin, 1772.
Various Documents illustrative of Irish affairs and of the V of I.

LOMBARD, PETER (Abp. of Armagh, 1601–25). De Regno Hiberniae, Sanctorum Insula, Commentarius. Ed. P. F. Moran. Dublin, 1868. (Copy in Harv. Lib.)

With introd. The text deals with Irish antiquities, geography, religion, early history, etc.

LYON, WM., Bp. of Cork. On the State of Ireland. In Cal. of State Papers, Ireland, 1596–97, pp. 13–20.

Maps of Ireland, contemporary:

Sp in his plan for the pacification of Ireland (V of I, Globe ed. of Sp, 652) mentions "the mappe of Ireland" used as a guide in his descriptions. The only printed maps available to Sp probably were

(1) Hibernia sive Irlanda insula. . . . . In one sheet, 259×175 mm. In Civitatum aliquot . . . . delineatio . . . . Venetiis, 1568. Very few names of places; no roads. Probably not used. Insufficient. MS note (B.M. copy) attributes this map to Zalterius, and dates it 1560. The title-page says of the Irish: "gens moribus incultior, bello, latrociniss, et musica gaudent."

(2) Hibernia Insula . . . . 1565. In corner, "Venetiis Aeneis formis Bolognini Zalterii Anno M.D. LXVI." In one sheet, 332×242 mm. In volume with no separate title-page. Like No. 1, but many more names of places in the southeastern part. In the same volume is

(3) Hybernia nunc Irlant. 342×257 mm. (Venice 1570): A copy of No. 2.

(4) Eryn. Hiberniae Britannicae Insulae, nova descriptio. Irlandt. . . . . In addimentum theatri orbis terrarum Abrahamus Ortelius. Antuerpiae, 1573. 476×357 mm. Based upon Giraldus Cambrensis. Many place-names (often different in form from those recited by Sp).

(5) MS map said to have been made by Laurence Nowell (d. 1576), the antiquary, Dean of Lichfield, and brother of Alex. Nowell. Much more detailed than the above. Possibly Sp had a copy. Lithographed and printed by the Ordnance Survey, c. 1861. One sheet, 444×327 mm.

See Dunlop, R., and Gilbert, J. T., above. See Westropp, below.

MERRILL, ELIZ. The Dialogue in English Literature. N.Y. 1911. Yale Diss. 64 f.

The Monitor, Dublin, II (1879), 19–27.

NICHOLSON, WM., Bp. The Irish Historical Library. Dublin, 1724. 4:

A brief note on the V of I and Walsh's criticism of it. This work is a bibliographical guide to the authorities for the history of Ireland.

Notes and Queries, Ser. IV, Vol. II (1868), 298:
>MS versions of the V of I.

O'DONOVAN, JOHN, ed. Topographical Poems. Pub. Irish Arch. and Celtic Soc. 1862.

O'FLAHERTY, RODERIC. Ogygia, or a Chronological Account of Irish Events . . . . written originally in Latin; trans. by James Hely. Dublin, 1793. II, Pt. III, ch. lxxvii (pp. 284–88):
>"The errors of Mr. Edmond Spencer,"—i.e. in the V of I, and chiefly in points of history and genealogy.

O'SULLIVAN BEAR, DON PHILIP. Ireland under Elizabeth . . . . transl. from the Latin by M. J. Byrne. Dublin, 1903.
>From the Irish-Catholic point of view. Tome III, Bk. I uses the V of I.

PADELFORD, F. M. In Journal of Eng. and Germ. Philology, XIV (1915), 412 ff.

PAYNE, ROBERT (fl. 1589). Brief Description of Ireland (1589). Dublin (Irish Arch. Soc.), 1841.
>By one of the undertakers, and written to induce Englishmen to join the undertakers. Cf. pp. vii+, and passim.

The Present State of Ireland. Lond. 1673.
>Copy in Harvard Lib. Ed. of 1689 in Huntington Lib.
>A historical discussion of Irish political problems; useful in illustration of Sp.

Quarterly Review, CLXXXIII (1896), 259, 283.

[RICH, BARNABE.] New Description of Ireland. Lond. 1610. Repr. 1624 as "A new Irish Prognostication." Copy in Harvard Lib.
>Illustrates the V of I, with the MS of which Rich (in 1610–24) was apparently unacquainted.

*RICH, BARNABE. The Irish Hubbub, 1617.

*RICH, BARNABE. Greenes Newes both from Heauen and Hell, 1593.

*RICH, BARNABE. Looking Glass for Ireland, 1599.

RICH, BARNABE. Remembrances of the State of Ireland, 1612. In Proc. Royal Irish Acad., XXVI (1906–7), Sect C. 125–42.

From Lansdowne MS 156, No. 6. Introd. by C. L. Falkiner (valuable), which refers to Rich's dialogue (MS) "The Anatomy of Ireland." Relates mostly to time of James I; but treats many of the abuses discussed by Sp. No influence of Sp?

SECCOMBE and ALLEN. The Age of Shakespeare. Lond. 1903. I, 201:

Prose style of the V of I.

SÉLINCOURT. Introd. to his one-volume Oxford ed. of Sp. P. xxxvii.

SHIRLEY, EVELYN P. Catalogue of the Library at Lough Fea. Chiswick Press, 1872.

A bibliography of books on Ireland (with indexes of subjects and of names).

SIDNEY. State Papers in relation to Sir Henry Sidney in Ireland. In Letters and Memorials of State, ed. Arthur Collins. Lond. 1746.

See esp. I, 18–31 (on the conditions of Ireland), and passim, esp. 89–97, 102–11, 112–18, 119–22, 279–83.

SNYDER, E. D. In Mod. Philol., XVII (1920), 698.

SOUTHEY, ROBT. Commonplace Book. Lond. 1876. 210–11.

STAFFORD, SIR THOS. Pacata Hibernia. Lond. 1633. Repr. Dublin, 1810.

A history of the wars in Ireland immediately after Sp's time. "Spenser" does not appear in the index.

STANYHURST, RICHARD. De Rebus in Hibernia gestis. Antwerp, 1584.

Also, Description of Ireland, in Holinshed's Chronicle, 1586–87, II, 9–45; also in ed. of 1807, VI, 1–69. Copy in Newberry Lib.

TODD's ed. of Sp, 1805, I, pp. cxxi–viii.

VALLANCEY, CHARLES. Collectanea de Rebus Hibernicis. Dublin, 1786–1804. (2d ed.) 6 v.

Much on Irish antiquities, customs, laws, etc. See III, No. xi: "Antient Topography of Ireland," with description (alphabetically) of ancient place-names (Celtic).

WALKER, Jos. C. Historical Memoirs of the Irish Bards. Dublin, 1786. Repr. 1818. II, 13, 69–75, 117, 124, etc.
> Cf. Gentleman's Magazine, LXX (1800), 1127 *n*.

WALSH, PETER. Prospect of the State of Ireland. Lond. 1682. Preface:
> On the errors of previous writers on Ireland, including Sp; censures the historical portions of the V of I; but "where he pursued the Political main design of this dialogue . . . . none could surpass him."

WARD, A. W. In Cambr. Hist. Eng. Lit., VII, 209–11:
> A general review of Sp's prose treatise. Notes Sp's interest in ballads and folk-lore (contrary to the common opinion).

WARE, SIR JAS., ed. The Historie of Ireland. Dublin, 1633.
> See Epistle Dedicatory: On Sp's competence to treat of Irish affairs. The Preface criticizes the V of I (first printed in this volume). See Ware's marginal notes.

WESTROPP, THOS. J. Early Italian Maps of Ireland. In Proc. Royal Irish Acad., XXX (1912–13), Sect. C, 361–428. With reproductions of maps. 361–428:
> A study of the origin and development of these maps. Mostly maps of harbors (for mariners); notes of names of places. Important.

VIRGIL'S GNAT

COLLIER, J. P. In his ed. of Sp, I, p. lxxxi.

EMERSON, O. F. A new Word in an Old Poet. In Mod. Lang. Notes, XXXII (1917), 250–51:
> On four lines in VG.

EMERSON, O. F. Spenser's Virgil's Gnat. In Journal of Eng. and Germ. Philology, XVII (1918), 94–118:
> The poem studied in relation to its original; textual comments; Sp's quality and methods as a translator.

GREENLAW, E. In Pub. Mod. Lang. Asso., XXV (1910), 557–59.

GROSART'S ed. of Sp, I, 93–94.

HUGHES, M. Y. Some Aspects of the Relation of Spenser's Poetry to Classical Literature. MS. Harv. Diss. App. II.

LISLE, WM. See "Criticism before 1651."

PALGRAVE, F. T. In Grosart's ed. of Sp, IV, pp. lxv f.

SARGENT, LUCIUS M., trans. The Culex of Virgil, with a Translation into English Verse. Bost. 1887. (Copy in Newberry Lib.)
    Latin text and Eng. translation. No mention of Sp.

SCOT, THOS. See "Criticism before 1651."

TODD's ed. of Sp, 1805, I, pp. lxxix–lxxx.

VISIONS OF BELLAY

Hadriani Junii Medici Emblemata. . . . Antwerpiae, 1565. (Copy in Univ. of Chicago Lib.)
    Cuts of emblems quite in the style of the cuts in the Visions of Bellay and Visions of Petrarch; several nearly identical.

KOEPPEL, E. See under "Visions of Petrarch."

NICHOLSON, B. Spenser's 1569 "Visions of Bellay," viii, ix. In Notes and Queries, Ser. VII, Vol. II (1886), 443–44:
    Emendations; Sp's version not from the Dutch. Cf. III, 262.

PALGRAVE, F. T. In Grosart's ed. of Sp, IV, pp. lxxiv f.

SCOTT, MARY A. In Pub. Mod. Lang. Asso., XI (1896), 406.

VISIONS OF PETRARCH

See also "Theatre of Worldlings."

DESHLER, C. D. Afternoons with the Poets. N.Y. 1879. 23–25.

EMERSON, O. F. In Pub. Mod. Lang. Asso., XXXII (1917), 309:
    That Sp intended to link the Visions and the Muiop., and "relate the whole to Lady Carey."

FLETCHER, J. B. Spenser and the Theatre of Worldlings. In Mod. Lang. Notes, XIII (1898), 409–15:
    In answer to Koeppel (see below); holds that Sp is the author of the versions of 1569.

JUSSERAND, J. J. Spenser's "Visions of Petrarch." In Athenaeum, Lond., May 10, 1902, I, 595–96:
    That Sp follows Marot and not Petrarch at first hand in these Visions.

KOEPPEL, E.   Ueber die Echtheit der Edmund Spenser zuge-
schriebenen "Visions of Petrarch" und "Visions of Bellay."
In Englische Studien, XV (1891), 53–81:
> That these poems are based (1) on Marot's version of Petrarch,
> and (2) a close translation of Bellay; Sp *not* the translator of the ver-
> sions of 1569. Cf. Fletcher, J. B., above.

KOEPPEL, E.   In Englische Studien, XXVII (1900), 100–111:
> In answer to J. B. Fletcher (see above). Maintains that Sp
> altered slightly the earlier versions, but that he did not write them,
> adding four sonnets translated freely and inaccurately by himself.

NICHOLSON, B.   Spenser's "Visions of Petrarch."   In Notes
and Queries, Ser. VII, Vol. III (1887), 262–63, 344:
> Sp's translations not directly from the Italian, but from the French
> version of 1568 (Van der Noodt publisher); a detailed comparison of
> the versions. Cf. 371.

PALGRAVE, F. T.   In Grosart's ed. of Sp, IV, pp. lxxv f.

VISIONS OF THE WORLD'S VANITY

BROWNE, WM.   Poems, Muses Library ed., II, 279 ff.
> "Visions" in the manner of Sp.

Notes and Queries, Ser. IX, Vol. IX (1902), 389, 433, 516–17;
X, 53, 218:
> On the meaning of "Tedula" in V. of W.V., iii..

PALGRAVE, F. T.   In Grosart's ed. of Sp, IV, pp. lxxii f.

SCATTERED VERSES

CONTARENO, GASPER.   The Commonwealth and Government of
Venice . . . . trans. by Lewes Lewkenor. Lond. 1599.
(Copy in Newberry Library, Chicago.)
> With commendatory verses: "The antique Babel, Empresse of
> the East," signed "Edw. [sic] Spencer."

HARVEY, G.   Fowre Letters and Certain Sonnets.   Lond. 1592.
> The first appearance of the Sonnet to Harvey of 1586.

The Historie of George Castriot, surnamed Scanderbeg. . . . .
Newly translated . . . . by Z. I. . . . . Lond. (Ponsonby),
1596.

> Sonnet by Sp prefixed: "Wherefore doth vaine antiquitie so vaunt."

Nennio, Or a Treatise of Nobility. . . . . Done into English by
William Jones. Lond. 1595. [By G. B. Nenne.]

> Sonnet by Sp prefixed: "Who so wil seeke by right deserts t'attain."

PALGRAVE, F. T. In Grosart's ed. of Sp, IV, pp. xciii f.; cvi f.

SÉLINCOURT. One-volume Oxford ed. of Sp, 603-4.

Spenser-Harvey Correspondence.

> For Sp's Latin verses and other experiments in verse.

IV
CRITICISM, INFLUENCE, ALLUSIONS

IV. CRITICISM, INFLUENCE, ALLUSIONS

IN GENERAL

See "Works, Editions," above.

The subject of Spenser's literary influence has been so fully treated by others, that I have not thought it necessary to give in the following pages many of the references to be found in their works. The list immediately following gives most of the works which discuss the subject:

ADAMS, E. D., ed. The Poet's Praise. Lond. 1894. 103–12. Cf. 146.

ALLIBONE, S. A. Dictionary of English Literature. Phila. 1899. II, 2202–8:
> Gives numerous citations of "critical opinions."

BASKERVILL, CHARLES R. The Early Fame of *The Shepheards Calender*. In Pub. Mod. Lang. Asso., XXVIII (1913), 291–313.
> Cf. under "Works," Greenlaw.

BAYNE, RONALD. In Cambr. Hist. Eng. Lit., VI (1910), ch. xiii, pp. 329–30, 335–36.
> "The relation of Spenser's art to the masque." (Influence of Sp.)

BEERS, HENRY A. A History of English Romanticism in the Eighteenth Century. N.Y. 1899. Ch. iii:
> "The Spenserians." One phase of the rise of Eng. romanticism historically studied. The interest, however, as is natural, is not cente˜ed in the study of the influence of Sp as such. See esp. 77–101: motives of the turn of taste toward Sp; history of his literary reputation in outline; chief instances of Sp's fertilizing influence, after 1650. Editions of Sp, commentaries, etc., in the period. The Spenserian imitations discussed in detail (83 ff.). The best treatment of Sp's influence in the period. But see Cory, below.

BEERS, H. A. A History of English Romanticism in the Nineteenth Century. N.Y. 1901.
> Similar plan. Touches upon Sp's influence in the period covered. See index.

BELL, JOHN, ed. Fugitive Poetry. Lond. 1789.

Vol. X: Poems in the Stanza of Spenser; XI: Poems Imitative of Spenser, and in the manner of Milton.

BÖHME, TRAUGOTT. Spensers literarisches Nachleben bis zu Shelley. Berlin (Palaestra, XCIII), 1911.

Interesting study of Sp's literary influence, in some detail. Cf. Engl. Studien, XLIV (1912), 403–8.

BROWN, P. F. The Influence of Edmund Spenser on the British Romantic Poets, 1800–40. Chicago. MS Diss. in Univ. of Chicago Lib.

BRYDGES, SIR EGERTON. Censura Literariā. Lond. 1815. See indexes.

CHURCH, R. W. Spenser. 137 ff. Cf. 100, 101, 165.

CORY, HERBERT E. The Influence of Spenser on English Poetry. MS Diss., 1910, in Harvard Lib.

"Modified and pub. in part as "Browne's 'Britannia's Pastorals' and Spenser's 'Faerie Queene,'" Univ. of Cal. Chron. 1911, 13: 189–200; "The Critics of Edmund Spenser," Univ. of Cal. Pub., Mod. Philol., 1911, 2: 81–182; "The Golden Age of the Spenserian Pastoral," Pub. Mod. Lang. Asso. Amer., 1910, 25: 241–67; "Spenser, Thomson, and Romanticism," ibid., 1911, 26: 51–91: "Spenser, The School of the Fletchers, and Milton," Univ. of Cal. Pub., Mod. Philol., 1912, 2: 311–373."

CORY, H. E. The Golden Age of the Spenserian Pastoral. In Pub. Mod. Lang. Asso., XXV (1910), 241–67.

A study of the influence of the Sh Cal on the Eng. pastoral, 1579–1700.

CORY, H. E. The Critics of Edmund Spenser. Berkeley, Univ. of Cal. Press, 1911.

Treats the criticism of Sp historically, to the nineteenth century: chiefly in Harvey and other contemporaries, in Hall, Jonson, Bolton, Davenant, Dryden, Addison, Pope, Hughes, the Wartons, Hurd, Scott, Hazlitt, Hunt, .etc. A substantial contribution, marred by faults of taste and style. Controverts Beers and Phelps; holds that the classical school consistently accepted Sp, and that the long line of "imitations" of Sp in the eighteenth century as such did not mark a romantic revival. See 129 ff., 159. Cf. Engl. Studien, XLIV (1912), 403–8.

CORY, H. E. Spenser, Thomson, and Romanticism. In Pub. Mod. Lang. Asso., XXVI (1911), 51–91.

That Sp was recognized as a classic in the eighteenth century, and was imitated by the classicists, as well as by the romanticists, although in a different way.

CORY, H. E. Spenser, the School of the Fletchers, and Milton. Berkeley, Univ. of Cal. Press, 1912.

CORSON, H. Primer of Eng. Verse. 87–142.

COURTHOPE, W. J. History of English Poetry. Lond. 1897 ff.

Passim, esp. III, 6, 29, 38, 40, 139, 360, 392, 504.

CRANE, R. S. Imitation of Spenser and Milton in the Early Eighteenth Century. In Studies in Philology, XV (1918), 195–206.

Dict. Natl. Biog., XVIII, 796:

That after pub. of Sh Cal "Spenser was at once admitted by critical contemporaries to the first place among English poets" (contra, Greenlaw); 804: "In England's Parnassus (1600) he is quoted 225 times, while Shakespeare is quoted only seventy-nine."

EATON, H. A. See "Works, Sh Cal."

FILON, A. Histoire de la littérature anglaise. Paris, 1883. 206–11:

"L'école de Spenser": That Sp's immediate disciples exaggerate his qualities and his faults; degeneration of allegory into emblem ("l'emblème, c'est l'allégorie poussée à outrance") in Quarles, Wither, etc.; Drayton the most successful of Sp's followers in reproducing his beauties.

FLEAY, FREDERICK G. Guide to Chaucer and Spenser. Lond. 1877.

Brief critical examination of the Life: Chronology (with table, test of verse-forms, and dates); Table of characters in Sh Cal, and in CCCHA, with attempted identifications; similarly for FQ; contemporary poets. Useful and compact.

FULTON, EDWARD. Spenser and Romanticism. In the Nation, N.Y. XCII (1911), 445:

Sp as a factor in the Romantic movement.

GREG, W. W. Pastoral Poetry and Pastoral Drama. Lond. 1906.

Passim, on Sp's influence (see index).

GROSART'S ed. of Sp, I, 122 ff.:
Contemporary criticism of Sp.

HALES, J. W.   In Ward's Eng. Poets.   Lond. and N.Y. 1880.
II, 104:
The School of Spenser, its characteristics.

HAMELIUS, P.   Die Kritik in der engl. Litt. des 17. und 18.
Jahrh.   Leipzig, 1897.   111-12, 114-15:
The course of Sp criticism in the neo-classical period.

HUNT, LEIGH.   Imagination and Fancy.   Lond. 1883.   66.

JUSSERAND, J. J.   French Ignorance of English Literature in
Tudor Times.   In Nineteenth Century, XLIII (1898),
590-603:
That Sp and other Elizabethan writers were unknown in contemporary France.

KOEPPEL, E.   Ben Jonson's Wirkung auf zeitgenössische Dra-
matiker.   Heidelberg, 1906.   80-93:
Sp's influence on the Elizabethan Drama.   Cf. 95 ff.

LOUNSBURY, THOMAS R.   Studies in Chaucer.   N.Y.   1892.
III, 114 f.:
Seventeenth and eighteenth century imitations of Sp.   Cf. 119,
125, 152 ff.

MARSH, GEO. L.   Imitation and Influence of Spenser in English
Poetry from 1765 to 1800.   MS Diss. 1899.   In Univ. of
Chicago Lib.

MASSON, DAVID.   Life of Milton.   Lond. 1881.
I, 263; 452-55, 575; III, 456, 515.

MORTON, E. P.   The Spenserian Stanza before 1700.   In Mod.
Philol., IV (1907), 639-54.

MORTON, E. P.   The Spenserian Stanza in the Eighteenth
Century.   In Mod. Philol., X (1913), 365-91.
See 371 ff. for a review of the 18th cent. criticisms of the stanza.

MOULTON, CHAS. W.   Library of Literary Criticism.   Buffalo,
N.Y., 1901-5.   I, 368-400:
Extracts from criticisms of Sp.

MULLINGER, J. B.   Introd. to Masterman's Age of Milton.
Lond. 1897.   P. xiv:

Sp's influence chiefly among the graver and more masculine spirits of the seventeenth century, and greater in the first half than that of Shakespeare.

MUNRO, JOHN. Spenser Allusions. In Notes and Queries, Ser. X, Vol. X (1908), 121.

NICHOLS, J. A Select Collection of Poems. Lond. 1780. See index under "Spenser," in Vol. VIII.

OLIPHANT, THOS. Musa Madrigalesca. Lond. 1837. 176, 207, 310:
Imitations of Sp.

OSGOOD, C. G. Concordance to Spenser. Preface, pp. v–vii:
Discusses the progress of the appreciation of Sp; Sp's many-sidedness as brought into relief by his various critics; his propagating and proselytizing genius; an originator of Eng. poetical diction.

PHELPS, WILLIAM L. The Beginnings of the English Romantic Movement. Bost. 1893.
Passim (see index), esp. ch. iv: "The Spenserian Revival." But see Cory, above.

RESCHKE, H. Die Spenserstanze im neunzehnten Jahrhundert. Heidelberg, 1918.
General introd. followed by study of use of the stanza in some twenty-five or thirty poets of the century.

REUNING, K. Das Altertümliche im Wortschatz der Spenser-Nachahmungen das 18 Jahrh. Strassburg (Quellen und Forschungen, CXVI), 1912.

REYHER, PAUL. Les Masques Anglais. Paris, 1909. 142–46:
Influence of FQ on the masques; general pictorial and symbolical quality of FQ, and its influence in detail on various masques of Jonson, Beaumont, Browne, Milton, etc. Effect on mise-en-scène, costumes, etc. Incidentally some excellent characterization of the poetical qualities of the FQ.

The Saturday Review, XLI (May 20, 1876), 640–41: Spenser in the Eighteenth Century.
Survey of the subject, historically treated; the admirers of Sp in the period; his imitators. Recent change in views: "It requires as much courage to call Spenser a bore at the present day as it then required to deny that he was barbarous." . . . . "In the worst of times Spenser was not entirely neglected."

SCHELLING, FELIX E. The Elizabethan Drama. Bost. 1908. II, 170.

SCHELLING, F. E. A Book of Seventeenth Century Lyrics. Bost. 1899. Pp. xv–xviii.

SCHIPPER, J. Grundriss der englischen Metrik. Wien und Leipzig, 1895. 359–67:

> "Die Spenserstanze und ihre Nachbildungen," etc. Cf. the English version: Schipper, A History of English Versification. Ox. 1910, 358–65.
> Fuller treatment, with more numerous instances of imitations, in Schipper's Neuenglische Metrik. Bonn, 1888. 766–801.

SCHRÖER, A. Zu Spenser im Wandel der Zeiten. In Die Neueren Sprachen, XIII (1905), 449–60:

> On Sp's later literary influence; esp. on "Spenser Redivivus," 1686; with excerpts; and on "Spensers Fairy Queen attempted in Blank Verse," 1783.

SCRIBNER, DORA A. The History of Spenser's Literary Reputation Chicago, 1906. MS Diss. in Univ. of Chicago Lib.

SÉLINCOURT. Introd. to his one-volume ed. of Sp. P. xl.

SHEAVYN, PHOEBE. The Literary Profession in the Elizabethan Age. Manchester, 1909. 157 n:

> Sp's literary success in aristocratic and literary circles.

SPURGEON, CAROLINE F. E. Five Hundred Years of Chaucer Criticism and Allusion (1357–1900). Lond. (Chaucer Soc. Pub.), 1914.

> Quotation of many comments on Sp, chronologically arranged. In addition to references to Miss Spurgeon's book in various references below, see I, 118, 132–33, 134, 161, 167, 176, 192, 194, 195, 224, 242, 244, 247, 248, 249, 257, 258, 262, 263, 266, 288, 314, 322, 349, 369, 391, etc.

STEPHEN, LESLIE. Eng. Thought in the Eighteenth Century. Lond. [1876]. 2d ed., 1881. II, 359.

SWINBURNE, A. C. Miscellanies. Lond. 1886. 6–10.

THOMPSON, ELBERT N. S. Between the Shepheards Calender and the Seasons. In Philological Quarterly, Univ. of Iowa, I (Jan. 1922), 23–30:

> On Robert Farlie's Lychnocausia, 1638, and his Kalendarium Humanae Vitae, 1638,—the latter partly fashioned after the Sh Cal.

THOMPSON, G. A. Elizabethan Criticism of Poetry. Menasha, Wis., 1914. Diss. Univ. of Chicago. Passim.

TODD'S ed. of Sp, 1805, I, pp. cliv ff.

TUCKWELL, WM. Spenser. Lond. 1906. 70, 78–79.

VAUGHAN, C. E. In Cambridge Modern History, VI (1909), 829 ff.:
Sp and the Romantic Movement.

WARD, ADOLPHUS W. Hist. Eng. Dram. Lit. Lond. 1899. I, 367; II, 119, 464, 583, 664.

WINDSCHEID, K. See "Works, Sh Cal."

CRITICISM BEFORE 1651

See below, Index, Part II.

ALABASTER, WM. Epigrammata. Bodleian MS No. 283:
One is "In Edouardum Spencerum, Britannicae poesios facile principem."
Cf. Catalogi Cod. MSS Bibl. Bodl., Partis Quintae. Oxon. 1893. Fasc. iii, p. 133:

> "Fors qui sepulchro conditur siquis fuit
> Quaeris uiator, dignus es qui rescias.
> Spencerus istic conditur, siquis fuit
> Rogare pergis, dignus es qui nescias."

(If you ask who's buried here, passerby, you deserve to hear. Spenser is buried here. If you go on to ask who he is you don't deserve to know.)
Text from rotograph copy. Translation by Professor Paul Shorey. These are perhaps another of the copies of verses thrown into Spenser's tomb.

ALCILIA, 1595. In Grosart's Occasional Issues, 1879. P. xxvi.

ALLOT, ROBT., ed. England's Parnassus. 1600. Repr. in Park's Heliconia. Lond. 1815. III.
A book of elegant extracts, arranged under topics. Quotations from Sp appear on almost every page (over 300 entries in all, mostly from the FQ, but with a fair number from the Four Hymns, Sh Cal, and other minor poems,—some 15 or 20). Following the alphabetical arrangement of topics are extracts in general classes grouped as Divisions of the Day, Poetical Descriptions, Poetical Comparisons (Similes),

etc., where Sp's rich art in handling the *materia poetica* in its details may profitably be studied in juxtaposition with that of his most esteemed contemporaries.

Cf. Chas. Crawford in Notes and Queries, Ser. X, Vol. XI, 4, 123, 204, 283, 383, 443, 502; XII, 235.

Cf. Shakspere Allusion Book, II, 474–75: corrects some of the attributions.

ANTON, ROBERT. The Philosophers Satyrs, 1616. Extract in Brydges' Brit. Bibliographer, I, 532–3 *n*.

"Sound searching Spencer with his Faierie frame."

B., R. Greenes Funeralls, 1594. Repr. ed. R. B. McKerrow. Lond. 1911. Pp. 73, 75.

Allusions to Sp?

BARNES, BARNABE. Parthenophil and Parthenophe, 1593. Repr. in Arber's Eng. Garner, V. See p. 445:

Among the shepherds,
> "Here Colin sits, beneath that oaken tree,
> Eliza singing in his lays."

BARNFIELD, RICHARD. Poems in divers humors, 1598. In his Poems, ed. Arber, 1882.

118: "Spenser to mee [is dear]; whose deepe Conceit is such,
> As passing all Conceit, needs no defence."

119: "A Remembrance of some English Poets."

Cf. Barnfield's Address to the Readers, p. 44: that his Cynthia (1595) "is the first imitation of the verse of that excellent poet, Maister Spencer, in his Fayrie Queene."

Cf. Brydges, Restituta, IV, 494, 499, 500; Collier's ed. of Sp, I, pp. cvi–cx.

BASSE, WM. (d. 1653?). Poetical Works, ed. R. W. Bond. Lond. 1893. Pp. xiv f. (Basse one of Sp's Circle), xxvii, 36, 58, 73, 164, 170.

Cf. The Academy, 23 Sept. 1893, 247. Cf. Greenwood, G. G. Is There a Shakespeare Problem? Lond. 1916. 399–400.

B[AXTER], N[ATHANIEL]. Sir Philip Sydneys Ourania. Lond. 1606. (Copy in Newberry Lib., Chicago). Sig. C (1):

Mention of Sp. The poem shows some influence of Sp. Introducing ladies of the court under pastoral names, it deserves study as a document of the Sidney-Spenser circle.

BEAUMONT, JOSEPH (1615–99). Complete Poems, ed. A. B. Grosart. Chertsey Worthies Lib. 1880. I, 10, 110; II, 207.

BEAUMONT, FRANCIS (1584–1616). A Letter from B., printed in Lady Newdigate-Newdegate's Gossip from a Muniment-Room. Lond. 1898. 132.
> Cf. Lounsbury's Chaucer, III, 59; C. M. Gayley, Francis Beaumont. Lond. 1914. See index, esp. p. 44.

BEAUMONT AND FLETCHER:
> The Knight of the Burning Pestle (c. 1610).
>> In part a satire on the FQ? "Dorus"=Sp?
>> Cf. Mézières, Contemporains et Successeurs de Shakespeare. Paris, 1881. 171.

> The Woman's Prize. (Before 1633.)
>> Act I, sc. iii, quotes from the FQ, I, i, 13.
>> Cf. A. W. Ward, Hist. Eng. Dram. Lit., 1899. II, 752.

BODENHAM, JOHN. Belvedere or the Garden of the Muses, 1600. Spenser Soc. Repr., 1875.
> One- or two-line extracts, similes, and examples, arranged topically, from the poets of the age, including Sp, "from many of their extant works, and some kept in privat."

BOLTON, EDMUND. Hypercritica (c. 1616). Pub. 1722. Repr. in Spingarn's Critical Essays of the Seventeenth Century, I, 82 ff. See p. 109. Also quoted in Warton's Hist. Eng. Poetry. Lond. 1871. IV, 205:
> "In verse there are Ed. Spencer's *Hymns*. I cannot advise the allowance of other of his Poems as for practick English." Bolton is discussing standards and models of English prose, especially for writers of history. He adds: "My judgment is nothing at all in Poems or Poesie."

BRANDON, SAMUEL. The Virtuous Octavia, 1598. Malone Soc. Repr. 1909.
> Ll. 895 ff. (mutability); 1960 ff. (Beauty and Love).

BRATHWAITE, RICHARD. A Strappado for the Diuell, 1615. Repr. ed. J. W. Ebsworth. Bost. (Eng.), 1878. 129 ff.:
> A satire on getting on in the world. Influence of MHT. Cf. Spenser, ed. Grosart, III, p. xxxi.

BRETON, NICHOLAS. Melancholic Humors (1600). In his Works, ed. Grosart, 1893.

> I, 15: "Epitaph upon Poet Spencer."
> Cf. J. P. Collier's ed. of Sp, I, pp. cxlvi ff.

BROWNE, WM. (1591–1643?). Poems, ed. G. Goodwin. Lond. (The Muses Lib.) 1894.

> I, 12: Commendatory verses by E. Heyward: calls Browne "A Second Colin Clout."
> 88: Britannia's Pastorals (1613), I, Song 3, ll. 179–92: pastoral praise of Colin Clout; 150.
> 154 ff., Id., I, Song 5, ll. 465 ff.: The House of Repentance, in the manner of FQ; 222; 225–26: fervent praise of Sp; 313.
> II, 51; 81: Commendatory verses by E. Johnson, on Sp and Sidney, the "Sole English makers," etc.; 237; 279–82: "Visions" in the manner of Sp; 313.
> Cf. F. W. Moorman, William Browne and the Pastoral Poetry of the Elizabethan Age. Strassburg, 1897. Passim, esp. 7, 18, 23–24, 26, 27, 29 ff., 42, 47 ff., 87, 90, 92 ff. (On Sp's "interpretation of nature"), 96 ff. (The "School of Spenser"), 114, 137, etc.
> Cf. H. E. Cory, Browne's Britannia's Pastorals and Spenser's Faerie Queene. In Univ. of Cal. Chronicle, 1911.

BRYSKETT, LODOWICK. Discourse of Civill-Life, 1606.

> See above, under "Life, General."
> See also his Pastorall Aeglogue (with the Astrophel volume), ll. 35–36.

BUTLER, CHARLES. Rhetoricae Libri Duo. Oxon. 1600, 1629, 1642, etc. Quoted in Shakspere Allusion Book, I, 473; also in Spurgeon, Chaucer Criticism, I, 162:

> Sp cited among the chief English poets, "quorum haec aetas uberrima est."
> Cf. Foster Watson, in Trans. of Bibliog. Soc. London, VI (1903), 209: Butler quotes from the FQ, "ut in illo Homeri nostri poemate." "Thus, through 11 editions of this school book written in Latin the attention of generations of schoolboys was called to these lines in Spenser, all the more emphatically for being surrounded by Latin on the technical terms of Rhetoric."

C., E. Emaricdulf, 1595. Repr. in A Lamport Garland. Roxburghe Club, 1881. Sonnet 40.

C., R.   The Times Whistle (c. 1615).   Repr. E.E.T. Soc. 1871.
Cf. Robert Anton, above.
Cf. Alden, Rise of Formal Satire, 207.

Caesar's Revenge, 1606.   Repr. Malone Soc. 1911.
Ll. 1451 ff., 2247.

CAREW, RICHARD (1555–1620).   Epistle on the Excellency of
the English Tongue.   In Camden's Remains, 1614.   Pr.
from MS in Gregory Smith's Elizabethan Critical Essays.
II, 293:
Sp the English Lucan.

CARLTON, R.   Madrigals to Five Voyces, 1601.   Quoted in
Fellowes, Eng. Madrigal Verse.   Ox. 1920.   70, 71:
Verses from FQ, VI, vii, 1; V, viii, 1–2; V, vii, 1; VI, viii, 1; set
to music.

Certain Elegies done by Sundrie excellent wits, with Satyrs and
Epigrams.   Lond.   1620.   Repr. ed. Utterson.   Beldornie
Press, 1843.   [25].

Certaine Worthye Manuscript Poems of Great Antiquitie Reserved long in the Studie of a Northfolke Gentleman and
now first published by J. S.   Lond. 1597.   (Copy in Harvard
Lib.)   Repr. 1812.
Dedicated (verso of Title) "To the worthiest Poet Maister Ed.
Spenser."
Cf. Mary A. Scott, Eliz. Translations from the Italian.   Bost. 1916,
150; Collier's ed. of Sp, I, pp. cxxxiii–vii; Hunter, Chorus Vatum, IV,
470, conjectures that "J.S." is Joshua Sylvester.

CHALKHILL, JOHN (fl. 1600).   Thealma and Clearchus. . . . . By
John Chalkhill, Esq.   An Acquaintant and Friend of Edmund
Spencer.   Lond. 1683.   Preface by Isaac Walton.   Repr. in
Saintsbury's Caroline Poets, II.
In prefatory verses to Walton Thos. Flatman promises that his
memory shall be secure
"As long as Spencer's noble flames shall burn,
And deep Devotions, throng about his Urn."
Allusions to or echoes of Sp (Colin) occur at pp. 3, 61, 99, 125, and in
the diction passim.   See Saintsbury's ed., 371, 374, 414, etc.
Cf. Drake, Shakespeare and his Times, I, 605–7.

CHAPMAN, GEO.   Monsieur D'Olive, 1606.

 Esp. Act IV, sc. i (Parody of Sp).   Cf. E. Koeppel, Ben Jonson's
Wirkung, 87.

CHETTLE, HENRY.   England's Mourning Garment, 1603.
Quoted in Collier's ed. of Sp, I, p. lxxix *n.*

CHURCHYARD, THOS.

 A Praise of Poetrie, 1595.   In Censura Literaria, 1815, I, 312:
"Spenser's morall Fairie Queene."
 The Challenge, 1593.   In Censura Literaria, 1815, I, 289: "Call
Spenser now the spirit of learned speech."

CLARKE, WM.   See below, Polimanteia.

CHUTE, ANTHONY.   Beawtie dishonoured [Shores' Wife], 1593.

 Quoted in Corser, Collectanea, IV, 394.

SIR CLYOMON and SIR CLAMYDES (c. 1580?).

 Cf. Schelling, Eliz. Drama, 1908, II, 399: "Sir Clyomon . . . .
wherein the world as it is conceived in the Faery Queen is transferred
to the stage."   (Influence, or source?)

COKE, EDWARD (1552–1634), Lord Chief Justice.

 Cf. The Library, Ser. IV, Vol. II (1922), 218: Coke had a copy of Sp
in his library.

*COLLINS, THOS.   The Tears of Love. Lond. 1615.   Cf.
Hunter's Chor. Vat.   IV, 469.

COOPER, D.   Commendatory verses upon the Royal Master,
1638.   In Jas. Shirley's Dramatic Works, ed. Dyce.   Lond.
1833.   I, p. lxxxiv.

COWLEY, ABRAHAM (1618–67).   Poems.   In Chalmers' Poets,
VII, 3:

 Dr. Johnson on Sp's influence on C.   There are few echoes of Sp in
C.   But cf. 74 b, a possible allusion; 141 b, the figure of Envy; 214,
"Of Myself": of his being made a poet by reading Sp as a boy—the
oft-quoted passage.

CUTWOODE, THOS.   Caltha Poetarum. Lond.   1599.   Repr.
Roxburghe Club Pub.   Lond. 1815.   Sig. A4b.

DANIEL, GEORGE, of Berwick (1616–57).

 A Vindication of Poesy.
 Essay Endeavouring to Ennoble our English Poesy.
 In his Poems, ed. Grosart, 1878.   I, 26–32, 79–84.

DANIEL, SAMUEL.
  Delia, 1591, No. 55.
  Civil Wars, 1595, Bk. IV (later = Bk V), st. 4–5.
  Musophilus, 1601.
  Cleopatra, 1623 (Dedicatory Verses).
  In his Complete Works, ed. Grosart, Spenser Soc. Pub., 1885–96. I, 73,
    239; II, 175; III, 26, 398.

DAVENANT, SIR WM.
  The Platonic Lovers, 1636. In his Dramatic Works. Edinb. (Drama-
    tists of the Restoration), 1872. II, 13.
  Preface to Gondibert, 1650. In Chalmers' Poets, VI, 350–51.

DAVIES, SIR JOHN. Orchestra, 1594. St. 128.
  In his Complete Poems, ed. Grosart. Lond. 1876. I, 212.

DAVISON's Poetical Rhapsody, 1600. Repr. ed. Bullen. Lond.
  1890. I, pp. lxxv, lxxxv, 62, 65, 67, 71, 76 ff, 136; II, 124–25:
    Reprints Sp's "Elegie in Trimetre Iambickes" from the Harvey-Sp
  correspondence, 1580.
  Cf. Cambr. Hist. Eng. Lit., IV, 125; Dict. Natl. Biog., XVIII, 797.

DEKKER, THOS. Whore of Babylon, 1607. In Dekker's Dramatic Works. Lond. 1873. II.
  .   E.g., pp. 187: Florimell, Paridel, etc.; 229: Satyran, etc.

  A Knight's Conjuring, 1606. Quoted in Sélincourt,
  Introd. to his one-volume Oxford ed. of Sp, p. xl.
    Cf. F. E. Schelling, The Eng. Chronicle Play. N.Y. 1902. 240;
  E. Koeppel, Ben Jonson's Wirkung, 91; Collier's ed. of Sp, I, p. cxliii;
  Mary L. Hunt, Thomas Dekker, a Study. N.Y. 1911. 5, 38, 134.

DICKENSON, JOHN. The Shepheardes Complaint (c. 1594).
  Repr. in Grosart's Occasional Issues, 1878. 14, 30–32, etc.

DIGBY, SIR KENELM (1603–65). Journal of a Voyage into the
  Mediterranean, 1628. Ed. J. Bruce. Camden Soc. 1868.
    "Digby beguiled the voyage out by reading Spenser." (Cambr.
  Hist. Eng. Lit., VII, 449.)

  Observations on the 22d stanza of the 9th canto of the
  2d Book of Spenser's Fairy Queen. Lond. 1644. Frequently
  reprinted in editions of Sp.
    Cf. Catalogi Codicum Manuscriptorum, Bibl. Bodleianae, Pars
  Quarta. Oxon. 1860. P. 899: Copy of a letter of Sir Kenelm Digby to
  Sir Edw. Stradling, on FQ, II, ix, 22.

A Discourse concerning Edmund Spencer. Brit. Mus. MS. Harl. No. 4153.

Digby's copy of Sp's Works, 1617, with his signature, was advertised in a London book auction sale, April, 1922.

DONNE, JOHN. Poems, ed. E. K. Chambers. Lond. and N.Y. 1896. II, 205: Satire VI (vii), c. 1603:

> "Here sleep's house by famous Ariosto,
> By silver-tongued Ovid, and many moe,
> —Perhaps by golden-mouthed Spenser too, pardie—
> (Which builded was some dozen stories high),
> I had repaired."

Cf. FQ, I, i, 39 ff. (The House of Sleep.) The fourth line apparently alludes to the plan of the FQ. The Stephens MS of Donne reads "two dozen stories,"—referring to the original plan of twenty-four books.

DRAYTON, MICHAEL. Poems, in Chalmers' Poets, IV.

Echoes of Spenserian images and phrases or references to Sp may be found on pp. 26a, 96a, 97b, 163b, 169a, 290 ff. (Polyolbion, song xv, Marriage of the Thames and the Isis: cf. Sp's Marriage of the Thames and the Medway), 298b, 300 ff. (Polyolbion, song xvii, the English rivers), 400b, 431b, 433, 434a, 436b, 438b, 440a, 443b; etc.

Cf. R. M. Alden, Rise of Formal Satire in England. Phila. 1899. 171: Drayton's Owl influenced by MHT.

Cf. J. P. Collier's ed. of Sp, I, pp. xcix f.; cxxi *n* (Drayton's copy of Sp's Works); L. Whitaker in Pub. Mod. Lang. Asso., XVIII (1903), 406–8.

DRUMMOND, WM. (1585–1649.) Poems, ed. W. C. Ward. The Muses Lib. 1894. Passim. Cf. I, p. xxxii.

Cf. D. Masson, Drummond of Hathornden, 1873. 19, 27, 67 ff., 80.

DYER, SIR EDWARD. Verses in the Phoenix Nest, 1593. In Miscellanies of the Fuller Worthies Lib. IV, Dyer, 51–53 (printed from MS):

In the manner of the Sh Cal.

EDWARDS, THOS. Cephalus and Procris. Narcissus. 1595. Repr. ed. W. E. Buckley. Lond. (Roxburghe Club), 1882. 4: Allusion to Tears of Muses?; 12 (cf. 224); 27–28 (cf. 253–54); 62. Cf. p. 25 ("Amoretta").

Cf. Charlotte C. Stopes in Mod. Lang. Review, XVI (1921), 209–23.

England's Helicon, 1600. Repr. ed. Bullen. Lond. 1887. Selections from Sp in this anthology occur at pp. 28, 38, 64.

The Faerie Leveller, or King Charles his Leveller descried and deciphered in Queene Elizabeth's Dayes. By her Poet Laureat Edmond Spenser, in his Unparaleld Poem, entituled The Faerie Queene, a lively representation of our Times. 1648. (Copy in Huntington Lib.)

"A twelve page tract in verse." See Preface: that the levellers (the Puritans) were hit off by "the Prince of English Poets *Edmund Spenser.*" His verses here revised; on the allegory of the FQ; quotes stanzas on Artegal and Talus (FQ, V, ii, 29–54); identifies Artegal as King Charles, Talus as "the king's forces or Gregory," Pollente as the Parliament, the Giant Leveller as "Col. Oliver Cromwell," etc.

FAIRFAX, EDWARD. Translation of Tasso's Jerusalem Delivered, 1600. Repr. ed. H. Morley. Lond. (Carisbrooke Lib.), 1890.

In style and phrasing this translation was deeply influenced by Sp, just as Sp was deeply influenced by its original, Tasso. Cf. Morley's Introd.; cf. E. Koeppel in Anglia, XII (1890), 105 ff.

FANSHAWE, SIR RICHARD. The Progress of Learning. 1647, and later eds. (1736 "improved"). With his Pastor Fido, 1648, Pp. 256–63:

Copy in Bost. Pub. Lib. and in Newberry Lib. In Spenserian stanzas. Line 1 =

"Tell me O Muse, and tell me Spencers ghost."

Father Hubberd's Tales, 1604. Repr. in Middleton's Works. ed. Bullen, VIII.

Cf. Collier's Poetical Decameron, I, 100.

First Booke of the Preservation of King Henry VII when he was but Earle of Richmond . . . . 1599. In Collier's Illustrations of Old Eng. Lit. Lond. 1866. II.

The address to the Reader discusses Eng. hexameters; regrets Sp's abandonment of them.

FITZGEOFFREY, CHARLES. Poems, ed. Grosart, Occasional Issues, 1881. 21:

Sir Francis Drake, 1596; cf. 22, 79, pp. xix–xx:
Affaniae, 1601.
Latin verses on Sp; transl., p. xxiii.
Cf. Brydges, British Bibliographer, II, 119–20.
Collier's Poet. Decameron, I, 32–33; Collier's ed. of Sp, I, p. cxlii *n.*

[FITZGEFFREY, HENRY.] Certain Elegies, 1620. Repr. 1843.
See above, Certain Elegies.

FLETCHER, GILES, JR. (1588–1623?). Complete Poems, ed.
Grosart. Lond. 1876.
> Echoes of Sp on almost every page. See esp. 115, 145, 169, 172–74
> (cf. Sp's Cave of Despair, FQ, I, ix), 178–83 (cf. Sp's Garden of Adonis,
> FQ, III, vi, and Gardens of Acrasia, FQ, II, v, etc.), 184 (cf. Cave of
> Mammon, FQ, II, vii, viii), 187 (cf. FQ, II, xii, 74 ff.), 189 (cf. FQ,
> II, xii, 71), 227.
> Cf. Cambr. Hist. Eng. Lit., IV, 167; J. D. Wilson, Giles Fletcher
> and "The Faerie Queene." In Mod. Lang. Review, V (1910), 493–94.

FLETCHER, JOHN. The Faithful Shepherdess, 1610. Esp. V, v.
> On imitations of Sp in this play cf. E. Koeppel, Quellen-Studien zu
> den Dramen Jonsons, Marstons, und Beaumont und Fletchers, Erlangen,
> 1895, 39–40; also A. W. Ward, Hist. Eng. Dram. Lit., II, 664.

FLETCHER, PHINEAS (1582–1650). Poems, ed. Grosart. Fuller
Worthies Lib. 1869.
> For passages conspicuously imitating Sp see I, 57: Britain's Ida,
> 1628, canto ii (cf. FQ, II, xii, Bower of Bliss, etc.); II, 72: The Locusts,
> 1627 (cf. FQ, I, ix, Cave of Despair); 241: Piscatorie Eclogues, 1633
> (cf. Sh Cal, Dec.); III, 216; IV: Purple Island, 1633; 37, 45–46, 58,
> 83 ff., 164, 166, 183–84, 186, canto vii, passim, 267, 327, 329–30, 349; etc.
> Cf. Grosart's excited and tasteless discussion of the literary relations
> of Fletcher and Sp, I, pp. clxxvi, cxcvii ff., ccxxii–xlviii.
> Cf. The Retrospective Review, II (1820), 341 ff.

FLORIO, JOHN. Second Fruits. Lond. 1591. Epistle Dedicatory. A 3:
> Copy in Brit. Mus. and in Huntington Lib.
> Praise of Leicester "which the sweetest singer of all our western
> shepheards hath so exquisitely depicted . . . . so I account him thrice
> fortunate in having such a herauld of his vertues as Spencer.   Curteous
> Lord, Curteous Spenser, I knowe not which hath purchased more fame;
> either he in deserving so well of so famous a scholler, or so famous a
> scholler in being so thankfull without hope of requitall to so famous a
> Lord."

*FRAUNCE, ABRAHAM. The Sheapheardes Logike: conteyning
the praecepts of that art put down by Ramus: examples fet
owt of the Sheapheards Kalender. Ded. to Edw. Dyer.
Brit. Mus. MS.

Described in Brydges, Brit. Bibliographer, II, 276–81.

Cf. Moore Smith's ed. of Fraunce's Victoria, p. xxxii.

Cf. Catalogue of Additions to MSS in Brit. Museum. Lond. 1894. No. 34,361.

*FRAUNCE, A. The Lawyers Logike. 1588.

Fraunce c.1580 wrote the Shepheardes Logike (see above). To this he refers in the epistle to this work: "I have reteyned those ould examples of the new Shepheards Kalender, which I first gathered." Copy in Newberry Lib.

FRAUNCE, A. Arcadian Rhetoricke. 1588.

Cites part of stanza 35 of Bk. II, canto iv, of the FQ (before the publication of the FQ).

The book is described, with quotations, in Gregory Smith's Eliz. Crit. Essays, I, 303–6, 422.

FREEMAN, THOS. Rubbe, and a Great Cast; Epigrams, 1614. Epig. 64:

"Of Spencer's Faiery Queene"; high laudation.

G., (E.). Verses, in M. Lluelyn, Men Miracles. Ox. 1646.

Quoted in Spurgeon, Chaucer Criticism, I, 225. Copy of ed. of 1656 in Newberry Lib.

GIBBONS, ORLANDO. First Set of Madrigals, 1612. Quoted in Fellowes, Eng. Madrigal Verse. Ox. 1920. 98:

Verses from the FQ (III, i, 49), set to music.

GILL, ALEX. Logonomia Anglicana, 1621. Repr. ed. O. L. Jiriczek. Strassburg (Quellen u. Forsch., XC), 1903.

Gill's treatise is in Latin, but is illustrated by quotations, in phonetic spelling, in English, esp. from Sp. See 103–29, 145.

Cf. Böhme, Spenser's lit. Nachleben, 1911, 3, 7–9: finds the "canonization of the Spenserian diction" in this work. Cf. Masson's Life of Milton, I, 79–81.

GREENE, ROBERT. Plays and Poems, ed. J. C. Collins. Ox. 1905. I, 70–82:

Collins' discussion of the relation of the Prologue to Greene's Alphonsus to Sp's Complaints, which in parts are imitated; similarly to Greene's A Maidens Dreame, 1591. Cf. the Prologue, pp. 79–82.

Grim the Collier of Croydon, c. 1600. In Hazlitt's Dodsley, VIII, 385 ff.

Introduces among the parts, Malbecco (ghost), from the FQ (III, ix, x). Cf. 393 ff., 467, 470.

Cf. Cambr. Hist. Eng. Lit., V, 329; Koeppel, Ben Jonson's Wirkung, 92; John C. Jordan, Robert Greene. N.Y. 1915. 175, 185–86.

GUILPIN, EDWARD. Skialetheia, 1598. Repr. in Grosart's Occasional Issues, 1878. 63: Satyre vi:

> "Some blame deep *Spencer* for his grandam words,
> Others protest that in them he records
> His maister-piece of cunning, giving praise
> And gravity to his profound-prickt layes."

Also in Collier's Illus. of Early Eng. Lit., III, 53.

H., R. [Richard Harvey?]. In obitum doctissimi viri venerabilisimmi Spenseri Carmen. MS (c. 1600). MS in Newberry Lib., Chicago.

> An exercise in rhetorical laudation. Nothing specific. Is this a copy of one of the sets of verses cast into Sp's grave at his funeral? Cf. C. Fitzgeoffrey, above.

HABINGTON, WM. Castara, 1634.

> In Chalmers' Poets, VI. See 481. Also in Arber's Reprints.

HALL, JOSEPH. Satires, 1597-98. Virgidemiarum, 1599. In his Complete Poems, ed. Grosart, 1879. P. 11. Also in his Works. Ox. 1839, Vol. XII; and in Chalmers' Poets, V.

> See (in Chalmers, V), 263, Introd.: Hall's muse does not deal with "elvish knights," or "misty moral types," or giants, enchantments, and "stories of ladies and adventrous knights" in "stately stanzas."
>
> 264-65 (Bk. I, sat. i): laudatory allusion to Sp's episode of the Marriage of the Thames and the Medway. (Cf. Warton, Hist. Eng. Po. Lond. 1871. IV, 369.)
>
> 266 (Bk. I, sat. iv): praise of Sp; 268 (Bk. II, sat. ii). Cf. Cory's Critics of Spenser, 95-97; K. Schulze, Die Satiren Halls. Berlin, 1910. Pp. 122, 125-26, 127, 129, 131, 151, 156, 254, 255, 259, 274.

HANCOCKE, GEO., 1615. In Spurgeon, Chaucer Criticism, I, 190.

HANNAY, PATRICK. Sheratine and Mariana, 1622. In his Poetical Works, Hunterian Club. Pub., 1875.

> A few echoes of Sp, esp. 149-50.

HARBERT, WM. A Prophesie of Cadwallader, 1604. In Miscellanies of the Fuller Worthies Lib. 1871. I, 93-94.

Harl. MSS 5353:

> In Spenseru[m].
> Famous alive, and dead here is y*e* ods
> Then God of Poets, nowe poet of y*e* Gods.
> (Transcript by H. R. Plomer.)

[HARINGTON, SIR JOHN?]. The Metamorphosis of Ajax. 1596.
Quoted in Collier's Poet. Decameron, I, 204. Repr.
Chiswick Press, 1814: In "An Anatomy of the Meta-
morphosed Ajax," p. 3 of "An Apology":

> A feigned conversation of Zoilus, Momus, etc. "They descanted
> of the new Faerie Queene, and the old both; and the greatest fault they
> could find in it, was that the last verse [i.e. of the stanza?] disordered
> their mouths, and was like a trick of seventeen in a sinkapace."

HARVEY, GABRIEL. Marginalia, ed. G. C. Moore Smith, 1913.
> See index, esp. 232 (popularity of the FQ).

HEATH, ROBERT. Clarastella. . . . . Epigrams. 1650. 48.

H[ENDERSON?, or HARRIS?], R[OBERT]. Arraignement of the
Whole Creature, 1631. 186.
> Copy in Newberry Lib.

A Herring's Tayle. Lond. for Mathew Lownes, 1598. (Copy
in Huntington Lib.)

> Mock heroic hexameter couplets. Possible allusion to Sp at B iv,
> verso: "Who list such know, let him *Muses Despencier* reede."

HEYLYN, PETER. Microcosmos. Ox. 1625. Quoted in Spurgeon, Chaucer Criticism, I, 194.

HEYWOOD, THOS. Love's Mistress, 1636.
> Cf. Koeppel, Ben Jonson's Wirkung, 89.

HOWES, EDMUND. John Stow's Annales . . . . continued to
the end of 1631, by E. H. Lond. 1631. 811:
> List of the Elizabethan poets, including Sp.

JONSON, BEN. Works, ed. Gifford and Cunningham. Lond.
n.d. (187–).

> I, 415: The Silent Woman, 1609: The gossip of women about con-
> temporary poets (cf. Whalley's note; cited ad loc.)
> III, 470: Conversations with Drummond, in 1619: Jonson's distaste
> for Sp's stanza and allegory; 475: Verses from the Sh Cal which J.
> had by heart; 478: Sp's last days; a point in the allegory.
> III, 58: Masque of Queens, 1609: "The grave and diligent Spenser."
> III, 398: Timber, or Discoveries, 1641 (mostly after 1630): Popular
> judgments on poetry would prefer "the water-rhymer's works
> against Spenser's"; 412: "Spenser, in affecting the ancients, writ
> no language; yet I would have him read for his matter, but as Virgil
> read Ennius."

III, 102: The Golden Age Restored, 1615: Invocation of
"You far-famed spirits of this happy isle, ...
That Chaucer, Gower, Lidgate, Spenser, hight."
Immediately "they descend" upon the scene. A bold treatment of
a person but sixteen years dead. And therefore high evidence of
Sp's poetical canonization.

III, 352: Underwoods, 1641. Epigram on Sir Kenelm Digby.
Cf. A. S. Cook, Faerie Queene I, Introd. 3, 5. In Mod. Lang. Notes,
XXII (1907), 209: an echo of Sp in Jonson. C. Crawford, Collectanea,
I, 45.

The King and Queenes Entertainement at Richmond, 1636.
Repr. ed. Bang and Brotanek. Louvain (Materialien, II),
1903.
Line 479 quotes from the FQ.

KIRBYE, GEORGE. First Set of English Madrigals, 1597.
Quoted in Fellowes, Eng. Madrigal Verse, 115:
Verses from Sh Cal, Nov., 177–86, set to music.

KYD, THOS. (1558?–94).
Cf. Kyd's Works, ed. Boas. Ox. 1901. P. xxiii.
Cf. G. Sarrazin, Thomas Kyd und sein Kreis. Berlin, 1892. 52–54.

KYNASTON, SIR FRANCIS. Leoline and Sydanis. Lond. 1642.
In Saintsbury's Caroline Poets. Ox. 1906. II. See pp. 70,
110, 119, 121.

L[ANE], J[OHN]. An Elegie upon the Death of . . . . our late
Soveraigne Elizabeth. Lond. 1603. Repr. in Huth's Fugi-
tive Tracts, 1875, 2d series.
Passim, e.g., "the Lady of the Faiery-land," "the songs of Colin
Clout," etc.

*LANE, JOHN. Triton's Trumpet, 1620.
Cf. C. W. Moulton, Lib. Lit. Crit., I, 369; cf. J. P. Collier's ed. of
Sp, I, pp. cl ff.

*LANE, JOHN. Spenser's Squiers Tale which hath been loste
. . . . now brought to light. Douce MS 170 (1616).
Cf. Spurgeon, Chaucer Criticism, I, 189.

LISLE, WM. Preface to Eclogues of Virgil, 1628. Quoted in
Introd. to V. Scholderer's "English Editions and Translations
of Greek and Latin Classics," Lond., Bibliog. Soc. Pub., 1911,
p. xxiv:

"Only Master Spenser long since translated the Gnat . . . . giving the world peradventure to conceive that he would at one time or other have gone through the rest of this poet's works; and it is not improbable that this very cause was it that made every man else so very nice to meddle with any part of the building which he had begun, for fear to come short with disgrace of the pattern which he had set before them."

LLOYD, LODOWICK. Poem on the Twelve Months. In Royal MS 17. B. XV, Brit. Mus.
Mention of Sp at pp. 83, 102 and 175 (H.R.P.)

LLOYD, THOS. In Kynaston's Amorum, 1635, MS.
Quoted in Spurgeon, Chaucer Criticism, I, 214.

LOCRINE, 1595. (See also Selimus, below.)
Cf. Cambr. Hist. Eng. Lit., V, 85–87 (and references).
Chas. Crawford, Edmund Spenser, Locrine, and Selimus. In his Collectanea, 1906, I, 47–100. Originally in Notes and Queries, Ser. IX, Vol. VII (1901), 61, 101, 142, 147, 202, 261, 324, 384.
Carrie A. Harper, Locrine and the Faerie Queene. In Mod. Lang. Review, VIII (1913), 369–71: further points of resemblance.
E. Koeppel, "Locrine" und "Selimus." In Shakespeare-Jahrbuch, XLI (1905), 196–98: copyings from Sp.
E.K.B., Locrine and the Faerie Queene. In the Nation, N.Y., CVII (1918), 296.

LODGE, THOMAS. Complete Works. Hunterian Club Pub., 1883.
I, Alarum against Usurers, 1584. 85: "My mournfull Muse, Melpomine." Cf. Sh Cal, Nov., l. 56.
Scillaes Metamorphosis, 1589. 36: Nymphs dancing in moonlit groves. Cf. Sh Cal, Apr., ll. 115 ff.; June, ll. 28–34. 37: allusion to Sp as "the shepheard in the shade"?
Rosalynde, 1590. 41,136: echoes of Sh Cal.
II, Phillis, 1593. 6, Stanza 7 of the Induction.
III, Fig for Momus, 1595. 15: "To reverend Colin."
IV, Wits Miserie, 1596. 57: characterizations of English authors. "Spencer, best read in ancient Poetry." Cf. Collier's Poet. Decameron, I, 181; Collier's ed. of Sp, I, pp. xc ff.

LOK, HENRY. Sundrie Sonnets of Christian Passions, 1597. In Miscellanies of the Fuller Worthies Lib., 1871. II.
Lok frequently uses the Spenserian sonnet-scheme (ababbcbccdcd ee). See 90 ff., 187–90, 197–98.

LYLY, JOHN (1553–1606). Complete Works, ed. R. W. Bond. Ox. 1902. I, 18–19:
Relations of Sp and Lyly. Cf. 62–63, 74, 516; II, 256.

LYTE, HENRY. The Light of Britayne, 1588. Repr. Lond. 1814.
The Epistle addresses Elizabeth as "Britomartis President of Britain."

MARKHAM, GERVASE. Marie Magdalens Lamentations, 1601. In Miscellanies of the Fuller Worthies Lib., 1871. II, 85:
"Colin in his graver Muse."

MARLOWE, CHRISTOPHER (1564–93). Works, ed. Bullen. Bost. 1885. I, 173, 183; III, 359.
Cf. Spenser, ed. Grosart, V, 124, 136; Crawford's Collectanea, I, 52 ff.; W. Creizenach, Gesch. des neueren Dramas, IV, 498; Georg Schoeneich, Der litterarische Einfluss Spensers auf Marlowe. Halle, 1907. Diss.

MARSTON, JOHN. The Scourge of Villainy, 1598. Satire VI. (On versifying, etc.), ll. 38, 59.

MARSTON, ROBERT. Tam Martis quam Artis Nenia. A MS elegy in 1614, printed in Brydges' Restituta, 1816. IV, 345.

A Maske presented . . . . at Coleoverton. Printed from a MS in the Dyce Collection. In Brotanek's Die englischen Maskenspiele. Wien, 1902. 328 ff.
Cf. 333: allusions to Sp (Artegall, Sir Guion, Calidore).

Maydes Metamorphosis, 1600. In A Collection of Old English Plays, ed. A. H. Bullen. Lond. 1882. I.
Many echoes of Sp. Cf. Bullen's Introd., 99; also 120, 156. Also in complete works of John Lyly, ed. R. W. Bond. Ox. 1902. III. Cf. Bond's Introd., 336.

*MERCER, WM. Angliae Speculum, 1646.
Copy in Huntington Lib. Cf. DNB, XIII, 267–69.

MERES, FRANCIS. Palladis Tamia, 1598.
Parts quoted in Arber's Eng. Garner, II, 95–96, 98, 99, 100. Also in Gregory Smith, Eliz. Critical Essays, II, 313, 315, 316, 318, 319, 321.

MIDDLETON, THOMAS. Works, ed. A. H. Bullen. Bost. 1886. VIII, 31 (the calling in of MHT); 53 (allusion to MHT).

MILTON, JOHN.

Poems:

Penseroso, ll. 116–20.

Milton's Latin Poem "Mansus," l. 32 (Warton, Hurd, etc., see here an allusion to Sp. Cf. Milton's Poet. Works, ed. Todd, VII, 360).

Prose: **Prose Works**, ed. J. A. St. John. Lond. (Bohn's Standard Lib.), 1884.

I, 346: reference to Talus—"by our poet Spenser . . . . feigned."
II, 68: The famous passage on "our sage and serious poet Spenser."
   505: reference to St. George and his "sail-winged" dragon.
III, 81: Cave of Mammon. 84: Application of passage from Sh Cal, May (quoted at length) on "that false shepherd Palinode" to the false prelates of Milton's day. 118: Milton's early reading "among those lofty fables and romances, which recount in solemn cantos the deeds of knighthood."
V, 175: A quotation from "our Spenser" (FQ, II, x, 24).

Milton's **Common-place Book**, ed. A. J. Horwood. Lond. 1876. 188, 242:

   References to the V of I.
      Cf. Cory, Herbert E. Spenser, the School of the Fletchers, and Milton. Berkeley, 1912.
      A study of Sp's influence on Milton, both directly and indirectly, through the first imitators of Sp. Based on the parallels accumulated by previous commentators, it attempts to generalize and trace this influence beyond the evidence of parallel passages. That at home in the Elizabethan poets rather than abroad was Milton's chief "source."
Crompton, Jas. In Manchester Quarterly, I (1882), 239–43.
Dryden's Preface to Fables. In Works, ed. Saintsbury, XI, 209–10.
Friedland, L. S. Milton's Lycidas and Spenser's Ruines of Time. In Mod. Lang. Notes, XXVII (1912), 246–50: That the elegiac parts of the R of T suggest Lycidas.
Greenlaw, Edwin. "A Better Teacher than Aquinas." In Studies in Philology, XIV (1917), 196–217: Sp's influence on Milton, esp. in Paradise Lost; the spiritual affinity of the two poets; analogous situations in FQ and PL (also in Paradise Regained).
Greenlaw, Edwin. Spenser's Influence on Paradise Lost. In Studies in Philology, XVII (1920), 320–59: On Sp's philosophy of Nature (330 ff.), as influencing Milton's views; Sp's cosmos; Milton's sources largely in the Four Hymns and the Cantos of Mutability.
Grosart's ed. of Sp, IV, p.c.; V, 197, 199, 212–13.

Hanford, J. H.   The Pastoral Elegy and Milton's Lycidas.   In Pub.
Mod. Lang. Asso., XXV (1910), 438 ff.: the influence of Sp's pastoral
vein on Milton.

Lowell, J. R.   Works, IV, 302, 305 *n*, 307 *n*, 333.

Masson, David.   Life of Milton. Lond. 1881.   I, 452 f., 749.   Cf.
80, 89, 263, 575, 817 *n*, and III, 456, 515, and passim.

Masterman, J.H.B.   The Age of Milton. Lond. 1897.   1–2: Milton's
plan of an allegorical romance, similar to Sp's.

Edw. Phillips.   See under "Criticism after 1650."

Raleigh, Walter.   Milton, N.Y. 1900.   7, 187 ff.

Thompson, E. N. S.   J. Milton, Topical Bibliography, 25, 69.

Tuckwell's Spenser, 28.

Warton, Thomas.   Observations, I, 336 ff., and passim.

MORE, HENRY (1614–87).
> Cf. F. Greenslet, Joseph Glanvill. N.Y. 1900.   23, 41.
> Coleridge, Miscellanies (Bohn Lib.), 332.
> Todd's ed. of Sp, 1805, I, p. clix.

MOSELEY, HUMPHREY.   "The Stationer to the Reader," prefixed
to the 1645 ed. of Milton's Poems.   Quoted in Masson's Life
of Milton, III, 456.

NASHE, THOMAS.   Complete Works, ed. Grosart.   Huth Lib.,
1883–84.
> II, 133–35 (Pierce Penilesse, 1592); 212. 233, 237, 274, 278.
> III, 50, 159, 160.
> IV, 13.
> Also Nashe's Works, ed. R. B. McKerrow. Lond. 1904.
> See index; esp. I, 282, 299, 327; III, 108, 323, etc.

NICCOLS, RICHARD.
> *Epicedium. A Funerall Oration. 1603. B 3, recto.
> The Cuckow, 1607:
> Cf. J. P. Collier's Bibliog. Account, II, 38. Cf. Corser, Collectanea,
Pt. ix, 67–78: states that it abounds in echoes and imitations of the FQ.
The echoes are doubtless there ("bower of bliss," "Adonis garden,"
"louting low," "soft winds and waters fall," etc.), and there is evident
effort to catch the note of Sp and of his poetic luxury (see esp., p. 29).
A poem of interest. Cf. Brydges, Restituta, II, 7.
> England's Eliza, 1610. Pt. V of the Mirror for Magistrates. See
Repr. ed. Haslewood. Lond. 1815. II, Pt. II, 823. Cf. 828 ("Fi-
dessa"). Cf. Corser.
> The Beggars Ape, 1627: imitates MHT, introducing the ape and
the fox. Cf. Collier, Bibliog. Account, II, 35–38.

NICHOLSON, SAMUEL. Acolastus his After-Witte, 1600. In Grosart's Occasional Issues. 1876.
> Slight influence of Sp, passim. Cf. 20 ff. with MHT.

NORDEN, JOHN. The Labyrinth of Man's Life, 1614. Quoted in Powell's Eng. Domestic Relations, 191.

O., (I). The Lamentation of Troy. 1594. A 3b, and B 2.

PASQUIL'S Palinodia, 1619. Repr. in Illustrations of Old Eng. Lit., ed. J. P. Collier. Lond. 1866. I.
> It opens with lines in parody of the opening verses of the FQ.

PEACHAM, HENRY. The Garden of Eloquence, 1593. 15:
> "Touching this part [Onomatopeia] I will refer the Reader to Chaucer *and* Gower, and to the new Shepherds calendar, a most singular imitation of ancient speech." Copy in Newberry Lib.

PEACHAM, H. The Compleat Gentleman. Lond. 1634 (1622). Ch. 10. "Of Poetry." Pp. 94–96:
> Recital of the chief English poets, including Sp. Ch. 10 is repr. in Spingarn, Critical Essays of the 17th Cent., I, 116–33.

PEACHAM, H. The Truth of Our Times. Lond. 1638. 37–38. See above under "Life, Gen. Refs."

Pedantius. Acted c. 1580. Cf. Moore Smith's ed. P. xlv:
> That Leonidas represents Sp.

PEELE, GEORGE. Works, ed. A. H. Bullen. Bost. 1888.
> I, 34–36: Echoes of Sh Cal in act III, sc. i, of the Arraignment of Paris, 1584.
> II, 318, The Honour of the Garter, 1593: Sp praised under the name of Hobbinol (sic, Bullen). Cf. 42, 244. Cf. A. W. Ward, Hist. Eng. Dram. Lit., I, 327, 367. Spenser, ed. Grosart, V, 77.

Polimanteia, 1595. Extracts in Brydges, The British Bibliographer. Lond. 1810. See I, 281, 284.

PORTER, THOMAS. Epigrams. MS of 1614. Cf. Report of Hist. MSS. Commission, IX, Pt. II, 362 a.

PUTTENHAM, GEORGE. The Arte of English Poesie, 1589. Repr. ed. Arber. Lond. 1869. Bk. I, ch. xxxi:
> A discussion of the best English poets to date, including "for Eglogue and pastorall Poesie, Sir *Philip Sydney* and Maister *Challener*, and that other Gentleman who wrate the late shepheardes Callender."

QUARLES, FRANCIS.
    A Feast for Wormes, 1626.
    Emblemes, 1643.
    Argalus and Parthenia, 1629.
    In Complete Works of Quarles, ed. Grosart, Chartsey Worthies Lib.
        1880. II, 18a; III, 91; 271 (Archimago).

R., H. [HENRY REYNOLDS?]. Mythomystes. n.d. (c. 1630).
    Extracts in Brydges, British Bibliographer, IV, 373-79.
      See p. 376: "I must approve the learned *Spencer*, in the rest of his
    poems no lesse than his *Fairy Queene*, an exact body of the *Ethicke*
    doctrine; though some good judgments have wisht (and perhaps not
    without cause) that he had therein beene a little freer of his fiction, and
    not so close rivetted to his Morall." Also in Spingarn's Crit. Essays
    of the 17th Cent., I, 141-79. See 147.

RALEIGH, SIR WALTER. Poems. Aldine ed. 8, 9:
    "Methought I saw the grave where Laura lay."
    Cf. under Life, "Spenser and Raleigh."

RANDOLPH, THOS. Eclogue on the noble Assemblies revived on
    Cotswold Hills. In Annalia Dubrensia, 1636. In R's
    Poetical and Dramatic Works, ed. W. C. Hazlitt. Lond.
    1875. 621-26:
      The interlocutors Colin and Thenot. Reference to "the *Shep-
    herd's Calendar.*"

The Returne from Parnassus, c. 1600. In Parnassus, Three
    Eliz. Comedies, ed. W. D. Macray. Ox. 1886. Pp. 58, 63:
      Academic parody on the popular "vayns" in poetry, including
    Spenser's and Shakespeare's. Gullio, the butt, says: "Let this dunci-
    fied worlde esteeme of Spencer and Chaucer, I'le worshipp sweet Mr.
    Shakspeare,"—where a hit may be intended at Shakespeare, but where
    the bracketing of Spenser and Chaucer is significant.
      84: "Judicio's" judgment on Sp—a passage of high praise.
      127: Parody of lines in the Cave of Despair passage (FQ, I, ix, 33).
      150: Spenserian lines imitated; reference to the Blatant Beast.
      Cf. Otto Ballmann in Anglia, XXV (1902), 45.

ROBINSON, THOMAS. Life and Death of Mary Magdalene, 1621.
    Ed. H. O. Sommer. Marburg, 1887. Passim, esp. 27, 51,
    63, 83. Also E.E.T. Soc. 1899.
      Cf. H. E. Cory, Spenser, The School of the Fletchers and Milton
    331-34.

*ROLLINSON. Silvanus, c. 1600. In Douce MSS in the Bodleian.
> Cf. Shakespeare-Jahrbuch, XXXIV (1898), 294–97: That it imitates
> (in Latin), the Sh Cal.
> Cf. Cambr. Hist. Eng. Lit., VI, 304–5.

ROUS, FRANCIS. Thule, 1598. Repr. Spenser Soc. Pub. 1878.
> Shows general influence of the FQ.

ROWLANDS, SAMUEL. Complete Works. Hunterian Club Pub.
1880. I. Greenes Ghost, 1602. Pp. 39–43:
> Quotations from Sh Cal to enforce the author's homily. R's Guy
> of Warwick, 1607, perhaps owes something to the FQ.

SCOT, THOMAS. Philomythie. Lond. 1616. Copy of ed. of
1622 in Univ. of Chicago Lib.
> Address to Reader, B i, recto: On the danger of writing verse
> which may be given a political application, so that
>> "The ghost of Virgil's Gnat would not sting so,
>> That great men durst not in the City go" . . . .
>> "If Spencer now were living, to report
>> His Mother Hubbert's tale, there would be sport:
>> To see him in a blanket tost, and mounted
>> Up to the starres."
> Cf. J. P. Collier, Bibliog. Account, II, 326.

SELDEN, JOHN. Notes on Drayton's Polyolbion, Sixteenth Song,
l. 43.

SELIMUS, 1594.
> See, above, under "Locrine."

SHAKESPEARE.
> See under Works, "Spenser and Shakespeare."
> Cf. Spedding, Wm., A Letter on Shakspere's Authorship of the
> Two Noble Kinsmen. Lond. 1876. 68: "His [Shakespeare's] early
> poems belong in design to Spenser's school, and their style is often
> imitative of his." Cf. p. 72.

SHEPPARD, S. The Times Displayed in Six Sestyads. 1646.
Extracts in Brydges' British Bibliographer. Lond. 1810.
I. See p. 332.
> Cf. Collier's ed. of Sp, I, p. clxviii.

SHIRLEY, JAMES (1596–1666). Dramatic Works and Poems, ed.
Dyce. Lond. 1833.
> Shirley leaves some traces of his reading of Sp. For examples see
> IV, 95 (Spenserian imagery); 366 ff. (Archimagus); VI, 351 ff.

SIDNEY, SIR PHILIP.
> See also above, under Life, "Spenser and Sidney."
> Apologie for Poetry, c. 1581.　Repr. of ed. of 1595, ed. Arber, 1868.
> It has several times been conjectured that this work gives the substance of Sp's lost English Poet.　Cf. its mention of the Sh Cal.

SMITH, WM.　Chloris, 1596.　Repr. in Arber's Eng. Garner, VIII, 171 ff.　Also S. Lee, Eliz. Sonnets, II, 321 ff.
> A complete disciple of Sp, to whom these sonnets are addressed; they contain many echoes of Sp (e.g., in Nos. 1, 15, 20, 35, etc.).　The last (No. 50) again addresses "Colin," apparently implying that Sp had "pleased" to be "the patron" of these poems.　See dedicatory sonnets.

SPEGHT, THOS.　Life of Chaucer, prefixed to ed. of C's Workes, 1602.　ciijb.　(Copy in Newberry Lib.)

STRADLING.　Joannis Stradlingi Epigrammatum libri quatuor. Lond. 1607.
> Quoted in Chalmer's Poets, III, 13.　See above under Works, "Lost Works."　Cf. Collier's ed. of Sp, I, p. cxli.　See under "Life."

SYLVESTER, JOSHUA (1563–1618).　Complete Works, ed. Grosart, Chertsey Worthies Lib., 1880.　I, 169; II, 314.
> Cf. Certain Worthy MS Poems, above.

TAYLOR, JOHN (The Water Poet).　Praise of Hemp-seed, 1620. In Workes, 1630.　III, 72:
> "Spencer and Shakespeare did in Art excell."

THYNNE, F.　Emblems and Epigrams, 1600.　Printed from MS, Early Eng. Text. Soc.　Lond. 1876.　71.
> Cf. Collier's ed. of Sp, I, p. cxlvi.

*T[OFTE], R[OBERT].　The Blazon of Iealousie.　1615.
> Quotes Sp.

The Valiant Welshman, 1615.　Repr. ed. V. Kreb. Erlangen (Münchener Beiträge, XXIII).　1902.
> Cf. Koeppel, Ben Jonson's Wirkung, 92.

Vindex Anglicus, 1644.　Repr. in Harleian Miscellany, 1809, II, 37–42:
> Sp the English Lucan.　Cf. Shakspere Allusion-Book, I, 494.

WARNER, WM.　See under "Life, General References."

WATSON, THOMAS. Meliboeus, An Eclogue upon the Death of
. . . . Walsingham, 1590. In Watson's Poems, ed. Arber.
Lond. 1870. 172–73.

Cf. J. W. Beach, A Sonnet of Watson and a Stanza of Spenser. In
Mod. Lang. Notes, XVIII (1903), 218–20: Sonnet 51 of Watson's
Tears of Fancie and FQ, II, vi, 12, 13; six identical lines in the two
passages; proof that Watson copies Sp.

Cf. Todd's ed. of Sp, 1805, I, p. xcix *n.*

WEBBE, WILLIAM. A Discourse of English Poetrie, 1586. Repr.
ed. Arber. Lond. 1870.

23: "Our late [i.e., lately] famous English Poet, who wrote the *Sheep-
heards Calender,*" etc.

35–36: "The rightest English Poet that ever I read: that is, the Auther
of the Sheepeheardes Kalender," etc. Cf. 37.

52–55: Praise of "Master *Sp:* Author of the *Sheepeheardes Calender,*"
comparing that work with Virgil's Eclogues point by point. Notes
the obscurity, even to contemporaries, of "much matter" therein,
"uttered somewhat covertly." Defends its author against misinter-
pretation.

59–61, 65: Illustrates "kyndes of English verses" from the Sh Cal.

81–84: Webbe's version of a lyric from Sh Cal, in English "*Saphick*
verse."

WEEVER, JOHN. The Mirror of Martyrs, 1601. Repr. in The
Hystorie of . . . . Plasidas and other Rare Pieces. Lond.
Roxburghe Club, 1873. 194.

Cf. Collier's Bibliog. Account, II, 497–98.

Epigrammes, 1599. Repr. ed. R. B. McKerrow. Lond. 1911.
11, 18, 81 (cf. 121), 101, 123. Cf. Collier, Bibliog. Account, II, 496.

"Was John Weever related to William Weever who wrote a
Discourse on Ireland, 1599?"—Edith Rickert.

WHETSTONE, GEORGE. Sir Phillip Sidney, his honorable Life,
his valiant Death, and True Vertues. 1586. Repr. in
Frondes Caducae. Auchinleck Press, 1816. B 2a.

Side Note: "The last Sheppard's Calender, the reputed worke of
S. Phil. Sydney,—a worke of deepe learning, judgement, and witte,
disguised in Shep. Rules."

*[WHITE, TRISTRAM.] The Martyrdome of St. George. 1614.
Cf. Collier's Bibliog. Account, II, 519–20.

WHITING, NATHANIEL. Il Insonio Insonnadado. In his Le
Hore di Recreatione. Lond. 1638. (Copy in Newberry
Lib.) Reprinted in Saintsbury's Caroline Poets, III. See
pp. 544, 550.

Willobie his Avisa, 1594. Preface by Hadrian Dorrell. Repr.
in Huth's Prefaces . . . . 1874. 160. Also in Grosart's
Occasional Issues, 1880.

Wily Beguiled. 1606. Repr. Malone Soc., 1912.
> Cf. E. Koeppel, Studien über Shakespeares Wirkung, 89 *n*.

WITHER, GEORGE (1588–1667). Juvenilia, 1626. Repr. Spenser
Soc. 1871. 17, 796.

Wits Recreations, 1640. 226, 275, 292.

WYBARNE, JOSEPH. The New Age of Old Names, 1609. Preface. Repr. in Huth's Prefaces. . . . Huth Lib., 1874.
224–25:
> "*Error's Denne*, celebrated by the penne of our second *Chaucer*."
> Cf. pp. 67, 113, of original ed.

ZOUCHE, RICHARD. The Dove. 1613. Repr. Ox. 1839. 51.

CRITICISM AFTER 1650

The Academy. Lond., LXV (1903), 248–49: "The Poet's
Poet."
> Scattered but excellent aperçus. That the archaism of Sp's diction
> is overestimated; Sp "rediscovered Poetry"; "Spenser is a mine of
> diction"; "The Spenserian subtlety of emotion"; his lyric gift.

ADDISON, JOSEPH. Works. ed. R. Hurd. Lond. 1811.
> See Epistle to Sacheverell, I, 29–30: An Account of the Greatest
> English Poets, 1694; II, 409; III, 384; V, 322 ff.: The Guardian
> No. 152: plan of an imitation of Sp's allegory.
> Cf. Cory, Critics of Sp, 130 ff.; Spence's Anecdotes. Lond. 1858.
> 38.

AMES, PERCY W. Spenser. In Trans. Royal Soc. of Lit.,
XXV (1904), 91–125. Unimportant.

Anecdotes of Polite Literature. Lond. 1764. II, 6:
> Censure of Sp's rustic style in pastorals.

Angliae Speculum Morale. [By Sir Richard Grahame?]
Lond. 1670. 67.
> Quoted in Sp ed. Todd, II, p. cxli. Copy of ed. of 1670 in Newberry
> Lib. See Mercer's Angliae Speculum, 1646. Cf. Spurgeon, Chaucer
> Crit., I, 257.

*ARNOLD, C. The Mirror, a Poetical Essay in the Manner of
Spenser. Lond. 1755.

ARNOLD, FREDERICK. Spenser as a Sacred Poet. In The Leisure
Hour, XIII (1864), 746–51.

ARNOLD, T. Spenser as a Text-book. In Dublin Review, Ser.
III, Vol. IV (1880), 321–32:
> A review of Kitchin's ed. of FQ, I and II. On bowdlerizing Sp
> for school use; contending Catholic and Protestant elements in Sp.
> By a pro-Catholic, anti-Spenser, writer. Cf. Grosart's ed. of Sp, I,
> 456–57.

Athenaeum, XXXIX (1862), 73–76:
> Fervent appreciation of Sp.

The Athenian Mercury, July 11, 1691. Quoted in Shakspere
Allusion Book, II, 378.

ATTERBURY, FRANCIS. Preface to Waller's Poems, 1690. In
Waller's Poems ed. G. Thorn Drury. Lond. 1893. P. xxiii.

AUSTIN, ALFRED. In Quarterly Review, CCX (1909), 418:
> The lyrical note, passim, in Sp. Cf. 168: "Spenser seems con-
> stantly on the verge of a well-bred smile."

AUSTIN, SAMUEL. Naps upon Parnassus, 1658. B5. (Copy
in Newberry Lib.) Quoted in Shakspere Allusion Book,
II, 78.

B., H. Commendatory Verses prefixed to Wm. Cartwright's
Comedies, 1651: "Platonick Spencer."

BAILEY, JOHN. Poets and Poetry, being articles reprinted from
the Literary Supplement to "The Times." Ox. 1911.
45–54:
> "Spenser": a review of W. B. Yeats' Select Poems of Sp. Sympa-
> thetic appreciation of Sp.

BANKS, ADELINE M. Spenser's Grave (a poem). In Gentleman's Magazine, CCLXXXVI (N.S., LXII) (1899), 443.

BARKER, JANE. Poetical Recreations, 1688. Poem by "Philaster," and Pt. II, 39.

BASCOM, JOHN. Philosophy of English Literature. N.Y. 1889. 106–14.

BAYNE, THOS. Spenser. In St. James Magazine, XXXVI (1879), 105–18:
A readable general essay, partly in criticism of R. W. Church on Sp.

BEATTIE, JAMES. The Minstrel, 1771. Preface.

*BEDELL, WM. A Protestant memorial . . . . a Poem in Spenser's Style. Lond. 1713:
Imitation of the Sh Cal. Cf. Malone's ed. of Shakespeare, 1821, II, 202 n.

BLACKLOCK, THOS. An Hymn to Divine Love. In Imitation of Spencer. In Chalmers' Poets, XVIII, 186–87.

BLACKMORE, SIR RICHARD. Preface to Prince Arthur, 1695.
In Spingarn, Crit. Essays of 17th Cent., III, 238:
Censure of Sp's allegory.

BLOUNT, THOS. The Academie of Eloquence. Lond. 1654. 4.

BLOUNT, SIR THOMAS POPE. De Re Poetica, 1694. I, 114; II, 52, 136, 137, 213–16:
Blount gives a string of citations from Dryden, Temple, Rapin, Rymer, Mulgrave, etc., arranged under headings and connected by a thin text of comment,—unoriginal, but a sort of commonplace book of the accepted critical ideas of his day.

BOSWORTH, WM. Arcadius and Sepha, 1651.
A 2: "The Divine Mr. Spencer"; A 4 verso: "Mr. Edmund Spencer, whom Sir Walt. Raleigh and S. Kenelm Digby were used to call the English Virgill." Repr. in Saintsbury's Caroline Poets, II.

*BOYLE, HON. R. Remarks on Spenser's Poems. Lond. 1734.

*BOYSE, SAMUEL. Cambuscan; or the Squire's Tale of Chaucer, 1741.
Continued by Geo. Ogle, "from the Fourth Book of Spenser's Fairy Queen," and by Joseph Sterling, in 1785. Cf. E. P. Morton, The Spenserian Stanza in the 18th Cent.

BRIGHT, JAS. W. In Mod. Lang. Notes, XXXI (1916), 189–91:
On some characteristics of Sp, and on Winstanley's ed. of FQ, I and II.

BROWN, T. E.   Spenser: A Causerie.   In The New Review, XVI (1897), 393–404:

Discursive comment, generally inconsiderable.   That the modern reader may be converted to Sp by (in order of merit) the Hymns, Prothalamion, Epithalamion, MHT, and Muiopotmos, rather than by the FQ.

BROWN, T. E.   Poems.   Lond. 1912.   8s.

*BROWNE, ISAAC.   Piscatory Eclogues, 1729.

Cf. Cory, Critics of Sp, 140–41.

*B[RYDGES] SIR E.   Sir Ralph Willoughby.   An historical Tale . . . . in which are inserted the dedicatory sonnets of E. Spenser.   Florence, 1820.   (See Brit. Mus. Cat.)

BUNYAN, JOHN.

Cf. O. Kötz, Faerie Queene und Pilgrims Progress.   In Anglia, XXII (1899), 33–80.   Also Halle, 1899.   Diss.: That Bunyan probably knew at least cantos 9 and 10 of Bk. I of FQ.   Their features in common.

Cf. Methodist Quarterly Review, N.Y., XL (1858), 209–27.

BURKE, EDMUND.   On the Sublime, Pt. V, sect. v.

Cf. John Timbs, Anecdote Biography.   Lond. 1860.   165:

"Edmund Spenser and Edmunde Burke": Burke's distant relationship to Sp; his reading the FQ as a boy in the ruins of Kilcolman. Cf. Gilfillan's ed. of Sp, II, p. xx.

BURNS, ROBERT.

Cf. O. Ritter, Quellenstudien zu Robert Burns.   Berlin (Palaestra, XX), 1901.   65, 155–56.

BYRON.   Works, ed. E. H. Coleridge.   Lond. 1898.

Poetry, I, 395: I1, pp. x, 4–5, and passim, for Spenserian diction; 40 n; III, 224, the stanza; 474 n.   Letters and Journals, II, 150, the stanza; III, 29.

Cf. J. Kindon, Byron versus Spenser, in Internatl. Journal of Ethics, XIV (1904), 362–77.

BYSSHE, EDWARD.   Art of English Poetry.   Lond. 1702.   2d ed., "corrected and improved," 1705.

Mainly a collection of poetical extracts (none from Sp?).   In the introductory Rules for making English Verse see p. 33 on the stanza.

CAMBRIDGE, RICHARD O.   Archimage; a Poem written in Imitation of Spenser.   In Chalmers' Poets, XVIII, 240–42.

*Cambuscan; or the Squire's Tale of Chaucer, modernized by Mr. Boyse, continued from Spenser's Fairy Queen by Mr. Ogle, and concluded by Mr. Sterling. Dublin, 1785.

> See "Boyse, Samuel," above.

CAMPBELL, THOS. Poems: "Chaucer and Windsor."

CAMPBELL, THOS. Specimens of the British Poets. Lond. 1845. 2d ed. Pp. liv–lvii, 45–47:

> Agreeably appreciative, but not penetrating estimate; "this Rubens of English poetry"; the FQ characterized. Cf. Grosart's Sp, I, 102 ff.

A Canto of the Fairy Queen. Written by Spenser. Never before published. Lond. 1739.

CARPENTER, W. BOYD. The Religious Spirit in the Poets, N.Y. 1901. Ch. iv: Edmund Spenser.

CHATTERTON, THOS.

> Cf. W. P. Ker, in Cambr. Hist. Eng. Lit., X, 235: "Chatterton's Debt to Spenser."

Choyce Drollery. Lond. 1656. Repr. ed. J. W. Ebsworth, 1876. 7.

> Quoted in Spurgeon, Chaucer Criticism and Allusion, I, 234.

CHURCH, R. W. Spenser. Lond. 1879, and N.Y. n.d. (Eng. Men of Letters).

> Excellent general treatment. Much good literary criticism. Cf. Thos. Bayne, above.

CHURCH, R. W. Introduction to Selections from Sp in Ward's English Poets. Lond. and N.Y. 1880. I, 275–83.

CLARK, J. SCOTT. A Study of English and American Poets. N.Y. 1900. 38–88. Spenser.

> Schematic study: a compilation; pp. 44 ff. on Sp's characteristics (quotations from various critics).

[CLEVELAND, H. K.] In North Amer. Review, L (1840), 174–206:

> Review of the First American edition of Sp, 1839. On the times of Sp; Sp as representative of his age; growth of Sp's literary reputation, etc.

[COBB, SAMUEL.] Poetae Britannici, c. 1700. In his Poems on Several Occasions. Lond. 1710. Quoted in Spurgeon, Chaucer Criticism, I, 271.

COCKAIN, SIR ASTON. 1658. Quoted in Chalmers' Poets,
III, 13.
> Cf. Brydges, Restituta. 1815. II, 139-40.

COLERIDGE, SAMUEL T. Poetical Works, ed. J. D. Campbell.
Lond. 1895. 46:
> "Lines in the Manner of Spenser," c. 1795; 61: Monody on the
> Death of Chatterton, 1829, ll. 36-40; 183: allusion to FQ, III, ii, 19; 208.

COLERIDGE, S. T.
> Lectures on Shakespeare, ed. T. Ashe. Lond. 1885.
> 17: comment on Cave of Care, FQ, IV, v; 67: Sp "out of space";
> 105 n: Sp's women, cf. 515; 109; 510-17: characteristics of Sp's
> verse; his descriptions; dream quality, etc.
> Table Talk, ed. T. Ashe. Lond. 1884. 45: Sp's verse.
> Miscellanies, ed. T. Ashe. Lond. 1885. 333: the stanza.
> Coleridge is one of the most suggestive and illuminating of Sp
> critics.

A Collection of Letters and Poems . . . . to the Late Duke
and Duchess of Newcastle. 1678. 160.

COLLIER, J. P. Poetical Decameron. Edinb. 1820.
> I, 31 ff., 46, 68, 91, 96 ff., 105, 181, 188, 204, 245, 252; II, 89, 115,
> 211. Various interesting comments.

COLLINS, WM. Poetical Works, ed W. M. Thomas. Lond.
1894. 33:
> The Story of Florimel's girdle; 73.

COOPER, E. The Muses Library, 1737.
> "A sort of Poetical Chronicle." Cf. pp. xii, 49, 89, 253 ff.

CORY, H. E. Edmund Spenser, a Critical Study. Berkeley
(Univ. of Cal. Press), 1917.
> See characterization of this book in Studies in Philology, XV (1918),
> 213-14; and in Mod. Lang. Notes, XXXV, 165-77; cf. Mod. Lang.
> Rev., XV, 3.

COURTHOPE, W. J. History of English Poetry. Lond. 1897 ff.
II, ch. ix: "Court Allegory: Edmund Spenser."
> A discussion of Sp's performance based on a peculiarly schematic
> neo-classical conception of the matter and function of poetry, with
> slight regard to the poetic essence of Sp's work. Disproportionate
> insistence on his "lack of unity" (external). 239 ff.: Sp's Allegory;
> 283 ff.: Place in History of Poetry.
> III, 127; 134: Sp's mediaeval spirit.

COURTHOPE, W. J.   In Cambr. Hist. Eng. Lit., III, ch. xi:
"The Poetry of Spenser." A good general treatment.

COURTHOPE, W. J.   Essay on the Genius of Spenser.   Ox. 1868.
Some power of generalization; lacking in subtler appreciation, but a valuable essay.

COWARD, W.   Licentia Poetica.   Lond. 1709.   77:
The FQ in its day "an approved Poem, tho' now unwarrantably imitable, without affectation of treading in the steps of antiquity."

CRABBE, GEORGE.   Poetical Works.   Lond. 1834.   II, 239–40.

CRAIK, GEORGE L.   Spenser and his Poetry.   Lond. 1845.   3 v.
In its day the best piece of work on Sp, and still useful. Good study of the Life, and excellent criticism.

CRAIK, G. L.   A Compendious History of English Literature. Lond. 1861.   I, 478–520:
Good general criticism: see on Sp's characteristics as a poet.

The Critical Review, Ser. III, Vol. VII (1806), 411–16:
A review of Todd's ed., by a lover of "gothic fables"; survey of criticism of Sp through the eighteenth century; finds it vitiated by the dominance of French "rules of criticism"; approves of Hurd.

CROFTS, ELLEN.   Chapters in the History of English Literature. Lond. 1884.   Ch. iv.

CROMWELL, OLIVER.   See "Life, General References."

[CROXALL, SAMUEL.]   An Original Canto of Spencer . . . . now made public by Nestor Ironside, Esq. 1713.   Also a second and third editions in 1714 (B.M. Cat.).   Repr. in facsimile. N.Y. (A. H. Nason), 1912.
Another Original Canto of Spencer.   1714.
Colin's Mistakes.   Written in imitation of Spenser's style. Lond. 1721.   Repr. in Nichols, A Select Collection of Poems. Lond. 1781.   VII, 345–49.

CULPEPPER, SIR THOS.   Essayes.   Lond.   1671.   Quoted in Spurgeon, Chaucer Criticism, I, 247–48.

CUNINGHAM, GRANVILLE C.   Bacon's Secret disclosed in Contemporary Books.   Lond. 1911.   77-127:
"Bacon and Edmund Spenser." The usual Baconian stuff. That Sp=Bacon; some peculiarities of the 1679 ed. of Sp discussed; that "Colin" in the Sh Cal=Bacon.   Copy in N.Y. Pub. Lib.

D., (E. M. L.). The Three Great English Poets, Spenser, Shakespeare, Milton. In Victoria Mag., XXV (1875), 856–68:
"Spenser and the Faerie Queene." Slight but of some interest; stresses Sp's constancy in friendship; the ethical system of the FQ. Cf. Vol. XXVI (1876), 29, on Milton's debt to Sp.

DANA, RICHARD H. Poems and Prose Writings. N.Y. 1850. II, 172–77.

DAVENANT, SIR WM. Preface to Gondibert, 1651. In Chalmers' Poets, VI; see pp. 350–51:
The objections to Sp's archaisms stated; "the unlucky choice of his stanza"; his allegory like "a continuance of extraordinary dreams" (cf. Coleridge, to this effect); lack of naturalness and so of usefulness in his "argument." Also in Spingarn, Crit. Essays, II, 1 ff.

DENHAM, SIR JOHN. On Mr. Abraham Cowley's Death, 1667. In Chalmers' Poets, VII, 247. See his "On Mr. Abraham Cowley."

DENNIS, JOHN. Studies in English Literature. Lond. 1876. Also 1883. 308, 405–8.

DE VERE, AUBREY. Essays, chiefly on Poetry. Lond. 1887.
I, ch. i: "Characteristics of Spenser's Poetry." Also in Grosart's Sp, I, 257–303.
Ch. ii: "Spenser as a Philosophic Poet." Valuable criticism.
Poetical Works. Lond. 1884. III, 347: "Chaucer."

DOBSON, W. T. The Classic Poets. Lond. 1879. 327–93.
Negligible.

DORR, JULIA C. R. When Spenser Died (a poem). In Poet-Lore, VII (1895), 183.

DOWDEN, EDWARD. Transcripts and Studies. Lond. 1888. 269–304:
"Spenser, the Poet and Teacher." Also in Grosart's ed. of Sp, I, 304–39.
305–37: "Heroines of Spenser."
Both contain valuable criticism. The former is regarded by H. E. Cory as the best essay on Sp.

DRAKE, NATHAN. Shakespeare and his Times. Lond. 1817. I, 645–49.

DRAKE, NATHAN. Literary Hours, 1798. Also, 1800, 1804, 1820. See index, esp. II, 91 (ed. of 1820).

DRYDEN, JOHN. Works, ed. Scott and Saintsbury. Edinb. 1882–93.

> IV, 23: Advantage to Sp of his supernatural "machinery," "and those enthusiastic parts of poetry"; beauty of the Bower of Bliss episode in the FQ.
> VI, 407.
> XIII, 16, 17–19: Essay on Satire, 1693: In heroic poetry "the English have only to boast of Spenser and Milton"; censure of the faulty design and lack of uniformity in the FQ; "his obsolete language, and the ill choice of his stanza"; yet, in spite of this, "his verses are so numerous, so various, and so harmonious, that only Virgil, whom he professedly imitated, has surpassed him among the Romans; and only Mr. Waller among the English." 324–25: Praise of the Sh Cal.
> XIV, 144: Defects of the FQ; 210: "Spenser wanted only to have read the rules of Bossu; for no man was ever born with a greater genius, or had more knowledge to support it." See also The Hind and the Panther, Pt. II, l. 230: allusion to "the blatant beast"; Pt. III, ll. 8–11:
>
> > "And Mother Hubbard in her homely dress
> > Has sharply blamed a British Lioness,
> > That Queen, whose feast the factious rabble keep,
> > Exposed obscenely naked and asleep."
>
> DuFresnoy, De Arte Graphica, translated by Dryden. Lond. 1695. 108: Among the books of most advantage to painters, especially "to warm the imagination," Sp's FQ, etc. Dryden's copy of Sp's Works is noticed in Allibone, II, 2204.
> Cf. Cory, Critics of Sp, 112 ff.

DUNHAM, S. A. Lives of the most eminent literary and scientific men of Great Britain. Lond. 1836. I, 312–51.

D[WIGHT], J. S. Review of First Amer. ed. of Sp. In Christian Examiner, XXVIII (1840), 208–23:

> Impressions (in the Romanticist vein) on reading Sp; the spirit of beauty the predominating note in Sp. "He is beautiful even while dull. His world is always fresh and young"; like the music of Haydn. Rather a noteworthy little critical essay.

Edinburgh Review, VII (1806), 203–17:

> Review of Todd's ed. A general discussion. Of some slight interest.

Edinburgh Review, XXV (1815), 59 ff.:

Sp and Chaucer, Sp and Ariosto, comparisons.

EDWARDS, THOS. In Correspondence of Samuel Richardson. Lond. 1804. III, 13:

Thos. Edwards to S. R. as to proposed (1751) edition of "my ever-honoured Spenser." Edwards' own project for an edition. Cf. 20.

ELLIS, GEO. Specimens of the Early Eng. Poets. Lond. 1801. II, 202–3:

Brief outline of the Life, and some conventional criticism. Negligible.

ELY, GERTRUDE H. Chaucer, Spenser, Sidney. N.Y. [1894]. "English Men of Letters for Boys and Girls."

37–76: "Spenser." For children, but many inaccuracies.

An Essay on the Poets. Lond. 1717. 10.

The European Magazine, LXXIX (1821), 525:

A good "Sonnet to Spenser," beginning,
"I thought of witcheries of olden days."

The Examiner Examin'd. . . . . Occasioned by the Examiner of Friday, Dec. 18, 1713. Upon the Canto of Spencer. Lond. 1713. See Croxall, above.

FAIRFAX, HENRY. Catalogue of his Library (c. 1660). Sloane MS 1872. Quoted in Shakspere Allusion Book, II, 82.

FELTON, HENRY. A Dissertation on Reading the Classics. Lond. 1718.

Mainly a discussion of style; fervent personal acknowledgment of Sp's charm (p. 215).

FLETCHER, JEFFERSON B. Spenser, the Cosmopolitan Poet. In the English Graduates Record. Columbia Univ., Oct. 1905. 65–80.

FLETCHER, J. B. The Painter of the Poets. In Studies in Philology, XIV (1917), 153–66:

Sp as a painter in words; his painter's eye; slight use of color, but skill in "plastic grouping and movement"; comparison of Sp with certain of the great painters; sources of his imagery in contemporary art and the "emblems." Cf. Leigh Hunt, below, on Sp as "The Poet of the Painters." Cf. New Monthly Magazine, XXXVIII (1833), 161–77.

FULLER, THOS. Worthies of England, 1662. Repr. Lond. 1840. II, 379:

"The many *Chaucerisms* used (for I will not say affected by him) are thought by the ignorant to be blemishes, known by the learned to be beauties, to his book. . . . ."

FULLER, THOS. Church History. Lond. 1655. Bk. IV, 152. Quoted in Spurgeon, Chaucer Criticism, I, 231.

GALLUP, MRS. ELIZ. W. The Bilateral Cypher of Sir Francis Bacon. Lond. 1899. 9–17:

"Spenser-Bacon" papers. Cf. App.

GAY, JOHN. The Shepherds' Week, 1714. In Chalmers' Poets, X. Cf. Cory, Critics of Sp, 138–40.

GAYTON, EDMUND. Pleasant Notes upon Don Quixot. Lond. 1654. 150. Quoted in Shakspere Allusion Book, II, 36–37.

GIBBON, EDWARD. Autobiography. In his Miscellaneous Works. Lond. 1814. I, 4.

The FQ "the most precious jewel" of the coronet of the noble family of the Spencers.

GILDON, CHARLES. The Complete Art of Poetry. Lond. 1718. Pt. VI:

"A Collection of the most beautiful Descriptions, Similes, Allusions, etc. from *Spenser*, and our best *English* Poets." Quotations from Sp occur, Vol. II, 3, 4, 6, 14, 16, 18, 19, 22, etc. See I, 149, 160, 271, 276.

GILFILLAN, G. In his ed. of Sp. Edinb. 1859. III, pp. v-xxii:

"The Genius and Poetry of Spenser": the allegory; dream-quality of Sp's imagination; Sp and Bunyan compared; Sp's poetical characteristics; "Diffusion is at once the power and the weakness of Spenser's style"; Sp's learning, language, and verse.

[GILMAN, S.] The Faerie Queene of Spenser. In North Amer. Review, V (1817), 301–9:

Interesting as an early example of American appreciation of Sp. Defends the allegory.

GLOVER, TERROT R. Poets and Puritan. Lond. 1915. 1–33.

GOLDSMITH, OLIVER. Spenser's Faerie Queene. In The Critical Review, VII (1759). Repr. in Goldsmith's Works, ed. Gibbs. Lond. 1885. IV, 333–37.

A Notice of Church's ed. of FQ, 1758: General effect of reading the FQ; "no poet enlarges the imagination more than Spenser"; his strong influence over other poets.

GOSSE, EDMUND. Spenser. In Chambers' Cyclopedia of English Literature. Phila. 1902. I, 293–304.
Unimportant.

GRAHAME, SIR RICHARD. See Angliae Speculum, above.

GRANGER, REV. I. A Biographical History of England. Lond. 1775. 2d ed. I, 257 ff.:
"Edmund Spencer." Sp's superiority as a poet in invention and "harmonious versification"; his peculiarities of style easily imitable; his "vigour of imagination"; the FQ as much a state poem as Virgil's Aeneid.

Great Thoughts, IX (1888), 178–82: "Edmund Spenser."
A mere popular essay. See also 3rd ser., II (1893–94), 467, 481, 513.

GREEN, J. R. History of the Eng. People. N.Y. 1882. II, 461–67.

GRIFFINHOOFE, C. G. Celebrated Cambridge Men. Cambr. 1910. 43–45:
Sp marshalled among the distinguished graduates of Cambridge.

HACKET, BP. In Notes and Queries, Ser. II, Vol. VII (1859), 235:
Verses on Sp, c. 1670.

HALLAM, HENRY. Literature of Europe. Lond. 1839–40. II, ch. v.
Conventional and barren criticism.

HANNAY, DAVID. The Later Renaissance. N.Y. 1898. 192–98:
Brief sketch; emphasizes Sp's originality.

HARMAN, E. G. Edmund Spenser and the Impersonations of Francis Bacon. Lond. 1914.
One of that group of books usually classed under the title of "The Sheakespeare-Bacon Controversy," all of which have certain earmarks in common and none of which are taken quite seriously by scholars. Much delving into Spenser-lore and Elizabethan literature and history to dig up evidence intended to prove (1) that Sidney's Apologie for Poetry is Sp's English Poet, (2) that Bacon wrote Sp's works, the allusions in which must all be re-explained from this datum, to which re-explanation a large part of the book is devoted, with fantastic results. (3) It also appears that Bacon wrote most of Sidney, Tarlton, "Leices-

ter's Commonwealth," Gascoigne, Lyly, Daniel, etc. A mad world, my masters!

Cf. The Saturday Review, CXVII (1914), 705–6:
"A learned but unconvincing book"; with brief critical remarks on Sp by the reviewer.

See also Cuningham, G. C., Gallup, E. W., and Woodward (Parker).

HART, J. S.   Essay on the Life and Writings of Edmund Spenser. N.Y. and Lond. 1847.

A thin commentary, with copious quotations. Negligible.

HARTLIB, SAMUEL.   Letter of Jan. 1, 1660. In John Worthington's Diary. Chetham Soc., I, 259; cf. 271, 279.

HAYES, JOHN R.   Edmund Spenser Poet of Country Life. In Book News Monthly, Phila., XXVI (1908), 911–15.

HAYLEY, WM.   Essay on Epic Poetry. Lond. 1782.   63–64.

HAZLITT, WILLIAM.   Collected Works, ed. A. R. Waller and A. Glover. Lond. 1902–6.   See index.

See esp. I, 39, 110, 358; IV, 244; V, 11, 19 ff., 46, 368, 370: Sp's characteristics; VII, 227; IX, 71: Sp and Rubens; X, 73–74: Sp's characteristics; 155: Sp's poetic diction; 242; XII, 30: the man vs. the poet.

One of the best and most sympathetic of the critics of Sp's poetry. Valuable.

Cf. Cory, Critics of Sp, 176–77; The Monthly Review, XCII (1820), 62–64.

HERFORD, C. H.   The Elizabethan Age.   In Quarterly Review, CCXVI (1912), 355 ff.   See 362–63:

Strictures on Jusserand's criticism of Sp.   369: Sp's early imitations.

HEYLIN, PETER.   France painted to the Life, 1657 (2d ed.). 309.   See also "Criticism before 1651."

HOFFMAN, F. A.   Poetry, its Origin, etc. Lond. 1884.   Ch. x.
"Spenser."   A mere text-book chapter.

HOLLAND, SAMUEL.   Don Zara del Fogo, a mock romance, 1656. Pp. 101–2:

Introduces various English poets. "Hereupon Spencer (who was very busy in finishing his *Fairy Queen*) thrust himself amid the throng and was received with a showt by Chapman, Harrington, Owen, Constable, Daniel and Drayton." . . . .

"Spenser waited upon by a numerous Troop of the best Bookmen in the world."

Cf. W. C. Hazlitt's ed. of Thos. Carew's Poems. 1870. P. xlvi. Cf. Todd's ed. of Sp, 1805, I, p. clix.

HOLLAND, S. Romancio-Mastrix: or a Romance on Romances, 1660.

The above under another title. Quoted in Brydges Restituta, 1816, IV, 199.

HOWARD, EDWARD. The British Princes, 1669. Sigs. A5b, A6.

HOWARD, ED. Caroloiades Redivivus. Lond. 1689. Sig. A4.

HUBBARD, WM. The Introspection and Outlook of Spenser. In Grosart's ed. of Sp, I, 373–400.

Mostly negative criticism.

HUGGINS, WM. See Observer, below.

HUGHES, JOHN. Life of Sp prefixed to his ed. of Sp, 1715.

Cf. Cory, Critics of Sp, 145–48.

HUME, D. History of England. Lond. 1826. 432–33.

The Humours and Conversations of the Town. 1693. 81–84.

HUNT, LEIGH.

Juvenilia. 1801. "The Palace of Pleasure . . . . in Imitation of Spenser."

Imagination and Fancy. Lond. 1883 (pub. 1844).

62–120: "Selections from Spenser, with Critical Notice." Highly sympathetic; Sp's characteristics. Mostly short appreciative comments on detached selections. Sp as the Poet of the Painters.

Cf. his Table Talk. Lond. 1882. 174–76.
Cf. his Autobiography. Lond. 1885. 71, 97, 369.
Cf. Cory, Critics of Sp, 177–78.

HUNT, THEODORE W. English Meditative Lyrics. N.Y. 1899. 26–33:

"The Lyrics of Edmund Spenser."

HUNTER, WM. An Anglo-Saxon Grammar . . . . with . . . . an Analysis of the Style of . . . . Spenser. Lond. 1832. 78–84.

Superficial.

HURD, RICHARD. Works. Lond. 1811. IV, 231 ff. "Letters on Chivalry and Romance."
> Good general romanticist criticism of Sp.
> Cf. Cory, Critics of Sp, 168–72.
> Phelps, Beginnings of Romantic Movement, 112–15.
> The Monthly Review, XXVII (1763), 89–94.

An Impartial Estimate of Upton's Notes on the Fairy Queen. Lond. 1759. 28 pp.
> Controversial; unimportant.

JACK, A. A. A Commentary on the Poetry of Spenser and Chaucer. Glasgow, 1920.

[JACOB, GILES.] Historical Account of the . . . . English Poets. Lond. 1719. Ed. of 1724, 195–204.

JOHNSON, SAMUEL. The Rambler (1751), No. 121, etc.
> Cf. Cory, Critics of Sp, 153.

KEATS, JOHN.
> Eve of St. Agnes.
> Imitation of Spenser.
> Sonnet: "Spenser! a jealous honourer of thine."
> Cf. Cambr. Hist. Eng. Lit., XII, 79, 86–87.
> S. Colvin, John Keats. N.Y. 1887. 12–13.
> W. M. Rossetti, Life of John Keats. Lond. 1887. 20, 163–64.
> W. A. Read, Keats and Spenser. Heidelberg, 1897. Diss.
> W. A. Read, Keats and Spenser. In Mod. Lang. Notes, XVIII (1903), 204–6.

KEBLE, JOHN.
> Lectures on Poetry. Ox. 1912. See index, esp. I, 123: the figure of Arthur in the FQ; 82: Sp "the English Virgil"; II, 102: Sp "at once the tenderest and most dignified of poets."
> Occasional Papers and Reviews. Ox. 1877. 98–102.
> Praelectiones. Ox. 1844. No. V (II, 415).

KEIGHTLEY, THOS. Edmund Spenser, his Life and Poetry. In British Quarterly Review, XXII (1855), 368–412:
> Discusses various aspects of the life and works. Of interest.

KINDON, J. Byron versus Spenser. In International Journal of Ethics, XIV (1904), 362–77.
> Negligible.

KINGSLEY, CHARLES. Westward Ho. (1855). Lond. 1894. Ch. ix:
> Digressions on Sp and artificial versifying, etc.; Sp and Raleigh introduced into the narrative.

KLEIN, J. L. Geschichte des englischen Dramas. Leipzig. 1876. II, 809 ff.
> Brief sketch of the Life and Works. Many errors. Without illumination or sympathy. Written in a cocky, expatiating style.

LAMB, CHARLES. "To the Poet Cowper," 1796.
> Cf. Lamb's letter to Wordsworth, June, 1806: "I have copied . . . . from a book of Chalmers on Shakespeare [the Supplemental Apology] a sonnet of Spenser's never printed among his poems. It is curious, as being manly, and rather Miltonic, and as a sonnet of Spenser's with nothing in it about love or knighthood." Cf. the sonnet to Harvey: "Harvey, the happy above happiest men." Cf. the letter to Wordsworth, Feb. 1, 1806.

LANDOR, WALTER SAVAGE. Works. Lond. 1874–76.
> II, 461–63: IV, 74; V, 90–96: "Essex and Spenser"; 151; 173–76: "Queen Elizabeth and Cecil"—apropos of Sp's pension; VIII, 318.
> Cf. Lounsbury, Studies in Chaucer, III, 214.

*LEIGH, EDW. A Treatise of Religion and Learning. Lond. 1656. Copy in Lib. of Congress.
> Bk. V, ch. 14 quotes Camden on Sp. Cf. Spurgeon, Chaucer Crit., I, 232.

LENZ, L. Wielands Verhältnis zu Edmund Spenser, Pope, und Swift. Hersfeld, 1903. Progr.

The Literary World, ed. John Timbs. Lond. II (1840), 96:
> General characteristics of Sp's poetry defined.

LOUNSBURY, THOS. R. Studies in Chaucer. N.Y. 1892. See index.

LOWELL, JAMES RUSSELL. Writings. Bost. 1891. See index.
> See esp. IV, 265–353: Essay on Spenser. One of the best. Highly stimulating, sympathetic, and valuable. Censured by Dowden (see his essay on Sp), and Cory, Critics of Sp, 178. Practically the same essay appeared first in the North Amer. Review, CXX (1875), 334–94. See also his Old English Dramatists. Bost. 1892.
> 10, 28–9: the contrast between Sp's earliest work and his later poems; Sp helped by his practice in translation and by his study of Italian

poets, from whom he gets the secret of the music of his verse, esp. of his lyrics; 33–34: Attraction of the FQ for Lowell the boy; 54: Sp's fondness for "luxury of sound" in proper names.

Cf. L's Letters, ed. C. E. Norton, N.Y. 1894. I, 9: "Spenser was always my favorite poet."

MACAULAY, THOS. B., Lord. Essays. "The Pilgrim's Progress." (1831.)
Unsympathetic.

MACKAIL, J. W. The Springs of Helicon. Lond. 1909. 73–133.
A first rate treatment. Well tempered. Sketches Sp's background and derivation and his historical place. Excellent as a vade-mecum for the appreciation of Sp, although lacking some of the intimate personal gusto and catholic receptivity of such Spenser lovers as Saintsbury, Wilson, Hazlitt, etc.

MACKINTOSH, SIR JAMES. Memoirs, ed. by his son. Lond. 1836. II, 241–43:
A brief appreciation. Cf. I, 168.

[MANNING, ANNE.] The Masque at Ludlow and other Romanesques. Lond. 1866. 97–195:
"Immeritus Redivivus": on Sp and Rosalind; a fantasy. Feigned letters of Sp to Harvey, from the north parts.

MARC-MONNIER. La Réforme. Paris. 1885. 405–11:
Intelligent brief appreciation. "La poésie de Spenser est peut-être la plus poétique qui fût jamais sortie de l'imagination d'un homme," etc.

MARVELL, ANDREW (1621–78). Satires, ed. G. A. Aitken. Lond. 1892. 13.

MASSON, ROSALINE O., ed. Three Centuries of English Poetry. Preface by David Masson. Lond. 1877. Pp. xi, 215–68.

MAYER, CARL. Edmond Spenser et la Critique de M. Taine. In Le Correspondant. NS. XLII (1869), 1124–50:
An interesting critique. "L'imagination prodigieuse et tout italienne de Spenser." The FQ fundamentally a political and historical rather than a moral poem; "l'histoire allegorisée du règne d'Elisabeth." This theme developed; censures Taine for neglecting it. Classicist and negative criticism. (Copy in Yale Lib.)

MEREDITH, GEO. Poems. N.Y. 1910. I, 27: "The Poetry of Spenser."

Methodist Review, N.Y., XL (1858), 209–27:
A comparison of Sp and Bunyan.

MICKLE, W. J. Syr Martyn; a Poem, in the manner of Spenser, 1767 (= The Concubine). In Chalmers' Poets, XVII, 541–52. Cf. 553–54.

MIEGE, GUY. Etat présent d'Angleterre. 1702. Quoted in Spurgeon, Chaucer devant la critique, 221, 304.

MILTON, JOHN. See "Criticism before 1651," above.

MINTO, WM., and F. J. SNELL. In Encycl. Britannica, 11th ed. XXV (1911), 639–43:
A careful and judicious account, with some good appreciation; the authors' opinions on some points are open to question, e.g., on the infelicity of the Spenserian stanza. One may prefer Shelley's judgment on this point.

MITCHELL, DONALD G. English Lands, Letters, and Kings. N.Y. 1891. 217–30:
The characteristics of Sp and the FQ,—"The criticism of a matter-of-fact man."

MONNIER. See Marc-Monnier.

MONTÉGUT, E. Essais sur la Littérature Anglaise. Paris, 1883. 59–60:
Personal testimony of enthusiasm on first reading Sp. Cf. 63, 66, 103.

The Monthly Review, XCII (1820), 62–64:
A hostile review of Hazlitt. Antipathetic criticism of Sp. "Spenser has had numerous imitators, many of whom surpass the model."

MORRIS, WILLIAM.
Cf. G. Saintsbury, A Calendar of Verse, 1893. Introd.

MOULTON, RICHARD G. Interpretative Studies in Spenser and Milton. Syllabus. Chicago, 1893.

NEELE, HENRY. Lectures on Eng. Poetry. Lond. 1830. 48–53.

NELMES, THOS. E. Kilcolman, or Raleigh's Visit to Spenser, and other Compositions in Verse. N.Y. 1875.
Agreeable verse-embroideries (58 pp.) on the theme of Raleigh's visit to Sp—prompted by a visit of the author to Kilcolman.

[NEVE, P.] Cursory Remarks on some of the Ancient English Poets. Lond. 1789. 17–25:
> Spenser, his sources and his imitations, etc.

New Monthly Magazine. A New Gallery of Pictures. Spenser, the Poet of the Painters. XXXVIII (1833), 161–77:
> Sp the "most pictorial" of the poets; his painter's instincts; the painter's poet; and the greatest of English painters; passages from Sp suggesting each of the great painters, e.g., FQ, I, 1, 13 = Rembrandt. An interesting study.

*A New Occasional Oratorio . . . . the words taken from Milton, Spenser, etc. 1746.

New York Review, VIII (1841), 50–73:
> Review of first Amer. ed. of Sp, 1839. General observations. Stresses purity, abundance and scope of Sp's language; on his characteristics and quality of his imagination. Interesting specimen of early American Criticism.

NEWCOMB, THOS. Bibliotheca, 1712. Repr. in Nichols' Select Collection of Poems. Lond. 1780. III, 33–34. Cf. IV, 355.

NOEL, RODEN. Selections from Spenser. Lond. 1887 (Canterbury Poets).
> See Preface, 7–41. Of interest.

North Amer. Review: see Cleveland, H. K.; Gilman, S.; above.

*The Observer Observed, or Remarks on a curious tract, entitled "Observations on the Faery Queene of Spenser." Lond. 1756 [by Wm. Huggins?].
> A rambling reply to Warton. Nothing of value.

OLDHAM, JOHN. Works. Lond. 1710. 102, 151, 296–305:
> "A Satyr. The Person of Spencer is brought in" . . . . etc.
> He speaks,
>> "In stile of satyr, such wherein of old
>> He the fam'd Tale of *Mother Hubberd* told."

OLDYS, WM. British Librarian. Lond. 1737. See index.

PACHEU, JULES. De Dante à Verlaine. Paris [1897] 1912. Ch. ii:
> "Idéalistes et mystiques: Dante, Spenser, Bunyan, Shelley." Spenser "vrai père de la poésie anglaise"; emphasizes Sp's idealism. But a mere superficial study as to Sp.

PAGE, THOS. Spenser and Shakespeare; their Lives and Literary Work. Lond. n.d.

Sp, 3–16. An elementary cram-primer.

PALMER, GEO. H. Formative Types in English Poetry. Bost. 1918. Ch. iii.

"Edmund Spenser." A significant general essay. Sp not a naturalist, but a moralist and idealist; "His home is in a world of ideas"; "We should approach him primarily as a painter or a musician"; his debt to Elizabethan pageantry; "Space and generality are essential elements of Spenser's power"; his broad and massive effects; favorite cadences; his effects like those of a musician; main currents in his life, esp. classical learning, Puritanism, and Plato. Contrasted with Chaucer. Sp's poetry "intentionally unreal, a refuge, a restorative."

PANCOAST, HENRY S. One Aspect of Spenser's "Faerie Queene." In Andover Review, XII (1889), 372–85.

Of the unreality of Sp's world. Negative criticism. Cf. Clark, Ellen U., under "Faerie Queene."

PHILIPS, AMBROSE. Pastorals, 1709. See Preface. In Chalmers' Poets, XIII.

Cf. Cory, Critics of Sp, 135 ff.

PHILLIPS, EDWARD. Theatrum Poetarum Anglicanorum, 1675. Repr. Canterbury, 1800. 148–54:

Important, as it is generally believed to express Milton's opinions.

PHILIPS, KATHERINE. Poems. Lond. 1678. 15, 22.

PHILISIDES. See Shepherds', below.

Poems on Affairs of State, 1703. II, 235, 274.

Poems on Several Occasions . . . . written by a Lady. 1727. 68–76:

"Pindarick Ode, in Imitation of Spencer's Divine Love."

POOLE, JOSUA. The English Parnassus. Lond. 1677.

A phrase-book of English poetry, with quotations from Sp and others, e.g., 604: "Names of beauteous women": Amoret, Florimel, Belphoebe, etc.

POPE, ALEXANDER.   Works, ed. Croker, Elwin, and Courthope. Lond. 1871.
> I, 189: On the allegorical poets; 235 ff.: Pastorals.
> III, 355: "Spenser himself affects the obsolete."
> IV, 425: Imitation of Sp.
>> Cf. Spence's Anecdotes. Lond. 1858. 6, 16, 18, 129, 210, 224, 225, 235 *n*.
>> Cf. Cory, Critics of Sp, 132 ff.

PRESCOTT, WM. H. Biographical and Critical Miscellanies. Bost. 1855.   414, 447–48, 451, 480, 508, 559, 599, 634.
> Passing allusions to aspects of Sp's poetry.   Unimportant.

PRIOR, MATTHEW. Poems, 1709.   273 ff.:   "An Ode . . . . written in Imitation of Spencer's Stile."   See the Preface. Repr. in Chalmers' Poets, X, 178.
> Cf. Cory, Critics of Sp, 143–45.

Quarterly Review, XXXII (1825), 225–28:
> Sp as a "sacred poet"; the allegory.

Quarterly Review, XLIII (1830), 486–88:
> Sp and Bunyan; the allegory.

Quarterly Review, LXV (1840), 353–55:
> On Hallam's criticisms of Sp; Sp's "redundance of power," and command of diction.

Quarterly Review, CLIII (1882), 438–40.

R. (G. S.).   Spenser on the Finance Bill.   In Saturday Review, CVIII (1909), 81–82:
> Quotations from FQ, V (application to measures of current politics suggested).

[RAMESEY, WM.]   The Gentleman's Companion.   Lond. 1672. 129.   (Copy in Newberry Lib.)
> Quoted in Shakspere Allusion Book, II, 184.

RANKE, L. VON.   History of England.   Ox. 1875.   I, 340:
> Sp's qualities briefly stated.

REED, HENRY.   Lectures on the British Poets.   Phila. 1857.   I, Lect. IV:
> In the appreciative spirit of Wilson (Christopher North) and Coleridge.   Readable

The Retrospective Review, 1825, XII, 142 ff.

RUSSELL, W. C. Book of Authors. Lond. 1871. 26–29:
  Brief quotations from various writers on Sp.

RYMER, THOS. The Whole Critical Works of Monsieur Rapin; newly translated into English by several Hands. Lond. 1706. [1674].
  Cf. the Preface of the Publisher, I, A2 verso. See II, 114–15. In Spingarn, Crit. Essays of the 17th Cent., II, 167–68.

SAINTSBURY, GEORGE. History of Elizabethan Literature. Lond. 1887. 82–96.
  Excellent short appreciation. One of the best.

SAINTSBURY, GEO. In Traill's Social England. N.Y. 1895. III, 513–16; IV, 112–13.

SARRAZIN, G. William Shakespeares Lehrjahre. Weimar, 1897. 133–34:
  Shakespeare's pictures in his Poems; suggest Renaissance painters like Titian, Botticelli, etc. Compare Sp's pictures. Cf. 146–47.

Saturday Review, LXXVI (1893), 299. A Spencerian "Canto of Mutabilitie":
  Political verses on the Irish Situation (a mere allusion—juggling with the title).

SAUNDERS, FREDERIC. The Story of Some Famous Books. Lond. 1887. 23–28.
  Negligible.

SCHELLING, F. E. English Literature during the Lifetime of Shakespeare. N.Y. 1910. Ch. iv.

SCHELLING, F. E. The English Lyric. Bost. 1913. 46 ff.:
  The lyrical in Sp. 76. See index.

SCOTT, SIR WALTER.
  Poetical Works . . . . ed. F. T. Palgrave. Lond. 1893. 98, 203, 214, 232, 362. Cf. 355 ff.
  Familiar Letters. Edin. 1894. I, 218, 378.
  Review of Todd's Edition of Spenser. In Edinburgh Review, VII (1806), 203–17. Repr. in Scott's Prose Works. Edin. 1835. XVII, 80–101: Mildly sympathetic criticism of Sp; reviews the plan and allegory of the FQ; urges need of a commentary on the View of Ireland. Unimportant.
  Cf. Lockhart's Life of Scott, ch. i.
  Cory, Critics of Sp, 173–76.

SCUDDER, VIDA D. The Life of the Spirit in the Modern English Poets. Bost. 1895. 96–144. (See also the index.)

A comparison of Sp, Dante, and Shelley. See 113 ff. on their ethical attitudes. "It is the Renaissance spiritualized which Spenser gives us."

SCUDDER, VIDA D. Social Ideals in English Letters. Bost. 1898. 83–86:

Sp's poetry the mirror of his times "at its best"; some underlying ideas. See also index.

SECCOMBE, T., and J. W. ALLEN. The Age of Shakespeare. Lond, 1903. I, 29–41:

Perfunctory account.

SÉLINCOURT, E. DE. Introd. to his one-volume Oxford ed. of Sp.

A judicious and sympathetic study of the Life and Works. One of the best criticisms of Sp.

SERRELL, GEO. Spenser, and England as he Viewed It. In Temple Bar, CVII (1896), 423–37. Also in Littell's Living Age, CCIX (1896), 154–63.

Negligible.

SHEFFIELD, JOHN, Duke of Buckinghamshire. Essay on Poetry, 1682. Last line. In Chalmers' Poets, X, 94.

Cf. Cory, Critics of Sp, 124.

SHELLEY, PERCY BYSSHE. Works, ed. H. B. Forman. Lond. 1880.

I, 92: Preface to Laon and Cythna, 1818: Why he adopts the stanza of Sp—"a measure inexpressibly beautiful"; 408–10.

VIII, 72: Letter of Jan. 26, 1819: allusion to FQ, V, ii.

Cf. Böhme, Spenser's lit. Nachleben. Berlin, 1911. Kap. VII, Abschnitt 5: Spensers Einfluss auf Shelley.

Richard Ackermann, Quellen, Vorbilder, Stoffe, zu Shelleys Poetischen Werken. Erlangen, 1890. 36–41, 56.

SHENSTONE, WM. Letters, 1769. 61, 63, 66, 120, 121.

Cf. W. S. Landor. Works, IV, 187.

The Shepherds' Calender, being twelve pastorals attempted in blank verse. The subjects partly taken from the select Pastorals of Spenser and Sir Philip Sidney. By Philisides. Dublin, 1758.

Parts of the Sh Cal, paraphrased in blank verse.

SMITH, JOHN. The Mysterie of Rhetorique Unveil'd. Lond. 1665.
> One or two "examples" from Sp, e.g. 183.

SMITH, J. J., ed. Cambridge Portfolio. Lond. 1840, I, 48:
> "A dream of the Poets," by R. A. Willmott, with praise of Sp.

SOAME, SIR WM., and JOHN DRYDEN. Translation of Boileau's Art of Poetry, 1680 (with amplifications). Repr. in The Art of Poetry, ed. A. S. Cook. Bost. 1892. 165. Also in Dryden's Works, 1892, XV, 228.
> The later 17th cent. view of Sp's services in refining verse.

SOUTHEY, ROBERT.
> Poetical Works. Lond. 1837. I. Pp. viii, xxv, 309, 318, 321, 323 ff.; II, 143, 230, 279; III, 31, 259; IV, 1, 219 ff. (Bk. VI), 247, 354, 404 ff., 419; IX, 10; X, 9, 82 ff., 141, 143, 164 ff., 234.
>
> The Doctor. Lond. 1848. 382 ff.
>
> Commonplace Book. Lond. 1850. III, 210–11: synopsis of the View of Ireland; 213.
>
> IV, 310–12: Scattered observations on the FQ, etc.; that the versification of Prothal. and Epithal. "was formed upon some of Bernardo Tasso's Canzoni"; of Sympson's projected variorum ed. of Sp; "Pageants and court masques accustomed the people to such personifications as Spenser's."
>
> Life and Correspondence. Lond. 1849–50. I, 85; III, 295.
>
> Review of Todd's Edition of Spenser. In The Annual Review, IV (1806), 544–55: A sympathetic review. Some of the notes are of interest.
>
> Cf. Recollections of the Table-Talk of Samuel Rogers, ed. A. Dyce. Lond. 1887. 209: "Southey told me that he had read Spenser through about *thirty* times."
>
> Southey's criticism of Sp is sympathetic and readable.

SPEED, SAMUEL. Fragmenta Circeris. Lond. 1674. F 4.
> Quoted in Shakspere Allusion Book, II, 206.

SPENCE, JOSEPH. Anecdotes. Lond. 1858. See index.

SPENDER, A. E. The Tercentenary of Edmund Spenser. In Westminster Review, CLI (1899), 85–92.
> Sketchy. Not significant.

SPRAT, THOS. Account of the Life of Cowley, 1668. Repr. in Spingarn, Crit. Essays of 17th Cent., II, 121, 145.

STEBBING, WM.   The Poets, Chaucer to Tennyson; Impressions.
Lond. 1907.   As, Five Centuries of English Verse.   Impressions.   Lond. 1913.   I, 32–41:
> "Edmund Spenser."   Fairish criticism.

STEELE, SIR RICHARD.   The Spectator, Nov. 19, 1712.   See
The Spectator.   Lond. 1797.   VII, 370–75:
> Appreciative criticism with brief exposition of the allegory.
> The Tatler, July 6, 1710.   See The Tatler.   Lond. 1797.   IV,
> 30–36: Comment on FQ, IV, x, with prose paraphrase.
> Cf. Cory, Critics of Spenser, 141–43.

STOBART, J. C.   The Age of Spenser.   Lond. [1906].
> An anthology, with extracts from Sp.

STOCKDALE, PERCIVAL.   Lectures on the Truly Eminent English
Poets.   Lond. 1807.   2 v.   Vol. I, lecture 1: "Spenser."
> A study of Sp's style and stanza.   Not significant.

SWANWICK, ANNA.   Poets the Interpreters of their Age.   Lond.
1892.   171–82.
> Negligible.

SWINBURNE, ALGERNON C.   Miscellanies.   Lond. 1886.   6–10.
> Sp and Dante contrasted; the allegory; "the discursive and
> decorative style of Spenser."

TAINE, HIPPOLYTE A.   History of English Literature, trans.
H. van Laun.   N.Y. 1872.
> Book II, ch. i.   Passim, esp. "Poetry," sections vi–vii: Stimulating
> appreciation of the peculiar and purely poetical qualities of Sp's
> imagination.   Excellent criticism.

TATE, NAHUM.   Poems.   Collected by N. Tate, 1685.   45, 47, 91.

The Tatler No. 194.   (July 6, 1710.)   See Steele, Sir Rich., above.

TAYLOR, H. O.   Thought and Expression in the Sixteenth Century.   N.Y. 1920.
> II, 210 ff., Sp and Raleigh; II, 230–37: Sp in his century; a
> poetic Platonist; "The Faerie Queene is an example of the veritable
> self-expression of a sixteenth century poet."

TEMPLE, SIR WILLIAM.   Essay: Of Poetry, 1685.   In Works.
Edin. 1754.   II, 316–52.   See p. 342:
> Sp one of the refiners of "Gothic" heroic poetry; his qualities and
> his defects.
> Also in Spingarn, Crit. Essays of 17th Cent., III, 99 ff.

TENNYSON, ALFRED, LORD.

Cf. J. C. Collins, Illustrations of Tennyson. Lond. 1891. 7, 24, 45, 78, 149.

W. S. Kennedy, Tennyson and other Debtors to Spenser's Faerie Queene. In Poet Lore, X (1898), 492–506.

Paul Leveloh, Tennyson und Spenser. Eine Untersuchung von Spensers Einfluss auf Tennyson mit Berücksichtigung von Keats. Marburg, 1909. Diss. Deals with Sp's influence in respect of language, style, metre, and material, esp. on Princess, Maud, and the Idyls. Parallel passages, etc.

THOMPSON, WM. Preface to a Hymn to May, 1757. In Chalmers' Poets, XV, 32.

Cf. Cory, Critics of Sp, 160.

THOMSON, JAMES.

Cf. Cambr. Hist. Eng. Lit., X, 105–6.

T. Cibber, Lives of the Poets, 1753. I, 99: Reports Thomson as saying "that he formed himself upon Spenser."

G. Cohen, Thomson's Castle of Indolence eine Nachahmung von Spensers Faerie Queene. Bonn, 1899. Diss.

TRENT, W. P. Longfellow and other Essays. N.Y. 1910. 51–71:

"Spenser." Repr. of the Introd. to his ed. of Sp.

TUCKWELL, WM. Spenser. Lond. (G. Bell & Sons), 1906.

A little primer of some merit. The Life follows the conventional lines, is sketchy, and to be used with caution (Query esp. pp. 13–14); the critical summary, pp. 69–80, is suggestive, esp. 75–76, on Sp's musical gift, 71 ff. on Sp's imagery and style, etc.

TWINING, THOS. Introd. to his ed. of Aristotle's Poetics. Lond. 1812. I, 19:

Example of "enargeia" from Sp, with chilling comment.

[JOHN UPTON?]. A New Canto of Spensers Fairy Queen, 1747.

[VANE, SIR HENRY, the younger? or Henry Stubbe?]. A Light shining out of Darkness. Lond. 1659.

Quotes from Sh Cal, May; that Palinode = the Presbyterian ministers. Cf. DNB, XX, 129.

VERE, AUBREY DE. Essays, chiefly on Poetry. Lond. (1887).

I, 1–47: Characteristics of Spenser's Poetry.

48–100: Spenser as a Philosophic Poet. Also in Grosart's ed. of Sp.

Victoria Magazine. See D (E.M.L.), above.

WALLER, EDMUND (1606–87). Poems, ed. G. Thorn Drury. Lond. (Muses Library), 1893. 71, 218.
> Cf. Cory, Critics of Sp, 112.

WALPOLE, HORACE. Letters, ed. Mrs. Paget Toynbee. Ox. 1914. VI, 198; XII, 274; XV, 343; etc.

WARTON, JOSEPH. Essay on the Genius and Writings of Pope (1756). 4th ed. Lond. 1782. II, 30–37:
> On Pope's imitations of Sp; contrast with the real characteristics of Sp; Sp compared with Rubens; nature of later imitations of Sp by others.

WARTON, THOMAS. Observations on the Fairy Queen of Spenser. Lond. 1807 (1752).
> The chief exponent of early romanticist criticism of Sp. Of interest for its study of Sp's "sources," Chaucer, the romances, Ariosto, etc., and of his allegory.
> See Warton's Pastoral "in the manner of Spenser." In Chalmers' Poets, XVIII, 99; cf. 101, 115.
> Cf. Cory, Critics of Sp, 161–68.
> Clarissa Rinaker. Thomas Warton; a biographical and critical study. Baltimore, 1915. Also Pub. Mod. Lang. Asso., XXX (1915), 79–109.
> The Monthly Review, XI (1754), 112–24.

WELSTED, LEONARD, trans. Longinus, Treatise on the Sublime. Lond. 1712. 149–50, 154, 169:
> Specimens of the "sublime" in Sp and Milton discussed.

WENDELL, BARRETT. The Temper of the Seventeenth Century in English Literature. N.Y. 1904. 25–28; 108–12:
> A few aperçus. Union of spirit of Reformation and Renaissance in Sp; his influence in form greater than in spirit, due to lack of grasp and of simplicity.

WESLEY, SAM. Maggots, 1685. 30, 32.

WHEELER, ETHEL. In Great Thoughts. 4th Ser., IX (1901–2), 75 ff.
> "The Fairy lands of the Poets." General appreciation; notes Sp's feeling for "the subtle beauty of matter."

WHIPPLE, E. P. The Literature of the Age of Elizabeth. Bost. 1891. 189–220. Cf. Atlantic Monthly, XXI (1868), 395–405.

WILKIE, WM. A Dream, in the Manner of Spenser, 1759. In Chalmers' Poets, XVI, 177–78.

WILMOT, JOHN, Earl of Rochester. Valentinian, 1696. 128.

WILLMOTT, R. A. See Smith, J. J., above.

WILSON, JOHN ("Christopher North"). In Blackwoods Magazine, XXXIV (1833), 830 ff.; XXXVI (1834), 408–30, 681–737; XXXVII (1835), 49–71, 540–56, 659–76.
Discussion of the works and of Sp's characteristics. Admirably appreciative and stimulating. Helpful.

WINBOLT, S. E. Spenser and his Poetry. Lond. 1912.
A primer for students.

WINSTANLEY, WM. Lives of the English Poets. Lond. 1687. 88–93. As in his England's Worthies, 1684.

WOODBERRY, GEO. E. The Torch. Lond. and N.Y. 1905. 113–36. "Spenser":
Sp as a "race-exponent" and center of spiritual history, using "the romanticism of a receding past," like Virgil; on scholarship (the assimilation of the great thoughts of mankind and the great forms) in the English poets, Spenser, Milton, Gray, Shelley, and Tennyson; Sp's poetic aim and performance; qualities of the FQ; his symbolism. Excellent general criticism. Suggestive.

WOODFORD, SAMUEL. Legend of Love. 1679. Pp. 54–118 of his Paraphrase upon the Canticles, etc. Lond. 1679.
Copy in Newberry Lib. Cf. Cory, Critics of Spenser, 89, 122–24; also his Spenser, the School of the Fletchers, and Milton, 342–43.

WOODWARD, PARKER. Euphues the Peripatician. Lond. 1907.
"Attributing to Francis Bacon the authorship of the works of Edmund Spenser" (Brit. Mus. Catalogue). See ch. ii; also p. 49: on the knowledge of law shown in Sp's works. See Harman, E. G., above.

WOODWARD, PARKER. Edmund Spenser's Poems. In Baconiana, Lond. N.S. IX (1901), 117–28, 177–85. See also pp. 21–26:
Baconian conjectures. Similar to those of G. C. Cuningham (q.v.). Also in his The Strange Case of Francis Tidir. Lond. 1901. 47–54.

WOODWARD, P. Tudor Problems. Lond. 1912. Ch. xiv.
On Sp. That Bacon published under the name of Sp—and others.

WORDSWORTH, WILLIAM.

    Poetical Works, ed. Wm. Knight. Edin. 1882.

      I, 22; III, 135, 178, 232, 287, 322; IV, 25, 35, 100, 256, 323, 337; V, 31; VI, 51, 85 *n*, 112; VII, 23, 109, 158; VIII, 90.

    Prose Works, ed. A. B. Grosart. Lond. 1876.

      I, 322; II, 111–12, 274; III, 76, 465.

    Cf. Lane Cooper, Concordance to Wordsworth. Lond. 1911. s.v. "Spenser."

    Wordsworth's loyalty to Sp is more constant than that of any of the greater English poets subsequent to Milton.

WORTHINGTON, JOHN. Diary and Correspondence, ed. Jas. Crossley. Chetham Soc. 1847–86. I, 259, 261–63, 271, 279; II, 76, 86, 345.

YEATS, WM. B. The Cutting of an Agate. Lond. 1919. 182–223. Repr. of Introd. to his ed. of Selected Poems of Sp.

    Sketchy and general. Stresses Sidney's influence; censures Sp's Irish views; "his genius was pictorial"; of his relation to his times; his allegory; his moral system "official and impersonal"; a servant of the state in all his work; Sp compared with Shelley and William Morris; Sp "seemed always to feel through the eyes, imagining everything in pictures."

V
VARIOUS TOPICS

V. VARIOUS TOPICS

For abstracts of several unprinted papers on Sp, see Pub. Mod. Lang. Asso.,
XXVIII (1913), p. xiii of "Proceedings."

Matson, H. References for Literary Workers. Chicago, 1892. 291–94.

Smythe-Palmer, A., ed. The Ideal of a Gentleman. Lond. 1908. Topically arranged extracts, including several from Sp.

PORTRAITS OF SPENSER

Of several classes, not easily reconcilable; some of doubtful authenticity; the evidence for each not yet sufficiently analyzed. Are the portraits all imaginary? If not, which portraits (or their originals) were made from the life? Evidence for this yet to be assembled. Is there any such evidence except tradition?

The Dupplin type: the oil painting owned by Earl Spencer at Althorpe, which is said to be a copy by Sir Henry Raeburn of the original at Dupplin Castle.

Two (?) pictures at Pembroke Hall.

Mr. Ellis H. Minns, Librarian of Pembroke College, writes me that so far as he knows there is only one, "hanging in the Hall, said to be given by William Mason, Gray's friend; it is a copy made by Benjamin Wilson after a lost original once belonging to George Onslow. Either it or (less probably) the original has been engraved."

Oil painting by Benj. Wilson, c. 1770 (after the Pembroke original).

The "reputed portrait" in the possession of the Right Hon. Lewis Harcourt.

The Tregaskis Catalogue No. 851 (1922) cites a copy of the 1750 ed. of Sp with inscription referring to a "picture of Spenser which General Guise presented to Speaker Onslow."

Portrait at Castle Saffron, County Cork (destroyed before 1818).

Portrait in Earl of Clarendon's gallery. Cf. Evelyn's Letter to Pepys, 12 Aug. 1689. (In Spingarn, Crit. Essays of 17th Cent., II, 320.)

Portrait "in the possession" of the Earl of Kinnoul (the Dupplin portrait).

Portrait, in the possession of Baring-Gould (engraving in large paper copy of Grosart's ed. of Spenser, Vol. II).

Portrait, the Fitzhardinge miniature. "Through Queen Elizabeth,"— in large-paper copy of Grosart's ed. of Spenser, Vol. VII. (The two are totally unlike.)

Is the fifth head from the top (No. 38), right-hand column (marked "E. S."), of the engraved title-page of Winstanley's England's Worthies, 1684, intended as a portrait of Sp?
For other portraits, see references below.

The Academy, LVI (1899), 67–68:
The Althorpe and Chesterfield portraits.

A.L.A. Portrait Index, Washington, 1906, p. 1372:
Some twenty references; the Earl Spencer (Althorpe) portrait and the Earl of Kinnoul portrait seem to be most often given.

Anthologia Hibernica. Dublin, 1793–94. I, 189.

BOURNE, H. R. FOX. Sir Philip Sidney. N.Y. 1891. 196:
"From an engraving by W. B. Scott, 1839."

Calendarium Pastorale . . . . T. Bathurst [d. 1651] n.d. (1653). Frontispiece: "G. Vertue, sculp."

CHALMERS, GEORGE. Supplemental Apology for the Believers in the Shakespeare-Papers. Lond. 1799. 23 n.
The portraits in Pembroke Hall.

COLLIER's ed. of Sp, 1862, I, p. clv.

CROKER, T. C. Researches in the South of Ireland. Lond. 1824. 111:
The portrait at Castle Saffron.

Dict. Natl. Biog., XVIII, 802:
"Four reputed portraits (in oils) are known": (1) Kinnoul, at Dupplin Castle (half length); (2) Carnarvon, at Bretby Park (three quarters length); (3) Copy by Benj. Wilson, presented by the poet Mason to Pembroke College, from Onslow's lost original; (4) Portrait ascribed to the Florentine Bronzino, the property of S. Baring-Gould. Several engravings described.

Effigies Poeticae, or the Portraits of the British Poets. Lond. 1824. 2 v. (Text by Bryan Waller Proctor.) I, 92:
Engraving from the Kinnoul portrait; II, 29, brief impressionistic comment on the portrait.

FLETCHER, C. R. L. Historical Portraits, 1400–1600. Ox. 1909. 165–66:
The Pembroke Hall portrait.

GARNETT, R., and E. GOSSE. English Literature, an Illustrated Record. N.Y. 1903–4. Vol. II, ch. iii.

Gentleman's Magazine, LXXXVIII (1818), 224:
> Portrait of Sp, in 1750 at Castle Saffron.

Grolier Club, Catalogue of an Exhibition of . . . . the Works
of Edmund Spenser. N.Y. 1899. 16–19:
> List of portraits of Sp; traces four types; each described.

GROSART, A. B.   Spenser, I, 242–43:
> Three described; no documentation.

GROSART, A. B.   Circular inviting subscribers to an engraved
portrait of Sp from the painting owned by the Countess of
Chesterfield.   Copy in Harvard Lib.
> That the Kinnoul portrait at Dupplin Castle is not Sp's; that "emi-
> nent authorities" agree that the Chesterfield portrait is authentic.

HUTTON, L.   Literary Landmarks of London.   N.Y. 1892.   286.

KNIGHT, CHARLES.   The Gallery of Portraits.   Lond. 1835.
IV, 194–200:
> The Kinnoul portrait.

KRANZ, H. S.   In Current Literature, XXXVIII (1905), 438:
> The Kinnoul portrait.

LEE, S.   Great Englishmen of the Sixteenth Century.   Lond.
1904.   154.

New Monthly Magazine, VI (1816), 327:
> A portrait of Sp in the possession of John Love of Saffron Waldron,
> near Kilcolman.

Notes and Queries, Ser. I, Vol. III (1851), 301:
> An attempt to classify the various portraits; IV (1851), 74, 101;
> X (1854), 205; Ser. XI, Vol. V (1912), 310, 417.

OSGOOD, C. G.   Concordance to Spenser: frontispiece:
> "A reputed portrait" in the possession of the Rt. Hon. Lewis
> Harcourt reproduced. The inscription on the portrait, following the
> old tradition of Sp's birth in 1510 (the early monument in Westminster
> Abbey) reads "1596: ÆT; 86." The face, however, bearded, with
> flowing hair, long nose, and high brow, is apparently that of a man in
> his forties.

PENNANT, THOS.   Tour in Scotland, 1772.   Chester, 1774–75.
II, 80.   Repr. in John Pinkerton's Collection of Voyages and
Travels.   Lond. 1809.   Cf. III, 398–99:
> The portrait of Sp at Dupplin Castle (near Perth), the seat of the
> Earl of Kinnoul.

SHELLEY, HENRY C. In The Outlook, N.Y., LXI (1899), 35–46:
> The Althorpe portrait; the Sp portraits discussed; two groups of portraits; the one at "Dublin" castle, and the one formerly owned by Lord Chesterfield.

SHELLEY, H. C. In Spenser's Footsteps. In his Literary By-paths in Old England. Bost. 1906. 53–55:
> Accepts the Dupplin portrait.

SMITH, CHARLES. The Ancient and Present State of . . . . Cork, 1750. Repr. by the Cork Hist. and Arch. Soc., 1893, I, 311–13.

SMITH, J. J., ed. Cambridge Portfolio. Lond. 1840. I, 48.

The Universal Magazine, XLIX (1771), 337.

WHITE, JAS. G. Historical and Topographical Notes. Cork, 1913. III, 264–73.

WOODWARD, P. Tudor Problems. Lond. 1912. 141.

WOTTON, MABEL E. Word Portraits of Famous Writers. Lond. 1887. 293–96:
> On the portraits of Sp.

AUTOGRAPHS

Calendars of State Papers, Ireland, 1574–85.
> 292, 293, 303, 381, 393: various papers certified by Sp.
> do do, 1588–92: pp. 198, 247: Sp's autograph.
> do do, 1598–99: pp. 401, 414, 467: despatches by the hand of Sp.

Catalogue of Additions to the Manuscripts in the British Museum. Lond. 1875+. No. 19,869, "with autograph signature."

Collier's ed. of Sp, I, pp. ciii–iv.

Dict. Natl. Biog., XVIII, 805–6.

GARNETT, R., and E. GOSSE. English Literature, an Illustrated Record. N.Y. 1904.
> Vol. II, ch. iii: facsimile of Sp's handwriting.

Gentleman's Magazine, CII (1832), 194, 305:
> Facsimile of Sp's autograph; a lease signed by Sp and with the seal of "several houses of Spencer." Important.

FROM LORD GREY'S LETTER TO THE QUEEN, DECEMBER 22, 1580.
STATE PAPERS, IRELAND, VOL. 79. 24 (1). BELIEVED TO BE
IN SPENSER'S HAND

GOLLANCZ, I. Spenseriana. In Proceedings of the British
  Academy, 1907–8, pp. 99–105:
> Sp's signature and holographs. Also in Archiv. f. d. Studium d.
> neueren Spr. u. Lit., CXLI (1921), 138–43; and The Athenaeum,
> No. 4180, 7 Dec. 1907, p. 732.

GREENWOOD, SIR GRANVILLE G. Is There a Shakespeare Problem? Lond. 1916. 322 *n;* 333.

GROSART'S ed. of Sp, I, 148:
> The frontispiece of the large-paper edition gives a facsimile of Sp's
> autograph.

Guide to Autographs, Letters, MSS, etc. in the British Museum.
  Lond. 1859 (also 1851, 1860, 1864, 1870, etc.). Ed. of
  1870, 17:
> Sp's grant to McHenry of the woods of Balliganim. "Holograph."
> Cf. Collier and Grosart, contra.

JENKINSON, HILARY. Elizabethan Handwritings. In The
  Library, Lond., 4th Ser., III (1922), 1 ff.
> At pp. 33–34 is a discussion (with a facsimile plate) of Sp's signa-
> ture and handwriting in the Brit. Mus. and Public Record Office.
> Important.

NETHERCLIFT, FREDK. G. Handbook to Autographs. Lond.
  1862. No. S. 11:
> Facsimile of Sp's autograph, from BM MS.

Notes and Queries, Ser. VI, Vol. X (1884), 502.

PLOMER, HENRY R.
> In a letter of Sept. 7, 1922, Mr. Plomer states his belief that a copy
> of a letter of Lord Grey written to the Queen is in Sp's handwriting (see
> facsimile opposite). "It is written in what Mr. Jenkinson calls the
> 'Secretary' hand, which was the universal hand for correspondence in the
> days of Elizabeth and appears to have been taught in all schools—and
> there was so little deviation from the settled form of this handwriting
> that it is extremely difficult and very hazardous to ascribe a document
> in this hand to any particular writer. Happily, however, human beings
> are not machines and individualism shows itself, even in this very stereo-
> typed handwriting. The copy of Lord Grey's letter to the Queen is
> written in this Secretary hand, and at first sight you may be inclined to
> reject it as being Spenser's, although it bears some points of resemblance

to the two authenticated examples of Spenser's handwriting in the Grant of Kilcolman in the British Museum and the Depositions at the Public Record Office. But to my mind there is one strong piece of evidence. On line 5 [line 6] from the bottom of the left hand page in the photograph you will see a capital B. If you compare that with the B in the Grant and the Depositions you will notice that they are made in exactly the same way. Now, so far as my examination of the documents in the Public Record Office has gone, and I have carefully been through some twenty-five volumes, I have not met with any other writer who made a capital B in that way. Another point must be borne in mind. Lord Grey's letter to the Queen was written in 1580, whereas both the document in the Museum and that at the Public Record Office were not written until c. 1589."

"Amongst others the following documents may be compared with the handwriting of Lord Grey's letter to the Queen:

State Papers, Ireland, Vol. 87. 64. Letters of Lord Grey to Walsingham dated from Dublin 29 Decr. 1581.

do do, Vol. 89. 18. Copy of John Nugent's Confession (6 pages).

do do, Vol. 89. 30. Lord Grey to the Privy Council.

do do, Vol. 89. 35. Lord Grey to the Privy Council."

Mr. Plomer writes Nov. 7, 1922: "I do not see how anyone can question the genuineness of the Kilcolman grant (BM), or the Depositions (PRO). It would not have paid anyone to forge those documents, and the Roche document is also clearly genuine."

STRONACH, GEO. Signatures of Spenser. In The Academy, LXXVII (1909), 519:

Of the two pieces of Sp's handwriting extant. With reference to Cal. of State Papers, Ireland, 1558–92, p. 198. On the MS of the View of Ireland in the Public Record Office and other Spenser papers there.

WARNER, GEO. F., ed. Facsimiles of Royal, Historical, Literary, and other Autographs in the . . . . British Museum. Lond. 1899.

No. 92 gives Sp's grant of the woods of Balliganim with his Signature (or, "entirely in Spenser's handwriting"); =B.M. Add MS 19869. Cf. Grosart's Spenser, I, 148: but Warner insists upon the genuineness of this document.

SPENSER POET LAUREATE

See *Amoretti*, sonnet 28 (also 29, line 3): that the laurel "is the badge which I do bear."

The Anti-Jacobin Review and Magazine, XXV (1807), 3.

AUSTIN, W. S., and JOHN RALPH. The Lives of the Poets-Laureate. Lond. 1853.
> Begins with Ben Jonson as the first poet laureate. Cf. Introd., pp. 34–35 for sketch of Sp's life. That Sp was not a poet laureate.

British Quarterly Review. See T. Keightley, below.

BROADUS, EDMUND K. The Laureateship. Ox. 1921. Ch. iv:
> That the laureateship technically began with Dryden. Analyzes the (late) tradition that Sp was poet laureate and the official sanction it has received, based on the fact of the pension.

COLLIER'S ed. of Sp, I, p. lxvii.

CORBETT, F. ST. JOHN. A History of British Poetry. Lond. 1904. 624:
> That Sp was the first poet-laureate.

The Faerie Leveller . . . . By her Poet Laureat, Edmond Spenser, 1648.
> An early mention of Sp as poet laureate.

The Grolier Club. Catalogue of an Exhibition of Selected Works of the Poets Laureate of England. N.Y. 1901. 7:
> Sp entered among "the Volunteer Laureates."

HAMILTON, WALTER. The Poets Laureate of England. Lond. 1879. 32–38:
> Places Sp with Chaucer, Skelton, etc., among "the volunteer laureates."

KEIGHTLEY, T. In Brit. Quar. Review, XXII (1855), 392 *n*.

MALONE, EDMOND. In the Prose Works of Dryden. Lond. 1800. I, 84:
> Sp not called Poet Laureate.

MITFORD, JOHN. In his ed. of Sp, 1839, I, p. xxii.

TANNER, THOS. Bibliotheca Britannico-Hibernica. Lond. 1748. 684:
> "Titulo poetae laureati a regina Elizabetha ornatus."

TODD'S ed. of Sp, 1805, I, pp. lxv f.:
> Cites contemporary allusions to Sp as laureate.

SPENSER AND PURITANISM: RELIGIOUS OPINIONS

The Hymn of Heavenly Love is Sp's chief religious poem. See Sh Cal passim, esp. May; MHT; FQ, VII, vii, 35; V of I (Grosart's ed.), 246.

BLACKWOOD'S MAGAZINE, XCIX (1866), 200–23: "Religio Spenseri."

    Sp and Ariosto compared, esp. as "witnesses to the religious condition of their respective countries." Also in Littell's Living Age, 3d Ser., Vol. XXXII (1866), 673–88.

BROOKE, STOPFORD A. English Literature. N.Y. 1897. 111.

CAMPBELL, D. The Puritan in Holland, England, and America. N.Y. 1892. II, 127:

    Sp and Milton, "both Puritans." Echoes the conventional view, without analysis.

DRAPER, J. W. In the Colonnade. N.Y. 1922. XIV, 45.

Edinburgh Review, CLXI (1885), 142–76. "Spenser as a Philosophic Poet."

    A review of Grosart's ed. of Sp. Analysis of Sp's philosophic opinions.

GROSART'S ed. of Sp, I, 33, 189, 314; IV, pp. xlviii, lii, lxix; IX, 246.

HICKEY, E. Catholicity in Spenser. In Amer. Catholic Quar. Review, XXXII (1907), 490–502:

    Sp not a Catholic or a Puritan; but in part his poetry expresses Catholic ideas, e.g., Hymn of Heavenly Beauty; in the House of Pride, etc.

HIGGINSON, J. J. Spenser's Shepherd's Calender. N.Y. 1912. Passim, esp. 16 ff., 150 ff.; discusses theories of Lowell, Church, Winstanley, and Padelford, on the subject.

HUGHES, M. Y. In Mod. Lang. Review, XIII (1918), 267–75.

HUNT, T. W. Edmund Spenser and the English Reformation. In Bibliotheca Sacra, LVII (1900), No. 1, pp. 39–53:

    Sp's attitude towards the classical paganism of the time and towards Romanism; also his attitude towards the Reformation, which was favorable to Calvinism and Puritanism, as distinct from Anglicanism. Cf. Higginson's Spenser's Shepherd's Calender, 155.

HUNT, T. W. See "Faerie Queene, Gen'l."

JACK, A. A. Chaucer and Spenser. 261–62.

KLEIN, ARTHUR J. Intolerance in the Reign of Elizabeth. Lond. 1917.
> A history of ecclesiastical-political affairs in the time of Elizabeth. See esp. chs. v–viii, and the Bibliography.

MORLEY, H. Eng. Writers, IX, 41 ff., 449.

PADELFORD, F. M. The Political and Ecclesiastical Allegory of the First Book of the Faerie Queene. Bost. 1911.
> Sp a Low-Church Calvinist.

PADELFORD, F. M. Spenser and the Puritan Propaganda. In Mod. Philol., XI (1913), 85–106:
> Nature of Puritanism in Sp's day; Puritan satire in Sp's poetry; Sp a Low Churchman.

PADELFORD, F. M. Spenser and the Theology of Calvin. In Mod. Philol., XII (1914), 1–18:
> Further on Sp's Puritanism; points in which Sp agrees with the Calvinistic theology.

PADELFORD, F. M. Spenser and the Spirit of Puritanism. In Mod. Philol., XIV (1916), 31–44:
> On Sp's relation to "the essential spirit" of Puritanism. Elizabethan distinguished from seventeenth century Puritanism; its various phases and divisions; movement for Calvinistic reform of the church dominant in it; its anti-Renaissance spirit; in theology Sp a Calvinist; in attitude towards life a man of the Renaissance. Sp takes middle ground, with Sidney, in the Puritan controversy over the stage.

POLLARD, A. F. Hist. of England, 1547–1603. Lond. 1915.
> Ch. xix, etc., and 497 (references).

SÉLINCOURT. Introd. to his one-volume Oxford ed. of Sp, p. liii n.

TOLMAN, A. H. The Relation of Spenser and Harvey to Puritanism. In Mod. Philol., XV (1918), 549–64:
> A review of preceding discussions of Sp's Puritanism. Sp a Low-Churchman, not opposed to Episcopacy. Harvey's views similar.

WHITMAN, C. H. Subject Index to Spenser. 195.

WINSTANLEY, LILIAN. Spenser and Puritanism. In Mod. Lang. Quarterly, III (1900), 6–16, 103–10:
> Attempts to define Puritanism in England, historically, and Sp's relation to it; that Sp accepts Calvinism; its doctrines in the FQ, etc.;

contrasts Marlowe; Sp a Puritan on questions of church discipline, and of morals and manners—unlike the dramatists, and like Milton; a didactic poet, but less severe in his later period and less of a Puritan.

SPENSER AND THE CHURCH

See above, "Spenser and Puritanism."

WHITMAN. Subject Index to Spenser, 52–53.

V of I, in Sp ed. Grosart, IX, 242:
"Iren. For religion lytle have I to say, my self being as I sayde, not professed therin." Cf. 132.

SPENSER'S PHILOSOPHY

See "Spenser and Puritanism," above.

See also "Works: Cantos of Mutability"; "Four Hymns."

DE VERE, A. Essays, I, 48–100: "Spenser as a Philosophic Poet."

DOWDEN, E. See "Faerie Queene, Gen'l."

Edinburgh Review, CLXI (1885), 142–76. "Spenser as a Philosophic Poet." See De Vere, above.

HOPE, C. See "Faerie Queene, Gen'l."

PADELFORD, F. M. See "Faerie Queene, Gen'l."

RUSKIN. Stones of Venice, Vol. II, ch. viii.

SPENSER AND THE LAW

See references, above, on the "Life, in General."

The View of Ireland, passim, evinces considerable knowledge of law. See esp. (Grosart's ed.), IX, 42 ff.

HARVEY, GABRIEL, Works, ed. Grosart, 1884. I, 139.
"So towarde a lawier"—with reference to Sp?

WHITMAN. Subject Index to Spenser, 140.

WOODWARD, PARKER. In Baconiana, Lond. N.S., IX (1901), 180–82.

WOODWARD, PARKER. Tudor Problems, Lond. 1912. 158.

SPENSER'S TREATMENT OF NATURE

See "Works: Cantos of Mutability," for Sp's philosophy of nature.

AMHERST, ALCILIA.   A History of Gardening in England.   Lond. 1896.   109–78:

> Chapters on English gardens in the 16th cent.; citations from Sp in illustration, at pp. 134, 149.

ECKERT, FLORENCE.   The Portrayal of Nature in Spenser. 1912.   MS.   Diss. in Univ. of Chicago Lib.

MOORMAN, F. W.   The Interpretation of Nature in English Poetry.   Strassburg (Quellen und Forschungen, XCV), 1905, ch. xii:

> Sp's general sources; his use of nature like Chaucer's, with additions; his pastoralism; sentimental interpretation of nature; feeling for the sea; use of simile; the FQ in a "land of *Weissnichtwo*"; romantic landscapes "shot with classic imagery." Cf. 195.

NICHOLS, ROSE S.   English Pleasure Gardens.   N.Y.   1902. Illus.   Ch. v: "The Elizabethan Flower Garden."

> Sp is not utilized, but it is useful for a study of this theme in Sp.

PALGRAVE, F. T.   Landscape in Poetry from Homer to Tennyson.   Lond. 1897.   133–37.

> Sp's landscapes = in a semi-classic style; his many "picturesque vignettes"; etc.

Quarterly Review, CLXXXIII (1896), 245:

> Flowers in Sp.

SCHRAMM, R.   Spensers Naturschilderungen.   Leipzig, 1908. Diss.

> Schematic treatment, with copious citations.

SÉLINCOURT.   Introd. to his one-volume Oxford ed. of Sp. Pp. lvii–lix.

WILSON, JOHN.   In Blackwood's Magazine, XXXIV (1833), 832.

COLOR IN SPENSER

ELTON, OLIVER. Notes on Colour and Imagery in Spenser. In Otia Merseiana. Lond. 1904. And in his Modern Studies, Lond. 1907. 67–77. Cf. 56–59.

FLETCHER, J. B. The Painter of the Poets. In Studies in Philology, XIV (1917), 153–66:
> That Sp has "the temperament of a painter at work in the medium of a poet"; analyzes his pictorial technic; of the various painters to whom Sp has been compared—Rubens, Paul Veronese, Turner, etc. F. compares him with Botticelli [cf. Galimberti, under "Sources, General," above] and Dürer; Sp's colors few and symbolic; sources of his imagery in Emblem books, etc. A suggestive essay.

HOTCHKISS, FLORENCE. Spenser as a Colorist. In Vassar Miscellany, XXVI (1897), 402–6.

PRATT, ALICE E. The Use of Color in the Verse of the English Romantic Poets. Chicago, 1898. Diss. 7–11:
> Use of color in Sp.

VIEWS ON ART, POETRY, ETC.

FLETCHER, J. B. In Studies in Philology, XIV (1917), 153–66.

GROSART's ed. of Sp, I, 281, 318 ff.; IX, 116–17.

HARVEY's Marginalia, 169.

LANGDON, IDA. Materials for a study of Spenser's Theory of Fine Art. Ithaca, N.Y. 1911.
> A classified collection of passages in Sp, etc., illustrating his views on art, including the art of poetry; with an Introd. (pp. i–lxiii) on Sp's "Theory of Fine Art." Cf. review by R. E. N. Dodge in Journal of Eng. and Germ. Philology, XII (1913), 341–43.

POPE, EMMA FIELD. Renaissance Criticism as Illustrated in the Faerie Queene, 1920. MS Diss. in Univ. of Chicago Lib.

THOMPSON, G. A. Elizabethan Criticism of Poetry. 1914. Univ. of Chicago Diss.
> Analysis of the Elizabethan and the Spenserian conception of poetry and literary art.

WHITMAN, C. H. Subject Index. 90 (and cross references).

SPENSER'S WOMEN

BEALE, DOROTHEA. Literary Studies of Poems, New and Old. Lond. 1902. 25–51: "Britomart, or Spenser's Ideal of Woman."

From papers written for a ladies' school. Pp. 49–51 summarize the writer's views on Sp's ideal of women.

DOWDEN, E. See "Criticism after 1650."

HUNTER, MARGARET. In Twentieth Century, Lond., III (1901), 198–212. (Copy in N.Y. Pub. Lib.)

On Sp's treatment of women in the FQ, esp. Medina, Belphoebe, and Alma.

PADELFORD, F. M. In Jour. Eng. and Germ. Philology, XVI (1917), 70–83.

SÉLINCOURT. Introd. to his one-volume Oxford ed. of Sp. Pp. lix f.

WHIPPLE, E. P. Lit. of Age of Eliz. 1891. 218.

CONCORDANCE AND SUBJECT INDEX

*MAXWELL, ANNIE A. A Glossary of the non-classical Proper Names of Spenser. MS Diss. 1904. In Cornell Univ. Lib.

OSGOOD, C. G. A Concordance to the Poems of Edmund Spenser. Washington (Carnegie Institution), 1915.

A monumental work, of the highest value in the minute study of Sp. A thorough index to all of Sp's poetry. Cf. Mod. Lang. Review, XII, 87–89.

WHITMAN, C. H. A Subject-Index to the Poems of Edmund Spenser. New Haven (Yale Univ. Press), 1918.

Very helpful. Indexes characters and names as well as subjects.

Cf. Studies in Philology, XVII, 255–56; Mod. Lang. Notes, XXXV, 429–32; H. S. V. Jones in Jour. Eng. and Germ. Philol., XXI, 702.

SPENSER'S LANGUAGE, ARCHAISMS, ETC.

See above, references under each of the Works, esp. Sh Cal.

See the following section.

BACKE, W. Essay on Spenser . . . . especially with regard to the Language. Stralsund, 1872.

BARROW, SARAH F. Studies in the Language of Spenser. 1902. MS Diss. in Univ. of Chicago Lib.

BAUERMEISTER, K. Zur Sprache Spensers auf Grund der Reime in der Faerie Queene. Freiburg, 1896. Diss.
>Cf. Englische Studien, XXVI, 2; Anglia, Beiblatt, X, 12.

BOEHM, K. Spensers Verbalflexion. Berlin, 1909. Diss.

BOHNE, K. Bemerkungen zur Grammatik Spensers. Geestemünde, 1884. Progr.

BRADLEY, HENRY. The Making of English. N.Y. 1904. 126-27:
>Sp's compound epithets. 227-29: Sp's neologisms; justification of his poetic diction; that his language, "pseudo-archaic as it may be called, was the only fitting vehicle for his tone of thought and feeling."

BRENDEL, H. Ueber die Konjunktionen bei Spenser. Halle, 1890. Diss.

BRUNNER, K. Die Dialektwörter in Spensers "Shepherds' Calendar." In Archiv. f. d. Studium d. n. Spr. u. Lit., CXXXII (1914), 401-4:
>That Sp uses few dialect words, but draws freely from the vocabulary of older Eng. literature for unusual words.

CHESTERFIELD, LORD. Letters, ed. Lord Mahon. Phila. 1892. I, 202-3:
>Letter dated Sept. 27, 1748: On Sp's obsolete English.

COVINGTON, F. F., Jr. See under "Works: V of I."

CULPEPPER, SIR THOS. Essayes. Lond. 1671. (Copy in Newberry Lib.) 118. Quoted in Spurgeon, Chaucer Criticism, I, 247-48:
>On Sp's archaisms.

DRAPER, J. W. See under "Sh Cal"; "V of I."

DÜRING, H. Ueber die Pronomina bei Spenser. Halle, 1891. Diss.

ELLIS, A. J. On Early English Pronunciation. Lond. 1869-89. Pt. III, 845-52, 858, 862-71:
>On Alex. Gill's Phonetic Writing, 1621, with an examination of Sp's and Sidney's rhymes. Reprints Gill's extracts in phonetic transcription from the FQ. Sp's pronunciation not to be determined from his

rhymes, which are frequently imperfect rhymes; Sp's diction apes that
of the 15th cent. Lists of eye-rhymes, assonances, and anomalous
rhymes in Sp.

ENGEL, H. Spenser's Relativsatz. Berlin, 1908. Diss.

FULLER, THOS. See "Criticism after 1650."

GABRIELSON, ARVID. Rime as a Criterion of the Pronunciation
of Spenser, etc. Uppsala, 1909.
> Cf. Englische Studien, XLI, 397 ff. See also Bauermeister; Ellis.

GREENOUGH, J. B., and G. L. KITTREDGE. Words and their
Ways in English Speech. N.Y. 1901. 118:
> Sp's archaisms.

GREG, W. W. Pastoral Poetry. Lond. 1906. 93–95.

GROSART'S ed. of Sp, I, 408–21.

GÜNTHER, F. Spenser's syntaktische Eigentümlichkeiten. In
Herrig's Archiv, LV.

GÜNTHER, G. Ueber den Wortaccent bei Spenser. Jena, 1889.
Diss.

HALL, FITZEDWARD. Modern English. Lond. 1873. 59, 180 n,
287 n:
> On certain neologisms in Sp.

HERFORD, C. H. Spenser's Use of In. In the Academy,
Lond., XXII (1882), 315.

HOFFMAN, FRITZ. Das Partizipium bei Spenser. Berlin, 1909.
Diss.

LIESE, R. Die Flexion des Verbums bei Spenser. Halle, 1891.
Diss.

LONG, P. W. In Modern Language Review, XII, 88:
> That Sp's archaisms "reside chiefly in antiquated spellings . . . .
> one questions whether page by page he be not more modern (with modern-
> ized spellings) than Shakespeare."

LOUNSBURY T. R. History of the English Language. N.Y.,
1894. 364:
> Sp's pronunciation; 412: Influence of some of his archaisms.

LOUNSBURY, T. R. Studies in Chaucer. N.Y. 1892. III, 59–65:

> Sp's archaisms and innovations in poetic diction. Penetrating criticism, but needing correction in important points. See Henry Bradley, cited above. The question of Spenser's diction in comparison with other poetic diction of the sixteenth century calls for a new and thorough investigation.

MARCH, FRANCIS A. Method of Philological Study. N.Y. 1886. 74–87.

MARSH, GEO. P. The Origin and History of the English Language. N.Y. 1892. 548–49:

> Sp's diction; his "nice sense of congruity in the choice and application of epithets."

MURRAY, J. A. H. Derring Do, Derring-do, etc. In The Nation, N.Y., LXI (Oct. 3, 1895), 239:

> Traces Sp's archaisms mostly to Lydgate.

ROYSTER, J. F. A Note on Spenser's Archaism and Cicero. In Mod. Lang. Notes, XXIV (1909), 30–31.

SAINTSBURY, GEO. History of Criticism. N.Y. 1902. II, 227.

SCHULTZ, VICTOR. Das persönliche Geschlecht unpersönlichen Substantiva bei Spenser. Heidelberg, 1913. Diss.

SKEAT, W. W. A Student's Pastime. Ox. 1896. 40.

STEININGER, M. Der Gebrauch der Präposition bei Spenser. Halle, 1890. Diss.

WAGNER, GEORG. On Spenser's Use of Archaisms. Halle, 1879. Diss.

WILLIS, JOHN. De lingua Spenseriana ejusque fontibus. Bonn, 1848. Diss.

WILKINSON, T. T. See "Life, General."

STYLE, DICTION, ETC.

See also the preceding section.

BÖHME, T. Spenser's Literarisches Nachleben. Berlin, 1911. 6.

BOLWELL, R. Notes on Alliteration in Spenser. In Journal Eng. and Germ. Philology, XV (1916), 421–22.

BRIE, FRIEDRICH. Ursprung der poetischen Beseelung. . . . .
In Engl. Studien, L (1917), 383–425:
Discusses the literature on personification; incidentally notes
Sp's use of this figure and his debt to Sidney (392, 398).

BAYNE, THOS. In St. James Mag., XXXVI (1879), 106–7.

The British Critic, XXII (1803), 380.

DRAPER, J. W. See "Works: Sh Cal."

HALES, J. W. In H. Craik, English Prose. N.Y. 1893. I,
453–56.

HEISE, W. See under "Faerie Queene."

JACK, A. A. Chaucer and Spenser. Glasgow, 1920. 346–62:
"Spenser's Similes," etc.

KING, EMMA C. Rhetorical Elements in the Poetry of Spenser.
1912. MS Diss. in Univ. of Chicago Lib.

LEWIS, EDWIN H. History of the English Paragraph. Chicago,
1894. Diss. 85–86:
Sp's prose-style.

The Monthly Review, XI (1754), 112–24:
A review of Warton, with comments on Sp's style and diction.

PALMER, G. H. Formative Types in English Poetry. Bost.
1918. 77:
Sp's poetic diction and the theory underlying it.

Quarterly Review, VII (1812), 192–94:
Native quality of Sp's diction; difficulty of imitating its effects.

Quarterly Review, CLIII (1882), 438–40:
"His chief glory must always be that he created a poetic language
for England."

RENWICK, W. L. The Critical Origins of Spenser's Diction.
In Mod. Lang. Review, XVII (1922), 1–16.
That Sp departs from the precepts of 16th cent. Eng. criticism in
his innovations in poetical diction, and follows the lead of the Pléiade.

RENWICK, W. L. Mulcaster and DuBellay. In Mod. Lang.
Review, XVII (1922), 282–87.
Mulcaster's influence on Sp's diction; their sources in Ronsard and
Du Bellay.

ROWE, FLORENCE E.   Spenser's Short Similes.   In Mod. Lang. Notes, XIV (1899), 16–24 (32–47).

SCHLEGEL, F.   Lectures on the History of Literature.   Lond. (Bohn Lib.), 1889.   273–74:
Sp's Germanic diction.

SÉLINCOURT.   Introd. to his one-volume Oxford ed. of Sp. P. xviii:
Sp's attempt to form a new poetic diction; xxxii: as modified in MHT; lxi f.: "The first conscious inventor of a distinct poetic diction."

SHERMAN, L. A.   Analytics of Literature.   Bost. 1893.   259, 265, 274, 356, 389, etc.:
Stylistic and linguistic peculiarities in Sp.

SPENCER, VIRGINIA E.   Alliteration in Spenser's Poetry discussed and compared with the Alliteration as employed by Drayton and Daniel.   s. l. [Zurich], 1898.   Diss.

STEEL, JAMES H.   Style in Spenser.   In Proceedings Royal Philos. Soc., Glasgow, XLVI (1914–15), 146–205.   (Copy in Boston Pub. Lib.):
Important technical study of Sp's style and verse.

VERSIFICATION, STANZA, ETC.

ALDEN, R. M.   English Verse.   N.Y. 1903.
Sp's several measures are analyzed in this book.   See index.

BARNFIELD, R.   See "Criticism before 1651."

BAYFIELD, M. A.   Elizabethan Abbreviation: Spenser.   In Times Literary Supplement, Lond. Sept. 1 and 8, 1921. 562, 578:
On some traits of Sp's versification; his use of "resolutions" and of the apostrophe mark; similar usages in Jonson; etc.

BEATTIE, JAMES.   The Minstrel, 1771.   Preface.   In Chalmers' Poets, XVIII, 572–82.   Cf. 522–23.   Cf. III, 3 n.
On the advantages of the Sp stanza.   "It admits both simplicity and magnificence of sound and language, beyond any other stanza that I am acquainted with.   It allows the sententiousness of the couplet, as well as the more complex modulation of blank verse"; etc.

Blackwood's Magazine, XCIX (1866), 200 *n:*
    Origin of the stanza = the stanza of Chaucer's Monk's Tale, plus
an Alexandrine.

BRIGHT, JAS. W., and R. D. MILLER. The Elements of English
    Versification. Bost. 1910. See Index.

The British Review, III (1812), 286–87.

BROOKE, TUCKER. Stanza-Connection in the *Fairy Queen.* In
    Mod. Lang. Notes, XXXVII (1922), 223–27.

BRYANT, WILLIAM CULLEN. Prose Writings, ed. Parke Godwin,
    N.Y. 1884. I, 65:
    Sp's verse; 152: Sp's poetic diction.

BRYDGES, SIR E. In Introd. to his ed. of Phillips, Theatrum
    Poetarum. Canterbury, 1800. P. xxv.

CHURCH, R. W. Spenser (Eng. Men of Letters), 148.

COLERIDGE. Lectures on Shakespeare, 512–13.

COLERIDGE. Miscellanies, 333.

COLLIER, J. P., ed. of Sp., 1862, I, pp. cv ff.

COLLIER, J. P. The Poetical Decameron. Edin. 1820. I, 91 ff.
    On "blank verse" in Sp (an error; it is a sestina).

CORSON, H. A. Primer of English Verse. Bost. 1892. 13–14:
    Alliteration in Sp; 41–43: his versification; 87–133: the stanza.
    Cf. 134 ff.; 182–83: verse of the Amoretti.

CORY, H. E. Spenser, the School of the Fletchers, and Milton.
    315 *n.*

COURTHOPE, W. J. Hist. Eng. Poetry. Lond. 1897. II, 279 f.

CRAIK, G. L. Spenser and his Poetry, III, 126, 129.

DAVIDSON, C. Studies in the English Mystery Plays. Yale
    Diss. 1892. 126–27.

The Eclectic Review, IX (1813), 220–21.

ERSKINE, J. The Elizabethan Lyric. N.Y. 1903. 110:
    Verse of Sh Cal, Aug.; 192: verse of Epithal.; 294; rhyme scheme
    of Sonnets, source in Marot; 298: Sp's lyrics.

GUEST, E. Eng. Rhythms, ed. Skeat, Bk. IV, ch. vii.

GUMMERE, F. B. In Amer. Journal of Philology, VII, 60–70.

HERFORD, C. H. In Academy, L (1896), 28:
> Sp's scansion of Chaucer's verse; the four-beat rhythm of Sh Cal, Feb., etc.

HOGG, JAMES. Works. Centenary Ed. Lond. n.d. II, 451.

KALUZA, MAX. Englische Metrik in historischer Entwicklung. Berlin, 1909. 358 ff.

LEGOUIS, E. Quomodo Spenserus ad Chaucerum se fingens in eclogis "Shepheardes Calender" versum heroicum renovarit ac refecerit. Paris, 1896.
> Cf. Anglia, Suppl. 1898–99; Academy, L (1896), 28; Mod. Lang. Notes, XIII (1898), 414.

LEWIS, C. M. Principles of English Verse. N.Y. 1906. 83–84.

LISLE, WM. Part of Du Bartas, 1625. Preface. Repr. in Prefaces, etc. Huth Lib. 1874. 321:
> Caesura in the Sp stanza.

LOCKHART, J. G. Memoirs of the Life of Sir Walter Scott. Bost. n.d. III, 153, 157 (in ch. xxii).

LOWELL, J. R. Works, IV, 328–31.

McKERROW, R. B. Classical Metres in Elizabethan Verse. In Mod. Lang. Quarterly, IV (1901), 174:
> Sp's part in classical versifying.

MORTON, E. P. See "Criticism, General."

PALMER, G. H. Formative Types in English Poetry. Bost. 1918. Ch. iii.
> Analysis of the stanza as an instrument of "voluminous emotion."

PATMORE, COVENTRY. Poems. Lond. 1897. II, 262.

RESCHKE, H. See "Criticism, General."

SAINTSBURY, GEO. Prosody from Chaucer to Spenser. In Cambr. Hist. Eng. Lit. Cambr. 1909. III, 285–88:
> Influence of Sp on versification of Eliz. poets; trisyllabic foot infrequent in Sp; his variety of effects, yet a prophet of regularity; "impeccable master of rhythm, time and tune."

SAINTSBURY, GEO. History of English Prosody. Lond. 1906.
> I, 62, 320, 350 ff., 408, 416, 419; II, 268, 510.
> I, 361: verse of the sonnets; 352–58: of the Sh Cal. Cf. III, 544–48: "The Metre of Spenser's 'February'"; I, 364 ff., 408, 412: of FQ.

SAINTSBURY, GEO. Historical Manual of English Prosody. Lond. 1910. 60–62, 169–72, 224, 313.

SAINTSBURY, GEO. The Earlier Renaissance. N.Y. 1901. 239.

SAINTSBURY, GEO. Short Hist. of Eng. Lit. 1898. 268–69.

SCHELLING, F. E. Book of Eliz. Lyrics. Bost. 1895. Pp. xlv, li, lxi.

SCHELLING, F. E. Eng. Lit. during the Lifetime of Shakespeare. N.Y. 1910. 60–61:
Advantages for narrative of the Sp stanza; "made up of successive vignettes"; *ritardo* effect of the Alexandrine; really less monotonous than blank verse.

SCHIPPER, JAKOB. Neuenglische Metrik. Bonn, 1888. See index.

SCHIPPER, J. Grundriss der englischen Metrik. Wien. 1895. 359 ff.

SCHIPPER, J. History of English Versincation. Ox. 1910. Bk. II, chap. vii, etc.

SCHRÖER, ARNOLD. In Anglia, IV (1881), 49–53:
Sp's blank verse of 1569.

SÉLINCOURT. Introd. to his one-volume ed. of Sp. Pp. lxii ff.

SKEAT, W. W. The Origin of the Spenserian Stanza. In Athenaeum, Lond., May 6, 1893. 574:
That the stanza derives from Chaucer's eight-line stanza (The Monk's Tale), plus the Alexandrine developed by Surrey.

STEEL, JAMES H. Style in Spenser. In Proceedings Royal Philos. Soc. Glasgow, XLVI (1914–15), 146–205:
Technical analysis of versification of Sh Cal, Four Hymns, T of M, MHT, CCCHA ("Spenser and the Middle Style"), V.G., Muiop., Prothal. and Epithal. ("odes"), the Sonnets, and (180 ff.) the Sp stanza. Copy in Boston Pub. Lib.

TABOUREUX, ETIENNE. The Spenserian Stanza. In Revue de l'Enseignement des langues vivantes. Le Havre, XV (1899), 499–505; XVI (1899), 14–21, 112–18, 163–72:
An intensive study of Sp's versification in the FQ; and on the Sp stanza after Sp. Copy in Newberry Lib.

TRENT, W. P. In his ed. of Sp's Works, p. xvii.

Todd's ed. of Sp, VIII, 540–42.

[Upton, J.] Letter concerning a new edition of the Faerie
Queene. Lond. 1751. 28 ff.:
> On "half verses" in Sp.

Warton, Thos. Observations on the Fairy Queen. Lond.
1807. (Repr. in Todd's ed. of Sp, II.) I, 157 ff.: on the
stanza.

Webbe, Wm. Discourse of Eng. Poetrie, 1586. Repr. ed.
Arber. Lond. 1870. 59–61, 65:
> Versification of Sh Cal, discussed in detail.

Wilson, J. D. A Note on Elisions in "The Faerie Queene."
In Mod. Lang. Review, XV (1920), 409–14:
> Apostrophes, abbreviations, and clipped forms in the verse of Sp
> and Shakespeare.

Wilson, John. In Blackwood's Magazine, XXXVI (1834),
420–22.

Stockdale, Percival. Lectures on the Truly Eminent English
Poets. Lond. 1807. 2 v.
> I, Lecture i, "Spenser." A study of Sp's style and stanza. Not
> significant. Cf. The Monthly Review, LIX (1809), 138 ff.—a review
> of this work; condemns Sp's stanza.

MISCELLANEOUS TOPICS; HOW TO READ SPENSER; ETC.

Carpenter, F. I. Desiderata in the Study of Spenser. In
Studies in Philology, XIX (1922), 238–43.

Child's ed. of Sp, I, pp. lvii–viii.

Grosart's ed. of Sp, I, 294, 321, 393.

North Amer. Review, L (1840), 188–90.

Tuckwell's Spenser. 43–44.

FURTHER TOPICS SUGGESTED

See also under "Life, Chronological Outline;" "Introduction."
> Cf. F. I. Carpenter, Desiderata in the Study of Spenser. In
> Studies in Philology, XIX (1922), 238–43.

Spenser as a Satirist.

Dress in Spenser's Writings.

Spenser's Personifications.

The Treatment of the Arthurian Legend in Spenser.

Spenser's Use of the Supernatural.

The Use of Geographical and other Proper Names in Spenser.

Character-drawing in the Faerie Queene.

The Original and the Conventional in Spenser's Poetry.

Spenser as a Fabulist.

Spenser's Marriage Hymns and their Prototypes.

The Bible and Christian Theology in Spenser. Was Spenser a Calvinist?

> Dr. Grace W. Landrum of the University of Richmond has under preparation a study of Spenser's Use of the Bible.

Metaphor, Simile and Epithet in Spenser's Poetry.

Place and Time in the Faerie Queene.

Are the Sonnets of the Theatre of Worldlings, 1569, not repeated in 1591, of Spenser's composition?

The Sources of the Woodcuts in the Theatre of Worldlings.

Spenser's Relations with his Publishers.

The Authorship of the Ruins of Rome.

Spenser's Circle and Associates.

Repetition and Parallelism in Spenser: (1) in phrase, (2) in ideas.

INDEX

INDEX

See generally pp. 84 ff. List of Sp's "Circle," and references following.
See Part II of Index, below, for chronological arrangement of early references to Spenser.

A. L. A. *See* American Library Asso.

Abram, W. A., 79

Academy, The (London), 28, 44, 80, 122, 142, 202, 230, 252, 284, 288, 302

Academy. *See* Royal Irish Academy

Ackerman, Richard, 28, 274

Adams, E. D., 223

Addison, Joseph, 252

Additional MSS, 28, 44, 126, 133, 207, 286. *See also* Catalogues

Aëtion, 144 ff., 180 ff.

Aikin, John, 24, 112, 113

Alabaster, Wm., 84, 180, 229

Alanus, 135

Alcilia, 229

Alcon, 181, 203

Alcyon, 181

Alden, Raymond M., 188, 233, 236, 300

Allegory, 118, 149 ff., 154, 175, 254 257, 272, 276. *See also* under "Faerie Queen, Gen'l Reference"

Allen, H. W., 135

Allen, Thomas, 28

Allibone, Samuel A., 28, 105, 223

Allot, Robert, 225, 229

Almack, Edward, 106

Altenburg, ——, 148

Althorpe, 283, 284

Amadis de Gaule, 166, 168, 172

American Journal of Philology, 131

American Library Asso., 284

Ames, Percy W., 252

Amherst, Alicia, 293

Amis and Amiloun, 166

Amoretti, 25, 108, 120, 123, 124, 175 ff.

Amyntas, 181 f.

Andrews, Lancelot, story of the fellowship competition, 29, 30, 48, 52, 54, 73, 84, 93

Anecdotes of Polite Literature, 252

Anglia, 115, 116, 117, 197, 296, 302

Angliae Speculum, 253. *See also* Mercer, W.

Anthologia Hibernica, 28, 83, 206, 284

Anti-Jacobin Review, 112, 289

Antiquarian (Walford's), 52

Antiquities of Ireland, 126

Anton, Robert, 230

Apocrypha, 129 ff

Arber, Edward, 79, 120, 122, 124, 130, 134, 146, 206

Arcadia, 149, 150, 154, 169, 172. *See also* Sidney

Archaeologia, 28

Archaisms, 295 ff., 298 ff.

Archdall, Merwyn, 29

Archiv für das Studium der neueren Sprachen und Literatur, 55, 56, 161, 169

Areopagus, 97 f.

Ariosto, 137, 138, 166, 168, 169, 261, 290

Aristotle, 136, 138, 152, 167, 173

Arnold, C., 253

Arnold, Frederick, 253

Arnold, T., 253

Arraignement of the Whole Creature, 241

Arthur and Arthurian Romances, 155, 158, 161, 171

Ascham, 173

Astrophel, 26, 120, 179

Athenaeum (London), 52, 56, 79, 83, 98, 114, 115, 117, 121, 159, 203, 205, 253

Stanley, Alice (Spencer), Countess of Derby, wife of Ferdinando Stanley, fifth Earl of Derby, 86, 88, 93
Stanley, Arthur P., 73
Stanley, Ferdinando, Earl of Derby, 85, 86, 180, 181
Stanley, Henry, 86
Stanley, Thomas, 184, 187
Stanyhurst, Richard, 86, 135, 209, 215
Stanza, 300 ff.
State Papers. *See* Calendars; *also* Public Record Office
Stationers Register. *See* Arber
Statius, 135, 167
Statutes at Large, 36
Statutes of Ireland, 36
Stebbing, William, 276
Steel, James H., 300, 303
Steele, Sir Richard, 276. *See also* Tatler
Steininger, M., 298
Stemmata Dudleiana, 126
Stephen, Leslie, 228
Sterling, Joseph, 254
Stewart, J. A., 146
Still, John, 86, 88
Stobart, J. C., 276
Stockdale, Percival, 276, 304
Stone, Nicholas, 53, 59
Stone, W. J., 98
Stopes, Charlotte C., 182, 204, 236
Stothard, Thos., 113, 148
Stow, John, 241
Strachey, J. St. Loe, 6
Stradling, Sir John, 127, 250
Strange, Lady, Countess of Derby. *See* Stanley
Stronach, George, 288
Stubbe, Henry, 277
Stubbs, John, 86, 92
Studies in Philology (Univ. of North Carolina), 118, 257, 295
Style, 298 ff.
Sully, James, 163
Swanwick, Anna, 276
Swinburne, Algernon C., 228, 276
Sylvester, Joshua, 233, 250
Symonds, John A., 98
Synot, Rich., 38

T. (R.). *See* Tofte
Taboureux, Etienne, 303
Taine, Hippolyte A., 6, 276
Tanner, Thomas, 73, 289
Tarlton, Richard, 86, 203
Tasso, Bernardo, 131, 275
Tasso, Torquato, 138, 139, 146, 164, 166, 169, 177
Tate, Nahum, 276
Tatler, 119, 276. *See also* Steele
Taylor, H. O., 100, 276
Taylor, John, the Water Poet, 250
Tears of the Muses, 202 ff., 236
Temple, Sir William, 276
Tennyson, Alfred, Lord, 277
Theatre of Voluptuous Worldlings, 12, 76, 106, 124, 129, 205 f., 305. *See also* Noot
Theocritus, 138, 179
Thestylis. *See* Mourning Muse
Thomas, Francis S., 73
Thomas, G., 187
Thompson, Elbert N. S., 228, 246
Thompson, G. A., 229, 294
Thompson, James Westfall, 4
Thompson, William, 277
Thomson, C. L., 118
Thomson, James, 277
Thorpe, M. J. *See* Calendars, Scotland
Three Letters. *See* Letters
Thynne, Francis, 250
Timbs, John, 255
Times, The (London), 56, 253, 300
Times' Whistle. *See* C. (R.)
Todd, Henry J., 6, 24, 30, 73, 84, 96, 101, 106, 112, 123, 126, 128, 173, 179, 181, 182, 183, 187, 190, 192, 195, 208, 215, 217, 229, 246, 251, 265, 275, 289, 304
Tofte, Robert, 250
Tolman, Albert H., 4, 291
Towerson, Maria, 69
Townshend, Dorothea, 73, 82, 84
Towry, M. H., 119, 128, 141, 148
Toynbee, Paget, 144
Transactions Bibliog. Soc., Lond., 75, 147
Transcript of Stationers Register. *See* Arber

1579	E. K., 107 (with Sh Cal)	
1579, etc.	Gabriel Harvey, 107, etc.	
c.1580	Abraham Fraunce, 238, 239	
c.1580	"Pedantius," 247	
c.1581	Sir Philip Sidney, 106, etc.	
1584	Geo. Peele, 247	
1584	Thos. Lodge, 243	
1586	Wm. Webbe, 251	
1586	Geo. Whetstone, 251	
1588	A. Fraunce, 239	
1588	Henry Lyte, 244	
1589	Thos. Lodge, 243	
1589	Geo. Puttenham, 247	
1590	Sir Walter Raleigh, 248	
1590	Thos. Watson, 251	
1591	Samuel Daniel, 235	
1591	John Florio, 238	
1591	Robert Greene, 239	
1592	Thos. Nashe, 246	
−1593	Christopher Marlowe, 244	
1593	Barnabe Barnes, 230	
1593	A. Chute, 234	
1593	Thos. Churchyard, 234	
1593	Michael Drayton, 236	
1593	Sir Edw. Dyer, 236	
1593	Henry Peacham, 247	
1593	Geo. Peele, 247	
1593	Thos. Lodge, 243	
−1594	Thos. Kyd, 242	
1594	B. (R.), Greenes Funeralls, 230	
1594	Sir John Davies, 235	
1594	O. (I.), 247	
1594	"Selimus," 249	
1594	"Willobie his Avisa," 252	
c.1594	J. Dickenson, 235	
1595	Thos. Churchyard, 234	
1595	S. Daniel, 235	
1595	Thos. Edwards, 236	
1595	"Emaricdulf," 232	
1595	"Locrine," 243	

1595	Thos. Lodge, 243	
1595	"Polimanteia," 247	
1596	Michael Drayton, 236	
1596	Chas. Fitzgeoffrey, 237	
1596	Sir John Harington, 241	
1596	Thos. Lodge, 243	
1596	Wm. Smith, 250	
1597	"Certaine Worthye MS Poems," 233	
1597	Geo. Kirbye, 242	
1597	Henry Lok, 243	
1597	Joshua Sylvester, 250	
1598	Rich. Barnfield, 230	
1598	Saml. Brandon, 231	
1598	M. Drayton, 236	
1598	Edw. Guilpin, 240	
1598	Jos. Hall, 240	
1598	"A Herring's Tayle," 241	
1598	John Marston, 244	
1598	Francis Meres, 244	
1598	Francis Rous, 249	
1599	Thos. Cutwode, 234	
1599	"First Book of the Preservation," 237	
1599	Jos. Hall, 240	
1599	John Weever, 251	
c.1599	Wm. Alabaster, 229	
c.1599	H. (R.), 240	
1600	Robt. Allot, 229	
1600	N. Breton, 232	
1600	John Bodenham, 231	
1600	Chas. Butler, 232	
1600	Davison's Poetical Rhapsody, 235	
1600	"England's Helicon," 236	
1600	Edw. Fairfax, 237	
1600	"Maydes Metamorphosis," 244	
1600	Saml. Nicholson, 247	
1600	Francis Thynne, 250	
c.1600	John Chalkhill, 233